Pastoral and Romance

MODERN ESSAYS IN CRITICISM

PASTORAL AND ROMANCE

MODERN ESSAYS IN CRITICISM

Edited by

Eleanor Terry Lincoln
Smith College

PRENTICE-HALL, INC.
Englewood Cliffs, New Jersey

PRENTICE-HALL ENGLISH LITERATURE SERIES
MAYNARD MACK, EDITOR

©1969 by PRENTICE-HALL, INC., Englewood Cliffs, N.J.

Library of Congress Catalog Card No.: 69–10869

Printed in the United States of America

Current printing (last number):
10 9 8 7 6 5 4 3 2 1

PRENTICE-HALL INTERNATIONAL, INC., London
PRENTICE-HALL OF AUSTRALIA, PTY. LTD., Sydney
PRENTICE-HALL OF CANADA, LTD., Toronto
PRENTICE-HALL OF INDIA PRIVATE LTD., New Delhi
PRENTICE-HALL OF JAPAN, INC., Tokyo

Contents

v

vi

Introduction

The definitions of pastoral and romance that are represented in the following essays need some clarification. They reflect
a new, and in some respects, revolutionary approach to genre that is,
in large part, an achievement of the second quarter of this century.

It is often assumed that pastoral literature disappeared with the
grasslands and romance with the last knight in armor or at the latest
with massive French novels. If there are traditions of pastoral and
romance that persist in modern literature, how must we extend our
definitions of these genres to accommodate them (or can they be
called genres in the accepted meaning of the word)? Genre, as generally defined, admits criteria of form, style, or subject matter. In the
light of contemporary practice we must add purpose or point of view.[1]

We are accustomed to consider tragic and comic elements in works
that are neither tragedy nor comedy and to recognize that they shape
and distinguish a work as significantly as form or structure can do.
Modern criticism seeks inner distinctions based on the view of life,
or the view of truth, that the work strives to present. We are beginning
to see that pastoral is not simply a shepherd's song but a reflection
on the strife between the world that God created and that which man
has made for himself; that romance is not merely a tale of adventure
or of love but a representation of forces beyond matter of fact.

The following studies explore the critical significance of pastoral
and romance in many kinds of poetry and fiction. The essays often
point to qualities that are present in only part of a work. And, one
final *caveat*, this collection includes excerpts from book length studies

---

[1]American and English critics have so far written little about the theory of genre.
A brief but very useful survey of the subject, which includes bibliography, will be
found in René Wellek and Austen Warren, *Theory of Literature*, Chapter XVII.

1

designed to illuminate a work or to provide a setting for the author's approach to his subject but not intended to be a complete consideration of the problems of genre. It may therefore be useful to add a few points of definition, which the essays assume or ignore.

Pastoral

The extension of pastoral to embrace figures as various as Eve in the Garden and Alice in Wonderland[2] has always been implicit. From the beginning, the *Idylls* of Theocritus and the *Eclogues* of Virgil described life beyond mountain meadows. The poetry of shepherds was written by and for sophisticates. The prose romance of *Daphnis and Chloe* is a story of lost aristocrats and their education. The shepherd in pastoral is, strictly speaking, never a shepherd. He is a musician, a poet, a prince, and a priest. Colin Clout is Spenser himself, and Adonais is Keats. Paris, Prince of Troy, makes the great choice as a shepherd on Mount Ida, and David and Christ are Christian figures of the shepherd-king and shepherd-priest.

In its widest sense pastoral becomes a figure for the contemplative life, a withdrawal from action that affords a perspective upon battlefield and market place. Its distinctions from other genres, like the distinctions between tragedy and comedy, ultimately rest on a view of life or a way of representing it. The shepherd may be a hunter, a fisherman, a king, a child, or a shipwrecked mariner; his circumstance is pastoral because he is separated by mountain or meadow, forest or sea, or by his youth from commitment to the sophisticated and active world of strife. The essentials that shape the pastoral are withdrawal to a place apart and from that place a perspective of what man has made of man. The viewer is at once sophisticate and shepherd, his "disguise" offers the double view that is necessary to contrast and that dramatizes the ironic differences implicit in the situation. Those ironies insist on a comparison of worlds—a reassessment of accepted values, which is an education, sometimes so sudden as to be a revelation. Shepherd and reader re-emerge from the place apart to return, strengthened and enlightened, to active engagement in the imperfect world. The return distinguishes significant pastoral. The resolution of the contrast and the reconciliation of the ironies are the achieved end where art imposes order and meaning on nature.

The pastoral genre then seems best defined as a figure for a condition in which the characters understand life in relation not to man's

[2]William Empson, *Some Versions of Pastoral*, Chapter VII.

activity but to the fundamental patterns of the created world: day and night, the seasons, birth and death, love and fear, fertility and drought—all that obtained in Eden but in Eden *after* the Fall. For in spite of our associations with the word idyll and with conceptions of bucolic bliss, the pastoral is not a literature of escape. Virgil's first *Eclogue* deals with the evil of political expropriation; Daphnis and Chloe are assailed by pirates, the shepherd piper complains of unrequited love and protects his sheep from marauding beasts. Properly understood pastoral has never avoided the realities of life nor has it been a picture of primitive innocence. The pastoral withdrawal that is central to the genre, whether made necessary by herding or by exile or accident, leads to new knowledge and is followed by a return "to fresh woods and pastures new" where endeavor will be informed by a rigorous experience. Pastoral is often introduced as an interlude in epic or active endeavor when the hero faces the crossroads of choice, when the battle appears in cosmic perspective, or when the sky opens to permit a revelation.

The recurring motif of the royal child exposed to the elements, suckled by a wolf or bear, rescued by a shepherd, then rediscovered and enthroned is more than a plot device. In the mountains and pastures vice is revealed and villainy rebuked; from there the child or the exile learns to rule his kingdom however great or small. It is no accident that truth is so often revealed by a shepherd (*Oedipus, The Winter's Tale*). The complexities of the active life are swept away in the world ruled by nature; the eternal and fundamental elements reveal man to himself.

The enlargement of the pastoral, recognized by Pope in his definition "an imitation of the action of a shepherd or one considered under that character,"[3] begins with the figure of the shepherd as musician controlling his sheep with his pipe, then as poet composing to his flute. Nature and art so united combine to reveal the relation of man to his universe. His life is equated with the seasons of the year represented by the shepherd-god whose birth is spring and his death is winter: Adonis, Attis, Osiris, or Orpheus, whose music restrained wild beasts and who challenged Death himself. In the perspective of the great elemental cycles—the mystery of spring and birth, the inevitability of winter and death—the sphere of man's ambition assumes its true proportion. The pastoral becomes the vehicle for his acceptance of his human condition.

[3]*Discourse on Pastoral.*

In view of this definition it is possible to trace the tradition of pastoral that has persisted, even as tragedy has done, although the shepherds like the kings have almost vanished from the earth.

Romance

It is easily and often assumed that romance exists to give pleasure, that it is the literature of a summer afternoon, dedicated to leisure and indulgence, its haphazard adventures making no demand on thought. Its early admirers made a virtue of its incredibility, which won the reader with attractions impossible in life, on land, or on sea. Stevenson describes it in such an attractive guise. It is, he says, a daydream, "absorbing and voluptuous." James recognized the enchantment of the hansom announced by the click of cab horses. Hawthorne admitted the charms of romance. Its author, he says, may "mingle the Marvellous... as an evanescent flower," but he adds that romance "sins unpardonably so far as it may swerve aside from the truth of the human heart,"[4] a dictum that points to the larger role it will play in subsequent criticism.

Romance as we know it begins with the knight in a land of faerie, alone and pale, on a mysterious quest, facing exotic and completely improbable trials that have, nevertheless, ritual implications. The object of the quest, be it a magic sword or the Holy Grail, is an image of the ideal, which is central to romance; it is a dream of glory. Exaltation of the hero, if it is sufficiently miraculous, becomes mythical or assumes canonical importance; the knight becomes St. George. The hero of romance is the image of the ideal, whether it is courage or piety, brawn or wit. The dragon, which is his antagonist, is similarly symbolic, the representation of all that is monstrous, evil, and fearful.

Hawthorne recognized that the enchantment of romance was a creation of the artist; he saw too that the artistic imagination unchecked by truth is self-destructive. In the middle ground between fantasy and realism, the close reader sees truth revealed by the romantic perception of elements within or transcending reality. In this view romance is an oblique approach to truth through its representation in metaphor. The theme of the ritual quest pursued by the novice knight persists from chivalric cycles to the romance novels of Melville and Henry James.

[4]*House of Seven Gables*, Preface.

In its most attractive manifestations the romantic imagination symbolizes the heroic possibilities to which man may aspire, but the idealist is subject to dismay; and imagination is fertile in the creation of chimaeras that are no less symbolic and, in an imperfect world, no less true. Every romance includes in some degree visions of both order and disorder. The decapitating of giants points to confidence that God is in His heaven and His sword has destroyed the fiend. The dark tarn and the dungeon testify instead to the triumph of Satan. On one hand romance moves amid the symbolism of confidence; on the other, amid representations of terror.

The definition of romance must be broad enough to include both the vision and the nightmare. Our twentieth-century condition is contributing to both of these opposite faces of imagination. The quest for order, born of innumerable threats to old patterns and accepted belief, has inspired a renewed search for truth in religion that, in turn, has fostered an urgent quest for symbolic meaning in myth and romance.

The romance of fulfillment defends faith in a cosmic or divine order above the smoke and clamor of the turmoil everywhere apparent in the visible world. When the vision fails, the disorder so conspicuous in crowding human life becomes a more prevailing theme. Emphasis upon the isolation of modern man, upon war, and upon the aberrations of which the mind is capable discredit the prospect of order. One of the most striking and certainly the most recent developments in romance is the burgeoning of Southern Gothic. This strain dominates modern American fiction, its violence awakening us to the prodigies that were concealed in the age of confidence; its antirealistic melodrama making it just possible to look upon unbearable truth.

It is tempting to believe that Gothic horror, since it so often moves to no resolution, is little more than an emotional indulgence. There are many examples in paper covers that justify this view. But the Gothic no less than the heroic romance reveals truth. It is simply a truth we are more reluctant to recognize. The monstrous elements in the human condition—at first concealed in images of the fabulous beast, the fire-breathing dragon, or in physical dangers, the black tarn and the wasteland—have turned human and moved near to reveal in ruthless appetite the subconscious impulses that shatter confidence in civilization. The exotic madness of the Northanger romances suggest to modern intelligence the uncertainties, even the horrors of our own subliminal experience. Romance, once remote, is today near-at-hand; the tingling terrors of a summer afternoon have moved from far away castles to every city street.

It may be tempting also to ask if romance is no longer an adventure. If we no longer ride out or sail away to encounter wild men and vampires, are the distorted histories in contemporary fiction true romance? Should we separate the fantasies of human achievement from the phantasms of human failure, relegating romance to the world of youthful exploit? But the abductions, the usurpations, and the cruelties of the Greek romances, the hallucinations and the suffering of the chivalric quests all reveal to the perceptive reader the persistent inescapable symbolism of the brand of Cain, pleasure in pain, magic in violence. Fear and horror have always provided the catharsis that makes romance enthralling, and apparitions will always reveal truth shrouded like the ghost in *Hamlet*.

W. W. GREG

Pastoral : A Literary Inquiry

In approaching a subject of literary inquiry we are often
able to fix upon some essential feature or condition which may serve
as an Ariadne's thread through the maze of historical and aesthetic
development, or to distinguish some cardinal point affording a fixed
centre from which to survey or in reference to which to order and
dispose the phenomena that present themselves to us. It is the disadvantage of such an artificial form of literature as that which bears the
name of pastoral that no such *a priori* guidance is available. To lay
down at starting that the essential quality of pastoral is the realistic
or at least recognizably 'natural' presentation of actual shepherd
life would be to rule out of court nine tenths of the work that comes
traditionally under that head. Yet the great majority of critics, though
they would not, of course, subscribe to the above definition, have yet
constantly betrayed an inclination to censure individual works for not
conforming to some such arbitrary canon. It is characteristic of the
artificiality of pastoral as a literary form that the impulse which gave
the first creative touch at seeding loses itself later and finds no place
among the forces at work at blossom time; the methods adopted by
the greatest masters of the form are inconsistent with the motives that
impelled them to its use, and where these motives were followed to
their logical conclusion, the result, both in literature and in life, became a byword for absurd unreality. To live at all the ideal appeared
to require an atmosphere of paradox and incongruity: in its essence the
most 'natural' of all poetic forms, pastoralism came to its fairest
flower amid the artificiality of a decadent court or as the plaything of
the leisure hours of a college of learning, and its insipid convention

From *Pastoral Poetry and Pastoral Drama,* by W. W. Greg, pp. 1–7. Published, 1905.
Reprinted by permission of Sidgwick & Jackson Ltd.

having become 'a literary plague in every European capital,' it finally disappeared from view amid the fopperies of the Roman Arcadia and the puerile conceits of the Petit Trianon.

Wherein then, it may be wondered, does the pastoral's title to consideration lie. It does not lie primarily, or chiefly, in the fact that it is associated with names of the first rank in literature, with Theocritus and Vergil, with Petrarch, Politian, and Tasso, with Cervantes and Lope de Vega, with Ronsard and Marot, with Spenser, Ben Jonson, and Milton; nor yet that works such as the *Idyls*, the *Aminta*, the *Faithful Shepherdess*, and *Lycidas* contain some of the most graceful and perfect verse to be found in any language. Rather is its importance to be sought in the fact that the form is the expression of instincts and impulses deep-rooted in the nature of humanity, which, while affecting the whole course of literature, at times evince themselves most clearly and articulately here; that it plays a distinct and distinctive part in the history of human thought and the history of artistic expression. Moreover, it may be argued that, from this point of view, the very contradictions and inconsistencies to which I have alluded make it all the more important to discover wherein lay the strange vitality of the form and its power of influencing the current of European letters.

From what has already been said it will be apparent that little would be gained by attempting beforehand to give any strict account of what is meant by 'pastoral' in literature. Any definition sufficiently elastic to include the protean forms assumed by what we call the 'pastoral ideal' could hardly have sufficient intension to be of any real value. If after considering a number of literary phenomena which appear to be related among themselves in form, spirit, and aim we come at the end of our inquiry to any clearer appreciation of the term I shall so far have attained my object. I notice that I have used the expression 'pastoral ideal,' and the phrase, which comes naturally to the mind in connexion with this form of literature, may supply us with a useful hint. It reminds us, namely, that the quality of pastoralism is not determined by the fortuitous occurrence of certain characters, but by the fact of the pieces in question being based more or less evidently upon a philosophical conception, which no doubt underwent modification through the ages, but yet bears evidence of organic continuity. Thus the shepherds of pastoral are primarily and distinctively shepherds; they are not mere rustics engaged in sheepcraft as one out of many of the employments of mankind. As soon as the natural shepherd-life had found an objective setting in conscious artistic

literature, it was felt that there was after all a difference between hoe-
ing turnips and pasturing sheep; that the one was capable of a particular literary treatment which the other was not. The Maid of Orleans
might equally well have dug potatoes as tended a flock, and her place
is not in pastoral song. Thus pastoral literature must not be confounded
with that which has for its subject the lives, the ideas, and the emotions
of simple and unsophisticated mankind, far from the centres of our
complex civilization. The two may be in their origin related, and they
occasionally, as it were, stretch out feelers towards one another, but
the pastoral of tradition lies in its essence as far from the human document of humble life as from a scientific treatise on agriculture or a
volume of pastoral theology. . . .

An insistence upon the objective pastoral setting is of prime importance in understanding the real nature of pastoral poetry; it not only
serves to distinguish the pastoral proper from the more vaguely idyllic
forms of lyric verse, but helps us further to understand how it was that
the outward features of the kind came to be preserved, even after the
various necessities of sophisticated society had metamorphosed the
content almost beyond recognition. No common feature of a kind to
form the basis of a scientific classification can be traced in the spontaneous shepherd-songs and their literary counterpart. What does
appear to be a constant element in the pastoral as known to literature
is the recognition of a contrast, implicit or expressed, between pastoral
life and some more complex type of civilization. At no stage in its
development does literature, or at any rate poetry, concern itself with
the obvious, with the bare scaffolding of life: whenever we find an
author interested in the circle of prime necessity we may be sure that
he himself stands outside it. Thus the shepherd when he sang did not
insist upon the conditions amid which his uneventful life was passed.
It was left to a later, perhaps a wiser and a sadder, generation to gaze
with fruitless and often only half sincere longing at the shepherd-boy
asleep under the shadow of the thorn, lulled by the low monotonous
rustle of the grazing flock. Only when the shepherd-songs ceased to be
the outcome of unalloyed pastoral conditions did they become distinctively pastoral. It is therefore significant that the earliest pastoral
poetry with which we are acquainted, whatever half articulate experi-
ments may have preceded it, was itself directly born of the contrast
between the recollections of a childhood spent among the Sicilian
uplands and the crowded social and intellectual city-life of Alexandria.

As the result of this contrast there arises an idea which comes perhaps as near being universal in pastoral as any—the idea, namely, of the 'golden age.' This embraces, indeed, a field not wholly coincident with that of pastoral, but the two are connected alike by a common spring in human emotion and constant literary association. . . .

The conception of a golden age of rustic simplicity does not, indeed, involve the whole of pastoral literature. It does not account either for the allegorical pastoral, in which actual personages are introduced, in the guise of shepherds, to discuss contemporary affairs, or for the so-called realistic pastoral, in which the town looks on with amused envy at the rustic freedom of the country. What it does comprehend is that outburst of pastoral song which sprang from the yearning of the tired soul to escape, if it were but in imagination and for a moment, to a life of simplicity and innocence from the bitter luxury of the court and the menial bread of princes.[1]

And this, the reaction against the world that is too much with us, is, after all, the keynote of what is most intimately associated with the name of pastoral in literature—the note that is struck with idyllic sweetness in Theocritus, and, rising to its fullest pitch of lyrical intensity, lends a poignant charm to the work of Tasso and Guarini. For everywhere in these soft melodies of luscious beauty, even in the studied sketches of primitive innocence itself, there is an undercurrent of tender melancholy and pathos:

> Il mondo invecchia
> E invecchiando intristisce.

I have said that a sense of the contrast between town and country was essential to the development of a distinctively pastoral literature. It would be an interesting task to trace how far this contrast is the source of the various subsidiary types—of the ideal where it breeds desire for a return to simplicity, of the realistic where the humour of it touches the imagination, and of the allegorical where it suggests satire on the corruption of an artificial civilization.

When the kind first makes its appearance in a world already old, it arises purely as a solace and relief from the fervid life of actuality,

---

[1]The tendency to form an ideal picture of his own youth is common both to mankind and man. The romance of childhood is the dream with which age consoles itself for the disillusionments of life. This it is that gives a peculiar appropriateness to the title of Mr. Graham's pictures of childhood in *The Golden Age*, a work of the profoundest insight and genius, as delightful as it is unique. I am not aware that there has ever been another author in English who could have written thus intimately of children without once striking a false note.

and comes as a fresh and cooling draught to lips burning with the fever of the city. In passing from Alexandria to Rome it lost much of its limpid purity; the clear crystal of the drink was mixed with flavours and perfumes to fit the palate of a patron or an emperor. The example of adulteration being once set, the implied contrast of civilization and rusticity was replaced by direct satire on the former, and later by the discussion under the pastoral mask of questions of religious and political controversy. . . .

HALLETT SMITH

Elizabethan Pastoral

Whatever may be said of other times and places, Elizabethan England saw a meaning in pastoral. This meaning was, or
constituted, a positive ideal. It was an ideal of the good life, of the
state of content and mental self-sufficiency which had been known in
classical antiquity as *otium*. The revival of this ideal is a characteristic
Renaissance achievement; it would have been impossible in the Middle Ages, when time spent in neither work nor communion with God
was felt to be sinful. By projecting this ideal, poets of the age of Shakespeare were able to criticize life as it is and portray it as it might be.
Their shepherds are citizens of the same Arcadia as that inhabited by
the shepherds of Milton and Matthew Arnold.

The Elizabethan mind took over its conception of pastoral from
many sources. The most general and the most obvious of these sources
was the Bible. In Genesis, the first great event after the fall of man is
one which involves a shepherd; it is the story of Cain and Abel. What
it meant to the Elizabethans is explained by Bacon:

> We see (as the Scriptures have infinite mysteries, not violating at
> all the truth of the story or letter), an image of the two estates, the
> contemplative state and the active state, figured in the two per-
> sons of Abel and Cain, and in the two simplest and most primitive
> trades of life; that of the shepherd, (who, by reason of his leisure,
> rest in a place, and living in view of heaven, is a lively image
> of a contemplative life,) and that of the husbandman: where
> we see again the favour and election of God went to the shepherd,
> and not to the tiller of the ground.[1]

Reprinted by permission of the publishers from Hallett Smith, *Elizabethan Poetry*.
Cambridge, Mass.: Harvard University Press, Copyright, 1952, by the President and
Fellows of Harvard College. Extract from pp. 2–14, 33–35, 40–41, 47, 60–61.

[1]James Spedding, R. L. Ellis, and D. D. Heath, eds., *Sir Francis Bacon, Works*, VI
(Boston: 1860–1864), p. 138.

Moreover, David, perhaps the most romantic figure in the Old Testament, was a shephered, as well as being the principal poet and singer of songs among the ancient Hebrews. Of his psalms, the twenty-third was of course a special favorite. It reflected not only the atmosphere of green pastures but also the doctrine of content as the greatest of God's blessings. "The Lord is my shepherd; I shall not want" was explained by the preachers as a pastoral metaphor expressing the truth of Christian content. [2]

In the New Testament there is the central pastoral imagery of Christ the Good Shepherd, and of course the episode of the shepherds hearing from heaven the good tidings of Christ's birth. As Michael Drayton wrote, "In the Angels Song to Shepheards at our Saviours Nativitie Pastorall Poesie seemes consecrated." [3]

Characteristically, the Renaissance mixed examples of the shepherd from Greek and Roman tradition and history with those from the Bible. In Mantuan's seventh eclogue, Moses and Apollo are mentioned in pastoral roles. [4] Paris, the son of Priam, King of Troy, was the most famous of all classical shepherds because from his actions sprang the whole epic narrative of the siege of Troy. Besides Paris, James Sandford's translation of Cornelius Agrippa (1569) cites Romulus and Remus, Anchises, and the emperor Diocletian as shepherds. Thomas Fortescue's translation from Pedro Mexía, *The Foreste* (1586) adds Galerius and Tamburlaine. A shepherd in Drayton's "Dowsabell" is described as resembling Tamburlaine in looks and Abel in temper. [5]

The Elizabethan attitude toward Paris reveals much of the meaning and significance of pastoral in the poetry of the age. The story of Paris is of course one of the great stories: how a king's son, living as a shepherd, is in love with the nymph Oenone; how he is chosen to be umpire among the three goddesses, Juno, Venus, and Pallas Athena, to decide which of them deserves the golden apple inscribed "For the fairest"; how he decides in favor of Venus and is given as a reward the love of the most beautiful of women, Helen; how he deserts Oenone,

[2]See, for example, Thomas Jackson, *Davids Pastorall Poeme: or Sheepeheards Song. Seven Sermons, on the 23. Psalme of David* (1603).

[3]J. W. Hebel, ed., "To the Reader of his Pastorals," in *The Works of Michael Drayton*, V (Oxford: 1931–1941), p. 4.

[4]W. P. Mustard, ed., *The Eclogues of Baptista Mantuanus*, (Baltimore: 1911), p. 97. Translations or adaptations of this passage are in Alexander Barclay's fifth eclogue (before 1530), lines 469–92; in Tubervile's translation (1567), sig. K_2^v; in Spenser's July eclogue in *The Shepheardes Calender* (1579), ll. 131–60; and in Francis Sabie's *Pan's Pipe* (1595), sigs. $D_2^v — D_3^r$.

[5]Hebel, *Works*, I, p. 89.

brings Helen to Troy, and precipitates the Trojan War with all of its consequences—this plot is surely one of the great achievements of the Western imagination.

Dramatic treatments of the story of Paris are mentioned by Saint Augustine;[6] the subject is inherently dramatic, both for the power of the rival claims of the goddesses and for the world-shaking consequences of Paris' choice. The death of Hector and Achilles, the destruction of Troy, the wanderings of Ulysses and of Aeneas, the founding of Rome (and of Britain, too, as the Elizabethans thought), all resulted from this one simple decision by a shepherd on the hills of Ida.

Purely as plot, then, the story of the shepherd's choice had color and vitality. But it was also symbolic, and an understanding of what was represented to the Elizabethan mind by the offers of Juno, Pallas, and Venus while Paris was trying to make up his mind is essential to an appreciation of poetic treatments of the myth. From classical times on down, the principal myths had been interpreted morally, if not allegorically, and the Judgment of Paris was one which lent itself to such treatment in a very natural way. Athenaeus says, in the *Deipnoso-phistae*, "And I for one affirm also that the Judgment of Paris, as told in poetry by the writers of an older time, is really a trial of pleasure against virtue. Aphrodite, for example—and she represents pleasure— was given the preference, and so everything was thrown into turmoil"[7]

Fulgentius, Bishop of Carthage, also moralized the myth of the Judgment of Paris. The three goddesses, he says, represent the three ways of life: the active, the contemplative, and the voluptuous. Jove himself, continues Fulgentius, could not make judgment among the three contending goddesses or the ways of life they represent; it is essentially a human dilemma. A shepherd, in Fulgentius' opinion, is the most suitable of all men to be the judge, though of course, accord-ing to the bishop, Paris made a foolish choice. Spenser agrees, and in the July eclogue of *The Shepheardes Calender* goes out of his way to condemn Paris:

> For he was proude, that ill was payd,
> (no such mought shepheards bee)
> And with lewde lust was ouerlayd:
> tway things doen ill agree.[8]

[6]*De civitate Dei*, XVIII, p. 10.

[7]C. B. Gulick, trans., *The Deipnosophists*, XII, 510 c, Loeb Classical Library, V (1922–1949) p. 295.

[8]The same point had been emphasized by Horace in *Epistles*, II, p. 10. The idea was also familiar to Renaissance Platonists and was elaborated by Ficino, for example, in his commentary on Plato's *Philebus*. See P. O. Kristeller, *The Philosophy of Marsilio Ficino* (New York: 1943), pp. 358–59.

To the Renaissance, Paris' mistake was intended as a powerful warning. Italian treatises on nobility considered the Judgment of Paris story to represent the choice which must actually be made by the young man deciding upon a course of life.[9]

In the most popular of the pastoral romances, the Judgment of Paris is a subject for debate; in Montemayor's *Diana*, for example, Delia and Andronius spend the greater part of a night in arguing the question whether Paris gave the apple to the right gooddess or not and whether the inscription on it referred to physical or mental beauty.[10] The shepherds and shepherdesses in Elizabethan pastoral poetry often allude to the Paris story or compare themselves with figures in it. An example is from "Phillidaes Loue-Call to her Coridon, and his replying," by "Ignoto" in *England's Helicon;*[11] another is Willye's compliment to Cuddie, the umpire of the singing match in Spenser's August eclogue:

> Neuer dempt more right of beautye I weene,
> The shepheard of Ida, that iudged beauties Queene.[12]

Drayton's Rowland, on the other hand, compares himself to the deserted Oenone.[13]

Whatever the faults of Paris' decision, the son of Priam remained, for the Elizabethan, the archetype of the shepherd. Spenser's Sir Calidore, when he takes off his armor and puts on shepherd's weeds in

[9]The passage in G. B. Nenna's treatise is so typical, and the reputation of his book in England is so amply attested to by Edmund Spenser, Samuel Daniel, George Chapman, and Angel Day, that it must be quoted: "Now let vs consider what fruit may be gathered by the shadowe of fables, especially of this which I euen now recited. For indeed vnder those vailes we may receiue no lesse pleasant then profitable instruction. . . . After that a man is once framed, and that he hath attained to that age, that hee beginneth nowe to discourse within himselfe, what kinde of life hee were best to followe as the most noble in account amongst men: whether that which is grounded vppon knowledge, which the Philosophers were wont to cal a contemplatiue kind of life: or otherwise, yt which guideth a man that addicteth himself only to worldly matters, which they terme actiue: or else that which consisteth wholy in pleasure, which they name delightfull. Then straightwaie discord entreth: of which three sortes of liues, Soueraigne Iupiter will not giue sentence which is the best, least that in approuing the one, he should condemne the other two; and so the life of man should rather be constrained then free, but hee leaueth them to the judgement of man, to the end that he may as pleaseth him, tie himselfe to that kind of life that shall best like him; it may be, shewing vs thereby, the free choice which is granted to vs by him. Of the which notwithstanding he that is caried away to follow the delightfull kind of life, doth bring vnto him selfe vnspeakeable detriment" (William Jones, trans., *Nennio, or a Treatise of Nobility* (1595), sig. H$_3$^{v}).

[10]Bartholomew Yong, trans., (1598), P. 53.

[11]Rollins, ed., I, p. 70.

[12]Lines 137–38.

[13]*Idea The Shepheards Garland* (1593), Eclogue IX, ll. 55–60.

order to woo Pastorella, suggests the obvious model, "Phrygian Paris by Plexippus brooke."[14]

The Judgment of Paris had of course been treated in medieval love allegories such as Froissart's *L'Espinette Amoureuse*, Machaut's *Le Dit de la Fontaine Amoureuse*, and Lydgate's *Reson and Sensuallyte;* there had been continental dramas on the subject in the fifteenth and early sixteenth centuries; and most important of all for the English pastoral, the Paris story was a common subject of the pageants—for Queen Margaret at Edinburgh in 1503, for the coronation of Anne Boleyn in 1533, and at a marriage masque in 1566.[15] It also appeared in the emblem-books. In Whitney's *Choice of Emblemes* the account of the Judgment is much abbreviated, but full justice is done to the interpretation.[16]

It is obvious, then, that the major Elizabethan treatment of the Paris story, George Peele's play *The Arraignment of Paris* (1584), is in a well-established tradition. It is in dramatic form, but it is so important as an indication of the significance of pastoral in the Elizabethan mind that it must be discussed briefly here.

In the temptation scene, when the three goddesses in turn offer their rewards to Paris, they are more abstract than personal. Juno offers the shepherd "great monarchies, Empires, and kingdomes, heapes of massye golde, scepters and diadems," symbolized theatrically by the appearance of a golden tree, the fruit of which is diadems. Pallas offers fame, wisdom, honor of chivalry and victory, "but yf thou haue a minde to fly aboue." The reward is symbolized by nine knights in armor treading a warlike Almain. Venus offers Paris the services of Cupid, kisses from herself, and finally (here the reward and the symbol become the same thing) Helen.[17] Paris is constantly a symbolic figure; he is suggestive. I do not mean that the artist had nothing to do with this suggestiveness and that the audience could be counted upon to do it all. A sixteenth-century Italian treatise on painting makes clear the artist's obligation in the matter and uses Paris as an example:

> Hence then the painter may learne how to expresse not onely the proper and naturall motions, but also the accidentall; wherein

[14]*Faerie Queene*, VI, ix, xxxvi.

[15]See C. R. Baskervill, "Early Romantic Plays in England," *MP*, XIV (1916–17), p. 483; T. S. Graves, "*The Arraignment of Paris* and Sixteenth Century Flattery," *MLN*, XXVIII (1913), pp. 48–49; A. H. Gilbert, "The Source of Peele's *Arraignment of Paris*," *MLN*, XLI (1926), p. 36; and Douglas Bush, *Mythology and the Renaissance Tradition in English Poetry* (Minneapolis: 1932), pp. 51–52.

[16]Ed. of 1586, p. 83.

[17]Sig. C^r.

consisteth no small part of the difficulty of the Arte, namelie in representing diversities of affections and passions in one bodie: A thing much practized, by the ancient Painters (though with greate difficulty) who ever indevored to leaue no iotte of the *life* vnexpressed.

It is recorded that *Euphranor* gaue such a touch to the counterfeit of *Paris*, that therein the beholder might at once collect, that hee was *Vmpire* of the three *Goddesses*, the *Courter of Helena*, and the slaier of *Achilles*.[18]

But Paris, with the alternatives clearly before him, chooses Venus. When he defends himself before the court of the gods, in Peele's play, he speaks first as a man, blaming his fault, if any, on the judgment of his eye. Then he adds a *reason:* that it was only for beauty he gave the ball, and if other virtues had been concerned he would have chosen Pallas or Juno. Furthermore, he says, he was tempted more than man ever was, and as a shepherd he was relatively immune to offers other than that of Venus.[19] The simplicity of the shepherd's conditions makes for an invulnerability to appeals in the name of wealth or of chivalry. It is only beauty, of the three ideals represented by the goddesses, which has any significant power in a pastoral life.

Paris is the judge precisely because the conditions of the pastoral life provide the greatest independence, the greatest security. The shepherd is not motivated by ambition or by greed. Free from these two common human passions, he enjoys "content," or the good life. Elizabethan pastoral poetry is essentially a celebration of this ideal of content, of *otium*. The contemplative state enjoyed a freedom, not only from ambition or greed, but from the vicissitudes of fortune. The popular tradition of the fall of princes, represented in Elizabethan literature by the *Mirror for Magistrates* and the poems added to it, had stressed ominously the dangers in the turn of Fortune's wheel. Kings and princes, the high and mighty, were exhibited in tragic circumstances, the victims of their own high position, their ambition, or their greed. The poetic tragedies of the *Mirror* therefore supported, negatively, the same ideal celebrated by pastoral. Occasionally the warning in a *Mirror* tragedy concludes with a direct endorsement of the quiet life of content. In one of the tragedies in Blenerhasset's *Mirror*, for example, the herdsman who kills Sigebert and is hanged for it concludes with the lesson:

[18]G. P. Lomazzo, *A Tracte Containing the Artes of Curious Paintinge*, trans., Richard Haydocke (1598), sig. Bb6[r].
[19]Sig. D_4^r.

> And happy he, who voyde of hope can leade
> A quiet lyfe, all voyde of Fortunes dread.

This makes the following Induction deal with the question of why it is that formerly the wisest men were content to be shepherds, but now "in these our dayes, none bee Heardmen but fooles, and euery man though his witte be but meane, yet he cannot liue with a contented mind, except he hath the degree of a Lorde."[20]

In order to respond adequately to the appeal of the Elizabethan ideal of the mean estate, content, and *otium*, it is necessary to feel the force of its opposite, a form of ambition which the sixteenth century called most commonly the aspiring mind. Marlowe's Tamburlaine is of course the great representative of the aspiring mind, as he is its philosopher:

> Nature that fram'd vs of foure Elements,
> Warring within our breasts for regiment,
> Doth teach vs all to haue aspyring minds.[21]

But there are many other examples of the concept in Elizabethan England. Mr. Secretary Walsingham, summing up the personal charges against Mary Queen of Scots, said that she had an aspiring mind;[22] and Queen Elizabeth herself, writing a poem about Mary, included the line

> But clowds of tois vntried, do cloake aspiring mindes.[23]

Blue, as the color of the sky, was symbolic of the aspiring mind, according to Lomazzo:

> Persius sat. 1. speaking of Blew garments, sheweth that they belong only to such persons, as aspire vnto high matters: and Cicero vsed sometimes to weare this color, giuing men thereby to vnderstand, that he bare an aspiring minde.[24]

There were many other Roman examples of the aspiring mind; a typical one is Pompey.[25] That the aspiring mind was a dangerous and

[20]L. B. Campbell ed., *Parts Added to the Mirror for Magistrates* (Cambridge, England: 1946), pp. 462–63.

[21]Lines 869–71. For evidence that Tamburlaine was a symbol of this Renaissance spirit before he appeared in Marlowe's play, see Hallet Smith, "Tamburlaine and the Renaissance," *Elizabethan Studies in Honor of George F. Reynolds* (Boulder, Colo: 1945), pp. 128–29.

[22]Conyers Read, *Mr. Secretary Walsingham and the Policy of Queen Elizabeth I.* (Oxford: 1925), p. 69.

[23]George Puttenham, *The Arte of English Poesie*, ed., Gladys D. Willcock and Alice Walker (Cambridge, England: 1936), p. 248.

[24]Haydocke, trans., *The Arts of Curious Paintinge*, p. 122.

[25]*Fennes Frutes* (1590), sig. E₃ᵛ.

possibly sinful state is made clear by Du Bartas, who contrasts it to the attitude of the angels.[26] The first example of the aspiring mind, according to Du Bartas, was in the hunter, Nimrod, "that was the first Tyrant of the world, after the time of Noah, the first Admiral of the worlde: his aspiring minde & practises in seeking the peoples fauour, his proud and subtle attempt in building the Tower of Babel, & Gods iust punishment thereof in confounding the language of the builders."[27]

The central meaning of pastoral is the rejection of the aspiring mind. The shepherd demonstrates that true content is to be found in this renunciation. Sidney expresses the preference in terms of a contrast between pastoral and court life:

> Greater was that shepheards treasure,
> Then this false, fine, Courtly pleasure.[28]

In the pastoral episode in Book VI of *The Faerie Queene*, Sir Calidore envies the apparent happiness of the shepherds; he comments that their life seems free from the "warres, and wreckes and wicked enmitie" which afflict the rest of the world.[29] In reply to this, the sage old Meliboee then answers with an analysis of the pastoral existence which is in effect a definition of "the good life." It consists of four elements: (1) being content with what you have, however small it is—this is the way taught by nature (contrast Tamburlaine's statement that nature teaches us to have aspiring minds); (2) enjoying freedom from envy of others and from excessive care for your own possessions (the flocks multiply without your doing much about it); (3) avoiding the dangers of pride and ambition and also the insominia that plagues those who hold positions of responsibility (see the testimony of Shakespeare's kings in 2 *Henry IV*, III, i, 1–31, and IV, v, 20–27; *Henry V*, IV, i, 266–90); (4) doing what you like. Old Meliboee does not speak from provincial ignorance, either. He once spent ten years at court, but returned to the pastoral life from choice.

The question of the moral validity of pastoral life when compared with life at court is not difficult to answer: the long tradition of dispraise of the court is always, by implication or by direct statement, an endorsement of the pastoral life. But there is a more difficult question when the alternatives are the quiet, retired life of the shepherd on the one

---

[26]Joshua Sylvester, trans., *The First Day of the Worldes Creation* (1595), sig. E1^v.

[27]William L'Isle, trans., *Babilon*, (1595), sig. A$_3$^{v}.

[28]Hyder E. Rollins, ed., "Disprayse of a Courtly life," first published in *A Poetical Rhapsody* (1602), I (Cambridge: Harvard University Press, 1931, 1932), p. 9–12.

[29]VI, ix, xix.

hand or a mission of chivalric and honorable achievement on the other. The pastoral romance, both in Sidney and in his sources like Montemayor's *Diana*, mingles pastoral and heroic elements. The question of the relative value of the two kinds of life is naturally raised. The pastoral sojourn of Erminia in the seventh book of Tasso's *Jerusalem Delivered* is used as a contrast to the heroic actions of the main part of the poem. It is also obvious that pastoral and heroic put a different light upon the feelings of love; these might or might not be a detriment to the heroic life, but they are sanctioned in the world of pastoral.

The commentators on the sixth book of Spenser's *Faerie Queene* have been at odds over the meaning of the pastoral interlude there, the Pastorella episode. T. P. Harrison says, "Spenser obviously censures Sir Calidore's pastoral aberration; yet he, like Sidney, is inclined to paint the rural picture sympathetically."[30] The opposite view is expressed by C. S. Lewis:

> The greatest mistake that can be made about this book is to suppose that Calidore's long delay among the shepherds is a pastoral truancy from Spenser's moral intention . . . . Courtesy, for the poet, has very little connection with court. It grows "on a lowly stalke"; . . . according to Spenser, courtesy, in its perfect form, comes by nature; moral effort may produce a decent substitute for everyday use, which deserves praise, but it will never rival the real courtesy of those who
>
> so goodly gracious are by kind
> That every action doth them much commend.[31]

Lewis is certainly right about Spenser's endorsement of the pastoral life, or his justification of Sir Calidore, for the opening stanzas of Canto x make it clear.[32] Spenser's own words do not, however, support conclusively the suggestion that courtesy is wholly natural. When in the beginning of Canto xii the poet makes a kind of apology for the wandering structure of the narrative, he is careful to defend the idea behind it.[33] The pastoral environment is a further test and demonstration of Sir Calidore's courtesy, but it is not its source. Calidore treats his shepherd rival, Coridon, with great generosity and magnanimity.[34] The pastoral ideal, then, is reconcilable somehow with the code of chivalry and honor, even though its emphasis is different. As the

[30]"The Relations of Spenser and Sidney," *PMLA*, XLV (1930), p. 720.
[31]*The Allegory of Love* (Oxford: 1936), pp. 350–53.
[32]VI, x, iii.
[33]VI, xii, ii.
[34]VI, ix, xlv.

climax and goal of a life of heroic effort there is a state of heavenly
contemplation not too different from the state of mind of the pastoral
ideal. But this state may be reached only after the knightly quest is
achieved, as we see in the tenth canto of Spenser's Book I.

Closer to pastoral is the Horatian praise of the country gentleman's
life, of which there are many examples in Elizabethan poetry. Wyatt's
first satire, a translation of Alamanni, and Thomas Lodge's "In Praise
of the Countrey Life," a translation of Desportes, are typical. This
type of poetry, like pastoral, proclaims the moral and emotional advantages of the country over the court. Lodge, for example, sings:

> Amidst the pallace braue puft vp with wanton showes
> Ambicions dwell, and there false fauors finde disguise,
> There lodge consuming cares that hatch our common woes:
> Amidst our painted feelds the pleasant Fayrie lies,
>   And all those powers diuine that with vntrussed tresses,
>   Contentment, happie loue, and perfect sport professes.[35]

This kind of thing moves in the direction of satire. . . .

The theme of the Golden Age is one of the great commonplaces of
Elizabethan literature.[36] The creation of an Arcadia which is primitive
and pastoral, which may be identified with the early period before the
birth of Jupiter, and which finally is a country located not so much in
central Greece as in some Utopian space, is a result of the work of
Polybius, Ovid, and Virgil.[37] There are many sources in antiquity for
the theme; it was especially popular among the Stoics, and it was congenial to Stoic thought because it explained the Law of Nature as a
survival from the Golden Age.[38] Accordingly, the best example of it
may be chosen from Seneca:

> 'Twas in such wise, methinks, they lived whom the primal age
> produced, in friendly intercourse with gods. They had no blind
> love of gold; no sacred boundary-stone, judging betwixt peoples,
> separated fields on the spreading plain; not yet did rash vessels
> plough the sea; each man knew only his native waters.[39]

[35]"Sonnets" appended to *Scillaes Metamorphosis* (1589), sig. D₄ʳ.

[36]For the general background, see A. O. Lovejoy and George Boas, *Primitivism and
Related Ideas in Antiquity* (Baltimore: 1935); Paul Meissner, "Das goldene Zeitalter in
der Englischen Renaissance," *Anglia*, LIX (1935), 351–67; E. Lipsker, *Der Mythos
vom goldenen Zeitalter in den Schäferdichtungen Italiens, Spaniens und Frankreichs zur Zeit
der Renaissance* (Berlin: 1933).

[37]Erwin Panofsky, "Et in Arcadia Ego," *Philosophy and History*, ed., Raymond
Klibansky and H. J. Paton (Oxford: 1936), pp. 225–27.

[38]See L. I. Bredvold, "The Naturalism of Donne in Relation to Some Renaissance
Traditions," *JEGP*, XXII (1923), pp. 471–502.

[39]F. J. Miller, trans., *Hippolytus*, in *Seneca's Tragedies*, Loeb Classical Library, I
(1916–17), pp. 525–39.

Spenser in the Proem to Book V of *The Faeri Queene* follows the convention of idealizing the Golden Age,[40] even though his friend Harvey was of the newer school of Jean Bodin, which thought that the earliest periods of history were the worst and that something like progress had taken place.

The first information given the audience about the pastoral atmosphere in Shakespeare's *As You Like It* compares pastoral life to the Golden Age; the wrestler Charles, informing Oliver, and at the same time the audience, of the circumstances of the banished Duke, says:

> They say he is already in the Forest of Arden, and a many merry men with him; and there they live like the old Robin Hood of England; they say many young gentlemen flock to him every day, and fleet the time carelessly, as they did in the golden world.[41]

The identification of the pastoral life with the conditions of the Golden Age was natural enough. One was a criticism of life by means of adopting the point of view of its simplest and purest elements; the other was a criticism of the present way of life by describing an ideal past.

. . .

The Shepheardes Calender appeared anonymously, with a dedication to Sir Philip Sidney; its authorship could hardly have been a secret long, but whether the success of the poem made the poet or only the poem famous is not a matter of much concern to us. The volume did appear, however, with the annotations of one E. K., whose identity has fascinated many antiquarians but has never been perfectly established. E. K., whoever he was, was a mixed blessing. His confusions and his errors have been straightened out by modern scholarship, but one of his contributions, a classification of the eclogues, seems to have been very little utilized.[42]

> These xij. Aeclogues euery where answering to the seasons of the twelue monthes may be well deuided into three formes or ranckes. For eyther they be Plaintiue, as the first, the sixt, the eleuenth, and the twelfth, or recreatiue, such as al those be, which conceiue matter of loue, or commendation of special personages, or Moral: which for the most part be mixed with some Satyrical bitternesse, namely the second of reuerence dewe to old age, the fift of coloured deceipt, the seuenth and ninth of dissolute shepheards and pas-

---

[40]V, Proem, ix.

[41]I, i, 109–14.

[42]There is no comment on the classification in the Spenser Variorum, 9 vols. (Baltimore: 1932–1949). O. Reissert, in "Bemerkungen über Spensers *Shepheards Calender* und die frühere Bukolik," *Anglia*, IX (1886), 205–24, takes up the eclogues according to E. K.'s classification but only for purposes of source study.

tours, the tenth of contempt of Poetrie and pleasaunt wits. And to this diuision may euery thing herein be reasonably applyed: a few onely except, whose speciall purpose and meaning I am not priuie to.[43]

The *Calender* begins and ends with plaintive eclogues. This is appropriate to the winter season of January and December, and it also sets the over-all tone for the series. The total effect must not be harsh and satirical, as the moral eclogues tend to make it, not gay and carefree, as the recreative eclogues would suggest. The poet is our sage and serious Spenser, but his seriousness must be conveyed in tone and mood; doctrine and belief must be expressed primarily as poetry, and for this purpose the tone of the complaint will best serve. . . .

[December] is dependent on Marot, but a more important influence is that of the calendars, with their symbolic representations of the four seasons as representing the stages of a man's life.[44] The career of Colin, which I take to be somewhat more fictional than the commentators do, is here summed up. In spring he experienced exuberance and freedom, felt pride in his songs. In summer he learned his craft, but was smitten with love. In harvest he reaped only a weedy crop of care. And now winter comes:

> Winter is come, that blowes the balefull breath,
> And after Winter commeth timely death.

The paradox here depends upon the idea of a calendar: it runs out as time runs out; and yet the calendar of months is still good, it records something which is permanent. Just so the poet, saying adieu to his delights, to his love, to his sheep and his woods, to his friend, as Colin does in the last stanza, is by the very form in which he says it achieving something that stops time, that contradicts and denies the Death which is the subject. The detachment or the "distance" between the content or argument and the poetry itself produces a paradoxical relationship between them. That Spenser's use of the calendar device was useful for "scale" was first pointed out, I think, by Pope: "The addition he has made of a Calendar to his Eclogues, is very beautiful: since by this, besides that general moral of innocence and simplicity, which is common to other authors of pastoral, he has one peculiar to himself; he compares human Life to the several Seasons, and at once exposes to his readers a view of the great and little worlds, in their various changes

---

[43]C. G. Osgood and H. G. Lotspeich, eds., "The Generall argument of the whole booke," Variorum *Minor Poems*, I (Baltimore: 1943, 1947), p. 12.

[44]See Mary Parmenter, "Spenser's *Twelve Aeglogues Proportionable to the Twelve Monethes*," *ELH*, III (1936), pp. 190–217, for an exposition of the background of calendar and season; the author's suggestion of Queen Elizabeth as Dido is less useful.

and aspects."[45] The missing emblem for Colin is explained by E. K.:
"The meaning wherof is that all thinges perish and come to theyr last
end, but workes of learned wits and monuments of Poetry abide for
euer."[46] This is clearly the implication of the whole eclogue and, as
summary, of the whole *Shepheardes Calender*. Shakespeare found in Ovid
the same commonplace and developed it in a non-pastoral setting in
his sonnets. The pastoral handling of the theme enjoys an added richness, for, as the reply to Marlowe's "Passionate Shepherd" shows, time
is the answer to the pastoral ideal. But what if, in poetry, there is an
answer to the answer? . . . Far from being escapist, pastoral poetry was
the most apt of all the kinds for serious humanistic purposes. . . . The
shepherd's life is always stressed as one in which the characteristics of
the mind and will are important; the conditions for human existence
are most favorable, and there are few dangers from pride or ambition,
but the goddesses still appear before a shepherd and demand that he
choose between them. A wrong choice is always possible. The shepherd
is still man seen simply, but his idyllic life is now put upon a basis of
moral responsibility, and the existence of evil is recognized. . . . The
shepherd as pastor is responsible for caring for his flock; he has his
reward in protecting them from the wolves. What, then, are the
responsibilities of the shepherd as poet? Shall he be content "to feede
youthes fancie, and the flocking fry" with his dapper ditties? Is he a
mere entertainer? No, Piers replies, he can influence them morally. . . .

Drayton is the most interesting of the followers of Spenser in pastoral, and he illustrates well enough the survival of interest in pastoral
poetry, even though the style of it changed, on into the seventeenth
century. . . . When Drayton proceeds to his description of the Golden
Age, he makes clear that it was the time when the pastoral ideal governed mankind. His description of the Golden Age is both pictorial-
idyllic and moral; simplicity and beauty went hand in hand with innocence. When the aspiring mind destroyed the pastoral *otium* and the
Golden Age was no more, poets began to write of "slaughtering broiles
and bloody horror." The corruption of more recent times may be seen
by the absence of the natural and simple in life. . . .

[45]Norman Ault, ed., "A Discourse on Pastoral Poetry," *The Prose Works of Alexander Pope* (Oxford: 1936), pp. 301–2.
[46]A. H. Gilbert, "The Embleme for December in the *Shepheardes Calender*," *MLN*,
LXIII (1948), pp. 181–82, gives reasons for thinking that *Merce non mercede*, at the end
of the book, is the misplaced December emblem. Whatever the case, we have the
meaning of the December emblem preserved for us in the Glosse, and it is the meaning
that is here important.

ERWIN PANOFSKY

Et in Arcadia Ego

I

In 1769 Sir Joshua Reynolds showed to his friend Dr. Johnson his latest picture: the double portrait of Mrs. Bouverie and Mrs. Crewe, still to be seen in Crewe Hall in England.[1] It shows the two lovely ladies seated before a tombstone and sentimentalizing over its inscription: one points out the text to the other, who meditates thereon in the then fashionable pose of Tragic Muses and Melancholias.[2] The text of the inscription reads: "*Et in Arcadia ego.*"

"What can this mean?" exclaimed Dr. Johnson. "It seems very nonsensical—I am in Arcadia." "The King could have told you," replied Sir Joshua. "He saw it yesterday and said at once: 'Oh, there is a tombstone in the background: Ay, ay, death is even in Arcadia.' "[3]

To the modern reader the angry discomfiture of Dr. Johnson is very puzzling. But no less puzzling is the quick understanding of George III, who instantly grasped the purport of the Latin phrase but interpreted it in a manner dissimilar to that which seems self-evident to most of us. In contrast to Dr. Johnson, we are no longer stumped by the phrase *Et in Arcadia ego.* But in contrast to George III, we are accustomed to reading a very different meaning into it. For us, the formula *Et in Arcadia ego* has come to be synonymous with such paraphrases as "Et tu in Arcadia vixisti," "I, too, was born in Arcadia,"

From *Philosophy and History, Essays Presented to Ernst Cassirer*, by Erwin Panofsky. Reprinted by permission of the Clarendon Press, Oxford, pp. 295–320.

[1]C. R. Leslie and Tom Taylor, *Life and Times of Sir Joshua Reynolds*, I, (London: 1865), p. 325.

[2]See E. Wind, "Humanitätsidee und heroisiertes Porträt in der englischen Kultur des 18. Jahrhunderts," *Vorträge der Bibliothek Warburg* (1930–1931), pp. 156 ff., especially pp. 222 ff.

[3]Leslie and Taylor, *op. cit.*

"Ego fui in Arcadia,"[4] "Auch ich war in Arkadien geboren,"[5] "Moi aussi je fus pasteur en Arcadie";[6] and all these and many similar versions amount to what Mrs. Felicia Hemans expressed in the immortal words: "I, too, shepherds, in Arcadia dwelt."[7] They conjure up the retrospective vision of an unsurpassable happiness, enjoyed in the past, unattainable ever after, yet enduringly alive in the memory: a bygone happiness ended by death; and not, as George III's paraphrase implies, a present happiness menaced by death.

I shall try to show that this royal rendering—"Death is even in Arcadia"—represents a grammatically correct, in fact, the only grammatically correct, interpretation of the Latin phrase *Et in Arcadia ego*, and that our modern reading of its message—"I, too, was born, or lived, in Arcady"—is in reality a mistranslation. Then I shall try to show that this mistranslation, indefensible though it is from a philological point of view, yet did not come about by "pure ignorance" but, on the contrary, expressed and sanctioned, at the expense of grammar but in the interest of truth, a basic change in interpretation. Finally, I shall try to fix the ultimate responsibility for this change, which was of paramount importance for modern literature, not on a man of letters but on a great painter.

Before attempting all this, however, we have to ask ourselves a preliminary question: how is it that that particular, not overly opulent, region of central Greece, Arcady, came to be universally accepted as an ideal realm of perfect bliss and beauty, a dream incarnate of ineffable happiness, surrounded nevertheless with a halo of "sweetly sad" melancholy?

There had been, from the beginning of classical speculation, two

---

[4]This form of the phrase is found in Richard Wilson's picture (in the collection of the Earl of Strafford), cited below, p. 43.

[5]This is the beginning of Friedrich Schiller's famous poem *Resignation* (quoted, for example, in Büchmann, *Geflügelte Worte*, 27th ed., pp. 441 f., with many other instances from German literature), where the frustrated hero has renounced Pleasure and Beauty in favor of Hope and Truth and unsuccessfully requests compensation. In English dictionaries of quotations, the passage is often erroneously ascribed to Goethe (by way of confusion with the motto superscribed on his *Italienische Reise*, for which see below, p. 45); cf., e.g., Burt Stevenson, *The Home Book of Quotations* (New York: 1937), p. 94; *A New Dictionary of Quotations*, H. L. Mencken, ed. (New York: 1942), p. 53 (here with the equally erroneous assertion that "the phrase begins to appear on paintings in the XVI century"); Bartlett's *Familiar Quotations* (Boston: 1947), p. 1043.

[6]Jacques Delille, *Les Jardins*, 1782, quoted, e.g., in Büchmann, *op. cit.* and Stevenson, *op. cit.*

[7]*The Poetical Works of Mrs. Felicia Hemans* (Philadelphia: 1847), p. 398. See also below, p. 44, Note 49.

contrasting opinions about the natural state of man, each of them, of course, a "Gegen-Konstruktion" to the conditions under which it was formed. One view, termed "soft" primitivism in an illuminating book by Lovejoy and Boas,[8] conceives of primitive life as a golden age of plenty, innocence and happiness—in other words, as civilized life purged of its vices. The other, "hard" form of primitivism conceives of primitive life as an almost subhuman existence full of terrible hardships and devoid of all comforts—in other words, as civilized life stripped of its virtues.

Arcady, as we encounter it in all modern literature, and as we refer to it in our daily speech, falls under the heading of "soft" or golden-age primitivism. But of Arcady as it existed in actuality, and as it is described to us by the Greek writers, almost the opposite is true.

To be sure, this real Arcady was the domain of Pan, who could be heard playing the syrinx on Mount Maenalus,[9] and its inhabitants were famous for their musical accomplishments as well as for their ancient lineage, rugged virtue, and rustic hospitality; but they were also famous for their utter ignorance and low standards of living. As the earlier Samuel Butler was to summarize it in his well-known satire against ancestral pride:

> The old Arcadians that could trace
> Their pedigree from race to race
> Before the moon, were once reputed
> Of all the Grecians the most stupid,
> Whom nothing in the world could bring
> To civil life but fiddleing.[10]

And from a purely physical point of view their country lacked most of the charms which we are wont to associate with a land of ideal pastoral bliss. Polybius, Arcady's most famous son, while doing justice to his homeland's simple piety and love of music, describes it otherwise as a poor, bare, rocky, chilly country, devoid of all the amenities of life and scarcely affording food for a few meager goats.[11]

[8]A. O. Lovejoy and G. Boas, *Primitivism and Related Ideas in Antiquity*, I (Baltimore: 1935).

[9]Pausanius, *Periegesis*, VIII, 36, 8: "Mount Maenalus is particularly sacred to Pan so that people assert that Pan could be heard there playing the syrinx."

[10]Samuel Butler, *Satires and Miscellaneous Poetry and Prose*, ed., R. Lamar (Cambridge: 1929), p. 470.

[11]Polybius, *Historiae*, IV, p. 20. For further authors emphasizing the negative aspects of primordial simplicity, see, for example, Juvenal, who characterized a peculiarly boring orator as an "Arcadian youth" (*Saturae*, VII, p. 160) and Philostratus, *Vita Apollonii*, VIII, p. 7, who calls the Arcadians "acorn-eating swine." Even their

Small wonder, then, that the Greek poets refrained from staging their pastorals in Arcady. The scene of the most famous of them, the *Idylls* of Theocritus, is laid in Sicily, then so richly endowed with all those flowery meadows, shadowy groves and mild breezes which the "desert ways" (William Lithgow) of the actual Arcady conspicuously lacked. Pan himself has to journey from Arcady to Sicily when Theocritus' dying Daphnis wishes to return his shepherd's flute to the god.[12]

It was in Latin, not in Greek, poetry that the great shift took place and that Arcady entered upon the stage of world literature. But even here we can still distinguish between two opposite manners of approach, one represented by Ovid, the other by Virgil. Both of them based their conception of Arcady to some extent on Polybius; but they used him in diametrically opposed ways. Ovid describes the Arcadians as primeval savages, still representing that period "prior to the birth of Jupiter and the creation of the moon," to which Samuel Butler alludes:

> Ante Jovem genitum terras habuisse feruntur
> Arcades, et Luna gens prior illa fuit.
> Vita ferae similis, nullos agitata per usus;
> Artis adhuc expers et rude volgus erat.[13]

"The Arcadians are said to have inhabited the earth before the birth of Jupiter; their tribe was older than the moon. Not as yet enhanced by discipline and manners, their life was similar to that of beasts; they were an uncouth lot, still ignorant of art." Very consistently, Ovid makes no mention of their one redeeming feature, their musicality: he made Polybius' Arcady even worse than it was.

Virgil, on the other hand, idealized it: not only did he emphasize the virtues that the real Arcady had (including the all-pervading sound of song and flutes not mentioned by Ovid); he also added charms which the real Arcady had never possessed: luxuriant vegetation,

---

musical achievements were disparaged by Fulgentius, *Expositio Virgilianae continentiae*, 748, 19, ed., R. Helm (Leipzig: 1898), p. 90, who by *Arcadicae aures* (the reading *Arcadicis auribus* is better documented than, and preferable to, *arcaicis auribus*) meant "ears not susceptible to real beauty." The much discussed question as to whether there had existed in Arcady a genuine pastoral or bucolic poetry preceding Theocritus' *Idylls* now seems to have been decided in the negative. In addition to the literature adduced in E. Panofsky, "Et in Arcadia Ego; On the Conception of Transience in Poussin and Watteau," *Philosophy and History, Essays Presented to Ernst Cassirer*, eds., R. Klibansky and H. J. Paton (Oxford: 1936), pp. 223 ff., see now B. Snell, "Arkadien, die Entstehung einer geistigen Landschaft," *Antike und Abendland*, I (1944), pp. 26 ff. An article by M. Petriconi, "Das neue Arkadien," *ibidem*, III (1948), pp. 187 ff., does not contribute much to the problem discussed in this essay.

[12]Theocritus, *Idylls*, I, pp. 123 ff.
[13]Ovid, *Fasti*, II, pp. 289 ff.

eternal spring, and inexhaustible leisure for love. In short, he transplanted the bucolics of Theocritus to what he decided to call Arcadia, so that Arethusa, the fountain nymph of Syracuse, must come to his assistance in Arcady,[14] whereas Theocritus' Pan, as mentioned before, had been implored to travel in the opposite direction.

In so doing, Virgil accomplished infinitely more than a mere synthesis of "hard" and "soft" primitivism, of the wild Arcadian pine trees with the Sicilian groves and meadows, of Arcadian virtue and piety with Sicilian sweetness and sensuousness: he transformed two realities into one Utopia, a realm sufficiently remote from Roman everyday life to defy realistic interpretation (the very names of the characters as well as of the plants and animals suggest an unreal, far-off atmosphere when the Greek words occur in the context of Latin verse), yet sufficiently saturated with visual concreteness to make a direct appeal to the inner experience of every reader.

It was, then, in the imagination of Virgil, and of Virgil alone, that the concept of Arcady, as we know it, was born—that a bleak and chilly district of Greece came to be transfigured into an imaginary realm of perfect bliss. But no sooner had this new, Utopian Arcady come into being than a discrepancy was felt between the supernatural perfection of an imaginary environment and the natural limitations of human life as it is. True enough, the two fundamental tragedies of human existence, frustrated love and death, are by no means absent from Theocritus' *Idylls*. On the contrary, they are strongly accentuated and depicted with haunting intensity. No. reader of Theocritus will ever forget the desperate, monotonous invocations of the abandoned Simaetha, who, in the dead of night, spins her magic wheel in order to regain her lover;[15] or the end of Daphnis, destroyed by Aphrodite because he has dared challenge the power of love.[16] But with Theocritus these human tragedies are real—just as real as the Sicilian scenery— and they are things of the present. We actually witness the despair of the beautiful sorceress; we actually hear the dying words of Daphnis even though they form part of a "pastoral song." In Theocritus' real Sicily, the joys and sorrows of the human heart complement each other as naturally and inevitably as do rain and shine, day and night, in the life of nature.

In Virgil's ideal Arcady human suffering and superhumanly

[14]Virgil, *Eclogues*, X, pp. 4–6.
[15]Theocritus, *Idylls*, II.
[16]Theocritus, *Idylls*, I.

perfect surroundings create a dissonance. This dissonance, once felt, had to be resolved, and it was resolved in that vespertinal mixture of sadness and tranquillity which is perhaps Virgil's most personal contribution to poetry. With only slight exaggeration one might say that he "discovered" the evening. When Theocritus' shepherds conclude their melodious converse at nightfall, they like to part with a little joke about the behavior of nannies and billy goats.[17] At the end of Virgil's *Eclogues* we feel evening silently settle over the world: "Ite domum saturae, venit Hesperus, ite, capellae";[18] or: "Majoresque cadunt altis de montibus umbrae."[19]

Virgil does not exclude frustrated love and death; but he deprives them, as it were, of their factuality. He projects tragedy either into the future or, preferably, into the past, and he thereby transforms mythical truth into elegiac sentiment. It is this discovery of the elegiac, opening up the dimension of the past and thus inaugurating that long line of poetry that was to culminate in Thomas Gray, which makes Virgil's bucolics, in spite of their close dependence on Greek models, a work of original and immortal genius. The Daphnis motif, for instance, was used by Virgil in two of his *Eclogues*, the Tenth and the Fifth. But in both cases, tragedy no longer faces us as stark reality but is seen through the soft, colored haze of sentiment either anticipatory or retrospective.

In the Tenth *Eclogue*, the dying Daphnis is boldly—and, it would seem, not without humor—transformed into a real person, Virgil's friend and fellow poet, Gallus. And while Theocritus' Daphnis is really dying because he has refused to love, Virgil's Gallus announces to a group of sympathizing shepherds and sylvan divinities that he is going to die because his mistress, Lycoris, has left him for a rival:

[17]Theocritus, *Idylls*, I, pp. 151 f.; V, pp. 147 ff.

[18]Virgil, *Eclogues*, X, p. 77: "Come home, you've had your fill; the evening star is here; come home, my goats." See also *Eclogues*, VI, pp. 84 ff.:

> Ille canit (pulsae referunt ad sidera valles),
> Cogere donec ovis stabulis numerumque referre
> Iussit et invito processit Vesper Olympo.

"[Silenus] sings, the echoing valleys wafting the sound to the stars, until Hesperus has ordered the flocks to be stabled and counted and, against Olympus' wishes, has pursued his course." The *invito Olympo* ("Olympus" here used for "the Olympians" as we use "the Kremlin" for the Russian government) has to be construed as an ablative absolute: the gods regret that the relentless progress of the evening star puts an end to the song of Silenus.

[19]Virgil, *Eclogues*, I, p. 83: "And longer fall the shadows from the mountains high."

she dwells in the dreary North but she is happy in the arms of her hand-some soldier, Antony; he, Gallus, is surrounded by all the beauties of Utopia but wastes away with grief, comforted only by the thought that his sufferings and ultimate demise will be the subject of an Arcadian dirge.

In the Fifth *Eclogue*, Daphnis has retained his identity; but—and this is the novelty—his tragedy is presented to us only through the elegiac reminiscences of his survivors, who are preparing a memorial ceremony and are about to raise a tombstone for him:

> A lasting monument to Daphnis raise
> With this inscription to record his praise:
> "Daphnis, the fields' delight, the shepherds' love,
> Renown'd on earth and deifi'd above;
> Whose flocks excelled the fairest on the plains,
> But less than he himself surpassed the swains."[20]

II

Here, then, is the first appearance of the "Tomb in Arcadia," that almost indispensable feature of Arcady in later poetry and art. But after Virgil's passing, this tomb, and with it Virgil's Arcady as a whole, was to sink into oblivion for many centuries. During the Middle Ages, when bliss was sought in the beyond and not in any region of the earth, however perfect, pastoral poetry assumed a realis-tic, moralizing and distinctly non-Utopian character.[21] The *dramatis personae* were "Robin" and "Marion" instead of "Daphnis" and "Chloe," and the scene of Boccaccio's *Ameto*, where more than thirteen hundred years after Virgil at least the name of Arcadia reappears, is laid near Cortona in Tuscany. Arcadia is represented only by an emissary, so to speak, and this emissary— a shepherd named Alcesto di Arcadia—limits himself to defending, after the fashion of the con-ventional "debates" (*concertationes* or *conflictus*), the Polybian and Ovi-dian ideal of rough and healthy frugality against the charms of wealth and comfort extolled by his rival, Achaten di Achademia from Sicily.[22]

In the Renaissance, however, Virgil's—not Ovid's and Polybius'— Arcady emerged from the past like an enchanting vision. Only, for the modern mind, this Arcady was not so much a Utopia of bliss and beauty distant in space as a Utopia of bliss and beauty distant in time.

[20]Virgil, *Eclogues*, V, pp. 42 ff., here quoted from Dryden's translation.

[21]For a brief summary of the development, see L. Levraut, *Le Genre pastoral* (Paris: 1914).

[22]Boccaccio, *Ameto*, V (Florence edition: 1529), pp. 23 ff.

Like the whole classical sphere, of which it had become an integral part, Arcady became an object of that nostalgia which distinguishes the real Renaissance from all those pseudo- or proto-Renaissances that had taken place during the Middle Ages:[23] it developed into a haven, not only from a faulty reality but also, and even more so, from a questionable present. At the height of the Quattrocento an attempt was made to bridge the gap between the present and the past by means of an allegorical fiction. Lorenzo the Magnificent and Politian metaphorically identified the Medici villa at Fiesole with Arcady and their own circle with the Arcadian shepherds; and it is this alluring fiction which underlies Signorelli's famous picture—now, unhappily, destroyed—which used to be admired as the *Realm of Pan.*[24]

Soon, however, the visionary kingdom of Arcady was reestablished as a sovereign domain. In Boccaccio's *Ameto* it had figured only as a distant home of rustic simplicity, and the Medicean poets had used it only as a classical disguise for their own country life. In Jacopo Sannazaro's *Arcadia*[25] of 1502 Arcady itself is the scene of the action and is glorified for its own sake; it is revived as an emotional experience *sui generis* and *sui juris* intead of serving as a classical pseudonym for the poet's and his patrons' own surrounding. Sannazaro's Arcady is, like Virgil's, a Utopian realm. But in addition it is a realm irretrievably lost, seen through a veil of reminiscent melancholy: "La musa vera del Sannazaro è la malinconia," as an Italian scholar puts it.[26] Reflecting the feeling of a period that, for the first time, had realized that Pan was dead, Sannazaro wallows in those funeral hymns and ceremonies, yearning love songs and melancholy memories which occur in Virgil only occasionally; and his very predilection for triple rhymes, technically known as *drucciolo* (a few lines of this kind will be quoted later), endows his verses with a sweet, lingering plaintiveness.

[23]See E. Panofsky, "Renaissance and Renascences," *Kenyon Review*, VI (1944), pp. 201 ff.

[24]For an analysis of Signorelli's painting, see F. Saxl, *Antike Götter in der Spätrenaissance, Studien der Bibliothek Warburg*, VIII (Leipzig and Berlin: 1927), pp. 22 ff.

[25]For Jacopo Sannazaro's *Arcadia*, see M. Scherillo's illuminating introduction to his edition of 1888. Sannazaro's poem—first published at Venice in 1502—is based on both Italian and classical sources (Petrarch and Boccaccio on the one hand, Virgil, Polybius, Catullus, Longus, Nemesius, etc., on the other), thereby resuscitating the Virgilian conception of Arcadia within the limits of a modern, more subjective *Weltanschauung*. Sannazaro's is the first postclassical pastoral actually staged *in* Arcadia, and it is a significant fact that the few allusions to the contemporary scene, the court of Naples, were added, or at least made explicit, only in the second edition of 1504.

[26]A. Sainati, *La lirica latina del Rinascimento*, I (Pisa: 1919), p. 184, quoted by Saxl, *ibidem.*

It was through him that the elegiac feeling—present but, as it were, peripheral in Virgil's *Eclogues*—became the central quality of the Arcadian sphere. One more step and this nostalgic but as yet impersonal longing for the unbroken peace and innocence of an ideal past was sharpened into a bitter, personal accusation against the real present. The famous "O bell'età de l'oro" in Torquato Tasso's *Aminta* (1573) is not so much a eulogy of Arcady as an invective against the constrained and conscience-ridden spirit of Tasso's own period, the age of the Counter-Reformation. Flowing hair and nude bodies are bound and concealed, deportment and carriage have lost touch with nature; the very spring of pleasure is polluted, the very gift of Love perverted into theft.[27] Here is the outburst of an actor stepping before the footlights and in the presence of all contrasting the misery of his real existence with the splendor of his role.

III

Almost exactly half a century later, Giovanni Francesco Guercino—not Bartolommeo Schidone, as stated in all "Dictionaries of Familiar Quotations"—produced the first pictorial rendering of the Death in Arcady theme; and it is in this picture, painted at Rome between 1621 and 1623 and now preserved in the Galleria Corsini, that we first encounter the phrase *Et in Arcadia ego*.[28] There are reasons to believe that the subject was of special interest to Giulio Rospigliosi (later Pope Clement IX), whose family palace, which housed Guido Reni's *Aurora*, must have been frequently visited by Guercino when he composed his own, more modern *Aurora* in the Casino Ludovisi; and Giulio Rospigliosi—a humanist, a lover of the arts, and a poet of no mean merits—may even be the inventor of the famous phrase, which is not classical and does not seem to occur in literature before it made its appearance in Guercino's picture.[29] What, then, is the literal sense of this phrase?

[27]Tasso, *Aminta*, I, 2, ed., E. Grillo (London and Toronto: 1924), pp. 90 ff.

[28]Guercino's picture is referred to as Schidone's in, for example, Büchmann, *op. cit.;* Bartlett, *op. cit.* (where, in addition, the inscription on Poussin's Louvre painting. is misquoted as *Et ego in Arcadia vixi*); and Hoyt's *New Cyclopedia of Poetical Quotations* (which has the text right but translates it as: "I, too, was in Arcadia"). For the correct attribution of the painting, see H. Voss, "Kritische Bemerkungen zu Seicentisten in den römischen Galerien," *Repertorium für Kunstwissenschaft*, XXXIV (1911), pp. 119 ff. (p. 121).

[29]For Giulio Rospigliosi, see L. von Pastor, *The History of the Popes*, trans., E. Graf, XXXI (London: 1949), pp. 319 ff.; for his poetical works, G. Cavenazzi, *Papa Clemente IX Poeta* (Modena: 1900). He was born in 1600 at Pistoia but educated at the Jesuits'

As was mentioned at the beginning, we are now inclined to translate it as "I, too, was born, or lived, in Arcady." That is to say, we assume that the *et* means "too" and refers to *ego*, and we further assume that the unexpressed verb stands in the past tense; we thus attribute the whole phrase to a defunct inhabitant of Arcady. All these assumptions are incompatible with the rules of Latin grammar. The phrase *Et in Arcadia ego* is one of those elliptical sentences like *Summum jus summa iniuria, E pluribus unum, Nequid nimis* or *Sic semper tyrannis,* in which the verb has to be supplied by the reader. This unexpressed verb must therefore be unequivocally suggested by the words given, and this means that it can never be a preterite. It is possible to suggest a subjunctive as in *Nequid nimis* ("Let there never be done too much") or *Sic semper tyrannis* ("May this be the fate of all tyrants"); it is also possible, though fairly unusual, to suggest a future as in Neptune's famous

---

College at Rome, subsequently studied at the University of Pisa, and taught philosophy there from 1623 to 1625 (which, of course, did not prevent him from visiting Rome at intervals). Soon after, he seems to have settled in Rome (in 1629 he composed poems on a Barberini-Colonna wedding) and obtained high offices at the Curia in 1632. After nine years as papal nuncio in Spain (1644–53), he became governor of Rome (1655), was created cardinal in 1657, elected pope in 1667, and died in 1669. That this cultured and unselfish prince of the Church—who patronized the first "Exhibition of Old Masters," organized by his brother, in the last year of his papacy (Pastor, p. 331)—was in some way involved with the *Et in Arcadia* subject is suggested by a passage in G. P. Bellori, *Le vite de' pittori, scultori, et architetti moderni* (Rome: 1672), pp. 447 f. After having described Poussin's *"Ballo della vita humana,"* now in the Wallace Collection at London, Bellori informs us that the subject of this *morale poesia* had been "suggested by Pope Clement IX, when still a prelate," and goes on to say that the painter did full justice to the *sublimità dell'Autore che aggiunse le due seguenti invenzioni,* to wit, *"La verità scoperta del Tempo"* (probably not identical with the painting now in the Louvre but with another version, transmitted through the engravings listed in A. Andresen, *Nicolaus Poussin; Verzeichnis der nach seinen Gemälden gefertigten Kupferstiche* (Leipzig: 1863), Nos. 407 and 408, the latter dedicated to Clement IX) and *"La Felicità soggetta a la Morte,"* that is to say, the *Et in Arcadia ego* composition. Barring a typographical error (omission of a *si* before *che aggiunse*), the "exalted" *Autore* can only be Giulio Rospigliosi (for Poussin is referred to, at the beginning of the same sentence, as *Niccolo*): according to Bellori it was he, Rospigliosi, who "added the two following inventions," that is to say, in addition to the *Ballo della vita Humana,* the *Vertià scoperta del Tempo* and the Arcadia subject.

The difficulty is that—as we know while Bellori probably did not—this subject had already been treated by Guercino between 1621 and 1623 while he was engaged upon his Aurora fresco in the Casino Ludovisi. Bellori's brief account may have simplified a situation which might be tentatively reconstructed as follows: Bellori knew from Poussin that Giulio Rospigliosi had ordered the Louvre version of the *Et in Arcadia ego* and had informed Poussin that he, Rospigliosi, was the actual inventor of the subject. Bellori took this to mean that Rospigliosi had "invented" the subject when ordering the Louvre picture; but what Rospigliosi had really claimed was that he had suggested it to Guercino (doubtless a frequent visitor to Guido Reni's *Aurora*) and, subsequently, asked Poussin to repeat it in an improved redaction.

Quos ego ("These I shall deal with"); but it is not possible to suggest a past tense. Even more important: the adverbial *et* invariably refers to the noun or pronoun directly following it (as in *Et tu, Brute*), and this means that it belongs, in our case, not to *ego* but to *Arcadia;* it is amusing to observe that some modern writers accustomed to the now familiar interpretation but blessed with an inbred feeling for good Latin—for instance, Balzac,[30] the German Romanticist C. J. Weber,[31] and the excellent Miss Dorothy Sayers[32]—instinctively misquote the *Et in Arcadia ego* into *Et ego in Arcadia*. The correct translation of the phrase in its orthodox form is, therefore, not "I, too, was born, or lived, in Arcady," but: "Even in Arcady there am I," from which we must conclude that the speaker is not a deceased Arcadian shepherd or shepherdess but Death in person. In short, King George III's interpretation is, grammatically, absolutely right. And with reference to Guercino's painting, it is also absolutely right from a visual point of view.

In this painting two Arcadian shepherds are checked in their wanderings by the sudden sight, not of a funerary monument but of a huge human skull that lies on a moldering piece of masonry and receives the attentions of a fly and a mouse, popular symbols of decay and all-devouring time.[33] Incised on the masonry are the words *Et in*

[30]Balzac, *Madame Firmiani:* "J'ai aussi aimé, *et ego in Arcadia*."

[31]C. J. Weber, *Demokritos oder hinterlassene Papiere eines lachenden Philosophen* XII (n. d.), 20, pp. 253 ff.: "Gräber und Urnen in englischen Gärten verbreiten die namliche sanfte Wehmut wie ein Gottesacker oder ein 'Et ego in Arcadia,' in einer Landschaft von Poussin," and the same erroneous reading, now fairly well explained, occurs in the earlier editions of Büchmann's *Geflügelte Worte* (in the 16th edition, for instance, on p. 582).

[32]Dorothy Sayers, "The Bone of Contention," *Lord Peter Views the Body* (New York: Harcourt, Brace & World, Inc.), p. 139. This feeling for Latin grammar seems to be widespread among British mystery-story writers. In Nicholas Blake's *Thou Shell of Death*, XII (Continental Albatross Edition: 1937), p. 219, an elderly nobleman says: "*Et ego*, Superintendent, *in Arcadia vixi*—what?"

[33]The significance of the mouse as a symbol of all-devouring time is already pointed out in Horapollo's *Hieroglyphica* I, 50, (now easily accessible in G. Boas, *The Hieroglyphics of Horapollo*, Bollingen Series, XXIII (New York: 1950), p. 80) and remained well known throughout the centuries (cf. the mediaeval allegory of human life known as "The Tree of Barlaam"; according to Condivi, *Vita di Michelangelo*, cap. xlv, even Michelangelo is said to have planned the inclusion of a mouse in the iconography of the Medici Chapel). Viewed through the medium of "Romantic irony" the motive of the Guercino picture looks as follows: "Ein gar herrliches 'Memento mori' ist . . . ein hübscher gebleichter *Menschenshädel* auf der Toilette. So ein leerer Hirnksten . . . müsste Wunder tun, wenn die Macht der Gewohnheit nicht noch stärker wäre. . . . Man würde zuletzt das Dasein des Totenschädels ganz vergessen, wenn nicht schon zu Zeiten *eine Maus* ihn wieder lebendig gemacht . . . hätte" (Weber, *op. cit.*).

Arcadia ego, and it is unquestionably by the skull that they are supposed to be pronounced; an old description of the picture mistakenly but understandably even places them on a scroll issuing from the skull's mouth.[34] The skull, now, was and is the accepted symbol of Death personified, as is borne out by the very fact that the English language refers to it, not as a "dead man's head," but as a "death's-head." The speaking death's-head was thus a common feature in sixteenth- and seventeenth-century art and literature[35] and is even alluded to by Falstaff (*Henry IV*, second part, ii, 4) when he answers Doll Tearsheet's well-intentioned warnings as to his conduct: "Peace, good Doll, do

[34]Leslie and Taylor, *op. cit.*, with reference to Reynolds' portrait of Mrs. Bouverie and Mrs. Crewe: "The thought is borrowed from Guercino where the gay frolickers stumble over a death's-head with a scroll proceeding from his mouth inscribed *Et in Arcadia ego*." The "scroll" allegedly proceeding from the mouth of the skull is obviously due to a misinterpretation of the mouse's tail. Only, as I don't know the Reynolds sketch (unfortunately the "Roman Sketchbook," formerly belonging to R. Gwatkin, see Leslie and Taylor, *op. cit.*, I, p. 51, could not be located), I cannot tell whether Reynolds misinterpreted the picture or Tom Taylor misinterpreted the sketch. In any case this very misinterpretation shows that even at a comparatively recent period an unbiased observer of the Guercino composition naturally assumed that the words *Et in Arcadia ego* were voiced by the skull.

[35]As to the significance of skulls and skeletons in connection with the general conception of life and destiny, see R. Zahn, *81. Berliner Winckelmanns-Programm* (1923); T. Creizenach, "Gaudeamus igitur," *Verhandlungen der 28 Versammlung Deutscher Philologen und Schulmänner* (Leipzig: 1872); C. H. Becker, "Ubi sunt qui ante nos in mundo fuere?," *Aufsätze zur Kultur- und Sprachgeschichte, vornehmlich des Islam*, Ernst Kuhn zum 70. Geburtstage gewidmet (1916), pp. 87 ff. It appears that the original significance of those morbid symbols, occurring on goblets and table decorations before they appeared on sepulchral monuments, was a purely hedonistic one, viz., an invitation to enjoy the pleasures of life as long as it lasts, and only subsequently was turned into a moralistic sermon of resignation and penitence. This development took place in ancient Egypt as well as in the civilizations deriving from classical antiquity, both occidental and oriental. In them, the inversion of the original idea was chiefly due to patristic writing. In point of fact, the *Vita brevis* idea is characterized by an intrinsic ambivalence implying both the Horatian *Carpe diem* and the Christian *surge, surge, vigila, semper esto paratus* (refrain of a song of 1267). From the later phase of the Middle Ages the "speaking" skulls and skeletons became so common a symbol of the *memento mori* idea (in the Camaldulensian sense of this formula) that these motifs invaded almost every sphere of everday life. Innumerable instances are not only to be found in sepulchral art (mostly with such inscriptions as *Vixi ut vivis, morieris ut sum mortuus* or *Tales vos eritis, fueram quandoque quod estis*), but also in portraits, on clocks, on medals, and, most especially, on finger rings (many instances adduced in the London Shakespeare edition of 1785 with reference to the notorious dialogue between Falstaff and Doll Tearsheet). On the other hand, the menace of a "speaking skull" could also be interpreted as a hopeful prospect for the afterlife, as is the case in a short stanza by the German seventeenth-century poet D. C. von Lohenstein, in which the *Redender Todtenkopff des Herrn Matthaus Machners* says: *Ja/ wenn der Höchste wird vom Kirch-Hof erndten ein/ So werd ich Todten-Kopff ein Englisch Antlitz seyn* (quoted in W. Benjamin, *Ursprung des deutschen Trauerspiels*, [1928], p. 215).

not speak like a death's-head; do not bid me remember mine end."

This "remember mine end" is precisely the message of Guercino's painting. It conveys a warning rather than sweet, sad memories. There is little or nothing elegiac about it, and when we try to trace the iconographic antecedents of the composition, we find them in such moralistic representations as the renderings of the Legend of the Three Quick and the Three Dead (known to all from the Camposanto at Pisa), where three young knights, setting out for a hunt, come upon three corpses that rise from their coffins and warn the elegant young men against their thoughtless enjoyment of life. As these mediaeval dandies are stopped by the coffins, so are Guercino's Arcadians stopped by the skull; the old description just mentioned even speaks of them as "gay frolickers *stumbling over* a death's-head."[36] In both cases Death catches youth by the throat, so to speak, and "bids it remember the end." In short, Guercino's picture turns out to be a mediaeval *memento mori* in humanistic disguise—a favorite concept of Christian moral theology shifted to the ideal milieu of classical and classicizing pastorals.

We happen to know that Sir Joshua Reynolds not only knew but even sketched Guercino's painting (ascribing it, incidentally, to its true author instead of to Bartolommeo Schidone).[37] It is a fair assumption that he remembered this very painting when he included the *Et in Arcadia ego* motif in his portrait of Mrs. Crewe and Mrs. Bouverie; and this firsthand connection with the very source of the phrase may account for the fact that its grammatically correct interpretation (as "Even in Arcadia, I, Death, hold sway"), while long forgotten on the Continent, remained familiar to the circle of Reynolds and, later on, became part of what may be termed a specifically English or "insular" tradition—a tradition which tended to retain the idea of a *memento mori*. We have seen that Reynolds himself adhered to the correct interpretation of the Latin phrase and that George III understood it at once. In addition, we have an *Et in Arcadia ego* composition by Giovanni Battista Cipriani, born in Florence but active in England from

[36]See the passage quoted in Note 34.
[37]See Leslie and Taylor, *op. cit.*, p. 260: "I find a sketch of Guercino's picture in Reynolds' Roman notebook." It was obviously from this sketch, probably bearing the usual explanatory note, that Tom Taylor learned about the Corsini picture and its author, and so surprising was this knowledge that a later biographer of Reynolds, ignorant as he was of the Guercino painting, ventured to state that Reynolds had been inspired by Poussin (W. Armstrong, *Joshua Reynolds*, übersetzt von E. von Kraatz, [n.d.], p. 89).

the end of his apprenticeship up to his death in 1785,[38] which shows the coat-of-arms of Death, the skull and bones, surmounted by the inscription "*Ancora in Arcadia morte*," which means: "Even in Arcady there is Death," precisely as King George had translated it. Even the ironic iconoclasm of our own century still draws, in England, from this original, sinister conception of the *Et in Arcadia* theme. Augustus John, who likes to designate portraits of Negro girls with such Arcadian names as "Daphne," "Phyllis," or even "Aminta," has affixed the title *Atque in Arcadia ego* (the unorthodox *atque* expressing the "even" still more emphatically than does the orthodox *et*) to a morbid, morning-after scene where Death has assumed the guise of a ghastly guitar player;[39] and in Evelyn Waugh's *Brideshead Revisited* the narrator, while a sophisticated undergraduate at Oxford, adorns his rooms at college with a "human skull lately purchased from the School of Medicine which, resting on a bowl of roses, formed at the moment the chief decoration of my table. It bore the moto *Et in Arcadia ego* inscribed on its forehead."

However, Cipriani, while faithful to the "insular" tradition in the translation of the Latin phrase, drew from another source for his pictorial composition. A thoroughgoing eclectic, he expanded the landscape and added sheep, dogs, and fragments of classical buildings; he increased the personnel by seven figures of a, generally speaking, Raphaelesque character (five of them women); and he replaced Guercino's artless masonry and actual death's-head by an elaborately classicizing tomb, with the skull and bones carved upon it in relief.

In doing all this, this rather indifferent artist shows himself familiar with the innovations of the one man whose pictures mark the turning point in the history of the *Et in Arcadia ego* theme: the great French painter Nicolas Poussin.

IV

Poussin had come to Rome in 1624 or 1625, one or two years after Guercino had left it. And a few years later (presumably about 1630) he produced the earlier of his two *Et in Arcadia ego* compositions, now in the Devonshire Collection at Chatsworth. Being a

[38]Cipriani produced, among other things, the illustrations of the famous Ariosto edition brought out by the Baskerville Press at Birmingham in 1773.

[39]J. Rothenstein, *Augustus John* (Oxford: n.d.), Fig. 71. The Negro portraits referred to are illustrated there in Figs, 66, 67, 69. According to a letter from Sir John Rothenstein, the titles given to Augustus John's works in his book were furnished orally by the artist.

Classicist (though in a very special sense), and probably conversant with Virgil, Poussin revised Guercino's composition by adding the Arcadian river god Alpheus and by transforming the decaying masonry into a classical sarcophagus inscribed with the *Et in Arcadia ego;* moreover, he emphasized the amorous implications of the Arcadian milieu by the addition of a shepherdess to Guercino's two shepherds. But in spite of these improvements, Poussin's picture does not conceal its derivation from Guercino's. In the first place, it retains to some extent the element of drama and surprise: the shepherds approach as a group from the left and are unexpectedly stopped by the tomb. In the second place, there is still the actual skull, placed upon the sarcophagus above the word *Arcadia*, though it has become quite small and inconspicuous and fails to attract the attention of the shepherds who—a telling symptom of Poussin's intellectualistic inclinations—seem to be more intensely fascinated by the inscription than they are shocked by the death's-head. In the third place, the picture still conveys, though far less obtrusively than Guercino's, a moral or admonitory message. It formed, originally, the counterpart of a *Midas Washing His Face in the River Pactolus* (now in the Metropolitan Museum at New York), the iconographically essential figure of the river god Pactolus accounting for the inclusion of its counterpart, the less necessary river god Alpheus, in the Arcadia picture.[40]

In conjunction, the two compositions thus teach a twofold lesson, one warning against a mad desire for riches at the expense of the more real values of life, the other against a thoughtless enjoyment of pleasures soon to be ended. The phrase *Et in Arcadia ego* can still be understood to be voiced by Death personified, and can still be translated as "Even in Arcady I, Death, hold sway," without being out of harmony with what is visible in the painting itself.

After another five or six years, however, Poussin produced a second and final version of the *Et in Arcadia ego* theme, the famous picture in the Louvre. And in this painting—no longer a *memento nori* in classical garb paired with a *cave avaritiam* in classical garb, but standing by itself—we can observe a radical break with the mediaeval, moralizing tradition. The element of drama and surprise has disappeared. Instead of two or three Arcadians approaching from the left in

[40]The comnection between Poussin's earlier *Et in Arcadia* composition, viz., the painting owned by the Duke of Devonshire, and the New York Midas picture was recognized and completely analyzed by A. Blunt, "Poussin's Et in Arcadia ego," *Art Bulletin*, XX (1938), pp. 96 ff. Blunt dates the Duke of Devonshire version about 1630, with which I am now inclined to agree.

a group, we have four, symmetrically arranged on either side of a sepulchral monument. Instead of being checked in their progress by an unexpected and terrifying phenomenon, they are absorbed in calm discussion and pensive contemplation. One of the shepherds kneels on the ground as though rereading the inscription for himself. The second seems to discuss it with a lovely girl who thinks about it in a quiet, thoughtful attitude. The third seems trajected into a sympathetic, brooding melancholy. The form of the tomb is simplified into a plain rectangular block, no longer foreshortened but placed parallel to the picture plane, and the death's-head is eliminated altogether.

Here, then, we have a basic change in interpretation. The Arcadians are not so much warned of an implacable future as they are immersed in mellow meditation on a beautiful past. They seem to think less of themselves than of the human being buried in the tomb—a human being that once enjoyed the pleasures which they now enjoy, and whose monument "bids them remember their end" only in so far as it evokes the memory of one who had been what they are. In short, Poussin's Louvre picture no longer shows a dramatic encounter with Death but a contemplative absorption in the idea of mortality. We are confronted with a change from thinly veiled moralism to undisguised elegiac sentiment.

This general change in content—brought about by all those individual changes in form and motifs that have been mentioned, and too basic to be accounted for by Poussin's normal habit of stabilizing and in some measure tranquillizing the second version of an earlier picture dealing with the same subject[41]—can be explained by a variety of reasons. It is consistent with the more relaxed and less fearful spirit of a period that had triumphantly emerged from the spasms of the Counter-Reformation. It is in harmony with the principles of Classicist art theory, which rejected "les objets bizarres," especially such gruesome objects as a death's-head.[42] And it was facilitated, if not caused, by Poussin's familiarity with Arcadian literature, already evident in the Chatsworth picture, where the substitution of a classical sarcophagus for Guercino's shapeless piece of masonry may well have been suggested by the tomb of Daphnis in Virgil's Fifth *Eclogue*. But the reverent and melancholy mood of the Louvre picture, and even a detail such as the

[41]The importance of this habit is, in my opinion, somewhat overestimated in J. Klein, "An Analysis of Poussin's 'Et in Arcadia ego,' " *Art Bulletin*, XIX (1937), pp. 314 ff.

[42]See, for example, H. Jouin, *Conférences de l'Académie Royale de Peinture et de Sculpture* (Paris: 1883), p. 94.

simple, rectangular shape of the tomb, would seem to reveal a fresh contact with Sannazaro. His description of the "Tomb in Arcadia"—characteristically no longer enclosing the reluctant shepherd Daphnis but a no less reluctant shepherdess named Phyllis—actually foreshadows the situation visualized in Poussin's later composition:

> ....farò fra questi rustici
> La sepoltura tua famosa e celebre.
> Et da' monti Thoscani et da' Ligustici
> Verran pastori ad venerar questo angulo
> Sol per cagion che alcuna volta fustici.
> Et leggeran nel bel sasso quadrangulo
> Il titol che ad tutt'hore il cor m'infrigida,
> Per cui tanto dolor nel petto strangulo:
> "Quella che ad Meliseo si altera et rigida
> Si mostrò sempre, hor mansueta et humile
> Si sta sepolta in questa pietra frigida."[43]

"I will make thy tomb famous and renowned among these rustic folk. Shepherds shall come from the hills of Tuscany and Liguria to worship this corner of the world solely because thou hast dwelt here once. And they shall read on the beautiful square monument the inscription that chills my heart at all hours, that makes me strangle so much sorrow in my breast: 'She who always showed herself so haughty and rigid to Meliseo now lies entombed, meek and humble, in this cold stone.'"

These verses not only anticipate the simple, rectangular shape of the tomb in Poussin's Louvre picture which strikes us as a direct illustration of Sannazaro's *bel sasso quadrangulo;* they also conform in an amazing degree to the picture's strange, ambiguous mood—to that hushed brooding over the silent message of a former fellow being: "I, too, lived im Arcady where you now live; I, too, enjoyed the pleasures which you now enjoy; I, too, was hardhearted where I should have been compassionate. And now I am dead and buried." In thus paraphrasing, according to Sannazaro, the meaning of the *Et in Arcadia ego* as it appears in Poussin's Louvre painting, I have done what nearly all the Continental interpreters did: I have distorted the original meaning of the inscription in order to adapt it to the new appearance and content of the picture. For there is no doubt that this inscription, translated correctly, no longer harmonizes with what we see with our eyes.

[43]Sannazaro, *Arcadia*, ed., Scherillo, p. 306, ll. 257–67. Further tombs occur in Sannazaro's poem on p. 70, ll. 49 ff., and p. 145, ll. 246 ff. (a literal translation of Virgil, *Eclogues*, X, pp. 31 ff.)

When read according to the rules of Latin grammar ("Even in Arcady, there am I"), the phrase had been consistent and easily intelligible as long as the words could be attributed to a death's-head and as long as the shepherds were suddenly and frighteningly interrupted in their walk. This is manifestly true of Guercino's painting, where the death's-head is the most prominent feature of the composition and where its psychological impact is not as yet weakened by the competition of a beautiful sarcophagus or tomb. But it is also true, if in a considerably lesser degree, of Poussin's earlier picture, where the skull, though smaller and already subordinated to the newly introduced sarcophagus, is still in evidence, and where the idea of sudden interruption is retained.

When facing the Louvre painting, however, the beholder finds it difficult to accept the inscription in its literal, grammatically correct, significance. In the absence of a death's-head the *ego* in the phrase *Et in Arcadia ego* must now be taken to refer to the tomb itself. And though a "speaking tomb" was not unheard of in the funerary poetry of the time, this conceit was so unusual that Michelangelo, who used it in three of his fifty epitaphs on a handsome boy, thought it necessary to enlighten the reader by an explanatory remark to the effect that here it is, exceptionally, "the tomb which addresses him who reads these verses."[44] It is infinitely more natural to ascribe the words, not to the tomb but to the person buried therein. Such is the case with ninety-nine per cent of all epitaphs, including the inscriptions of the tomb of Daphnis in Virgil and the tomb of Phyllis in Sannazaro; and Poussin's Louvre picture suggests this familiar interpretation—which, as it were, projects the message of the Latin phrase from the present into the past—all the more forcibly as the behavior of the figures no longer expresses surprise and dismay but quiet, reminiscent meditation.

Thus Poussin himself, while making no verbal change in the inscription, invites, almost compels, the beholder to mistranslate it by relating the *ego* to a dead person instead of to the tomb, by connecting the *et* with *ego* instead of with *Arcadia*, and by supplying the missing verb in the form of a *vixi* or *fui* instead of a *sum*. The development of his pictorial vision had outgrown the significance of the literary formula,

[44]See the discussion between W. Weisbach, "Et in Arcadia ego," *Gazette des Beaux-Arts*, ser. 6, XVIII (1937), pp. 287 ff., and this writer, "'Et in Arcadia ego' et le tombeau parlant," *ibidem*, ser. 6, XIX (1938), pp. 305 f. For Michelangelo's three epitaphs in which the tomb itself addresses the beholder ("La sepoltura parla a chi legge questi versi") see K. Frey, *Die Dichtungen des Michelagniolo Buonaroti* (Berlin: 1897), No. LXXVII, 34, 38, 40.

and we may say that those who, under the impact of the Louvre picture, decided to render the phrase *Et in Arcadia ego* as "I, too, lived in Arcady," rather than as "Even in Arcady, there am I," did violence to Latin grammar but justice to the new meaning of Poussin's composition.

This *felix culpa* can, in fact, be shown to have been committed in Poussin's own circle. His friend and first biographer, Giovanni Pietro Bellori, had given, in 1672, a perfectly correct and exact interpretation of the inscription when he wrote: "*Et in Arcadia ego, cioè, che il sepolcro si trova ancora* in Arcadia, e la Morte a luogo in mezzo le felicità"[45] ("*Et in Arcadia ego*, which means that the *grave is to be found* [present tense!] *even* in Arcady and that death occurs in the very midst of delight"). But only a few years later (1685) Poussin's second biographer, André Félibien, also acquainted with him, took the first and decisive step on the road to bad Latinity and good artistic analysis: "Par cette inscription," he says, "on a voulu marquer que *celui qui est dans cette sépoulture a vécu* en Arcadie et que la mort se rencontre parmi les plus grandes félicitez"[46] ("This inscription emphasizes the fact that the *person buried in this tomb has lived* [past tense!] in Arcady"). Here, then, we have the occupant of the tomb substituted for the tomb itself, and the whole phrase projected into the past: what had been a menace has become a remembrance. From then on the development proceeded to its logical conclusion. Félibien had not bothered about the *et;* he had simply left it out, and this abbreviated version, quaintly retranslated into Latin, survives in the inscription of a picture by Richard Wilson, painted at Rome in 1755: "Ego fui in Arcadia." Some thirty years after Félibien (1719), the Abbé du Bos rendered the *et* by an adverbial "cependant": "Je vivais cependant en Arcadie,"[47] which is in English: "And yet I lived in Arcady." The final touch, it seems, was put by the great Diderot, who, in 1758, firmly attached the *et* to the *ego* and rendered it by *aussi:* "Je vivais aussi dans la délicieuse Arcadie,"[48] "I, too, lived in delightful Arcady." His translation must thus be considered as

---

[45]G. P. Bellori, *op. cit.*

[46]A. Félibien, *Entretiens sur les vies et les ouvrages des peintres* (Paris: 1666–1685) (in the edition of 1705, IV, p. 71); see also the inscription of Bernard Picart's engraving after Poussin's Louvre picture as quoted by Andresen, *op. cit.*, No. 417.

[47]Abbé du Bos, *Réflexions critiques sur la poésie et sur la peinture*, I, section VI (first published in 1719), in the Dresden edition of 1760, pp. 48 ff.

[48]Diderot, "De la poésie dramatique," *Oeuvres complètes*, J. Assézat VII (Paris: 1875–1877), p. 353. Diderot's description of the painting itself is significantly inaccurate: "Il y a un paysage de Poussin où l'on voit de jeunes bergéres qui dansent au son du chalumeau [!]; et à l'écart; un tombeau avec cette inscription '*Je vivais aussi*

the literary source of all the late variations now in use, down to Jacques Delille, Johann Georg Jacobi, Goethe, Schiller, and Mrs. Felicia Hemans."⁴⁹

Thus, while—as we have seen—the original meaning of *Et in Arcadia ego* precariously survived in the British Isles, the general development outside England resulted in the nearly universal acceptance of what may be called the elegiac interpretation ushered in by Poussin's Louvre picture. And in Poussin's own homeland, France, the humanistic tradition had so much decayed in the nineteenth century that Gustave Flaubert, the great contemporary of the early Impressionists, no longer understood the famous phrase at all. In his beautiful description of the Bois de la Garenne—"parc très beau malgré ces beautés factices"—he mentions, together with a Temple of Vesta, a Temple of Friendship, and a great number of artificial ruins: "sur une pierre taillée en forme de tombe, *In Arcadia ego*, non-sens dont je n'ai pu

---

dans la délicieuse Arcadie.' Le prestige de style dont il s'agit, tient quelquefois à un mot qui detourne ma vue du sujet principal, et qui me montre de côté, comme dans le paysage du Poussin, l'espace, le temps, la vie, la mort ou quelque autre idée grande et mélancolique jetée toute au travers des images de la gaieté" (See also another reference to the Poussin picture in Diderot's "Salon de 1767," *Oeuvres*, XI, p. 161; later on the misplaced *aussi* became as much a matter of course in French literature as the misplaced *Auch* in Germany, as illustrated by Delille's *Et moi aussi, je fus pasteur dans l'Arcadie*). The picture described by Diderot seemed to bear out his well-known theory of the *contrastes dramatiques*, because he imagined that it showed the shepherds dancing to the sound of a flute. This error is due either to a confusion with other pictures by Poussin, such, for example, as the *Bacchanal* in the London National Gallery of the *Feast of Pan* in the Cook Collection at Richmond, or to the impression of some later picture dealing with the same subject. Angelica Kauffmann, for instance, in 1766 exhibited a picture described as follows: "a shepherd and shepherdess of Arcadia moralizing at the side of a sepulchre, while others are dancing at a distance" (See Lady Victoria Manners and Dr. W. C. Williamson, *Angelica Kauffmann* (London: 1924), p. 239; also Leslie and Taylor, *op. cit.*, I, p. 260).

⁴⁹For Jacques Delille, Goethe and Schiller, see above, Notes 5, 6. As to Mrs. Felicia Hemans (See Note 7), the motto superscribed on her poem appears to confuse Poussin's Louvre picture with one or more of its later variations: "A celebrated picture of Poussin represents a band of shepherd youths and maidens suddenly checked in their wanderings and affected with various emotions by the sight of a tomb which bears the inscription 'Et in Arcadia ego.'" In the poem itself Mrs. Hemans follows in the footsteps of Sannazaro and Diderot in assuming that the occupant of the tomb is a young girl:

> Was some gentle kindred maid
> In that grave with dirges laid?
> Some fair creature, with the tone
> Of whose voice a joy is gone?

découvrir l'intention,"[50] "on a stone cut in the shape of a tomb one reads *In Arcadia ego*, a piece of nonsense the meaning of which I have been unable to dicover."

We can easily see that the new conception of the Tomb in Arcady initiated by Poussin's Louvre picture, and sanctioned by the mistranslation of its inscription, could lead to reflections of almost opposite nature, depressing and melancholy on the one hand, comforting and assuaging on the other; and, more often than not, to a truly "Romantic" fusion of both. In Richard Wilson's painting, just mentioned, the shepherds and the funerary monument—here a slightly mutilated *stele*—are reduced to a *staffage* accentuating the muted serenity of the Roman Campagna at sundown. In Johann Georg Jacobi's *Winterreise* of 1769—containing what seems to be the earliest "Tomb in Arcady" in German literature— we read: "Whenever, in a beautiful landscape, I encounter a tomb with the inscription *Auch ich war in Arkadien*, I point it out to my friends; we stop a moment, press each other's hands, and proceed."[51] And in a strangely attractive engraving by a German Romanticist named Carl Wilhelm Kolbe, who had a trick of constructing wondrous jungles and forests by magnifying grass, herbs or cabbage leaves to the size of bushes and trees, the tomb and its inscription (here, correctly, *Et in Arcadia ego* although the legend of the engraving consists of the erroneous "Auch ich war in Arkadien") serve only to emphasize the gentle absorption of two lovers in one another. In Goethe's use of the phrase *Et in Arcadia ego*, finally, the idea of death has been entirely eliminated.[52] He uses it, in an abbreviated version ("Auch ich in Arkadien") as a motto for his famous account of his blissful journey to Italy, so that it merely means: "I, too, was in the land of joy and beauty."

[50]Gustave Flaubert, "Par les chants et par les grèves," *Oeuvres complètes* (Paris: 1910), p. 70; the passage was kindly brought to my attention by Georg Swarzenski.
[51]See Büchmann, *op. cit.*
[52]See also Goethe's *Faust*, III, 3;

> Gelockt, auf sel'gem Grund zu wohnen,
> Du flüchtetest ins heiterste Geschick!
> Zur Laube wandeln sich die Thronen,
> Arcadisch frei sei unser Glück!

In later German literature this purely hedonistic interpretation of Arcadian happiness was to degenerate into the trivial conception of "having a good time." In the German translation of Offenbach's *Orphée aux Enfers* the hero therefore sings "Als ich noch Prinz war von *Arkadien*" instead of "Quand j'étais prince de *Béotie*."

Fragonard, on the other hand, retained the idea of death; but he reversed the original moral. He depicted two cupids, probably spirits of departed lovers, clasped in an embrace within a broken sarcophagus while other, smaller cupids flutter about and a friendly genius illumines the scene with the light of a nuptial torch. Here the development has run full cycle. To Guercino's "Even in Arcady, there is death" Fragonard's drawing replies: "Even in death, there may be Arcady."

RENATO POGGIOLI

The Pastoral of the Self

I

No Reader of *As You Like It* is likely to forget the double
repartee by which Shakespeare wittily closes the lively exchange
between two characters of that comedy, either of whom stands for a
peculiar version of the pastoral ideal:

JAQUES: I'll tarry no longer with you. Farewell, good Signior Love.
ORLANDO: I am glad of your departure. Adieu, good Monsieur Melancholy.

If Shakespeare calls *Monsieur* the gentleman who hails a loveless solitude as the supreme grace of pastoral life, and *Signior* the one who
blesses that life for its power to join two lonely hearts together, it is
only because the Christian names by which the poet had already
baptized the two speakers are the French Jaques in one case and the
Italian Orlando in the other. Yet it is difficult to treat as a mere coinci-
dence this naming of the representative of the erotic pastoral as
Signior Love, since the main business of the Italian poets of the late
Renaissance, especially Tasso and Guarini, had been to reduce the
manifold variations of the idyllic fancy to the common denominator or
single archetype of the pastoral of love.

As You Like It ends with a rather Pyrrhic victory of Signior Love over
Monsieur Melancholy. Yet one could say that one of the tasks of
European seventeenth-century literature was to reverse that outcome:
or, to speak less metaphorically, to liberate the pastoral from the
excessive or exclusive concern with passion and sex which had shaped
the bucolic vision of the Italians. The writers of that age succeeded in
doing so first by taking up its neglected variants, such as the pastorals of

From *Daedalus*, Vol. 88 (Winter, 1959), 686–99. Reprinted by permission of the
editors of *Daedalus* and the American Academy of Arts and Sciences.

melancholy and solitude, which they developed in either contact or contrast with the Italian example; and then by creating a novel variant, such as the pastoral of the self, which in the end transcended all previous traditions of the genre. The achievement of this double task was the particular merit of a few masters of the literatures of England and Spain: and from this viewpoint Shakespeare would have done better if instead of a French he had given an English or Spanish name to his Jaques, and addressed him as *Sir* or *Don* in lieu of *Monsieur*. One should, however, never forget that the ultimate representative of the pastoral of the self was bound to be another and less fictitious Jacques— the greatest literary figure of the eighteenth century, Jean-Jacques Rousseau, who wrote in French, and who would certainly deserve being called *Monsieur Soi-Même*.

Yet in a process such as the one to be described, what count most are the preliminary and transitional stages. The text that best documents the opening phase may well be the story that forms the climax of the most important of *Don Quixote's* bucolic interludes. That story, based on the conflict between the pastoral of love and the pastoral of solitude, ends with the victory of the latter, which for the first time is represented not by a shepherd, but by a shepherdess. Since the Spanish word for solitude is feminine, one could then say that in this case it is *Doña Soledad* who conquers *Signior Love*.

II

We enter the main "pastoral oasis" of *Don Quixote* at the end of Chapter X of the First Part, when Don Quixote and Sancho, suddenly surprised by darkness while still in open country, decide to spend the night outdoors, in the company of a group of goatherds. Thus with the traditional motif of peasant hospitality Cervantes opens the chief bucolic episode of his masterpiece. The travelers have just shared the simple fare of their hosts when a lad by the name of Pedro, whose job is to bring provisions for his fellow goatherds, comes from the village and relates to his companions and their guests that a gentleman farmer of a neighboring village has just died and has left a strange will. From Pedro's report, which is devoid of any logical order, and even more from his answers to Don Quixote's searching questions, we learn that the dead man, named Grisóstomo, had been young, handsome, and rich. He had studied at Salamanca, from where he had brought home great learning as well as the art of writing poetry. Shortly after his return, Grisóstomo had lost his father, who had left him property in land and cattle, in goods and cash. In the goatherds' village there was a girl named Marcela, no less handsome and young than Grisóstomo, who had also lost her parents, although earlier in life, and had inherited from them even greater wealth. She had been brought up by her uncle, the village priest, a good-natured old man who had never tried to force her resolute will to marry no one. But one day, without changing her mind, Marcela did change her way of life, in a manner best described in Pedro's words:

> But, lo and behold, when we least expected it, the modest Marcela suddenly appeared dressed like a shepherdess and, in spite of her uncle and everyone in the village, who tried to dissuade her, off she went into the fields with the other village shepherdesses and started to tend her flock.*

Grisóstomo and Marcela are the two leading characters of the pastoral fable we are about to be told: and it may well be worthwhile to examine how far they have now satisfied the stock requirements of their roles. They certainly seem to do so in full: Cervantes has endowed both of them with the supreme pastoral privileges—beauty and youth. If the author bestows on them even the blessings of class and wealth, which pastoral poetry at its most literal treats as parallel curses, it is only because, like many of his recent predecessors, Cervantes tends to relate the pastoral calling to the moral and social status of the landed gentry, and wishes to emphasize that such a calling appeals to those who are poor "in spirit" rather than in fact. This is obvious enough: yet Cervantes avoids attracting any attention to the outstanding divergence of his own story from the stock pastoral situation. It is true that literary shepherds are often born outside the pastoral state, into which they enter by an act of will, or at least by imitiating the action already taken by someone they admire or befriend. In this case the divergence, almost without precedent in the whole of pastoral literature, is seen in the fact that the willing or unwilling leader, the person taking the initiative, or at least setting an example, is a woman and not a man. Now we know that in the pastoral story we are about to hear there will be, not simply two leading characters of different sex, but an antagonist and a protagonist, which is extravagant enough; and we also know that by an even more extraordinary exception the latter will be a feminine one.

By the way he talks we realize that the simple-minded Pedro takes

*All Cervantes passages are reprinted by permission from *Cervantes: Don Quixote*, trans. J. M. Cohen (Baltimore: Penguin Books, Inc.).

it almost for granted that quite a few wealthy and well-born youths, whether boys or girls, may turn into shepherds at a moment's notice. Yet he cannot help finding it strange that at least some of them may do so for other than erotic motives. It is through Pedro's wonder at this deviation from the normal path that Cervantes betrays his awareness that he is now straying far away from the central vision of the Italian Renaissance idyll, according to which any pastoral retreat is a retreat into love, or at least into love's dream. As we know, the latter alternative occurs in the "pastoral oasis" of Tasso's *Gerusalemme Liberata*, which Cervantes must have kept well in mind while writing these pages. That famous episode deals with Erminia's stay among the shepherds. While Erminia is a passive heroine, Marcela is an active one: she decides to become a shepherdess forever, after refusing all her old suitors and without even thinking of new ones. What is wholly novel is that Marcela, unlike Erminia, changes her pastoral retreat into a retreat from both the reality and the dream of love. It is with due emphasis that Pedro points out this fact:

> Now you mustn't think that because Marcela adopted this free and unconstrained way of life, with little or no privacy, her modesty or her virtue had fallen under any shadow of suspicion. Far from it; she guards her honor so well that no one of her many suitors has boasted—nor has the right to boast—that she has given him the slightest hope of obtaining his desire.

The ironical consequence of Marcela's decision is that by acting as she did, she was bound to win all the hearts of her fellow shepherds without ever losing her own. This is why all of them had been calling her cruel and unkind: and no one had blamed her so harshly as the late Grisóstomo, who had finally died out of despair as soon as he realized that Marcela would never change her friendship into love. Although Pedro fails to say so, it is evident to everybody that Grisóstomo had put an end to his life by his own hand. If a reader asks for proof, he should be referred to the shepherd's request to be buried elsewhere than in consecrated ground. The discretion with which Cervantes alludes to all this is perhaps to be explained by theological considerations: we must never forget that the character was born a Christian, and that the author wrote in an age of religious dogmatism and fanatic zeal. Yet, besides being a Christian, Grisóstomo was a shepherd too, and any reader well acquainted with the pastoral tradition will immediately realize that his suicide is a literary transgression as well as a mortal sin. One could convey the sense of that transgression by anachronistically defining Grisóstomo as the first and last Werther to appear in the pastoral world. In brief, within the economy of the bucolic genre, Grisóstomo's suicide is no less arbitrary and unique than Marcela's decision to become a shepherdess in order to deny even more fully the rule of love.

The reader senses as much from the very tone of Pedro's words:

> ... and the strange thing is that he has directed in his will that he's to be buried in the fields like a Moor, at the foot of that rock where is the spring of the cork tree, because, the rumor goes—and they say they had it from his lips—that it was the spot he saw her for the first time. He has left other requests, such odd ones that the clergy says they mustn't be carried out; and quite right so, because they have a heathenish smack about them.

The narrator further relates that, all this notwithstanding, Ambrosio, who had been Grisóstomo's best friend, has stated his intention to fulfill his duty and do everything according to his poor friend's wishes. Pedro ends his report by informing his listeners that the following morning all his fellow shepherds will bring Grisóstomo's spoils to the spot he had chosen for his eternal rest. Hearing this, both Don Quixote and the goatherds decide to attend the ceremony.

Ambrosio, who is in charge of the proceedings, pronounces a funeral eulogy, and announces that he will burn his friend's manuscripts, as he had promised. Yet another fellow shepherd, Vivaldo, takes one of the dead man's papers containing one of his poems, and reads it aloud to the crowd. This poem is a *canción desesperada* in an extremely conventional style: and the effect of its reading over the grave of the man who wrote it is both absurd and grotesque. There is no doubt that by this and other details Cervantes wants to suggest to the reader the unseemly character of the funeral we are now witnessing. The strange obsequies of the shepherd Grisóstomo are devoid not only of Christian reverence but of pagan piety as well. It is only when Vivaldo is about to read aloud another of the poems left by the dead man that the scandal is interrupted by an unforeseen event. This was, as Cervantes says.

> ... a miraculous vision—for such it seemed—which suddenly appeared before their eyes. For on the top of the rock in which they were digging the grave appeared the shepherdess Marcela, looking even more beautiful than she had been described.

As soon as Ambrosio sees Marcela, he wrathfully calls her "fierce basilysk of these mountains," and reproaches her for adding scorn to injury by her presence. To which Marcela replies that she has come only to defend herself from the accusation that she is responsible for Grisós-tomo's suffering, and that she had caused his death. Marcela's long peroration begins with the acknowledgement that beauty inspires love, but also with the denial that it must return the love it inspires. The reason for this is not only that beauty is a grace which is granted without exacting the price of any responsibility toward others. What really matters is that such a grace disappears unless beauty involves the spiritual as well as the physical side. Without such adornments of the soul as modesty and virtue, loveliness cannot reside even in the most beautiful body. By yielding to man's desire, woman loses the very charms by which she attracts him. Having made these points, Marcela proclaims her moral independence in pastoral terms:

> ... I was born free, and to live free I chose the solitude of the fields. The trees on these mountains are my companions, the clear water of these streams my mirrors; to the trees and the waters I disclose my thoughts and my beauty.

Marcela affirms that she has always undeceived by her own words those attracted by her looks, and maintains that if love for her led any man to his undoing, it was the fault of his obstinacy rather than of her supposed cruelty. To Grisóstomo himself, when he declared his love for her on that very spot, far from beguiling him with false hopes or flattering promises, she had unequivocally stated her decision to lead a solitary existence, in communion only with nature and her own soul:

> ... I told him that my will was to live in perpetual solitude, and that only the earth would enjoy the fruit of my chastity and the spoils of my beauty.

Marcela ends her speech with an eloquent plea, picturing the pastoral calling as a state by which the soul attains its ideal perfection and purity:

> ... If I preserve my purity in the company of the trees, why should he who would have me keep the company of men desire me to lose it? I, as you know, have riches of my own, and covet no one else's. I have a taste for freedom and no wish for sub-jection. I neither love nor hate any man. ... I enjoy the modest company of the village shepherdesses and the care of my goats. My desires are bounded by these mountains; and if they extend beyond them, it is to contemplate the beauty of the sky, a step by which the soul travels to its first abode.

Everybody is both moved and astounded by the speech of Marcela, who leaves the scene as soon as she has uttered her last word. As for

Don Quixote, acting as if Marcela were a damsel in distress, he puts his hand on his sword hilt, forbidding all present to follow or persecute her, and loudly proclaiming the justice of her argument and the right-eousness of her cause. After this the funeral rites proceed according to plan, including the burning of Grisóstomo's manuscripts. Before leaving, Ambrosio announces that later he will replace the rock by which they have sealed the grave with a tombstone to be engraved with a rhymed epitaph he has already prepared. That epitaph will claim forever, as if nothing had happened, that his friend had died because of his beloved's disdain, or, as Ambrosio puts it, of *desamor*. By such an ironical ending Cervantes seems to intimate the persistence of the bucolic illusion, or the persistent refusal on the part of its devotees to heed the lesson of life and to face the challenge of death.

In brief, what counts in the story is not Grisóstomo's illusion, which is at once sentimental and literary, but Marcela's spiritual and per-sonal truth. And we find it significant that this shepherdess preaches her creed by exalting values directly opposed to those exalted in *Aminta's* first chorus. If Tasso preached sexual freedom, Marcela preaches instead freedom from love. If Tasso condemned honor, which enforces chastity and purity and makes both men and women unhappy by preventing the free play of love, Marcela praises honor, chastity, and purity as the highest of all pastoral virtues. Yet in doing so she changes those virtues into something strangely new. For her, honor is no longer a social tie controlling moral conduct from outside, but an inner power ruled by no other law than itself. Chastity and purity are not the exterior signs of the ethical will, but spiritual manifestations of the integrity of the person, of the perfection of the soul. It is then by a total reversal of the pastoral casuistry of love that Marcela brings forth what seems to be one of the earliest versions of the pastoral of the self. While affirming the lofty values of the latter, she denies, however, something higher than mere bucolic love. The erotic idyll is a masculine dream: "disappointed hedonism" may often lead a rejected swain to misogyny, to that hatred for the female which is but love for woman turned sour.

Marcela seems to avoid the pitfalls of sexual hatred by her proscrip-tion of sexual love. This is what she means when she proudly states that she neither hates nor loves any man, or when she simply acknowledges that the most she can offer to any other human being is but a casual fellowship, to which she prefers the silent company of nature or the soul's intercourse with itself. Friendship is not a substitute for charity:

and Marcela's way of life may well imply a denial of the Christian command to love, as well as of the pastoral one. An excessive concern with selfhood ends all too often in self-love: and no other detail proves this as eloquently as the fact that Marcela attends Grisóstomo's funeral merely because it is also her trial. If she comes, it is not to pay the tribute of pity at the grave of a dead friend, but to use that grave as a tribune from which to plead the cause of the self.

That plea attains its climax in Marcelas' avowal that there is neither love nor hatred in her heart. Yet such an avowal reveals that, while refusing to imitate the male hating the female who fails to respond to his love, Marcela cannot avoid the far worse pitfall of misanthropy, which is the negative complement of concern with the self. Now, both self-love and misanthropy are perhaps the most important components of the pastorals of melancholy and solitude. All too often self-love dons the mantle of purity, while misanthropy garbs itself all too easily in self-righteousness. If the latter is primarily an ethical disguise, the former is predominantly a religious mask. If this is true, then we cannot take too seriously the claim Marcela makes at the end of her speech, when she says that one of her life tasks will be that heavenly contemplation which initiates a mortal's soul into its immortal bliss. It is obvious that Marcela's mysticism carries an impurity and a worldliness of its own. Before that single, final allusion to the contemplation of heaven, she has spoken far more extensively and eloquently of the contemplation of nature, which she considers the most suitable mirror for reflecting the beauty of her own soul. In brief, not unlike the devotees of Eros, she treats her far less carnal but no less profane passion as if it were a form of sacred love.

III

There is a short English lyric which is a document of no lesser importance in the history of the Baroque pastoral than the long Spanish prose tale on which we have just commented. That text is Andrew Marvell's *The Garden*, which deserves an intensive analysis, not only for its significance and quality but also because the poem's brevity contributes to the complexity of its statement.

The Garden opens with a Baroque conceit by which the poet turns to his advantage the gnomic commonplaces of the pastoral of innocence, especially those indicting the social passions of vanity and ambition. How frequently and intensely does man exert himself (complains the poet rhetorically) to win the palm of the warrior, the oak of the statesman, the laurel of the poet, or the "single herb or tree" which is the symbolic reward of his efforts! Yet, as Marvell sententiously observes, the shadow projected by those leafy emblems of fame is far less lasting and lovely than the one produced by a grove where all plants join together to weave not coronets of glory but "garlands of repose." The only place where such a grove can be sought is the garden into which the poet has just withdrawn from the weariness and dreariness of the world. There he has found not only the two lovely sisters who are the fairest of all nymphs, peace and innocence, but also their sacred plants, which, unlike the symbolic flora of man's vanity, belong to the real vegatation of this earth. It is in their midst that the poet is now enjoying a solitude more delightful than the most tender or refined fellowship:

> Fair quiet, have I found thee here,
> And innocence, thy sister dear!
> Mistaken long, I sought you then
> In busy companies of men.
> Your sacred plants, if here below,
> Only among the plants will grow.
> Society is all but rude,
> To this delicious solitude.

Up to the second stanza of his poem Marvell treats his own withdrawal into the garden as a flight from society. But in the following stanzas he claims that the main motivation of his escape is to find rest and relief from the labors and sorrows of love. Later, by using jointly the devices of personification and paradox, he describes his own retreat from love as if it were Love's retreat from itself:

> When we have run our passion's heat,
> Love hither makes his best retreat.

Since he has chosen to convey the positive, novel experience of sexual abstention and renunciation under the imagery of the withdrawal of love, Marvell has no other alternative but to depict his own stay in the garden as Love's successful attempt to find there new and different objects—not fair women but "fair trees," whose beauty far exceeds that of his sweetheart. The lover of woman has turned into a lover of trees: and when indulging in the pastoral pastime of engraving their trunks, the letters he inscribes will not evoke or invoke any absent womanly being, but merely spell out the names by which those trees are known.

Having thus changed his love objects from human creatures into botanical ones, the poet compares himself to those gods who pursued a maid or a nymph only to see her transformed into a flower or a plant. Marvell builds this comparison into a striking anticlimax: reversing the meaning of the fables to which he refers, he treats the botanical metamorphosis by which they end as if it were a consciously expected or willfully provoked outcome: the fulfillment, rather than the frustration, of the god's desire. In brief, if a god persecuted a maid or a nymph, it was only because he wanted to see the creature he loved metamorphosed into a vegetable being:

> The gods, that mortal beauty chase,
> Still in a tree ended their race.
> Apollo hunted Daphne so,
> Only that she might laurel grow.
> And Pan did after Syrinx speed
> Not as a nymph, but as a reed.

It is at this stage that the poet finally discards the imagery of love, but only after drawing a last comparison between nature and woman, which is, in regard to the latter, an invidious one. The poet now looks not at the individual plants but at the whole grove, at the impersonal mystery of vegetation, at a landscape completely submerged in the anonymity and unanimity of the coloring which dominates the vegetable kingdom and the life of the earth. Yet at its first apparition the poet cannot help contrasting nature's dye to the tints of woman's complexion; and he insists that nature's color is more lovable than the hues of feminine beauty, which are the colors of love:

> No white nor red was ever seen
> So amorous as this lovely green.

In the lines that follow, any erotic suggestion, even of a negative kind, seems to disappear forever. The subject's passive and passionless contemplation of the garden's greenery seems now to abolish any other substance or appearance,

> Annihilating all that's made
> To a green thought in a green shade.

Here the poem reaches its critical point, and seems to anticipate some of the tendencies of the modern mind with its all too morbid wish to merge with the world soul or sink into mother nature's womb. Yet the two preceding stanzas prove that Marvell still thinks in conventional pastoral terms, as is shown by the sudden metamorphosis of this all too Italian garden—not into an English park, but into an orchard offering its juicy fruits for the asking to the joy of man. Both figuratively and literally, nature here remains all too fenced in: while its boundless fertility requires no human labor, its beauty, as shown by the closing vision of the flower bed which a "skillful gardener" has laid out in the shape of a sundial, may still need the artifices of man's wit and the control of his hand. Yet it is precisely as *hortus conclusus* that nature becomes the best abode of the soul. If in the golden age or in the Earthly Paradise of yore man could proudly wander abroad in the splendid nakedness of his body, here he may dwell or linger outdoors in the luminous pure nudity of his spirit:

> Here at the fountain's sliding foot,
> Or at some fruit tree's mossy root,
> Casting the body's vest aside,
> My soul into the boughs does glide.

At this point, as if to make it move and abide at greater ease among the boughs, the poet changes his soul into a bird. The metamorphosis is more metaphoric than symbolic: and since the image does not become *figura*, we should not conclude that this bird is the dove of the spirit. Marvell's awareness that the emblem he is using was originally religious in essence appears in the allusion to the "longer flight" the bird-soul will undertake when its stay in this or other gardens comes to an end. Yet such an allusion is to be taken even less literally than Marcela's closing reference to that "contemplation of heaven" by which the soul prepares itself for its final ascent. That Marvell's is a bird of different feather than the one standing for the Christian soul is shown by its main concern—to groom its gorgeous plumage and make it shine like a rainbow in the changing light. Except for its small size, we would at first think this feathery creature a peacock. Later we realize that this could not be so for other reasons. The peacock, after all, is barely able to fly, which our bird can easily do, although at present it prefers to rest in the garden, perching on one of its trees. There, with no thought of flying away, with no other care than delighting in its own beauty, it sings aloud, as no peacock can do, of its newly found bliss. Far from being an allegory of the religious soul, which trains itself through contemplative life to fly back to its eternal abode, Marvell's bird stands for an all too human and personal psyche, which retreats from the world of society into the world of nature so as to be less distracted from the bemused contemplation of its own loveliness:

> There like a bird it sits, and sings,
> Then whets, and combs its silver wings;
> And, till prepared for longer flight,
> Waves in its plumes the various light.

By nursing and reflecting its beauty within the intimacy of a nature so enclosed as to become a private reserve, the soul changes its own hermitage into a sort of outdoor boudoir. In literary terms, this simply means that at such a turning point the pastoral of solitude gives way to the pastoral of the self. While the former rejects man's love for woman, the second repudiates all love for any object other than the subject itself. This is the reason why at the poem's end the poet looks back at pastoral love. By that retrospective glance he wants to deny the old dispensation more fully and definitely than he has done before. The poet succeeds in doing so by changing the temporal perspective, by making the new dispensation the older of the two. While in the earlier stanzas he had treated the withdrawal of the self into the garden as an event occurring after the extinction of passion or the consummation of desire, now he views that withdrawal as a happening that took place in the remotest of all ages, when love had not yet made its appearance in the world.

In brief, the poet likens his own retreat to man's state in the Garden of Eden before the Fall, thus suggesting that pastoral innocence existed from the beginning of life itself. Marvell goes even further: to establish a perfect equation between the pastoral of solitude and the pastoral of the self, and to make both of them absolutely, rather than relatively, independent of the pastoral of love, he compares his own *hortus conclusus* to the Garden of Eden as it was, not simply before the Fall but before the very creation of Eve:

> Such was the happy garden-state
> While man walked there without a mate:
> After a place so pure, and sweet,
> What other help could yet be meet!
> But 'twas beyond a mortal share
> To wander solitary there;
> Two paradises 'twere in one
> To live in Paradise alone.

As the closing lines intimate, Marvell faces here the very issue Cervantes avoided by choosing a maidenly heroine as protagonist of his tale. Unlike the Spanish writer, the English poet builds the pastoral of the self on the cornerstone of misogyny, as well as on the more general foundations of misanthropy. Marvell the moderate puritan knew, as Milton did, that woman is a necessary evil, and that not even in Paradise will man ever live alone. Yet here he seems to think that the dream of a pure and sweet solitude may be realized within space and time, if we measure the former within the narrow range of an orchard or garden and reckon the latter within the brief span of the day, the hours of which are symbolized by the "herbs" and "flowers" of the botanical sundial appearing at the end of the poem. Marvell's acknowledgment that pastoral bliss can be only a momentary experience is made almost without regret, since the pastoral of the self must transcend that contrast between happiness and unhappiness which is at the very root of the pastoral of love. This is the reason why Cervantes ignored the tragicomic implications of the Marcela-Grisóstomo story or why Marvell neglects the very dialectics Milton has exemplified in his famous diptych, *L'Allegro* and *Il Penseroso*. Melancholy and solitude are one and the same thing; and the soul is at once pensive and mirthful when it keeps its own rendezvous with itself.

IV

By rephrasing a line by Dante one could say that according to the traditional Christian view the blessed, and the blessed alone, are *anime fatte belle*, and that it is God who makes them so. On the contrary, Cervantes treats his Marcela, and Marvell the birdlike psyche he celebrates in *The Garden*, as souls which have been born beautiful or have been made so by no other grace than an inner one. Then, at least potentially, they are already *belles âmes* in the sense that term will definitely acquire in eighteenth-century France, particularly in the hands of Rousseau. Actually Rousseau's *belle âme* is emancipated even more than are Cervantes' and Marvell's exemplars from the residual controls of the mind and the will. This is particularly true of his two main psychological archetypes, who are the Saint-Preux of *La Nouvelle Héloïse* and the autobiographical protagonist of the *Confessions* and the *Rêveries d'un promeneur solitaire*. Despite his claim to be the friend of mankind, the author of those works based his own conception of the *belle âme* on an almost hypochondriac misanthropy. Yet if he refused to sweeten that misanthropy with the balm of friendship, he also refused to embitter it further with the harsh medicine of misogyny. The task he had set out to accomplish was, after all, to bring back passion as the chief ingredient of the bucolic vision of life: the test of a *belle ame* was for him an uninterupted effusion of feeling, overflowing and overwhelming all its vessels and objects.

In brief, Rousseau re-established and reinforced the broken tie between the pastoral of love and the pastoral of the self. This explains his youthful admiration for such an old-fashioned pastoral romance as *Astrée*, of which he speaks at length at the beginning of the *Confessions*.

This also explains his love for Italian poetry, testified by the frequent quotations from Petrarch, Tasso, and Metastasio to be found in *La Nouvelle Héloïse*, as well as his passion for Italian music, especially for the opera, which in his time was but an idyll in courtly dress. It was by turning back to the Italians that Rousseau reintroduced into the pastoral the concern with sex, which he fused with the concern with the self. Sexual love is but a form of self-love, and in the *Rêveries*, when left without a sexual object, Rousseau found that object within himself. It was only with him that the pastoral of the self turned once and for all into the literary vehicle of an extreme and absolute narcissism, replacing the fables and myths of his Renaissance predecessors with the autobiographical and introspective concerns of modern literature. Rousseau transformed Narcissus, literally and unambiguously, into Jean-Jacques, as other and later poets, no longer committed to pastoral traditions and conventions, were to transform him into their Werthers or Renés. And the external mirror within which this new Narcissus would reflect his *belle âme* would no longer be a garden or an idyllic countryside, but a nature as wild and boundless as the romantic view of the self.

WILLIAM EMPSON

Proletarian Literature

Proletarian literature usually has a suggestion of pastoral, a puzzling form which looks proletarian but isn't. I must worry the meaning of the term for a moment. One might define proletarian art as the propaganda of a factory-working class which feels its interests opposed to the factory owners'; this narrow sense is perhaps what is usually meant but not very interesting. You couldn't have proletarian literature in this sense in a successful socialist state. The wider sense of the term includes such folk-literature as is by the people, for the people, and about the people. But most fairy stories and ballads, though 'by' and 'for,' are not 'about'; whereas pastoral though 'about' is not 'by' or 'for.' The Border ballads assume a society of fighting clans who are protected by their leaders since leaders can afford expensive weapons; the aristocrat has an obvious function for the people, and they are pleased to describe his grandeur and fine clothes. (This pleasure in him as an object of fantasy is the normal thing, but usually there are forces the other way.) They were class-conscious all right, but not conscious of class war. Pastoral is a queerer business, but I think permanent and not dependent on a system of class exploitation. Any socialist state with an intelligentsia at the capital that felt itself more cultivated than the farmers (which it would do; the arts are produced by overcrowding) could produce it; it is common in present-day Russian films, and a great part of their beauty (for instance the one called *The General Line* when it came to England). My reason for dragging this old-fashioned form into the discussion is that I think good proletarian art is usually Covert Pastoral.

. . .

From *Some Versions of Pastoral*, by William Empson. pp. 6, 9–23. All rights reserved. Reprinted by permission of New Directions Publishing Corporation and Chatto & Windus Ltd., Publishers.

61

It would be as well then to consider a few books written outside England, which are not definite propaganda and might be called proletarian. One would expect the democratic spirit of America to have produced proletarian literature some time ago, but so far as I know the central theme is always a conflict in the author's mind between democracy and something else. . . . William Faulkner writes direct moralistic tragedy or melodrama, and tends to take poor or low characters merely because their lives more than most are grindingly and obviously ruled by Fate; this is supposed to make us feel that the same is true of every one. Most writers on Fate play this trick; it uses a piece of pastoral machinery which is generally dignified into bad metaphysics. Whereas in André Malraux's *La Condition Humaine* (*Storm in Shanghai*) the heroes are communists and are trying to get something done, but they are very frankly out of touch with the proletariat; it is from this that they get their pathos and dignity and the book its freedom from propaganda. The purpose behind a Hemingway character is to carry to the highest degree the methods of direct reporting—his stoical simple man is the type who gets most directly the sensations any one would get from the events. This is a very general method for stories of action and has a touch of pastoral so far as it implies 'the fool sees true.' It is irritating when Hemingway implies that his well-to-do heroes should be praised for being boors, but even that is supported by a backwoods pioneer feeling which seems as much aristocratic as proletarian. Céline's *Voyage au Bout de la Nuit* is a more interesting case, not to be placed quickly either as pastoral or proletarian; it is partly the 'underdog' theme and partly social criticism. The two main characters have no voice or trust in their society and no sympathy with those who have; it is this, not cowardice or poverty or low class, which the war drives home to them, and from then on they have a straightforward inferiority complex; the theme becomes their struggle with it as private individuals. In the first half of the book the hero is crazy, and seems meant to be, from the idea that everybody is attacking him, and in consequence is as brutal as they are. He becomes conscious of this and ashamed of it when he goes off and leaves the girl in Detroit, so sets to work and becomes a doctor. From then on the underdog theme is carried by his double Robinson, whom he is trying to save, and who finally, in a second refusal of a girl's love, accepts death. The hero respects this but is far from the need to imitate it; it somehow releases him and ends the book. Life may be black and mad in the second half but Bardamu is not, and he gets to the real end of the night as critic and spectator. This change is masked by unity of style and by a humility which will not allow that one can claim to be sane while living as part of such a world, but it is in the second half that we get Bardamu speaking as Céline in criticism of it. What is attacked may perhaps be summed up as the death-wishes generated by the herds of a machine society, and he is not speaking as 'spokesman of the proletariat' or with any sympathy for a communist one. It may be true that under a communist government many fewer people would have this sort of inferiority complex, but that does not make a new sort of literature; and before claiming the substance of the book as prole-tarian literature you have to separate off the author (in the phrase that Gorki used) as a man ripe for fascism.

The essential trick of the old pastoral, which was felt to imply a beautiful relation between rich and poor, was to make simple people express strong feelings (felt as the most universal subject, something fundamentally true about everybody) in learned and fashionable lan-guage (so that you wrote about the best subject in the best way). From seeing the two sorts of people combined like this you thought better of both; the best parts of both were used. The effect was in some degree to combine in the reader or author the merits of the two sorts; he was made to mirror in himself more completely the effective ele-ments of the society he lived in. This was not a process that you could explain in the course of writing pastoral; it was already shown by the clash between style and theme, and to make the clash work in the right way (not become funny) the writer must keep up a firm pretence that he was unconscious of it. Indeed the usual process for putting further meanings into the pastoral situation was to insist that the shep-herds were rulers of sheep, and so compare them to politicians or bishops or what not; this piled the heroic convention onto the pastoral one, since the hero was another symbol of his whole society. Such a pretence no doubt makes the characters unreal, but not the feelings expressed or even the situation described; the same pretence is often valuable in real life. I should say that it was over this fence that pastoral came down in England after the Restoration. The arts, even music, came to depend more than before on knowing about foreign culture, and Puritanism, suspicious of the arts, was only not strong among the aristocracy. A feeling gradually got about that any one below the upper middles was making himself ridiculous, being above himself, if he showed any signs of keeping a sense of beauty at all, and this feeling was common to all classes. It takes a general belief as harsh and as unreal as this to make the polite pretence of pastoral seem necessarily absurd. Even so there was a successful school of mock-pastoral for so long as the upper and lower classes were consciously less Puritan than the middle. When that goes the pastoral tricks of thought take refuge in child-cult.

One strong help for the pastoral convention was the tradition, coming down from the origin of our romantic love-poetry in the troubadours, that its proper tone is one of humility, that the proper moments to dramatise in a love-affair are those when the lover is in despair. (Much theorising might be done in praise of this convention; some of it comes into Poe's absurd proof that melancholy is the most poetical of the tones. For one thing the mere fact that you don't alto-gether believe in the poet's expressions of despair makes you feel that he has reserves of strength.) Granted this, the low man has only to shift his humility onto his love affairs to adopt the dignity of a courtly convention. There is a good example in *As You Like It;* we see Corin[1] for a moment bewailing his hopeless love with an older shepherd, and then the gentry try to get food out of him.

CLOWN: Holla! you, clown!
ROSALIND: Peace, fool, he's not thy kinsman.
CORIN: Who calls?
CLOWN: Your betters, sir.
CORIN: Else they are very wretched.

Rosalind has heard the previous conversation, but no doubt she would understand this anyway; the shepherd is giving himself airs rather than being humble, but he has every right to it, and the court clown is silenced for the rest of the scene.

The convention was, of course, often absurdly artificial; the praise of simplicity usually went with extreme flattery of a patron (dignified as a symbol of the whole society, through the connection of pastoral with heroic), done so that the author could get some of the patron's luxuries; it allowed the flattery to be more extreme because it helped both author and patron to keep their self-respect. So it was much parodied, especially to make the poor man worthy but ridiculous, as often in Shakespeare; nor is this merely snobbish when in its full form. The simple man becomes a clumsy fool who yet has better 'sense' than his betters and can say things more fundamentally true; he is 'in contact

[1]The example from *As You Like It* is a mistake; Corin is the old shepherd, not the young one in love. However, the collapse of the example does not affect the princi-ple.

with nature,' which the complex man needs to be, so that Bottom is not afraid of the fairies; he is in contact with the mysterious forces of our own nature, so that the clown has the wit of the Unconscious; he can speak the truth because he has nothing to lose. Also the idea that he is in contact with nature, therefore 'one with the universe' like the Senecan man, brought in a suggestion of stoicism; this made the thing less unreal since the humorous poor man is more obviously stoical than profound. And there may be obscure feelings at work, which I am unable to list, like those about the earth-touching Buddha. Another use of the clown (itself a word for the simple countryman) should be mentioned here; the business of the macabre, where you make a clown out of death. Death in the Holbein Dance of Death, a skeleton still skinny, is often an elegant and charming small figure whose wasp waist gives him a certain mixed-sex quality, and though we are to think otherwise he conceives himself as poking fun; he is seen at his best when piping to an idiot clown and leading him on, presumably to some precipice, treating this great coy figure with so gay and sympathetic an admiration that the picture stays in one's mind chiefly as a love scene. It is a far cry from pastoral, but the clown has such feelings behind him among his sources of strength.

Thus both versions, straight and comic, are based on a double attitude of the artist to the worker, of the complex man to the simple one ('I am in one way better, in another not so good'), and this may well recognise a permanent truth about the aesthetic situation. To produce pure proletarian art the artist must be at one with the worker; this is impossible, not for political reasons, but because the artist never is at one with any public. The grandest attempt at escape from this is provided by Gertrude Stein, who claims to be a direct expression of the Zeitgeist (the present stage of the dialectic process) and therefore to need no other relation to a public of any kind. She has in fact a very definite relation to her public, and I should call her work a version of child-cult, which is a version of pastoral; this does not by any means make it bad. The point is to this extent a merely philosophical one, that I am not concerned to deny any practical claim made for what is called proletarian literature so long as the artist had not been misled by its theory; I only call it a bogus concept. It may be that to produce any good art the artist must be somehow in contact with the worker, it may be that this is what is wrong with the arts in the West, it may be that Russia is soon going to produce a very good art, with all the vigour of a society which is a healthy and unified organism, but I am sure it will not be pure proletarian art and I think it will spoil itself if it tries to be.

It seems clear that the Worker, as used in proletarian propaganda, is a mythical cult-figure of the sort I have tried to describe. This is not peculiar to one party. As I write, the Government has just brought out a poster giving the numbers of men back at work, with a large photograph of a skilled worker using a chisel. He is a stringy but tough, vital but not over-strong, Cockney type, with a great deal of the genuine but odd refinement of the English lower middle class. This is very strong Tory propaganda; one feels it is fair to take him as a type of the English skilled worker, and it cuts out the communist feelings about the worker merely to look at him. To accept the picture is to feel that the skilled worker's interests are bound up with his place in the class system and the success of British foreign policy in finding markets. There is an unfortunate lack of a word here. To call such a picture a 'symbol,' like a sign in mathematics, is to ignore the sources of its power; to call it a 'myth' is to make an offensive suggestion that the author is superior to common feelings. I do not mean to say that such pictures are nonsense because they are myths; the facts of the life of a nation, for instance the way public opinion swings round, are very strange indeed, and probably a half-magical idea is the quickest way to the truth. People who consider that the Worker group of sentiments is misleading in contemporary politics tend to use the word 'romantic' as a missile; unless they merely mean 'false' this is quite off the point; what they ought to do is to produce a rival myth, like the poster. In calling it mythical I mean that complex feelings, involving all kinds of distant matters, are put into it as a symbol, with an implication 'this is the right worker to select and keep in mind as the type,' and that among them is an obscure magical feeling 'while he is like this he is Natural and that will induce Nature to make us prosperous.' The point is not that myths ought not to be used but that their use in proletarian literature is not as simple as it looks.

The realistic sort of pastoral (the sort touched by mock-pastoral) also gives a natural expression for a sense of social injustice. So far as the person described is outside society because too poor for its benefits he is independent, as the artist claims to be, and can be a critic of society; so far as he is forced by this into crime he is the judge of the society that judges him. This is a source of irony both against him and against the society, and if he is a sympathetic criminal he can be made to suggest both Christ as the scapegoat (so invoking Christian charity) and the sacrificial tragic hero, who was normally above society rather than below it, which is a further source of irony. Dostoevksy is always using these ideas; perhaps unhealthily, but as very strong propaganda. But I doubt whether they are allowed in pure proletarian literature; the communists do not approve of them, either as tragic or Christian, both because they glorify the independent man and because they could be used against any society, including a communist one.

I am trying here to deal with the popular, vague but somehow obvious, idea of proletarian literature, which is what is influential; there may be a secret and refined definition which disposes of what I have to say. What seems clear from the varying accounts of the position of authors in Russia is that no one definition is generally accepted. Sympathisers tell you there is an arrangement by which authors are expected to do journalistic jobs, writing up conditions in a distant chain of factories or what not, and in their private writing have only to avoid active sedition; this seems healthy if the government would stick to it but not of much critical interest. Gorki, in his speech to the 1934 All-Union Congress of Soviet Writers, made a wider use of the crucial formula of proletarian literature, 'socialist realism.'

> To invent means to extract from the totality of real existence its basic idea and to incarnate this in an image; thus we obtain realism. But if to the idea extracted from the real is added the desirable, the potential, and the image is supplemented by this, we obtain that romanticism which lies at the basis of myth and is highly useful in that it facilitates the arousing of a revolutionary attitude towards reality, an attitude of practically changing the world.

I hope that this use of the word 'myth' will show that my use of it is not a distortion. The idea of the wheel going on revolving, even if you add dialectical materialism by saying that this gives it progress along the ground, is one that a communist must not push too far—revolutionary proletarian literature, in intention at any rate, is obviously a product of transition; and the second sentence might be misunderstood as an appeal for lying propaganda. But the only real trouble about this as an account of proletarian literature is that it applies to any good literature whatever. When communists say that an author under modern capitalism feels cut off from most of the life of the country, and would not under communism, the remark has a great deal of truth, though he might only exchange a sense of isolation for a sense of the waste of his powers; it is certainly not so completely true as to make the verse from Gray pointless to a man living under communism.

The way this sense of isolation has been avoided in the past is by the conventions of pastoral with which I am concerned. (Even Alice in Wonderland, though her convention corresponds to a failure in the normal tradition of pastoral, does indeed stand for something that produces a feeling of solidarity between classes.) When they say that a proletarian writer is the 'spokesman and representative of the proletariat' this is something like a definition; but once everybody is proletarian he is merely the representative of man; and in any case a representative is conscious that he is not the same as what he represents. When Radek in his speech at the same congress appealed for the help of foreign writers in the production of a great proletarian literature of 'love to all oppressed, hate toward the exploiting class. . . . Into this literature we will pour the soul of the proletariat, its passions and its love . . .' his rhetoric is meant to shift from a political idea to a universal one. To say that the only way a present-day writer can produce good work is by devoting himself to political propaganda is of course another thing from defining proletarian literature, and in some cases is true. But it seems fair to say that there is some doubt about the definition.

The poetic statements of human waste and limitation, whose function is to give strength to see life clearly and so to adopt a fuller attitude to it, usually bring in, or leave room for the reader to bring in, the whole set of pastoral ideas. For such crucial literary achievements are likely to attempt to reconcile some conflict between the parts of a society; literature is a social process, and also an attempt to reconcile the conflicts of an individual in whom those of society will be mirrored. (The belief that a man's ideas are wholly the product of his economic setting is of course as fatuous as the belief that they are wholly independent of it.) So 'fundamentally true' goes to 'true about people in all parts of society, even those you wouldn't expect,' and this implies the tone of humility normal to pastoral. 'I now abandon my specialised feelings because I am trying to find better ones, so I must balance myself for the moment by imagining the feelings of the simple person. He may be in a better state than I am by luck, freshness, or divine grace; value is outside any scheme for the measurement of value because that too must be valued.' Various paradoxes may be thrown in here; 'I must imagine his way of feeling because the refined thing must be judged by the fundamental thing, because strength must be learnt in weakness and sociability in isolation, because the best manners are learnt in the simple life' (this last is the point of Spenser's paradox about 'courtly';

the Book of Courtesy takes the reader among Noble Savages). Now all these ideas are very well suited to a socialist society, and have been made to fit in very well with the dogma of the equality of man, but I do not see that they fit in with a rigid proletarian aesthetic. They assume that it is sometimes a good thing to stand apart from your society so far as you can. They assume that some people are more delicate and complex than others, and that if such people can keep this distinction from doing harm it is a good thing, though a small thing by comparison with our common humanity. Once you allow the arts to admit this you will get works of art which imply that the special man ought to be more specially treated, and that is not proletarian literature.

It is for reasons like these that the most valuable works of art so often have a political implication which can be pounced on and called bourgeois. They carry an implication about the society they were written for; the question is whether the same must not be true of any human society, even if it is much better than theirs. My own difficulty about proletarian literature is that when it comes off I find I am taking it as pastoral literature; I read into it, or find that the author has secretly put into it, these more subtle, more far-reaching, and I think more permanent, ideas.

It would be interesting to know how far the ideas of pastoral in this wide sense are universal, and I think that to attempt a rough world-view brings in another point about the communist aesthetic. With the partial exception of *Alice* they are all part of the normal European tradition, but they might seem dependent on that, especially as dependent on Christianity. In my account the ideas about the Sacrificial Hero as Dying God are mixed up in the brew, and these, whose supreme form is Christianity, mainly belong to Europe and the Mediterranean. *The Golden Bough* makes a clear distinction between this hero and the Sincere Man as One with Nature, who is also sacrificial so far as national calamity proves that the emperor is not sincere, but refuses to try to separate them; it seems clear that they are at home respectively in the West and the East. On the other hand interest in the problems of the One and the Many, especially their social aspects, is ancient and obvious in the East, and many of the versions of pastoral come out of that. The idea of everything being included in the humble thing, with mystical respect for poor men, fools, and children, and a contrasting idea of everything being included in the ruling hero, were a main strand of Chinese thought by the third century B.C.; before Buddhism and not limited to Taoism. In China the feeling that everything is everything so nothing is worth doing, natural to this mode of thought, was balanced by the Confucian stress on the exact performance of local duties and ceremonies. One can make a list of European ideas with the same purpose, of making the immediate thing real, all of which stress the individual more or less directly and are denied in the East. God is a person; each separate individual is immortal, with the character he has acquired in this life; so one must continually worry about whether he is free; and he is born in sin so that he must make efforts; and because of this only a God, individual like the rest of us, is worthy to be sacrificed to God. These ideas were knocking about Europe before they were Christian, and the rejection of Christ may well be a less dangerous element in the communist position than the acceptance of Hegel. Gorki said in the early days of the Soviets that the great danger for Russia is that she may 'go East,' a pregnant remark even if the East itself is inoculated against this sort of philosophy. It may be said that men always go in droves, and that all versions of the claim to individualism are largely bogus; but that gives the reason why the prop of individualist theory is needed. Once you have said that everything is One it is obvious that literature is the same as propaganda; once you have said that no truth can be known beyond the immediate dialectical process of history it is obvious that all contemporary artists must prepare the same fashionplate. It is clear too that the One is limited in space as well as time, and the no less Hegelian Fascists are right in saying that all art is patriotic. And the dialectical process proceeds through conflicts, so we must be sure and have plenty of big wars. Of course to talk like this is to misunderstand the philosophy, but once the philosophy is made a public creed it is sure to be misunderstood in some such way. I do not mean to say that the philosophy is wrong; for that matter pastoral is worked from the same philosophical ideas as proletarian literature—the difference is that it brings in the absolute less prematurely. Nor am I trying to say anything about the politics and economics, only that they do not provide an aesthetic theory.

In following essays I shall try to show, roughly in historical order, the ways in which the pastoral process of putting the complex into the simple (in itself a great help to the concentration needed for poetry) and the resulting social ideas have been used in English literature. One cannot separate it from the hero business or from the device of 'pantification' (treating the symbol as everything that it symbolises, which turns out to be everything). . . .

WALTER R. DAVIS

Masking in Arden

One element in the delicate poise that raises Lodge's
Rosalynde a cut above the other Elizabethan pastoral romances is the
way in which it manages to embody its theme in the net of puzzling
disguises so essential to the machinery of a romance plot, instead of
allowing them to remain separate (hence making one or the other
extraneous) as the usual pastoralist did. Lodge's theme he received
from the pastoral tradition; his way of embodying it was quite new.

The Renaissance pastoral romance formed a perfect vehicle for
adjusting the actual and the ideal in life because it always placed the
real and the ideal side-by-side (with the usual result of implying that
the "real" was only apparent, the "ideal" really true). Its setting was
always dual: it juxtaposed directly the actual world of human experience—whether stylized or naturalistically represented—to a kind
of inner circle, a purified abstraction of that world, or "Arcady,"
often with a shrine or some supernatural place at its center to indicate
its central purity. Thus we have, in Sannazaro's *Arcadia*, Naples against
Arcadia, or in Montemayor's *Diana*, a stylized Spain against the pure
fields of Ezla, and so forth. The inner pastoral circle represented, more
or less concretely, a realization of more than usual possibilities in life,
of the natural in accord with the ideal. Descriptive passages stress
wonderment at the supernormal or supernatural quality of the natural
world assimilated to some ideal of order, of the mutable expressing
the permanent, as in this passage from Sidney's *Arcadia:*

> Do you not see how all things conspire to make this countrie
> a heavenly dwelling? Do you not see the grasse, how in colour
> they excell the Emeralds, every one striving to passe his fellow,
> and yet they are all kept of an equall height?... Certainely,

From *Studies in English Literature*, Vol. 5, 151–63. Published, 1965, by Rice University. Reprinted with the permission of the editors of *Studies in English Literature*.

certainely, cousin, it must neede be that some Goddesse in-
habiteth this Region, who is the soule of this soyle: for neither
is anie lesse then a Goddesse, worthie to be shrined in such a
heap of pleasures: nor anie lesse then a Goddesse could have made
it so perfect a plotte of the celestiall dwellings, . . .[1]

or this from Lodge's *Rosalynde:*

Round about in the forme of an Amphitheater were most curiouslie planted Pine trees, interseamed with Limons and Citrons,
which with the thicknesse of their boughes so shadowed the place,
that PHOEBUS could not prie into the secret of that Arbour;
so united were the tops with so thicke a closure, that VENUS
might there in her jollitie have dallied unseene with her deerest
paramour.[2]

More generally, the supernatural showed itself in a strange coöpera-
tion of art and nature, as in Sannazaro's cave of Pan, Centorio's
fountain, Guarini's or Sidney's central cave.[3] The plot of pastoral
romance usually consisted of the hero's mere experience of two worlds:
his entrance into "Arcady" full of the pain and turmoil he contracted
in the actual world, his experience of calm self-analysis in the inner
pastoral circle, and his return to the outer world in harmony with
himself. This action really amounts to the hero's observation of himself in two contexts—an actual and an ideal one—or to his living two
lives, actual and possible; and this action is symbolized by a pastoral
disguise of the new self he assumes upon entering the pastoral land.
To this pattern correspond Sannazaro's *Arcadia*, Montemayor's
Diana, Centorio's *L'Aura Soave*, Gil Polo's *Diana enamorda*, and even
Canto XIX of *Orlando Furioso*. The most familiar examples of it in
English are Shakespeare's *As You Like It* and *The Winter's Tale* (along
with his non-pastoral romance *The Tempest*, and Ben Jonson's strange
oblique romance, *The New Inn*, Sidney's *Arcadia*, Greene's *Pandosto*,
and Book VI of *The Faerie Queene*.
It is important to realize that the English romances exhibit an
emphasis new to the pastoral romance tradition, and that is the explicit
intellectualizing or moralizing of the plot. Sidney is, of course, the
first to show this trait; in his *Arcadia*, the setting becomes openly expressive of values, of ideas; the inner circle becomes the realm of love

[1]*Arcadia* (Folio of 1598), pp. 31–32.
[2]*Rosalynde*, in the Hunterian Club edition of Lodge's *Works*, ed., Edmund Gosse,
I, part 5 (Glasgow: 1883), p. 39.
[3]See Sannazaro, *Arcadia*, ed., Michele Scherillo (Turin: 1888), p. 195; Ascanio
Centorio, *L'Aura Soave* (Venice: 1556), p. 11; Guarini, *II Pastor Fido*, trans., Fanshawe
(London: 1647), p. 104; Sidney, *Arcadia* (Folio of 1598), p. 337.

and contemplation, the violent world around it, the realm of heroic action. Therefore his heroes fittingly discuss such matters as the active and contemplative lives and the nature and operation of love before entering the pastoral retreat. And in the other English works—even in the most unphilosophical of them—there is at least an initial lecture about the values of humility or simplicity. Hence the pastoral disguise signifies not only the discovery of a new aspect of the self, but the conscious acceptance of new values as well. Therefore it is no exaggeration to say that in Elizabethan romances, the pastoral land is first and foremost a symbol of an explicit ideal or a desirable state of mind, and that the purpose of the pastoral is to dramatize a state of mind through correspondence of a man's life to his context. Greene's *Menaphon* is able to rise to a sense of this fact:

> Content sitteth in thy minde as *Neptune* in his Sea-throne, who with his trident mace appeaseth everie storme. When thou seest the heavens frowne thou thinkest on thy faults, and a cleere skie putteth thee in minde of grace; the summers glorie tels thee of youths vanitie, the winters parched leaves of ages declining weaknes. Thus in a myrrour thou measurest thy deedes with equall and considerate motions.[4]

Then the action of the hero in dressing himself as a shepherd and going to live in this land can best be defined as an exploration of his mind, especially touching the relation between what his mind is and the state it might achieve. This is what the action meant to a later pastoral moralist:

> When he went to the pond, Thoreau struck an attitude and did so deliberately, but his posturing was not to draw the attention of others to him, but rather to draw his attention more closely to himself. "I learned this at least by my experiment: that if one advances confidently in the direction of his dreams, and endeavors to live the life which he has imagined, he will meet with a success unexpected in common hours." ... *Walden*, subtitled "Life in the Woods," is not a simple and sincere account of a man's life, either in or out of the woods; it is an account of a man's journey into the mind. . . .[5]

The possibility of striking an attitude in order to clarify one's sense of one's self or position was even more available to the Elizabethans than to Thoreau. Popular prose, for instance, was permeated with

[4]Edward Arber, ed., *Menaphon*, The English Scholar's Library of Old and Modern Works., 12 (London: 1880), p. 24. See also the song "O sweet woods" at the end of the Second Eclogues in Sidney's *Arcadia*.
[5]E. B. White, "Walden—1954," *The Yale Review*, XLIV (1954), 15, 16.

histrionics, since the writer usually assumed a fictional situation in which he could confront his audience directly in order to demand their praise, direct asides to them—"Gentle Readers (looke you be gentle now since I have cald you so)"[6]—ask questions of them and give answers, threaten them, and so forth; the pamphleteer, in short, conceived of himself as an actor in a role:

> Hollow there, give me the beard I wore yesterday. O beware of a gray beard and a balde head: for if such a one doo but nod, it is right dudgin and deepe discretion. But soft, I must now make a grave speach.[7]

Then, too, one of the salient characteristics of the poetry of this period is its liberal use of masks, whether the poet is operating solely beneath the mask of pastoral swain or epic bard or Petrarchan lover, or whether within the poem the speaker assumes a mask only to drop it at the end for a fuller realization of his situation, as in *Astrophel and Stella* XLVII or LXXIV or Drayton's "Since there's no help." But more important to our interests here are the situations where the hero of drama or fiction conceives of himself as acting. D. A. Traversi has written that "there is a sense, common in Elizabethan stage heroes and villains, of the speaker playing up to a dramatically acceptable picture of himself";[8] and the Elizabethan stage is filled with characters who take on roles which distort their personalities meaningfully in the sense that they exaggerate or straiten their personalities in order to enable their real powers—Richard III, Othello, Kent and Edgar in *Lear*, Bosola in *The Duchess of Malfi*, Vindice in *The Revengers Tragedy*, for instance. We find this histrionic self-awareness in Euphuistic fiction too, where the extreme dichotomizing pressure frequently forces an act of choice into a decision to embrace one of two opposite dramatic roles, roles which have beneath them contrasting ethical bases. When Euphues decides to court Lucilla, his decision involves not only the betrayal of a friend for love but leaving the whole moral realm of his part as "The Friend" for the uncertain a-moral world of "The Passionate Man"; he must set the roles side-by-side and try to neutralize the dislogistic *exempla* of Tarquin and Paris which point to the role he will embrace. So too must Saladyne, near the beginning of *Rosalynde*, deliberately cast aside his proper role of natural son and protective

---

[6]Nashe, *The Unfortunate Traveller* in *Works*, ed., R. B. McKerrow, II (London: 1904–10), p. 217.

[7]Lyly, *Pappe with an Hatchet* in *Works*, ed., R. Warwick Bond, III (Oxford: 1902), p. 403.

[8]D. A. Traversi, *Shakespeare: The Last Phase* (London: 1954), p. 7.

elder brother for the role of self-loving villain (a role he is just as suddenly released from later) in order to pursue his purposes.

These considerations suggest that conscious artifice, the deliberate playing of a role through a mask, may be of the utmost importance, in Elizabethan literature, to the exploration of human possibilities. And it is Lodge's *Rosalynde* that utilizes histrionics in the interests of ethical clarification more fully than any other work of Elizabethan prose fiction, pastoral or otherwise.

Rosalynde makes nonsense of the usual easy distinctions between "realism" and "stylization "or "natural" and "artificial." Any pastoral work will do this; for while the pastoral land is always assumed to be free from the taints of man's arts, and hence "natural," it is also ideal, completely unreal—because no such natural state has ever existed since the Fall—and hence "artificial." The country will present a natural ideal artifically, the city the vices of artifice in stylization. But in *Rosalynde* the boundary between natural and artificial is blurred more radically and explicitly than in any other Elizabethan romance— so much so, in fact, as to make the blurring thematic. The forest of Arden is a world that never was, pure artifice; in descriptions of the scenery there, the natural is almost completely subordinated to arti- ficial arrangement: "Passing thus on along, about midday they came to a Fountaine, compast with a grove of Cipresse trees, so cunninglie and curiouslie planted, as if some Goddesse had intreated Nature in that place to make her an Arbour. . . ." (36)[9] The keynote here, as in other romances, is the supernormal status of real growing things corresponding to an ideal arrangement. Yet there is a contrary ten- dency in narrative style, for where country and city meet Lodge seems to have distinguished them by giving the former a more natural and colloquial diction and syntax, the latter higher diction with Euphuistic *similia* and schemes (as in the passage of transition on p. 50).

Furthermore, the expected divisions between "artificial" and "na- tural" do not apply to the cast of characters. They split, of course, into two groups: the native inhabitants of Arden like Coridon, Mon- tanus, and Phoebe, and the disguised court people Rosalynde, Alinda, Rosader, and Gerismond. Yet to say that the first group acts and speaks "naturally" and the second "artificially" is a gross oversimplification. For one thing, there are degrees of artifice within each group. While the old shepherd Coridon comes as close as anyone in the Elizabethan

[9]All quotations from *Rosalynde* are from the Hunterian Club edition of Lodge's *Works*, ed., Gosse; parenthetical references are to pages in Vol. I, part 5.

romances to the actual sixteenth-century rustic, Montanus and Phoebe (whose upbringing is never shown to have been any different from Coridon's) conduct their affairs in the highest courtly style, replete with sonnets, postures, and Euphuistic talk. And while Rosader's conduct as a disguised shepherd is totally stylized, Rosalynde's is not at all; further, Gerismond's pose as a Robin Hood figure allows him to exist in the relaxed greenwood milieu of vigor and plenty.

The presence of degrees of artifice within each group allows some rather surprising crossings between groups; for instance, the disguised kind Gerismond playing his role is less stylized in his deeds and speech than the native Montanus and Phoebe. Rosader's and Montanus's approaches to love operate on the same high level, their poetic styles are indistinguishable, and they speak the same Euphuistic prose—this in spite of the fact that one of them is a nobleman playing a part while the other is a shepherd simply being himself. Or, to take a more radical example, Rosalynde is the most fully disguised person in the plot— first as page, then as pastoral swain—yet her actions are the least stylized, the most spontaneous and free from conventional forms. In Arden she shows more wit and common sense than anyone else; beneath her mask she can approach her love for Rosader directly and humorously, reject Phoebe with dispatch and a homely image, and manage a dénouement with delight and tact. Furthermore, her speech approaches the colloquial in diction and syntax more closely than anyone else's in the book; here for example is her way of handling Rosader: "How now Forrester, have I not fitted your turn? Have I not plaide the woman handsomely, and shewed my selfe as coy in graunts, as courteous in desires, and been as full of suspition, as men of flatterie? And yet to salve all, jumpt I not up with the sweete union of love?" In fact, we find that the disguised characters who deliberately swathe themselves in artifice are no more stylized than the undisguised characters, and frequently act with less attention to conventions and codes than the others. It is perhaps less a matter of who you are and where you come from than where you are and what you are doing at present. This consideration leads us to the interesting hypothesis that for Lodge a conscious pose may be a way of being "natural."

Since it is a place—Arden—that determines the pose, we may be better able to discern the function of the pose in *Rosalynde* after inspecting the major differences in values inherent in its two settings, the city of Bordeaux and the countryside of Arden. For though the manners and the styles of the court and country are not clearly distinguished, the significant ideas for which they stand are. For one thing, different kinds of events happen to people in Bordeaux and Arden. Since Bordeaux is in the hands of a usurper, it is fittingly the realm of division and strife, where Torismond has banished Gerismond and later banishes Rosalynde and his own daughter, and then oppresses Saladyne, who likewise has forced his brother into exile; where death rules over Sir John of Bordeaux and the victims of the Norman wrestler; and where constant violence erupts between brothers. The state of Arden under the true kind is, in direct contrast, a place of union and mutual aid: Adam helps Rosader; Rosader saves Adam with the aid of Gerismond, who prevents them both from starving; Rosader saves Saladyne, Saladyne then saves Rosader; Rosalynde helps Montanus, and so forth. The values that cause these events appear clearly in Sir John's legacy at the opening of the book:

> Climbe not my sonnes; aspiring pride is a vapour that ascendeth hie, but soone turneth to a smoake: they which stare at the Starres, stumble upon stones. . . . Low shrubbes have deep rootes, and poore Cottages great patience. Fortune looks ever upward, and envie aspireth to nestle with dignitie. Take heed my sonnes, the meane is the sweetest melodie; . . . levell your thoughts to be loyall to your Prince. (11)

As his terms show, the court is ruled by the selfish pride later exhibited by Torismond and Saladyne, while the country exhibits the humility which opens the way to love and giving: Montanus's generosity in giving up Phoebe to Ganimede or Gerismond's largesse proceeding from his content "with a simple Cottage, and a troupe of revelling Woodmen for his traine." One very practical result of the contrasting values is that Bordeaux denies sustenance to the needy while Arden is the inn where homely food is given to all who ask, whether it be at Gerismond's banquet or Alinda's cottage supper. Another is the restriction of natural desires—and hence their complication—in the city as against the peculiar liberty which allows one to act as he feels in the country. The contrast is felt especially in regard to love: in the city Rosader's love for Rosalynde was obscured by his familial misfortunes, while the country allows him free expression and even offers trees to hang sonnets from; Rosalynde's love at court is complicated by her position—"But consider ROSALIND his fortunes, and thy present estate"—while in the freedom of Arden she can even become the wooer. Alinda relates the difference between city and country love to appearance and reality:

> But sir our countrey amours are not like your courtly fancies,
> nor is our wooing like your suing: for poore shepheards never
> plaine them till Love paine them, where the Courtiers eyes is
> full of passsion when his heart is most free from affection; they
> court to discover their eloquence, we wooe to ease our sor-
> rowes; (108)

and she is right, for pride is the result of man's illusions fostered by
dumb fortune, whereas humility represents the actual nature of human-
kind.

Two recurring terms, each involving both personal and cosmic
application, will help us to take the contrast to the general level; they
are Fortune, referring both to individual luck and the Goddess Fortuna,
and Nature, meaning both one's human nature and the Creation.
Bordeaux is the realm of Fortune, Arden the realm of Nature. The
forces are not exclusive, but rather interact differently in each place;
in the one Fortune suppresses Nature, in the other Nature operates
freely to overcome Fortune (just as, in the beginning of the pastoral
tradition, Virgil's eclogues demonstrated that human suffering was
ameliorated by the influence of the natural world). In the city Fortune
tempts Saladyne into villainy with her promises, makes love impossible
for Rosalynde, and keeps Rosader's natural nobility obscure, causing
him to exclaim:

> Nature hath lent me wit to conceive, but my brother denied me
> arte to contemplate . . . those good partes that God hath bes-
> towed upon me, the envie of my brother dooth smother in
> obscuritie: the harder is my fortune, and the more his froward-
> nesse. (17)

Nature can emerge here only in acts of extreme jeopardy—such as
Rosader's wrestling or his defense of the manor against law and order—
or in flight. In Arden, Fortune frequently smiles, as when she leads
Rosader to Gerismond, Rosalynde to Rosader, or Rosader to Saladyne;[10] when she does not, as when she seeks "to have a bout" with the
lovers by the instrumentality of the outlaws, she is so successfully
defeated by the brotherly nature of Saladyne and Rosader that she
turns "her frowne into a favour" (92).

What Arden "means" is that in the natural world (the world as it
was intended to be at the Creation, totally unlike what it has become)
one's true human nature emerges. Saladyne's nature is not really
villainous (as Torismond's is); therefore, upon awakening from his

[10]See pp. 56, 62, and 83.

dangerous dream beneath the lion to find himself confronted by Rosader in Arden, he suddenly asks his brother for forgiveness and reforms.
And his subsequent life in Arden, playing the part of a swain and
wooing Alinda, is expressive of his true generous nature in a way that
his "real-life" status as landowner and elder brother was not. The
same is true of Rosader as a forester acting out his loyalty to his outlaw
king and giving full vent to his loyalty to his supposedly absent mistress,
or of Rosalynde playing the witty downright swain, or of Gerismond or
Alinda. Each of the roles, it should be noticed, transforms the merely
privative state of those who have lost their place in society into a
positive ideal of unrestricted action. To return to the hypothesis I
proposed a few pages back: it is in this way that, for Lodge, any disguise
or conscious role which enables a character to adjust his life to the
world of human and cosmic Nature becomes, in effect, a means for
expressing his true nature.

A consideration of Lodge's plot-structure will extend our understanding of the relation between the ideal and the disguise. The plot of
any pastoral romance is essentially defined by the movement out of
the civilized world into the pastoral world; in *Rosalynde* this amounts to
leaving the realm of pride, discord, and a human nature distorted by
the appearances of Fortune for the land of humility, love, and true
nature. As in so many pre-novelistic fictions, the plot is multiple. We
have first the "envelope-plot" of Gerismond and Torismond: the
selfish brother usurps the good brother's throne and drives him to
Arden, where he recovers, reconstructs a government on the natural
Robin Hood model, and emerges to reinstate himself. The Saladyne-
Rosader plot reinforces this one by parallel on the private level: the
avaricious elder brother first oppresses and then exiles the good brother, but then repents in response to his generosity, helps and rein-
states him. The main amorous plot of Rosader and Rosalynde shows
how love, dampened by the reversals of Fortune under selfish repres-
sors (Saladyne and Torismond) arises whole, fresh, and triumphant in
the natural world. The two other love plots expand this one: the Sala-
dyne-Alinda plot parallels it but emphasizes social and economic
conditions; the Montanus-Phoebe plot shows the separation of lovers
because of Phoebe's pride yielding to union by Montanus's triumphant
humility and Rosalynde's charity. All five plots are of course individual
variations on the single theme of separation brought about by selfishness yielding to union by means of love, which arises so "naturally" in
Arden. Or as Lodge himself puts it:

> Heere Gentlemen may you see in EUPHUES GOLDEN
> LEGACIE, that ... division in Nature as it is a blemish in
> nurture, so tis a breach of good fortunes; that vertue is not
> measured by birth but by action; that yonger brethren though
> inferiour in yeares, yet may be superiour to honours; that con-
> cord is the sweetest conclusion, and amitie betwixt brothers more
> forceable than fortune. (139)

Lodge wove his five variations together in a way most proper to his
theme. He divided his book structurally into two parts, separation and
reconstruction. The first part, as befits the theme of separation, proceeds by large separate sections of parallel plotting, a series of extrusions
from the City to the Forest like that of *King Lear*—first Rosalynde's
banishment, then Rosader's escape, then Saladyne's exile (Gerismond's
banishment is anterior to the book's opening). The second part, in
keeping with the growth of unity, proceeds by much closer interweaving, as Rosader, Saladyne, Alinda, Montanus, Phoebe, and Rosalynde
approach their unions in the climactic scene at the end.

Now the hinge on which the plot turns is the *rapprochement* of
Rosader and Rosalynde; and that occurs in a delicate interlude at the
exact structural center, just after the final extrusion of Saladyne and
immediately preceding the first movement toward reconcilation,
Rosader's discovery of Saladyne and the lion. The central interlude is
the most detached and stylized incident in the whole book; its language
is heightened, for it is in verse, in a "wooing eclogue," that they come
together; and while Rosader is merely operating out of his woodland
pose, though in verse, Rosalynde is stalking behind a whole system of
masks—Rosalynde as Ganimede "playing" Rosalynde. Yet it seems
that the very masking of identities and feelings is the only condition
under which true feelings can come to light; for on this level Rosalynde
feels that she can set aside maidenly modesty and act out the truth.
Therefore the wooing eclogue begins by Rosader's frank persuasions
matched by "Ganimede's" equally frank fears, proceeds to stichomy-
thiạ, and ends in a harmony marked by the intimate sharing of a
broken stanza:

ROSADER: Oh gaine more great than kingdomes, or a crowne.
ROSALYNDE: Oh trust betraid if *Rosader* abuse me.
ROSADER: First let the heavens conspire to pull me downe,
    And heaven and earth as abject quite refuse me.
    Let sorrowes streame about my hateful bower,
    And restlesse horror hatch within my brest,
    Let beauties eye afflict me with a lowre,

> Let deepe despaire pursue me without rest;
> Ere *Rosalynde* my loyaltie disprove,
> Ere *Rosalynde* accuse me for unkinde.
> ROSALYNDE: Then *Rosalynde* will grace thee with her love,
> Then *Rosalynde* will have thee still in minde.
> ROSADER: Then let me triumph more than *Tithons* deere,
> Since *Rosalynde* will *Rosader* respect:
> Then let my face exile his sorrie cheere,
> And frolicke in the comfort of affect:
>> And say that *Rosalynde* is onely pitifull,
>> Since *Rosalynde* is onely beautifull. (79–80)

Questions about the relation of fact to fiction come to center on this eclogue. Before entering on it Rosalynde had tested the degrees of conventionality and sincerity in Rosader's love by this pretext:

> I pray thee tell me Forrester, what is this ROSALYNDE, for whom thou pinest away in such passions? Is shee some Nymph that waits upon DIANAES traine, whose chastitie thou hast decyphred in such Epethetes? Or is she some shepheardesse that haunts these plaines, whose beautie hath so bewitched thy fancie, whose name thou shaddowest in covert under the figure of ROSALYNDE, as OVID did JULIA under the name of CORINNA? Or say mee for sooth, is it that ROSALYNDE, of whome we shepheards have heard talke, shee Forrester, that is the Daughter of GERISMOND, that once was King, and now an Outlaw in this Forrest of *Arden*. (62–63)

And the issue of the eclogue is, ironically, to turn fiction into fact:

> And thereupon (quoth ALIENA) Ile play the priest, from this day forth GANIMEDE shall call thee husband, and thou shalt call GANIMEDE wife, and so weele have a marriage. Content (quoth ROSADER) and laught. Content (quoth GANIMEDE) and changed as redde as a rose: and so with a smile and a blush they made up this jesting match, that after proovde to a marriage in earnest; ROSADER ful little thinking he had wooed and wonne his ROSALYNDE. (81)

Here in the wooing-eclogue, "fact" and "fiction," the "real" and the "ideal" merge, just as the restricted real-life status of Rosader the youngest son of Sir John and Rosalynde the lost daughter of a deposed king blend into the larger dimensions of themselves which the roles of open rural lover and saucy swain (which may be characterized as the free dream-personalities of the lost) allow. Such is the idealism of Lodge's book, assuming as it does that a more idealistic version of the self is also a truer version of the self, that to raise the situation by masks to a level of supernormal freedom and ingenuousness is also to give its problem more real and lasting solutions than would be otherwise possible. Hence, the wooing eclogue is the symbolic watershed of a plot where the problems of the unnatural "real" world become solved easily by a series of appeals to the true, natural, and "ideal" nature of each character. And the action of the eclogue is synecdochic of the entire plot where one takes up a pose that expresses his real nature (allowing him freedom and loyalty, hence natural love), comes to terms with himself and others in that pose, and eventually drops it by returning to quotidian life. As the lovers use a formal song to test their love, so the whole of *Rosalynde* uses fictional roles as means for testing the availability of an ideal of human conduct.

Lodge, like Sidney, attempted to explore and extend the possibilities of human existence; his thesis, the possibility he explored, was that the world as we know it, with its selfishness and violence, is only the apparent world, whereas the real world is something we never see, an ideal of humility and love. Such a thesis presupposed a Platonic view of reality, and in order to test it Lodge created for each of his major characters an artificial role of ideal generosity or humility or self-sacrifice. W. B. Yeats wrote in his *Autobiography*,

> There is a relation between discipline and the theatrical sense. If we cannot imagine ourselves as different from what we are and assume that second self, we cannot impose a discipline upon ourselves, though we may accept one from others. Active virtue as distinguished from the passive acceptance of a current code is therefore theatrical, consciously dramatic, the wearing of a mask.[11]

I believe that something like this is presented in *Rosalynde:* in order to escape the heartless current codes of Bordeaux, each character enters Arden under a conscious mask, finds his true self and thus achieves meaningful discipline. Each of them therefore finds his proper nature by acting it out dramatically. Saladyne, in acting out the part of a humble and loyal forester, discovers the true nature of an elder brother in protection and self-sacrifice. Rosalynde, in acting out the role of the open and charitable swain, finds for herself the true part of the lover in frank and direct giving. And Gerismond acts out as Robin Hood the true nature of kingship, in giving sustenance to his subjects.

[11]Yeats, *Autobiography* (New York: 1938), pp. 400–401.

EDWIN GREENLAW

Shakespeare's Pastorals

To many critics it has seemed that the pastoral element in
Shakespeare's plays has small significance because he nowhere
intoduces, with seriousness, the conventions of the *genre*. Pastoral
drama in England is represented, according to this view, by the
Arraignment of Paris or *The Faithful Shepherdess*, but not by *As You Like
It* or *The Winter's Tale*.[1] Such an exclusion, however, is surely illogical.
To say that because Autolycus is unlike Corin and Daphnis, therefore *The Winter's Tale* has little or no relation to pastoral literature is
no more reasonable than to say that because in the Henry V trilogy
we are more interested in Falstaff or Fluellen or Justice Shallow
than in the strictly historical material, therefore these plays do not
belong to the chronicle history group. Shakespeare extended and

From *Studies in Philology*, Vol. 13, 122–26; 129–33; 136–37; 141; 145–54. Published,
1916, by the University of North Carolina Press. Reprinted with the permission of
the publisher.

[1]As examples of many expressions of such views compare Smith, "Pastoral Influence on the English Drama," in *Publications of the Modern Language Association* (1897),
pp. 378–81: "In *The Winter's Tale* the pastoral element borrowed from Greene's
Pandosto is so completely subordinated that we can hardly say it exists at all. Who
would speak of Perdita as an Arcadian?" He makes a similar remark concerning
As You Like It. Schelling, *English Literature During the Lifetime of Shakespeare*, p. 386,
says that *As You Like It* is no true pastoral, since the genius of its author "could not be
bound within the conventions of a form of literature so exotic and conventional";
and of *The Winter's Tale* (pp. 389–90) he says that the outdoor scenes "are pastoral only
in the sense that they deal with shepherds and their life." Greg, *Pastoral Poetry and
Pastoral Drama*, p. 411, says: "It is characteristic of the shepherd scenes of that play
(*sc. Winter's Tale*), written in the full maturity of Shakespeare's genius, that, in spite of
their origin . . . they owe nothing of their treatment to pastoral tradition, nothing to
convention, nothing to aught save life as it mirrored itself in the magic glass of the
poet's inspiration;" and his comment (pp. 412–13) on *As You Like It* mainly consists of
generalizations about the beauty of "the faint perfume of the polished Utopia of the
courtly makers."

enlarged the scope of comedy, history, and tragedy, yet the classi-fication of the First Folio is convenient and not inaccurate. In *As You Like It, Cymbeline,* and *The Winter's Tale* he dealt with material drawn from pastoral romance in such a way as to deepen and enrich certain characteristics of this *genre*; he did not write pastorals of the conventional Renaissance type, yet the pastoral element in his plays is both considerable and important.

In the present study I shall discuss two topics: first, the relation of Shakespeare's pastorals to a well-defined type of plot-structure which, originating in *Daphnis and Chloe* and modified by certain Italian and Spanish elements, found its first complete English expression in Sidney's *Arcadia,* and, second, Shakespeare's development from a criticism of the absurdities of pastoralism coupled with a somewhat conventional use of the country vs. town motif to a much deeper interpretation of one of the most interesting phases of Renaissance thought.

Daphnis and Chloe supplied the chief elements in the plot of a type of pastoral which was used, with some modifications, by Sidney, Spenser, and Shakespeare. The romance is too well-known to need detailed exposition; the main points may be summarized as follows:

> Two foundlings are brought up by rustics whom they regard as their parents; their childhood is described in detail, and the man-ner in which they became lovers; the purity and sweetness of this love idyl are emphasized; character contrast is supplied by means of a rude lover, the rival of the hero, who is also a coward; disguised as a wolf, he attacks the girl, who is rescued by the hero. Later, wicked men attempt without success to kidnap the boy, the rival being slain in the encounter, and the incident is repeated in the captivity of the heroine by outlaws. At length the lovers are reunited; wealthy parents come and recognize them, and they are happily married.

This is the story, in brief, of the only true Greek pastoral which influenced English literature; other Greek romancers, such as Helio-dorus and Achilles Tatius, stressed the wanderings of the lovers and introduced various other elements which are without significance in the present study. The Italian and Spanish pastoral romances, such as the *Ameto,* the *Arcadia,* and the *Diana,* have little relation to this plot; they introduce various love idyls and go back to the Virgilian eclogues. But with them the element of allegory is introduced; there is the further important influence of style, particularly the inter-weaving of prose and verse; and in the introduction of the author, often as a disappointed lover who is living for the time among shepherds, a noteworthy addition to the *dramatis personae* was made.

From these various sources, all well known in the England of Sidney's time, a composite plot was formed, the essentials of which are as follows:

1. A child of unknown parentage, usually a girl, is brought up by shepherds. As a variant, the heroine may merely be living in seclusion among shepherds.

2. A lover is introduced, who may be a foundling, or, more commonly, a man of high birth who falls in love with the heroine and for her sake adopts the dress and the life of a shepherd or a forester.

3. This love story is complicated by the rivalry of a blundering shepherd, usually characterized as a coward, his function being to supply comedy and to serve as a foil for the hero.

4. Melodramatic elements are supplied by the attack of a lion or a bear, and this affords the hero another opportunity to prove his prowess.

5. A captivity episode is usually introduced; the heroine is stolen by pirates or outlaws; the hero goes to her rescue.

6. At length it develops that the girl is of high birth, and she marries the hero.

7. From Italian and Spanish sources comes an extra character, not vitally connected with the plot, often the author of the romance; usually this man is afflicted with melancholy and is living among shepherds because of his woes.

Sidney's *Arcadia* is often referred to as a pastoral; in reality it is a heroic "poem," according to the standards of Sidney and his circle, in which a pastoral episode is introduced. The action opens, in the midst of the story, with this pastoral, but that the pastoral is not the chief element in the story is evidenced not only by the space given in books I and II to the epic history of Pyrocles and Musidorus but by the fact that throughout book III, the most important of the entire work, the pastoral completely disappears.[2] The plot[3] of this pastoral portion of *Arcadia* follows closely the type outlined above:

1. A king, or, in the first version, a duke, lives with his daughters in pastoral seclusion.

2. Two princes come to the place; in order to get access to the maidens one disguises himself as a shepherd, the other as an Amazon.

3. A blundering shepherd, guardian of one of the girls, supplies comic interest; his cowardice is especially dwelt on.

[2] Except for the fact that the Captivity motif is pastoral; this motif is used, however, merely at the introduction. I have discussed the construction of this romance at some length in "Sidney's *Arcadia* as an Example of Elizabethan Allegory," in *Anniversary Papers by Colleagues and Pupils of George Lyman Kittredge*, pp. 327–37.

[3] The numbers used in my analysis correspond to the incidents in the typical plot.

4. Melodramatic incidents are supplied by the advent of a lion and a bear; the heroes save the maidens.

5. Two illustrations of the captivity motif are given: there is an incursion of the rabble by which the lives of the heroines are greatly endangered; the attempt, however, is foiled by the heroes. Later, by a ruse, the girls are abducted and are kept in captivity for a long time; the Amazon is also captured, but the shepherd goes to the aid of his lady. Here the pastoral disappears and a long series of chivalric adventures takes its place.

6. At length the heroines are released and marriages follow.

7. A melancholy shepherd named Philisides (Sidney), who has no part in the main action, is living in this pastoral seclusion because of an unhappy love affair (Stella).

The variations in this plot are not significant. There is a quartet of lovers, and the complications are, of course, increased thereby. The boorish shepherd is the guardian, not a suitor. The foundling motif is absent; the heroines are ladies of high rank. But the disguise of the lover as a shepherd; the character contrast supplied by Dametas; the incidents of the wild beasts, the rabble, and the captivity; the melancholy shepherd who is not connected directly with the action,— all these are based directly upon the special type of pastoral plot outlined above.[4]

We have now to consider two important but apparently overlooked illustrations of the influence of this part of the *Arcadia*. The first is the Pastorella-Calidore episode in *Faerie Queene* VI; the second is supplied by *As You Like It*. The Pastorella-Calidore story is important not only because it is closely parallel to some of Shakespeare's pastorals in plot and in its interpretation of pastoralism, but also because there are indications that it had direct influence on Shakespeare. In view of its importance, I give the plot of this episode in some detail; the numbers prefixed to the sections indicate the relations

---

[4]The long story of the Captivity is very similar to the last book of *Amadis*. In that romance Oriana is captured by Amadis and is taken to his castle, with other ladies. Her father raises a great force and lays siege to the castle. In both *Arcadia* and *Amadis* this mustering of forces by the leaders on both sides is stressed and is too characteristic to escape notice; the high chivalry with which the preparations for the battle, and the battle itself, are conducted, contributes to the similarity in atmosphere, while the central situation, a lady held in captivity by her lover while her father attempts her rescue, is precisely the same. In Sidney's romance, Amphialus, son of the wicked Cecropia, is himself a man very similar to Amadis; his love for Philoclea is not returned, but though Oriana stays voluntarily and Philoclea is detained against her will, the debt of Sidney to the most famous chivalric romance of his time is unquestionable. The Captivity in *Amadis*, like the corresponding portion of *Arcadia*, is the culmination of the romance; but in *Amadis* it is chivalric throughout, while in *Arcadia* it develops from the pastoral, and the lover who had been disguised as a shepherd joins the father in the attempt at rescue.

existing between Spenser and the typical plot already outlined, but I have not altered the sequence of events.[5]

1. Calidore, in pursuit of the Blatant Beast, comes upon a group of shepherds. Among them is a damsel wearing a crown of flowers and clad in home-made greens that her own hand had dyed; she sits on a hillock, and all around are country lads and lasses. Calidore is fascinated by her beauty, and in the evening gladly goes home with her and the old shepherd who is reputed to be her father. Spenser here explains that this shepherd is not really her father, but had found her in open fields, "as old stories tell."

2. After supper, Calidore and the old shepherd discourse on the charms of pastoral life; love for the fair Pastorella so inflames the knight that he seeks permission to remain. Thus Calidore, forgetting his quest, becomes a shepherd, and passes a long time in this idyllic existence.

3. Pastorella has many lovers, chief among them Coridon, who is in every way unworthy of her. The rivalry between Calidore and this shepherd is stressed, especially in such a way as to bring out the superiority of Calidore in courtesy and prowess.

4. On one occasion a tiger attacks Pastorella. Coridon acts the part of a coward, but Calidore slays the beast with his sheep-hook. By this means he wins the love of the maiden.

5. After a long period of happiness, brigands capture Pastorella and Coridon in Calidore's absence. The captain of the thieves loves the shepherdess but she foils him. In the meantime Calidore is searching far and wide. In an attack upon the brigands by some merchants who have come to buy slaves, Coridon escapes, the old shepherd is killed, and Pastorella is left for dead. Coridon finds Calidore, but is afraid to go back to the place where, he says, Pastorella was slain. He is forced to do so, however, and to the great joy of the knight he finds his lady and rescues her from the thieves.

6. Calidore restores the flocks to Coridon and takes Pastorella to the castle of Belgard where he leaves her with Sir Bellamore and his lady while he takes up once more his quest of the Beast. It soon appears that Pastorella is the long lost daughter of Bellamore and Claribell. The story is left incomplete by Spenser, since the remainder of the book, the last part of the *Faerie Queene* completed by Spenser, is taken up with the account of Calidore's quest; there is no doubt whatever that Spenser intended later to have Calidore return and claim Pastorella as his bride.

7. A shepherd named Colin (Spenser) has no part in the main action; Pastorella is fond of his music, and on one occasion Calidore comes upon him piping merrily to a bevy of maidens, who however disappear on the approach of a mortal.

That this plot corresponds very closely to the type is instantly apparent. There are variations, of course, but they do not affect the conclusion that *Daphnis and Chloe*, *Arcadia*, and the story of Pastorella are closely related. In the Greek pastoral both hero and heroine are

[5]The passage in the *Faerie Queene* begins with the ninth canto.

ignorant of their parentage, while in *Arcadia* a king adopts pastoral life in order to keep his daughters from marrying, so that although the hero becomes a shepherd it is in order to deceive the father, not the girl; in the *Faerie Queene* the girl is a foundling but the lover is a knight like Musidorus. These variants are due to the fact that in both *Arcadia* and *Faerie Queene* the pastoral is an episode in a chivalric romance.

II

Since the plot of *As You Like It* is drawn from Lodge's *Rosalynde*, a discussion of its relations to the type outlined in the preceding section is of importance only in so far as Shakespeare departs from his source. Lodge owed much to Sidney, but his romance is wholly lacking in those epic elements which characterize *Arcadia* and the *Faerie Queene*.[6] More important than this, for our present purpose, is the fact that though Lodge uses a number of the incidents found in the type plot, two of the three omitted by him are supplied by Shakespeare, while the third, the captivity, is not needed for the dénouement either in Lodge or in Shakespeare. William and Audrey, true rustics as compared with the gentility in disguise or with the eclogue shepherdess and swain, are supplied by Shakespeare and furnish the comic relief which is the function of the blundering shepherd in Sidney and Spenser. And the extra shepherd, melancholy, having no part in the main action yet deeply significant as one of the pastoral *dramatis*

[6]While the plot is not closely parallel, many of the essentials are present: (1) A girl of high rank, compelled to flee, lives among shepherds disguised as a swain; she is accompanied by a friend who becomes a shepherdess. There is the praise of country life by an old shepherd, as in Tasso and Spenser, and like Erminia, Rosalynde is disguised as a man and is oppressed by love. (2) The lover comes; there is a pretty variation from type in his fancied wooing of Ganymede for Rosalynde. Aliena (Celia) later has a love affair which is strictly typical. (3) This incident is wanting in Lodge. (4) A lion attacks, not the girl, but Saladyne (Oliver); he is more gentlemanly than the usual pastoral lion, since he waits throughout the long "meditation" of Rosader (Orlando). (5) Captivity is wanting, but in the attack on Aliena by the rabble, with her rescue by Saladyne, we have a pretty close imitation of *Arcadia* II, where this incident precedes the real captivity episode. (6) The recognition and marriage are present. (7) The extra shepherd is wanting. To this plot is added the Phoebe-Montanus complication. The entire setting reminds one of *Arcadia*, where there are also four lovers. Zelmane (Pyrocles) the amazon loves Philoclea, apparently of her own sex; so here the Rosader-Ganymede relation. Again, the Aliena-Saladyne story (shepherdess loved by hero disguised as a forester) corresponds to the Pamela-Musidorus story. Finally, Phoebe loves Ganymede, who is really a woman, corresponding to the love of Basilius for Zelmane, really a man. Thus Lodge has situations strikingly similar to those of *Arcadia*, with the sex-mystifications precisely reversed. The usual statement, therefore, that except for those portions which he drew from *Gamelyn* Lodge's story is original, ought to be considerably modified.

personae, the Philisides of *Arcadia* and the Colin of the *Faerie Queene*, is omitted by Lodge but in Shakespeare is no less a personage than the melancholy Jaques.

Jaques is always said to be the creature of Shakespeare's imagination, having no "source." Like Hamlet he is a mystery variously interpreted, and next to Hamlet he is Shakespeare's most perplexing character. Some critics, for example Professor Herford, find in him a promise of a "deeper, more comprehensive pity, the stuff of which in the next years the great tragedies were to be wrought."[7] Grant White and others have thought his "melancholy" to be "a sullen, scoffing, snarling spirit"; Hudson, on the other hand, thinks him "a philosopher with something of the fool in him," while Dowden sees a reincarnation of him in Laurence Sterne.[8]

A brief review of the points brought out in the previous section of this study will indicate *a priori* grounds for supposing that Jaques was introduced by Shakespeare in imitation of Sidney and Spenser. These points are as follows: 1. The stock character of the extra shepherd, not immediately connected with the main plot, a man who is not a real shepherd but is living among them because of melancholy due to a past love experience, derives ultimately from *Ameto, Arcadia* (Sannazaro), and *Diana*. 2. By Sidney this element was grafted on a plot of the *Daphnis and Chloe* type. 3. In English pastoral romances such a character is found in *Arcadia, Faerie Queene VI*, and *As You Like It*, but not in the romances of Greene or Lodge. 4. The source of the Calidore-Pastorella plot is not Tasso or Greene but Sidney's *Arcadia*. Colin, introducing the author, is similar to Philisides. 5. The pastoral plots of *Arcadia* and of *As You Like It* are very similar in their main outlines. By the introduction of William and Audrey, as well as of Jaques, Shakespeare makes his plot conform even more closely to that of Sidney, i.e., *As You Like It*, so far as the general plot is concerned, goes beyond *Rosalynde* in conformity to the typical plot of Sidney and Spenser.

We now turn to more direct proof. In the first version of *Arcadia*, Philisides occupies a more prominent place than in the version which we have.[9] Under this name Sidney represents himself as sojourning for a time among the Arcadian group because of his love melancholy.

[7]Introduction to the Eversley edition of *As You Like It*.
[8]Cited by Rolfe, in his edition of the play, p. 252.
[9]For an account of his discovery, in 1907, of several MSS copies of *Arcadia* as Sidney first wrote it, see Mr. Bertram Dobell's article in *The Quarterly Review*, CCXI, pp. 76 ff. The romance was originally of much simpler construction than in the form with which we are familiar, lacking the epic history of the heroes and the captivity.

He has no part in the main action, but describes himself as a man of good birth who had been educated as a gentleman; he had been a traveller to ripen his judgment, and had returned "to use the benefitt of a quyet mynde" when love came to divert the course of his tranquillity and to plunge him into melancholy.[10] He takes part in the amusements arranged for the Duke,[11] singing eclogues on the woes of love; he is characterized as melancholy, and his fondness for moralizing in his songs may well suggest the melancholy and moral Jaques. In the present version, Philisides appears only in connection with the "pastorals" at the end of each book; thus he is even more distinctly an extra character, having no close connection with the action, yet so characterized that it is difficult to avoid the belief that he is the original of Shakespeare's portrait.

This parallel is most striking in the pastorals at the end of Book I. After a conventional singing match by Lalus and Dorus, Basilius called to a young shepherd who neither danced nor sang, but lay on the ground at the foot of a cypress tree, "in so deep a melancholy, as though his mind were banished from the place he loved to be in prison in his body." Thus summoned, Philisides sings a strange song which he says he got from Lanquet (Languet):

> In the olden time, the beasts were the only inhabitants of earth, and were privileged to act in all ways without let or hindrance. They had a commonwealth, "for nothing can endure where order n' is"; in this commonwealth
>
>> The beasts with courage clad
>> Like Senators a harmless empire had.
>
> Despite the mildness of this government they desired a change, so all the other beasts prayed Jove for a king. After telling them that this would lead to trouble, Jove granted their request; so man was created. Each beast brought some gift to the new king, and all of them voluntarily relinquished the power of speech. Soon man turned the commonwealth into a tyranny; the more powerful beasts, imitating the bad example, preyed on their lesser brethren and finally were driven into waste places, enemies of man and beast alike. The weaker animals became beasts of burden, were deprived of their fur or feathers, were killed for food, and at length were even killed for sport:
>
>> At length for glutton taste he did them kill:
>> At last for sport their sillie lives did spill.

[10]See Jaques' account of the nature of his melancholy, "compounded of many simples," of his travels, and Rosalind's scornful remarks thereon. (IV, i).

[11]In the first *Arcadia* the exile is called merely the "Duke," on which see *As You Like It*.

Then the "moral" is phrased:

> But yet o man, rage not beyond thy neede;
> Deeme it no gloire to swell in tyrannie.
> Thou art of blood; joy not to see things bleed:
> Thou fearest death; thinke they are loth to die.
> A plaint of guiltlesse hurt doth pierce the skie.
> And you poore beastes, in patience bide your hell,
> Or know your strengths, and then you shall do well.

With this passage compare *As You Like It*, II. i. Amiens and "First Lord" came upon Jaques "as he lay along under an oak"; near by a poor sequestered stag, the prey of hunters,

> Much marked of the melancholy Jaques,
> Stood on the extremest verge of the swift brook,
> Augmenting it with tears.

The Duke inquires,

> What said Jaques?
> Did he not moralize this spectacle?

To which "First Lord" replies,

> O, yes, into a thousand similes.
> First, for his weeping into the needless stream:
> "Poor deer," quoth he, "thou mak'st a testament
> As worldlings do, giving thy sum of more
> To that which had too much." Then, being there alone,
> Left and abandoned of his velvet freinds:
> " 'Tis right," quoth he; "thus misery doth part
> The flux of company." Anon a careless herd,
> Full of the pasture, jumps along by him,
> And never stays to greet him. "Ay," quoth Jaques,
> "Sweep on, you fat and greasy citizens,
> 'Tis just the fashion; wherefore do you look
> Upon that poor and broken bankrupt there?"
> Thus most invectively he pierceth through
> The body of the country, city, court,
> Yea, and of this our life, swearing that we
> Are mere usurpers, tyrants, and what's worse,
> To fright the animals and to kill them up
> In their assign'd and native dwelling-place.

So they left him, "weeping and commenting upon the sobbing deer."

That Shakespeare had Sidney's Philisides in mind in his characterization of Jaques is, I think, clear for the following reasons:

1. The two characters are introduced under similar circumstances: Philisides is lying under a cypress tree when called upon; Jaques under an

oak. Moreover, Philisides is called, wherever he appears, "the melancholy shepherd," while the regular name for Shakespeare's character, throughout the drama, is "the melancholy Jaques."

2. The two passages are very like in content. Both refer to a beasts' commonwealth in which man is a usurper. Sidney stresses this more than Shakespeare, since he treats of the origin of the tyranny of man over beasts, but it is absolutely plain in Shakespeare. In addition to such references as those in the speech of Jaques, compare the Duke's words immediately preceding:

> Come, shall we go and kill us venison?
> And yet it irks me the poor dappled fools,
> Being native burghers of this desert city,
> Should in their own confines with forked heads
> Have their round haunches gored.

.   .   .

In two of the so-called dramatic romances, *Cymbeline* and *The Winter's Tale*, Shakespeare introduces pastoral episodes of great interest. These plays belong to his latest period, dating 1609–1611; they illustrate a return to a pastoralism quite different from that which appears in *As You Like It;* and they present interesting problems in source study. The source of one of these episodes, the Perdita-Florizel story, has long been recognized, but Shakespeare's changes are such as to alter materially the story as told in *Pandosto*. . . . This story [of *Cymbeline*] is as follows:

1. A courtier banished by the king steals for revenge the two baby princes. These lads he brings up as his own children; all three live in the wilderness, being hunters. Twenty years after his banishment the boys are restless and desire to go to the court to seek adventures; he dissuades them by praising the advantages of their present life over the wickedness and corruption of the city. At this time a beautiful youth comes to them, weary and in need of food. This youth is really a princess in disguise. She remains with them, assisting with the cooking and other housework.

2. The lover of the princess living in this forest seclusion is absent, therefore the pastoral love idyl does not figure in the story. But because of a misunderstanding with her lover, the heroine is oppressed by love-melancholy.

3. An unworthy suitor finds out where the heroine is and plans to attack her and force her to yield to him. But his attempt is foiled by the youths, really her brothers, instead of by her lover.

4. The potion scene, the trance, and the burial take the place of the usual pastoral incidents.

5. A Roman captain and his soldiers take the heroine into captivity; they are kind to her, and help her to return to her home.

6. At length she is restored to her lover and all are happy.

In general, this story conforms with sufficient accuracy to the typical plot to make clear that it was influenced by pastoral romance and perhaps drawn from some definite pastoral. The exiled Belarius reminds one of the banished Duke in *As You Like It;* the young princes brought up as woodsmen, thinking Belarius to be their father and ignorant of his rank, are true pastoral characters; the praise of the purity and sincerity of country life is closely similar to the speech of Melibee in *Faerie Queene* VI, and is an expansion of the thought expressed by the Duke in *As You Like It.* That Belarius and his two sons are not watchers of sheep with poetry and love as their avocation need not trouble us; there is in this episode, closely linked as it is to the tragic story of Imogen, no place for artificiality and shepherd gallantry. Furthermore, it is thoroughly characteristic of Shakespeare, even from the days of *As You Like It,* to stress the more active physical life of foresters and hunters rather than the elegant trifling of the artificial pastoral. It is a more robust pastoral, but it is pastoral none the less.

. . .

[The Imogen story] not only assists in giving the utmost complexity to the entire plot, thus carefully and deliberately preparing for what is in many respects the most remarkable dénouement in the entire list of Shakespeare's plays, and not only aids in binding the wager story and the *Romeo and Juliet* rifacimento to the historical material, but also, as I shall show . . . [later], is a means through which Shakespeare expresses some of his maturest and most characteristic thought about the meaning of life.

If Imogen is like Erminia, compelled because of separation from her lover and by great danger to her life to live for a time among rustics, Perdita resembles Pastorella in that ignorant of her high station she is brought up by an old shepherd as his daughter. In Perdita's story we have no problem of sources; the relation of *The Winter's Tale* to Greene's romance has long been known. But it is sometimes held by students of pastoral drama that the Florizel-Perdita episode is not a pastoral, though these same critics speak of *Pandosto* as a pastoral romance.[12] The fact is that Greene's story is

[12]Greg, for example (p. 411), speaks of the Perdita-Florizel story as only "apparent pastoral," and continues, "It is characteristic of the shepherd scenes of that play, written in the full maturity of Skakespeare's genius, that, in spite of their origin in Greene's romance of *Pandosto*, they owe nothing of their treatment to pastoral tradition." And Smith, *Publications of the Modern Language Association* (1897), p. 378 n., says that in *The Winter's Tale* "The pastoral element borrowed from Greene's *Pandosto* is so completely subordinated that we can hardly say it exists at all. Who would ever speak of Perdita as an *Arcadian*?" Certainly, and who would ever speak of *Hamlet* as a tragedy of blood, or of the scenes at the Boar's Head in Eastcheap as chronicle history?

much farther removed from true pastoral than Shakespeare's; what
has really happened is that Shakespeare has transformed a romance
of adventure which patronizes the "homely pastimes" of shepherds,
"shepheards ragges," and the garlands woven of shepherd's "homely
flowers" into the most exquisite and satisfying pastoral in Elizabethan
literature.

At first sight, Greene's story follows the pastoral rules in several
important respects. The shepherdess who is ignorant of her true
station, the high-born lover who for her sake dons pastoral attire,
the praise of shepherd life—all seem to belong to the realm of Pastorella and of Chloe. But beyond a bare mention of the gathering of
all the "Farmers Daughters of Sycilia" and their homely pastimes,
there is no introduction of other pastoral characters; the story is
almost devoid of incident except for the troubles of Dorastus about
his honor and his clothes, and it concludes with an elopement planned
chiefly by the ambitious shepherdess. The spirit is worldly, not pastoral. Porrus charges his wife not to tell of the gold found with the
child, lest claimants appear. With the money he buys land and flocks
and becomes a man of substance. Fawnia, in consequence, has many
rich stuitors, but she cares for none until the Prince comes. Her love
for Dorastus is very real, but she suspects him, even when he appears
in "shepheards ragges," of intending to betray her, and it is this
suspicion that makes her say, "This attire hath not made Dorastus
a shepherd, but to seeme like a shepherd." Even when she saw him
coming for the first time in this guise she began to forget Dorastus
and "to favor this pretty shepheard, whom she thought she might both
love and obtaine." He convinces her, at last, of his sincerity, but she
is also plainly impressed by his plea, in the manner of Herrick's advice
to the virgins, that her beauty will pass and she had better love be-
times. The plan for the elopement is mainly hers. Thus Fawnia is a
Pamela of the Richardsonian type, concerned about her virtue,
ambitious yet suspecting the intent of the Prince; her reputed father,
a worthy predecessor of Pamela's father, is wholly different from the
old shepherd in *The Winter's Tale*, for he suspects that the prince has
designs upon his daughter's virtue. As to Dorastus, he is utterly unlike
Calidore or Musidorus. "His honor wished him to cease from such
folly, but Love forced him to follow fancy." He procured a shepherd's
coat and hid it in a grove; when he went to call on his lady he put
it on, cursing his "base desires and homely attires." "Thy thoughtes,"
he says, "are fit for none but a shepheard, and thy apparell such as

only becomes a shepheard. A strange change, from a Prince to a pesant." Thus the true spirit of the pastoral love idyl is wanting; Dorastus does not go to live among shepherds in order to woo his lady, he merely puts on a shepherd's coat when he pays his visits, changing back to his "riche apparel" when the call is over. We are not surprised that after the betrothal Fawnia's chief thought is joy to have won "the love of a Prince, hoping in time to be advaunced from the daughter of a poore farmer to be the wife of a riche King." Greene's story is interesting as an early attempt to substitute psychological analysis, the conflict of motives, for such time-worn sensational incidents as the rescue of the maiden from a lion or a band of robbers, but it reminds us less of pastoral than of some modern romances in which a poor boy goes to the city, makes a fortune, marries his daughter to a foreign nobleman, and prides himself on being a self-made man. How completely all this is changed by Shakespeare needs no illustration. The single point that I wish to make is that, far from rejecting pastoral romance as a theme unworthy of the maturity of his genius, he converted Dorastus into Florizel, and Fawnia into Perdita.

. . .

Bacon speaks in one place of the story of Cain and Abel as an allegory of the contest between active life, represented in the husbandman, and the contemplative life, represented in the shepherd, and says that the favor of heaven was vouchsafed to the pastoral ideal.[13] In another passage, however, he combats the idea of Greek philosophy that the contemplative life is preferable: "But men must know that in this theatre of man's life it is reserved only for God and the angels to be lookers on. . . ."[14]

Even more pronounced is the apparent conflict between Elizabethan concreteness and sense of fact and Elizabethan sentimentality as manifested in the sonnets and the pastorals. Sidney is ambitious to be an explorer, a colonizer, a statesman, a military hero, and he also represents himself as the melancholy Philisides; he addresses to the Queen a state paper showing admirable grasp of the problems confronting England in a delicate situation, and he also writes sentimentally of his hopeless love for Stella. Elizabeth distinguishes herself for her careful economy in administration and proves a worthy match for Catherine of France and Philip of Spain, both consummate politicians; she also delights in being praised as a Diana, a Venus, a Queen

[13]*Advancement*, I, vi, 7.
[14]*Ibid.*, II, xx, 8.

of Faerie, a subject for the most fulsome flattery at the Princely Pleasures at Kenilworth. . . . Spenser, we say, is the dreamer, the poet
of allegory, the poet's poet; Bacon is the man of science, interested
in fact, with no illusions; Shakespeare is the purely objective poet,
whose facts come from the psychological laboratory, not from Bacon's
world of sense or from Spenser's faerie. In spite of the simplicity of
this mode of classification, it is not altogether borne out by the facts,
for Spenser does not inhabit a realm remote from the life that England
was living, his allegory of Gloriana is based upon one aspect of the
new English nationalism which none of his contemporaries phrased
more completely or more accurately; while the symbol and illusion of
faerie romance find a place in Bacon's quest of truth and in Shakespeare's quest of the springs of human action.

A complete study of the relation of Shakespeare to this apparent
duality of Elizabethan thought would take us far beyond the limits
of the present study, but certain aspects of his use of pastoralism
contribute something toward an understanding. In *As You Like It*,
for example, there is a keen sense of the absurdities of the *genre*. Lodge's
Rosader, who brings sonnets to read in order to show "what a poetical
fury love will inspire into a man," remains much the same in Shakespeare, excepting that Orlando's sonnets are converted into a sort of
verse that Touchstone says he could imitate for eight years together,
dinners and suppers and sleeping-hours excepted. Rosalind is not
the conventional shepherds' mistress, she has too much humor; she
believes in the sincerity of Orlando's love, but she lets fly the shafts
of her wit upon his imitation of the love-lorn swain. The portrait of
the melancholy Jaques is edged with satire. Touchstone's affair
with Audrey parallels in broad farce the "love" of the great ones,
and he parodies the effects of unrequited love as set forth by Silvius.
Comparison with Lodge shows how in the story of Phebe and Silvius,
both representative of the eclogue type of shepherdess and shepherd,
Shakespeare has heightened the impression of artificiality. Thus
"love" is approached from different angles, all of them showing
Shakespeare's familiarity with the rules observed by the best literary
practitioners and the test of silvery laughter to which he subjects
them. The seriousness of the *Shepheards Calender* is wholly wanting,
likewise the unreal agonies of *Arcadia* and the Petrarchism of Lodge.
Rosalind assures Orlando that her frown would not injure a fly;
Touchstone approves of the shepherd's life in respect of itself, "but
in respect that it is a shepherd's life, it is naught."

In *Cymbeline* and *The Winter's Tale* a deeper note is struck. Charming as it is as a romance, and witty as it is in its satire of certain literary conventions, *As You Like It* is deficient in thought. The Duke's speech on the uses of adversity is a lovely rendering of a motif frequently met, but it springs from no deep and passionate conviction. The unrealities of artificial pastoral formed no medium through which Shakespeare could express his thought; he had either to satirize or to transform. The pastoral episodes of these two late plays, however, form the vehicle for a noble defence of the contemplative ideal. This defence is the climax of the exposition of a theme which runs through a number of the plays. In *Richard II* Shakespeare had echoed Marlowe's conception of the dignity of high position. Kingship is a personal privilege; the crown is the symbol of earthly glory. In *Henry V* the essential worthlessness of such an ideal of glory is shown in Henry's great speech on ceremony, which is an expression, in magnificent verse, of the oft-repeated idea that the peasant is happier than the king—the very essence of the idea which Melibee expresses to Calidore, the old shepherd to Erminia, and that runs through the criticism of the court found in *Colin Clout*. In *Lear*, the idea recurs, but more poignantly expressed, in the old king's words to Cordelia. In prison, he says, they can find happiness:

> And pray, and sing, and tell old tales, and laugh
> At gilded butterflies, and hear poor rogues
> Talk of court news; and we'll talk with them too,
> Who loses and who wins; who's in, who's out;
> And take upon's the mystery of things,
> As if we were God's spies; and we'll wear out,
> In a wall'd prison, packs and sets of great ones
> That ebb and flow by the moon.

Other illustrations come readily to mind, but these are sufficient to show how Shakespeare's historical plays and tragedies reflect a progression from the Renaissance idea of glory to a conviction that happiness does not depend on place or power. This conception is closely akin to the fundamental principle of pastoral idealism. It is true that at first sight these and other similar passages in Shakespeare seem merely expressions of a well-known Elizabethan convention. No motif is more commonly met, beginning with Wyatt's version of the Town Mouse and the Country Mouse, than this dispraise of court and exaltation of the purity and simplicity of life in the country. But Shakespeare does not sentimentalize about country life; he would

not, if living to-day, write books for tired city clerks on "Five Acres
and Liberty." The very passage in *Henry V* in which the king attacks
so bitterly the emptiness of ceremony praises only the sound health
and the freedom from care of the peasant, not his "vacant mind";
if the only advantage in being a king consists in "ceremony,"

> Such a wretch,
> Winding up days with toil and nights with sleep,
> Had the fore-hand and vantage of a king.
> The slave, a member of the country's peace,
> Enjoys it, but in gross brain little wots
> What watch the king keeps to maintain the peace,
> Whose hours the peasant best advantages.

And in *Lear* we do not get the full power of the lines about the possibility of happiness, even in prison, unless we bear in mind that earlier
Lear, autocratic, imperious, who thought that he was great because
he was dressed in a little brief authority, but not learning until he
had been broken by suffering that ay and no is no good divinity and
that a king is not ague-proof.

In *Cymbeline* this theme is even more prominent. Belarius praises
their life in the wilderness for its security and its honesty. But Guiderius
replies,

> Out of your proof you speak; we, poor unfledg'd,
> Have never wing'd from view o' the nest, nor know not
> What air's from home. Haply this life is best
> If quiet life be best, sweeter to you
> That have a sharper known.

And Arviragus,

> What should we speak of
> When we are old as you? when we shall hear
> The rain and wind beat dark December, how
> In this our pinching cave shall we discourse
> The freezing hours away? We have seen nothing.

To which Belarius:

> Did you but know the city's usuries
> And felt them knowingly; the art o' the court,
> As hard to leave as keep, whose top to climb
> Is certain falling or so slippery that
> The fear's as bad as falling; the toil o' the war,
> A pain that only seems to seek out danger
> I' the name of fame and honour; which dies i' the search,
> And hath as oft a slanderous epitaph
> As record of fair act.

Here, then, the debate between the old shepherd and the youth, familiar in English pastorals since the time of Barclay, acquires new intensity. Later, when the youths wish to get into the battle, like Percival ambitious to seek Arthur's court, Belarius tries to keep them away, but Arviragus cries,

> What pleasure, sir, find we in life, to lock it
> From action and adventure?

The true significance of these passages becomes clear if we compare with the young princes Cloten the princely fool. Cloten is unable to understand why he fails to win Imogen's love, since the clothes once worn by Posthumus fit him perfectly. When Guiderius challenges him, he says,

> Thou villain base,
> Know'st me not by my clothes?

And, a moment later,

> To thy further fear,
> Nay to thy mere confusion, thou shalt know
> I am son to the queen.

Here, then, is the man of noble birth, but a fool, relying upon his tailor and his name for respect; over against him are set those whom he despises as "rustic mountaineers," but in whom innate nobility has produced character independent of position or the appearance and veneer of culture. Belarius looks with delight upon these evidences that his two charges are in reality noble:

> How hard it is to hide the sparks of nature!
> These boys know little they are sons to the king,
> Nor Cymbeline dreams that they are alive.
> They think they are mine; and though train'd up thus meanly
> I' the cave wherein they bow, their thoughts do hit
> The roofs of palaces, and nature prompts them
> In simple and low things to prince it much
> Beyond the trick of others.

And after they have slain Cloten:

> These two princely boys . . . 'Tis wonder
> That an invisible instinct should frame them
> To royalty unlearn'd, honour untaught,
> Civility not seen from other, valour
> That wildly grows in them but yields a crop
> As if it had been sowed.

Cloten, brought up at court and with every advantage, is yet a fool; Guiderius and Arviragus, ignorant of their descent, their only companion an old man whose wound still poisons his faith in his fellows, are fitted for a life of action through this withdrawal from the world. Place and power are relative: Richard could not command respect, wearing his crown; Lear could not command respect lacking his crown; Cloten gains nothing from his clothes; the two mountain youths possess a royalty of nature that dignifies their rustic garb.[15]

If, finally, we consider this material in connection with the preceding sections of this essay, the following conclusions may be drawn. In the first place, the pastoral element in Shakespeare's plays is constant and pervasive. He has little of the conventional; the artificiality seen in the eclogues and in the romances and dramas drawn therefrom has no attraction for him. Neither does he use the pastoral, as Spenser and others used it, as a medium for courtly allegory or for satire of church and state. He satirizes the conventional literary pastoral, but his sympathy for the sweetness, the purity, and the sincerity of life away from the heated atmosphere of court is shown in his Perdita, his Imogen, and in "that noble pair of brothers." He looks upon country life without the sentimentality of many modern writers; he indulges no illusions concerning it; the countryman is not made noble because he lives in the presence of natural beauty any more than the king is noble because he wears a crown. Yet one gets an impression of a value to be attached to what the Elizabethans called the contemplative life as a preparation for active life, not merely in the fact that one may find sermons in stones, but through the education which the young charges of Belarius received. Lastly, the whole idea is linked with that perception of the illusion of worldy place and honor which so informs much of his major work. In this he is

[15]This philosophy of clothes recurs frequently in *Cymbeline* and *The Winter's Tale*. Posthumus disguises himself as a peasant, saying,

> Let me make men know
> More valour in me than my habits show. . . .
> To shame the guise o'the world, I will begin
> The fashion, less without and more within.

In *The Winter's Tale* (IV, iv) the old shepherd and his son are impressed by the borrowed magnificence of Autolycus, and wonder if he is a courtier: "Seest thou not the air of the court," he says, "in these enfoldings? hath not my gait in it the measure of the court? receives not thy nose court-odour from me? reflect I not on thy baseness court-contempt?" And after they have been rewarded for their services, the shepherd and his son reflect on the delight of being gentlemen born. Meeting Autolycus again (V, ii), the clown says: "You denied to fight with me the other day, because I was no gentleman born. See you these clothes? say you see them not and think me still no gentleman born; you were best say these robes are not gentlemen born; give me the lie, do, and try whether I am not now a gentleman born."

one with his greatest contemporary. Back of the fact Spenser saw
always the symbol. There is a certain pathos in the story of how
Colin attained at last the vision of beauty for which he had searched
so long, only to see it disappear at the approach of a mortal. And
Shakespeare, in like case aware that the visions evoked by his imagination must fade into the light of common day, also comes to feel what
is at the very basis of the lovely vision of the *Faerie Queene*, that not
only are worldly standards of success and happiness illusory, but that

> Like the baseless fabric of this vision,
> The cloud-capp'd towers, the gorgeous palaces,
> The solemn temples, the great globe itself,
> Yea, all which it inherit, shall dissolve,
> And, like this insubstantial pageant faded,
> Leave not a rack behind.

HAROLD JENKINS

As You Like It[1]

A masterpiece is not to be explained, and to attempt to
explain it is apt to seem ridiculous. I must say at once that I propose
nothing so ambitious. I merely hope, by looking at one play, even in
what must neccessarily be a very fragmentary way and with my own
imperfect sight, to illustrate something of what Shakespeare's method
in comedy may be. And I have chosen *As Like You It* because it seems
to me to exhibit, most clearly of all the comedies, Shakespeare's
characteristic excellences in this kind. This is not to say that *As You
Like It* is exactly a representative specimen. Indeed I am going to
suggest that it is not. In this play, what I take to be Shakespeare's
distinctive virtues as a writer of comedy have their fullest scope; but
in order that they may have it, certain of the usual ingredients of
Shakespeare's comedy, or indeed of any comedy, have to be—not
of course eliminated, but very much circumscribed. In *As You Like It*,
I suggest, Shakespeare took his comedy in one direction nearly as
far as it could go. And then, as occasionally happens in Shakespeare's
career, when he has developed his art far in one direction, in the comedy which succeeds he seems to readjust his course.

If our chronology is right, after *As You Like It* comes, among the
comedies, *Twelfth Night*, And while we may accept that *Twelfth Night*
is, as Sir Edmund Chambers says, very much akin to *As You Like It*
"in style and temper", in some important respects it returns to the
method and structure of the previous comedy of *Much Ado About
Nothing*. Sandwiched between these two, *As You Like It* is conspicuously

From *Shakespeare Survey VIII*, edited by Harold Jenkins, pp. 40–51. Published, 1955,
by Cambridge University Press. Reprinted by permission of the author and the
publisher.

[1]A lecture delivered to the Shakespeare Conference at Stratford-upon-Avon, 18
August, 1953.

lacking in comedy's more robust and boisterous elements—the pomps of Dogberry and the romps of Sir Toby. More significantly, it has nothing which corresponds to the splendid theatricalism of the church scene in *Much Ado*, nothing which answers to those crucial bits of trickery by which Benedick and Beatrice in turn are hoodwinked into love. Even if, as may be objected, they are not hoodwinked but merely tricked into removing their hoods, still those stratagems in Leonato's orchard are necessary if the happy ending proper to the comedy is to be brought about. These ambushes, if I may call them so—they are really inverted ambushes—are paralleled, or should one say parodied, in *Twelfth Night* in the scene where Malvolio is persuaded that he too is beloved. And this ambush too is necessary if, as the comedy demands, Malvolio is to have his sanity called in question and his authority undermined. The slandering of Hero in *Much Ado* also is to have its counterpart in *Twelfth Night*. For the slandering of Hero, with its culmination in the church scene, forces one pair of lovers violently apart while bringing another pair together. And in *Twelfth Night* the confusion of identities holds one pair of lovers—Orsino and Viola—temporarily apart, yet forces another pair—Olivia and Sebastian—with some violence together. A satisfactory outcome in *Much Ado* and *Twelfth Night* depends on such embroilments; and the same is even more true in an earlier comedy like *A Midsummer Night's Dream*. In *As You Like It* I can hardly say that such embroilments do not occur, but they are not structural to anything like the same degree. Without the heroine's masculine disguise Phebe would not have married Silvius any more than in *Twelfth Night* Olivia would have married Sebastian; but the confusions of identity in *As You Like It* have no influence whatever upon the ultimate destiny of Rosalind and Orlando, or of the kingdom of Duke Senior, or of the estate of Sir Rowland de Boys. Yet these are the destinies with which the action of the play is concerned. It is in the defectiveness of its action that *As You Like It* differs from the rest of the major comedies—in its dearth not only of big theatrical scenes but of events linked together by the logical intricacies of cause and effect. Of comedy, as of tragedy, action is the first essential; but *As You Like It* suggests that action is not, if I may adapt a phrase of Marston's, "the life of these things". It may be merely the foundation on which they are built. And *As You Like It* further shows that on a very flimsy foundation, if only you are skilful enough, a very elaborate structure may be poised. But the method has its dangers, and though Shakespeare's skill conceals these dangers from us, *Twelfth Night*, as I said, returns to a more orthodox scheme.

The story which provides the action for *As You Like It* belongs to the world of fairy-tale or folk-lore. This is a world which supplied the plots of a number of Shakespeare's plays, including the greatest, notably *King Lear*. And fairy-tales have many advantages for the dramatist, among which is their total disregard of practical probabilities. In fairy-tales, for example, evil is always absolute, clearly recognized, and finally overthrown; all of which may have something to do with the Aristotelian theory that while history records what has happened, poetry shows what should happen. Relaxing the more prosaic demands of verisimilitude, the fairy-tale invites the imagination. It can certainly provide a convenient road into the Forest of Arden. And this is not less true for Shakespeare because the road had already been built for him by Lodge.

A man has died and left three sons. Three is the inevitable number, and though Shakespeare, like Lodge, forgets to do much with the middle one, he is not therefore unimportant. The eldest brother is wicked, the youngest virtuous—and does fabulous feats of strength, notably destroying a giant in the shape of Charles the wrestler, who has torn other hopeful youths to pieces. Orlando therefore wins the princess, herself the victim of a wicked uncle, who has usurped her father's throne. This is the *story* of *As You Like It*. And Shakespeare, making the journey of the imagination far more quickly than Lodge, gets most of it over in the first act. That is what is remarkable. By the time we reach the second act Rosalind has already come safe to the Forest of Arden, by the aid of her man's disguise. From this disguise, as everybody knows, springs the principal comic situation of the play. But such is the inconsequential nature of the action that this comic situation develops only when the practical need for the disguise is past. The course of true love has not run smooth. But most of its obstacles have really disappeared before the main comedy begins. It only remains for the wicked to be converted, as they duly are at the end, all in comedy's good but arbitrary time, when the wicked eldest brother makes a suitable husband for the second princess. Or a most *un*suitable husband, as all the critics have complained. But this, I think, is to misunderstand. Instead of lamenting that Celia should be thrown away on Oliver, he having been much too wicked to deserve her, we should rather see that Oliver's getting this reward

is a seal set on his conversion, and a sign of how good he has now
become.

The first act of *As You Like It* has to supply the necessary minimum
of event. But, Quiller-Couch notwithstanding, this first act is something more than mechanical.[2] It is for one thing a feat of compression,
rapid, lucid and, incidentally, theatrical. In fifty lines we know all
about the three brothers and the youngest is at the eldest's throat.
In three hundred more we know all about the banished Duke and
where and how he lives, and the giant has been destroyed before
our eyes. But there is more to the first act than this. Before we enter
Arden, to "fleet the time carelessly, as they did in the golden world",
we must be able to contrast its simple life with the brittle refinement
of the court. This surely is the point of some of what 'Q' called the
"rather pointless chop-logic"; and also of the courtier figure of Le
Beau, a little sketch for Osric, with his foppery of diction and his
expert knowledge of sport. Le Beau's notion of sport provokes Touchstone's pointed comment on the courtier's values. "Thus men may
grow wiser every day: it is the first time that ever I heard breaking of
ribs was sport for ladies." This *is* the callousness one learns at a court
ruled by a tyrannous Duke, whose malevolent rage against Rosalind
and Orlando not only drives them both to Arden but completes the
picture of the world they leave behind.

This first act, then, shows some instinct for dramatic preparation,
though we may grant that Shakespeare's haste to get ahead makes
him curiously perfunctory. He is in two minds about when Duke
Senior was banished; and about which Duke is to be called Frederick;
and whether Rosalind or Celia is the taller. He has not quite decided
about the character of Touchstone. I do not think these are signs
of revision. They simply show Shakespeare plunging into his play with
some of its details still but half-shaped in his mind. The strangest
of these details is the mysterious middle brother, called Fernandyne
by Lodge but merely "Second Brother" in *As You Like It*, when at
length he makes his appearance at the end. Yet in the fifth line of
the play he was already christened Jaques. And Shakespeare of course
afterwards gave this name to someone else. It seems clear enough
that these two men with the same name were originally meant to be
one. As things turned out Jaques could claim to have acquired his

[2]Quiller-Couch, *Shakespeare's Workmanship* (1918), p. 130. In spite of some radical
disagreement, I have got a number of hints from "Q"'s essay.

famous melancholy from travel and experience; but I suspect that it really began in the schoolbooks which were studied with such profit by Jaques de Boys. Though he grew into something very different, Jaques surely had his beginnings in the family of De Boys and in such an academy as that in Navarre where four young men turned their backs on love and life in the belief that they could supply the want of experience by study and contemplation.

Interesting as it might be to develop this idea, the important point of comparison between *As You Like It* and *Love's Labour's Lost* is of another kind. And to this I should like briefly to refer before I come to discuss the main part of *As You Like It*. *Love's Labour's Lost* is the one play before *As You Like It* in which Shakespeare sought to write a comedy with the minimum of action. Four young men make a vow to have nothing to do with a woman; each breaks his oath and ends vowing to serve a woman. That is the story; far slighter than in *As You Like It*. Yet, in contrast with *As You Like It*, the careful and conspicuous organization of *Love's Labour's Lost* distributes its thin action evenly through the play. And the characters always act in concert. In the first act the men, all together, make their vow; in the second the ladies, all together, arrive and the temptation begins. The climax duly comes, where you would expect it, in a big scene in Act iv, when each in turn breaks his vow and all together are found out. *Love's Labour's Lost* is the most formally constructed of all the comedies. When the ladies and gentlemen temporarily exchange partners, this is done symmetrically and to order. Indeed the movement of the whole play is like a well-ordered dance in which each of the participants repeats the steps of the others. But this is exactly what does *not* happen in *As You Like It*, where the characters do *not* keep in step. When they *seem* to be doing the same thing they are really doing something different, and if they ever echo one another they mean quite different things by what they say—as could easily be illustrated from the little quartet of lovers in the fifth act ("And so am I for Phebe.—And I for Ganymede.—And I for Rosalind.—And I for no woman"), where the similarity of the tune they sing conceals their different situations. The pattern of *As You Like It* comes not from a mere repetition of steps, but from constant little shifts and changes. The formal parallelisms of *Love's Labour's Lost* are replaced by a more complex design, one loose enough to hold all sorts of asymmetries within it.

But of course the effect of variations upon a theme instead of simple repetitions is not new in *As You Like It*. It is the tendency of Shakespeare's comedy from the start. In *Love's Labour's Lost* itself the courtly gestures of the four young men are burlesqued by those of a fantastic knight, and while the four young men are vowing not to see a woman, Costard the clown is "taken with a wench". Moreover, one of the four, though he goes through the movements with the others, has some trouble to keep in step, and is always threatening to beak out of the ring. Even when he makes his vow with the others, he knows that necessity will make him break it. As he joins in their purposes he knows them to be foolish and he mocks at ideals which he at the same time pursues. Human activity offers itself to the dramatist in a large variety of forms and the same individual can play contradictory parts. The drunken tinker in *The Taming of the Shrew* does not know whether he may not really be a noble lord. Although Shakespeare did not invent this situation, it was just the thing to appeal to him. For he knew that a man is very easily "translated". In the middle of his fairy play he put a man with an ass's head. In perhaps the most remarkable encounter in Shakespeare the daintiest fairy queen caresses a man turned brute, who, with a fairy kingdom around him, can think only of scratching his itch. When the animal appears in a man it may terrify his fellows; it may also attract to it his finest dreams and fancies, corrupting them, or being uplifted by them to a vision of new wonder. Shakespeare of course does nothing as crude as *say* this. He knows as well as the Duke in Arden that sermons may be found in stones, but much better than the Duke that it is tedious to preach them, a thing, incidentally, he does not permit the Duke to do. What Shakespeare characteristically does in his comedy is to set together the contrasting elements in human nature and leave them by their juxtaposition or interaction to comment on one another.

In *As You Like It* the art of comic juxtaposition is at its subtlest. It is to give it fullest scope that the action can be pushed up into a corner, and the usual entanglements of plotting, though not dispensed with altogether, can be loosened. Freedom, of course, is in the hospitable air of Arden, where convenient caves stand ready to receive outlaws, alfresco meals are abundantly provided, with a concert of birds and running brooks, and there is no worse hardship than a salubrious winter wind. This is "the golden world" to which, with the beginning of his second act, Shakespeare at once transports us, such a world as has been the dream of poets since at least the time of Virgil when, wearied with the toilings and wranglings of society, they yearn for the simplicity and innocence of what they choose to think man's natural state.[3] It is of course a very literary tradition that Shakespeare is here using, but the long vogue of the pastoral suggests that it is connected with a universal impulse of the human mind, to which Shakespeare in *As You Like It* gives permanent expression. But this aspect of the play is merely the one which confronts us most conspicuously. There are many others. *As You Like It* has been too often praised for its idyllic quality alone, as though it were some mere May-morning frolic prolonged into a lotos-eating afternoon. A contrast with the ideal state was necessitated by the literary tradition itself, since the poet seeking an escape into the simple life was expected to hint at the ills of the society he was escaping from. That meant especially the courts of princes, where life—it was axiomatic—was at its most artificial. And the vivid sketching in of the courtly half of the antithesis is, as I have shown, an important function of *As You Like It*'s maligned first act. With the first speech of the banished Duke at the opening of the second act, the complete contrast is before us; for, while introducing us to Arden, this speech brings into sharp focus that first act which has just culminated in the usurper's murderous malice. "Are not these woods more free from peril than the envious court?" Though the contrast is traditional, it comes upon us here, like so many things in Shakespeare, with the vitality of fresh experience. The Forest of Arden comes to life in numerous little touches of the country-side, and the heartless self-seeking of the outer world is concentrated into phrases which have the force of permanent truth. The line that 'Q' admired—"And unregarded age in corners thrown"— might have come from one of the sonnets, and when Orlando observes how "none will sweat but for promotion" we recognize the fashion of our times as well as his. As the play proceeds, it is easy enough for Shakespeare to keep us ever aware of the forest, what with Amiens to sing for us, the procession home after the killing of the deer, an empty cottage standing ready for Rosalind and Celia, surrounded by olive-trees beyond a willow stream, and a good supply of oaks for Orlando or Oliver to lie under. It cannot have been quite so easy

[3]This is not to imply that Shakespeare's "golden world" is at all the same as the primitive life of the mythical golden age, in which, by contrast with the Forest of Arden, there was no winter wind, sheep went unshorn, and man, at peace with all creatures, neither killed the deer nor was theatened by the snake and lion. Virgil associated the simplicity of pastoral life with the golden age, and the two ideais were frequently combined, not to say confused, by later pastoralists. (Cf. Roy Walker, *The Golden Feast* (1952), p. 133.)

to keep us in touch with the court life we have now abandoned; but nothing is neater in the construction of the play than those well-placed little scenes which, by despatching first Orlando and then Oliver to the forest, do what is still required by the story and give the illusion that an action is still going briskly forward, while at the same time they renew our acquaintance with the wicked world. After the first scene in the ideal world of Arden and a sentimental discourse on the deer, there is Frederick again in one of his rages, sending for Oliver, who, an act later, when we are well acclimatized to the forest, duly turns up at court. Then occurs a scene of eighteen lines, in which Shakespeare gives as vivid a sketch of the unjust tyrant as one could hope to find. The tyrant prides himself upon his mercy, punishes one man for his brother's sins, and finds in his victim's excuses further cause of offence. Oliver's plaint that he had never loved his brother brings the instant retort, "More villain thou. Well, push him out of doors." As this eruption dies down, there appears in the Forest of Arden the cause of all the trouble quietly hanging his verses on a tree.

The contrast between court and country is thus presented and our preference is very plain. Yet as a counterpoise to all this, there is one man in the country-side who actually prefers the court. Finding himself in Arden, Touchstone decides: "When I was at home, I was in a better place." It is no doubt important that he is a fool, whose values may well be topsy-turvy. But in one word he reminds us that there are such things as domestic comforts. And presently we find that the old man whom society throws into the corner is likely in the "uncouth forest" to die of hunger and exposure to the "bleak air". There is clearly something to be said on the other side; the fool may anatomize the wise man's folly. And there is also Jaques to point out that the natural life in Arden, where men usurp the forest from the deer and kill them in their "native dwelling-place", while deer, like men, are in distress abandoned by their friends, is as cruel and unnatural as the other. When Amiens sings under the greenwood tree and turns "his merry note unto the sweet bird's throat", inviting us to shun ambition and be pleased with what we get, Jaques adds a further stanza to the song which suggests that to leave your "wealth and ease" is the act of an ass or a fool. Most of us, I suppose, have moods in which we would certainly agree with him, and it is a mark of Shakespeare's mature comedy that he permits this criticism of his ideal world in the very centre of it. The triumphal procession after the killing of the deer, a symbolic ritual of the forester's prowess, is accompanied by a mocking song, while the slayer of the deer is given its horns to wear as a somewhat ambiguous trophy.

It is Jaques, mostly, with the touch of the medieval buffoon in him, who contributes this grotesque element to the songs and rituals of Arden. Like Touchstone he is not impressed by Arden, but unlike Touchstone he does not prefer the court. Indeed, as we have seen, he is able to show that they are very much alike, infected by the same diseases. No doubt his is a jaundiced view of life, and it is strange that some earlier critics should have thought it might be Shakespeare's. Shakespeare's contemporaries would hardly have had difficulty in recognizing in Jaques a variant of the Elizabethan melancholy man—the epithet is applied to him often enough—though I remain a little sceptical when I am told by O. J. Campbell that from the first moment they heard Jaques described, the Elizabethans would have perceived "the unnatural melancholy produced by the adustion of phlegm".[4] Whatever its physiological kind, the important thing about his melancholy is that it is not the fatigue of spirits of the man who has found the world too much for him, but an active principle manifesting itself in tireless and exuberant antics. Far from being a morose man, whether he is weeping with the stag or jeering at the huntsman, he throws himself into these things with something akin to passion. His misanthropy is a form of self-indulgence, as is plain enough in his very first words:

JAQUES: More, more, I prithee, more.
AMIENS: It will make you melancholy, Monsieur Jaques.
JAQUES: I thank it. More, I prithee, more. I can suck melancholy out of a song.

His own comparison with a weasel sucking eggs suggests what a ferocious and life-destroying thing this passion is. Shakespeare's final dismissal of Jaques is profound. Far from making Celia a better husband than Oliver, as George Sand apparently thought, he is the person in the play who could not be allowed to marry anyone, since he can have nothing to do with either love or generation. His attempt to forward the nuptials of Touchstone and Audrey serves only to postpone them. He is of course the one consistent character in the play in that he declines to go back with the others to the court that they have scorned. Yet how *can* he go back when the court has been converted?

[4]*Huntington Library Bulletin*, VIII (1935), 85.

Jaques's occupation's gone. And he will not easily thrive away from the social life on which he feeds. It is notable that the place he really covets, or affects to, is that of the motley fool, licensed to mock at society, indulged by society but not of it. Yet, seeking for a fool, he has only to look in the brook to find one; and it is the romantic hero who will tell him so.

Shakespeare, then, builds up his ideal world and lets his idealists scorn the real one. But into their midst he introduces people who mock their ideals and others who mock *them*. One must not say that Shakespeare never judges, but one judgement is always being modified by another. Opposite views may contradict one another, but of course they do not cancel out. Instead they add up to an all-embracing view far larger and more satisfying than any one of them in itself.

Now when Orlando tells Jaques that he may see a fool by looking in the brook, this is not the first time that Jaques and Orlando meet; and the relations between the two of them are worth a moment's glance. Their first encounter occurs in public when the Duke and his retinue are met for one of their forest repasts. Jaques has just been eloquent about the vices of mankind and is justifying the satirist who scourges them, when he is confronted with the romantic hero in his most heroic attitude, rushing into the middle of the scene with drawn sword,[5] crying, "Forbear, and eat no more." But Jaques is not the man to be discomposed, even when a sudden interruption throws him off his hobby-horse. When he has inquired, "Of what kind should this cock come of?", the heroic attitude begins to look extravagant. The hero stands his ground: "Forbear, I say: He dies that touches any of this fruit"; at which Jaques nonchalantly helps himself to a grape, saying, "As you will not be answered with reason (raisin), I must die." Heroism now appears thoroughly deflated, or would do if Jaques were attended to by the company at large. The hero is in fact saved by the Duke's "civility"; and their talk of "gentleness" and "nurture" even throws back into perspective Jaques's recent attack upon society. The situation as a whole retains its equilibrium. And yet as a result of this little incident we are bound to feel that the romantic hero is very vulnerable to the ridicule of the satirist, until their duel of wit in the following act readjusts our view by allowing Orlando his retort.

There is a formal point to notice here, easy to miss but full of mean-

[5]"*Enter Orlando*" says the Folio simply, but the dialogue justifies Theobald's "*with Sword drawn.*"

ing. The wit-combat between Jaques and the hero is matched an act or so later—there is no strict regularity about these things—by a similar wit-combat between Jaques and the heroine. On each occasion Jaques is worsted and departs, leaving Rosalind and Orlando to come together. In fact the discomfiture of Monsieur Melancholy by one or other of the lovers is the prelude to each of the two big love-scenes of the play. And this arrangement makes a point more prettily than any action-plot involving Jaques could do. The mocking words of Jaques's farewell are in each case illuminating: "Farewell, good Signior Love"; and "Nay, then, God be wi' you, an you talk in blank verse." The gibe at blank verse is not an incidental or decorative jest. It makes it clear that, however we judge of them, the melancholy spirit of Jaques and the romantic emotion of Rosalind and Orlando cannot mingle. Shakespeare dismisses the melancholy man before he gives the lovers their scope. And in this I follow his example.

So far I have dealt only with the immigrants to Arden. There is of course a native population. The natural world of the poet's dreams has always been inhabited by shepherds, who from the time of Theocritus have piped their songs of love. And Rosalind and Celia have been in the forest for only twenty lines when two shepherds appear pat before them. In an earlier comedy perhaps these might have been a similar pair singing comparable love-ditties. But in *As You Like It*—Shakespeare making the most of what is offered him by Lodge—they are a contrasting pair. One is young and one is old, one is in love and one is not. The lover is the standard type. But the notion of love has undegone a change since classical times and the shepherds of Renaissance pastorals have all been bred in the schools of courtly love. So young Silvius is the faithful abject lover who finds disdain in his fair shepherdess's eye and sighs "upon a midnight pillow"— Shakespeare always fixes on a detail in which a whole situation is epitomized. There are of course many other lovers in the play, but the story of Silvius and Phebe is of the pure pastoral world, the familiar literary norm against which all the others may be measured. First against Silvius and Phebe are set Rosalind and Orlando, and the immediate result of this is that Rosalind and Orlando, though they clearly belong to the pastoral world, seem much closer to the ordinary one. Indeed, since Silvius and Phebe relieve them of the necessity of displaying the lovers' more extravagant postures, Rosalind and Orlando are freer to act like human beings. Rosalind need only play at taunting her adorer while allowing her real woman's heart to be in love with him in earnest. In an earlier comedy like *The Two Gentle-men of Verona* the heroes themselves had to undergo those "bitter fasts, with penitential groans, With nightly tears and daily heart-sore sighs", and these are what, as H. B. Charlton says, may make Valen-tine look a fool. But with Silvius to take this burden from him, Orlando can really be a hero, performing the traditional hero's fabulous feats, and upon occasion may even be a common man like ourselves. He has, for example, the very human trait of unpunctuality; he is twice late for an appointment. And although on one occasion he has the perfect excuse of a bloody accident, on the other he has nothing to say, beyond "My fair Rosalind, I come within an hour of my promise." Such engaging casualness is of course outside Silvius's range. And although Orlando has his due share of lovers' sighs and is indeed the "unfortunate he" who hangs the verses on the trees, in so human a creature these love-gestures appear not as his *raison d'être* but as an aberration. A delightful aberration, no doubt—"I would not be cured, youth", he says—still an aberration that can be the legitimate subject of our mockery. Lying contemplating his love under an oak, he seems to Celia "like a dropped acorn", and both the ladies smile at his youthful lack of beard. But Orlando is robust enough to stand their mockery and ours, and Shakespeare's superb dramatic tact arranges that Orlando shall draw our laughter towards him so that he may protect the fragile Silvius from the ridicule which would destroy *him*. Rosalind alone is privileged to make fun of Silvius; and that because searching his wounds, she finds her own. The encounters which do not occur have their significance as well as those which do: Touchstone is only once, and Jaques never, allowed a sight of Silvius before the final scene of the play. Silvius has not to be destroyed or the play will lack something near its centre.

If in a pastoral play the ideal shepherd is satirized it must be indirectly. But that he is, through his complete unreality, a likely target for satire has been commonly recognized by the poets, who have therefore had a habit of providing him with a burlesque counter-part to redress the balance and show that they did know what rustics were like in real life. As Gay was to put it in his proem to *The Shepherd's Week*, the shepherd "sleepeth not under myrtle shades, but under a hedge"; and so when Gay's shepherd makes love it is in a sly kiss behind a haycock to the accompaniment of the lady's yells of laughter. This may have been the method of Shakespeare's William, for, far from inditing verses to his mistress, William is singularly tongue-tied;

though he is "five and twenty" and thinks he has "a pretty wit", the biggest of his eleven speeches in only seven words long. And his partner is just as much a contrast to the shepherdess of pastoral legend. She thanks the gods she is not beautiful, does not even know the meaning of "poetical" and her sheep, alas, are goats.

Shakespeare, then, presents the conventional pastoral, and duly burlesques it. But with a surer knowledge of life than many poets have had, he seems to suspect that the burlesque as well as the convention may also miss the truth. Do shepherds really sleep under hedges? In order to be unsophisticated, must they be stupid too? So among his varied array of shepherds, Silvius and Ganymede and William, Shakespeare introduces yet another shepherd, the only one who knows anything of sheep, whose hands even get greasy with handling them. It does not matter that Shakespeare got the hint for Corin from Corydon in Lodge. For Lodge found Corydon in literature and for Corin Shakespeare went to life. Lodge's Corydon, though he may make the king smile with his clownish salutation, has evidently been bred at court himself. Would he ever else accost a lady in distress in strains like these

> If I should not, fair damosel, occasion offence, or renew your griefs by rubbing the scar, I would fain crave so much favour as to know the cause of your misfortunes.

Shakespeare's Corin speaks at once of grazing and shearing and an unkind master; and when he talks about the shepherd's life he shows that he knows the value of money and that fat sheep need good pasture. His greatest pride is to see his ewes graze and his lambs suck. This is the note of his philosophy, and if it has its limitations, it is far from despicable and is splendidly anchored to fact. His attitude to love is that of the fully sane man undisturbed by illusions. Being a man, he has been in love and can still guess what it is like; but it is so long ago he has forgotten all the details. How little he belongs to Arcadia may be discovered from Sidney, whose shepherd-boy went on piping "as though he should never be old". In *As You Like It* perpetual youth is the happiness of Silvius, and his fate. *That* much of the difference between Silvius and Corin is apparent from the short dialogue of twenty lines which first introduces them together to us.

In Corin Shakespeare provides us with a touchstone with which to test the pastoral. Corin's dialogue with the Touchstone of the court, dropped into the middle of the play, adds to the conventional antithesis between courtier and countryman a glimpse of the real thing. Our picture of the court as a place of tyranny, ambition and corruption is no doubt true enough. But its colours are modified somewhat when Touchstone gives us the court's plain routine. For him, as he lets us know on another occasion, the court is the place where he has trod a measure, flattered a lady, been smooth with his enemy and undone three tailors. Though Touchstone seeks to entangle Corin in the fantastications of his wit, his arguments to show that the court is better than the sheepfarm have a way of recoiling on himself. What emerges from the encounter of these two realists is that ewe and ram, like man and woman, are put together and that though the courtier perfumes his body it sweats like any other creature's. In city or country, *all* ways of life are at bottom the same, and we recognize a conclusion that Jaques, by a different route, has helped us to reach before.

The melancholy moralizings of Jaques and the Robin Hood raptures of the Duke, though in contrast, are equally the product of man's spirit. There has to be someone in Arden to remind us of the indispensable flesh. It was a shrewd irony of Shakespeare's to give this office to the jester. Whether he is wiser or more foolish than other men it is never possible to decide, but Touchstone is, as well as the most artificial wit, the most natural man of them all; and the most conscious of his corporal needs. After the journey to the forest Rosalind complains of a weariness of spirits, to which Touchstone retorts "I care not for my spirits, if my legs were not weary." And when he displays his wit at the expense of Orlando's bad verses, saying "I'll rhyme you so eight years together", he remembers to add "dinners and suppers and sleeping-hours excepted." A "material fool", as Jaques notes. This preoccupation with the physical makes Touchstone the obvious choice for the sensual lover who will burlesque the romantic dream. So Touchstone not only deprives the yokel William of his mistress, but steals his part in the play, making it in the process of infinitely greater significance. However, Shakespeare from the beginning cast Touchstone for this burlesque role, though he may not have seen at first what form the burlesque would take. When Silvius first exhibits his love to us, and reminds Rosalind of hers, Touchstone completes the trio on his discordant note:

> I remember, when I was in love I broke my sword upon a stone and bid him take that for coming a-night to Jane Smile; and I remember the kissing of . . . the cow's dugs that her pretty chopt hands had milked.

This sort of extravagance—in the burlesque-chivalrous vein—is not, I think developed; but an indecent jest about a peascod does point forward to the animal lust which propels him towards Audrey, and his amour with her forms the perfect contrast to the three idealized courtships of the play. If we need a formal juxtaposition of the two kinds of love to point the matter further, I note that it is just when Rosalind has met Orlando in the forest and Orlando has promised to woo her "by the faith of [his] love" and "with all [his] heart" that we see Touchstone courting the goat-girl, regretting that fair women should be honest and talking of sexual desire.

The fool is not only a material touchstone; he is also the time-keeper of the play. At least, in the forest, where "there's no clock", he carries a time-piece with him; and it provokes the reflection: "It is ten o'clock . . . 'Tis but an hour ago since it was nine, And after one hour more 'twill be eleven." The people of Arcadia will do well to take note of this, but if all you can do with your hours is to count them, this undeniable truth may seem a trifle futile. Touchstone, to do him justice, goes on: "And so, from hour to hour, we ripe and ripe, And then, from hour to hour, we rot and rot." He dares to speak in Arcadia, where one can never grow old, of Time's inevitable processes of maturity and decay. By this the ideal life of the banished Duke is mocked, and since Touchstone's words are repeated by Jaques with delighted and uproarious laughter, the mockery is double. Yet, in accordance with the play's principle of countering one view with another, there are two things that may be noted: first, that in a later scene Touchstone, who sums up life as riping and rotting, is compared by Rosalind to a medlar, which is rotten before it is ripe; and second, that it is at this very point, when the ideal life is doubly mocked, that the Duke administers to the mocker Jaques a direct and fierce rebuke, charging the mocker of the world's vices with having lived a vicious life himself.

The satirist, of course, is far from silenced: it is now that he ridicules the romantic hero, and presently he delivers his famous speech on the seven ages of man, brilliantly summing up the course of human life, but omitting to notice anything in it that is noble or even pleasant. However, as has often been observed, though the seven ages speech ends with a description of man's final decrepitude—"sans teeth, sans eyes, sans taste, sans everything"—it has not yet left the speaker's tongue when an aged man appears who is at once addressed as "venerable". There is always this readjustment of the point of view. Senility and venerableness—are they different things or different ways of looking at the same? Certainly the entry of the venerable Adam does not disprove what Jaques says; Shakespeare seeks no cheap antithesis. "Sans teeth"—Adam himself has admitted to being toothless, Orlando has called him "a rotten tree", and his helplessness is only too visible when he is *carried* on to the stage. Yet he *is* carried, tenderly, the master whom he has followed "to the last gasp, with truth and loyalty". Here is the glimpse of human virtue that the seven ages speech omitted. And then it is upon this moving spectacle of mutual affection and devotion that Amiens sings his song, "Blow, blow, thou winter wind, Thou art not so unkind As man's ingratitude." Placed here, this lovely lyric, blend of joy and pathos, has a special poignancy.

The arrangement of the play depends upon many such piquant but seemingly casual juxtapositions. *As You Like It* contemplates life within and without Arden, with numerous shifts of angle, alternating valuations, and variations of mood. As for action, incident—life in the Forest of Arden does not easily lend itself to those. I have suggested that Shakespeare does something to supply this want by a glance or two back at what is happening at court. And departures from the court are matched by arrivals in the forest. For events, of course, even in Arden do sometimes occur. Orlando arrives dramatically, even melodramatically. Presently Rosalind learns that he is about. A little later on they meet. Later still Oliver arrives and is rescued from a lioness. Shakespeare still keeps up a sense of things going on. But the manner of the play, when once it settles down in the forest, is to let two people drift together, talk a little, and part, to be followed by two more. Sometimes a pair will be watched by others, who will sometimes comment on what they see. Sometimes of course there is a larger group, once or twice even a crowded stage; but most often two at a time. When they part they may arrange to meet again, or they may not. Through the three middle acts of the play, though there are two instances of love at first sight (one of them only reported), it is rare that anything happens in any particular encounter between these people of the sort that changes the course of their lives, anything, that is to say, that goes to make what is usually called a plot. Yet the meetings may properly be called 'encounters', because of the impact the contrasting characters make on one another and the sparkle of wit they kindle in one another. What is important in each meeting is our impression of those who meet and of their different attitudes to one another or to one another's views of life, an impression which is deepened or modified each time they reappear with the same or different partners. As I describe it, this may all sound rather static, but such is the ease and rapidity with which pairs and groups break up, re-form, and succeed one another on the stage that there is a sense of fluid movement. All is done with the utmost lightness and gaiety, but as the lovers move through the forest, part and meet again, or mingle with the other characters in their constantly changing pairs and groups, every view of life that is presented seems, sooner or later, to find its opposite. Life is "but a flower in spring time, the only pretty ring time", but for the unromantic Touchstone there is "no great matter in the ditty" and he counts it but time lost—his eye no doubt still on his timepiece—"to hear such a foolish song". A quartet of lovers avowing their love is broken up when one of them says

> Pray you, no more of this; 'tis like the howling of Irish wolves against the moon.

And the one who says this is she who cannot tell "how many fathom deep" she is in love. Dominating the centre of the play, playing both the man's and woman's parts, counsellor in love and yet its victim, Rosalind gathers up into herself many of its roles and many of its meanings. Around her in the forest, where the banished Duke presides, is the perfect happiness of the simple life, an illusion, much mocked at, but still cherished. She herself, beloved of the hero, has all the sanity to recognize that "love is merely a madness" and that lovers should be whipped as madmen are, but admits that "the whippers are in love too". Heroine of numerous masquerades, she is none the less always constant and never more true than when insisting that she is counterfeiting. For she is an expert in those dark riddles which mean exactly what they say. Though things are rarely what they seem, they may sometimes be so in a deeper sense. What is wisdom and what is folly is of course never decided—you may have it "as you like it". Or, as Touchstone rejoined to Rosalind, after her gibe about the medlar, "You have said; but whether wisely or no, let the forest judge."

It may be possible to suggest that the forest gives it verdict. For if *As You Like It* proclaims no final truth, its ultimate effect is not negative. Longing to escape to our enchanted world, we are constantly brought up against reality; sanity, practical wisdom sees through our illusions. Yet in *As You Like It* ideals, though always on the point of dissolving, are for ever recreating themselves. They do not delude the eye of reason, yet faith in them is not extinguished in spite of all that reason can do. "I would not be cured, youth."

MARY LASCELLES

Shakespeare's Pastoral Comedy

Lodge's *Rosalynde*, the immediate precursor and substantial source of *As You Like It*, is a gay and graceful mixture of the old stories of Sherwood justice with the new, fashionable, pastoral romances. Lodge, an adventurous reader, was familiar with *Gamelyn*, Sidney's *Arcadia* (probably in manuscript) and, we may be sure, popular versions of the Robin Hood legend. And he had his share of the authentic Elizabethan magic, 'gilding pale streams with heavenly alchemy'. He has caught the happy timelessness of pastoral; any of his characters might say with Orlando: 'There's no clock in the forest.'[1] It has become the realm of 'love in idleness'. Replacing the 'wife good and fair' whom Gamelyn married in the last line but four—and a line is all she is allowed—princesses and shepherdesses (the princesses disguised as shepherdesses, the shepherdesses as courtly in their bearing as the princesses) await the approach of their suitors, sonnet in hand. And these are better love-poems than Orlando's. Was it Shakespeare's whim, or was it his wisdom, to give us the very poetry of love—and not allow so much as one of his lovers to write a respectable piece of verse? Perhaps his motive was akin to Chaucer's, when he took for himself the Tale of Sir Thopas.

These unreckoned riches of pastoral leisure belong rather to narrative than to drama, and I think there are signs that Shakespeare recognized this as a problem confronting him. Orlando, though he is driven from his brother's house within the narrow compass of the play, is indeed the lost child of traditional romance: he has been reared as though a foundling; nevertheless 'he's gentle, never schooled and yet

From *More Talking of Shakespeare*, edited by John Garrett. London: Longmans, Green & Co., Ltd.: New York: Theatre Arts Books. © 1959 by Longmans, Green & Co., Ltd., pp. 79–86. Reprinted by permission of Theatre Arts Books.

[1]III, ii, 321.

119

learned, full of noble device'.[2] Then, time-inconsistencies have been apparent to the critics, and by some set down to revision:[3] the rightful Duke's banishment seems to be news when Charles tells it to Oliver—yet, by Celia's account, it happened when she was too young to plead for her cousin; and the Duke himself speaks of his forest life as though it had endured the season's change. Presently, the usurping Duke gives Oliver a year in which to find his brother, though our impression of the play's duration is a few fleeting days. (The change from winter to summer, in a recent production, was—to my thinking—an innovation enjoyable while fresh, but not fit to establish a new theatrical tradition). Is it fanciful to suggest that Shakespeare, when he began to write, had hardly counted the cost of the alterations he must make and, if he later noticed discrepancies, did not care to efface them, preferring a *past-indefinite* tense? The passage of the seasons, especially as it is reflected in the talk of the older men (Duke Senior and Adam), signifies an acceptance of the terms of mortal life:

> my age is as a lusty winter,
> Frosty, but kindly.[4]

The condition of this acceptance of change is the contented mind. In Arden, love fosters its own peculiar impatience, but those who are free 'fleet the time carelessly, as they did in the golden world'.[5] Their contentment extends even to little things: Jaques' failure to disturb the equanimity of any but the lovers—and *they* give as good as they get. I suspect that a small illustration of this has been swept away in the process of tidying the text, and I would plead for its restoration. Who *should* sing the third stanza of 'Under the greenwood tree'? Jaques offers it to Amiens who, according to the First Folio, agrees to sing and launches into it with the words, 'Thus it goes.' But the subsequent Folios and modern editions and (so far as I can tell) stage tradition have transferred those three words, together with the stanza, to Jaques—only the New Cambridge editors offering a hesitant defence of the Folio text in a note. Now, the actor who plays Jaques is rarely a singer, and the stanza is usually declaimed to a little audience (Amiens and anyone else who can be mustered) with such acrimony that Amiens' subsequent question loses its point. But, let Jaques put a paper into Amiens' hand, and let *him* sing innocently this parody of his own two

[2]I, i, 175.
[3]Notably by the New Cambridge editors.
[4]II, iii, 52.
[5]I, i, 127.

stanzas, asking with unruffled good humour, at the close, 'What is Ducdame?'—and there is some reason for Jaques' exasperated retort: 'Tis a Greek invocation to call fools into a circle.'[6] The satirist is baffled by the world of comedy.

Unexpectedness ranks high among the distinctive qualities of *As You Like It*. The play tingles with questions. I deny altogether the claim that it is a satire on pastoral convention. True, it returns an echo to the pastoral idea; but the tone of this echo has not the heart-searching melancholy of Raleigh's:

> If all the world and love were young,
> And truth in every Sheepheards tongue,
> These pretty pleasures might me move,
> To live with thee, and be thy love—

nor the scorching irony of Donne's:

> Come live with mee, and bee my love,
> And wee will some new pleasures prove. . . .

It is the tone rather of a brisk challenge—one to which the sequel may yet be: 'Pass friend, and all's well,' and, if the pastoral idea is challenged, that is because it *is* an idea, a pattern for living laid up in the mind, and such ideas are in full flight, and the people of the play in full cry after them, all up and down the glades of Arden. Everything is set off by contrasts; and the alternations are so swift that we might as well try to tell the colour of a field of ripening barley combed by the wind as capture any of the successive moods by definition. If the idealism of the Duke is called in question by Jaques, why, so is the cynicism of Jaques by the Duke. Rosalind, herself 'many fathom deep in love' and pursued by Celia's keen raillery, undertakes to turn every convention of love-making inside-out; and against her romantic friendship with Celia is set her astringent treatment of Phoebe. None of the disputants has the last word; but, with the possible exception of Jaques, none of them wants it. The pursuer lets the quarry escape, sure that he will not go far, for fear of ending the pursuit. This is indeed Coleridge's 'intellectual wealth squandered in the wantonness of sport without an object'. How is it to be reconciled with the need inherent in romance, to resolve all discords in a full close?

In the first place, it is necessary that all the characters should go back where they belong. Do not quarrel with this; it is required by the pattern of loss and recovery. Dekker confuses this issue when—turning

[6]II, v, 48–58.

the story of patient Griselda into a play—he makes her father's home, to which she returns bringing her children, a place of pastoral felicity, where the loveliest of all his songs is sung. Only her brother, a spoiled scholar and a character of Dekker's own invention, is ignorant of what Griselda knows:

> ... adversity
> Dwells still with them that dwell with misery,
> But mild content hath eas'd me of that yoke;
> Patience hath borne the bruise, and I the stroke.[7]

Thus, when the story is pulled back into its course, we are haunted by remembrance of his pastoral world and would be glad to return to it. But the ring which is the proper symbol of pastoral romance is not rounded into completion until each of the characters has fulfilled the destiny to which he, or she, was born; and, to this end, the Duke must reassume his office—in a court where (as Professor Jenkins points out)[8] goodness has been restored and Jaques' occupation's gone, Rosalind must reign after him with Orlando, the dispossessed man come to his own again, and benignant powers must operate.

Now, I freely admit that Hymen is not a very impressive counterpart even of the *romantic* oracle. Nevertheless, I find it significant that Shakespeare should have employed, for the ending of *As You Like It*, these three agents: a symbolical figure, speaking such archaic verse as he gives to Jupiter and the ghosts in *Cymbeline*, Juno and Ceres in *The Tempest*; a mood of half-belief in Rosalind's tale of her uncle the magician ('most profound in his art and yet not damnable'); and a pattern of riddling stipulations, propounded by Rosalind in her character as *magician's boy*, to which the lovers must subscribe—and which, being fulfilled, resolve all discords.

The oracle in *Cymbeline* has proved a stumbling-block; and—not to pursue this question further than our purpose requires—it performs its function awkwardly: it bears no intelligible relation in time to those confessions by which the skein of the plot will presently be unravelled, nor any in place to that ideal country which Imogen has found and lost again, where outlaws offer refuge to the oppressed, and recognize an imposter, even in a true man's clothes. And yet I believe the use of this device to be in keeping with those pastoral intimations—with Imogen's wish, before ever she set out on the journey which led to the outlaw's cave, that she and Posthumus had been herdsmen's children;

---

[7]*Patient Grissill* (arrtibuted to Dekker, Chettle, and Haughton), V, ii.
[8]*Shakespeare Survey* 8, p. 45. (See above pp. 110–11.)

with the mountain-bred boy's victory over the court-bred ruffler and braggart. Suppose that Shakespeare was finding his way back to a source of imaginative fulfilment which had charmed him some years earlier, but was cumbered with too weighty and intricate a story, and had to rest content with something short of his full purpose.

Within a year or so, he recognized what he sought, hidden away in that old-fashioned and unprepossessing little tale, Greene's *Pandosto*. It had something he needed: an oracle which, as a source of infallible truth, could be credited with authority, even sanctity; which would inevitably punish the unbeliever and yet—so far had tragedy given ground to romance—let punishment teach repentance, and repentance cherish hope; and shepherds, the traditional guardians of that place of refuge in which hope might be realized.

To show why I believe that *The Winter's Tale* transcends the models on which it is framed by obtaining their ultimate purpose, I shall have to ask a question which must sound very simple and matter-of-fact: in those ancient tragic stories which turn upon oracular prediction, what would have happened if the people whom it threatens had taken no notice of it? If King Acrisius, warned that he would be killed by his grandson, had not imprisoned his daughter, nor, when her child was born, put them both to sea in an open boat, Perseus would not have caused the death of an unknown man, and found himself the slayer of his grandfather. For the point of these stories seems to be that it is a man's efforts to avert his fate which fasten it upon him. We are therefore (I take it) to understand that a man so visited can no more desist from struggling than could an animal caught in a trap. Does Shakespearian pastoral comedy shirk this knowledge, or see beyond it?

All I can now attempt is to point out some ways in which oracular truth—absolute truth regarding past, present, even future events—operates in *The Winter's Tale*. Notice, first, that Leontes no sooner acknowledges his suspicions than he sends to the oracle, supposing that he will obtain confirmation of them—a departure from *Pandosto*, in which the Queen asks that Apollo be consulted. Next, the crucial scene representing the messengers on their way back from 'the Isle of Delphos' is set as prelude to Hermione's trial: in some twenty lines it conveys an extraordinary impression of serenity and sanctity. Cleomenes and Dion are unshakeably convinced of the truth of the sealed statement they carry; convinced, also, that it will clear the Queen.[9] It is evidently established that, while we remain in Sicily—that is, until

[9] III, i,

the end of Act III, Scene ii—things are what they seem, to us and to everyone in the play, *except* Leontes.

Now, if I may revert to my simple question: what would have happened if Leontes had accepted the truth thus delivered? The prediction that 'the king shall live without an heir' would have been inexplicable; indeed, at the time when it was entrusted to the messengers, Leontes would still have a wife and two children with him. But, possessed by the insane conviction that he and oracular truth are ranged together against false seeming, he does not wait for the revelation: he condemns the child he supposes Polixenes' to death. It is Shakespeare's way to accept character as the ultimate source of event. Therefore, when truth is revealed and he finds himself standing alone, Leontes is already committed to the utterance of his final, fatal blasphemy: 'There is no truth at all i' the oracle.'[10] Immediately and inexorably, the wheels begin to turn: word comes of Mamilius's death, and he interprets it as divine retribution:

> Apollo's angry; and the heavens themselves
> Do strike at my injustice.

Paulina's 'this news is mortal to the Queen' threatens complete fulfilment of the prediction, and Leontes' public confession and vow of amendment are answered by her passionate cry that repentance prolonged beyond the span of mortal life would not atone. Nothing further is said of reparation, nor is the oracle's stipulation, 'if that which is lost be not found', remembered again until the very eve of finding. It is mere critical officiousness to demand an oracular injunction against second marriage; Leontes has accepted the full implications of his misdeed.

Presently, a speaker only less august than the oracle intervenes. Time, in appropriately archaic verse, explains his own function as composed of contrarieties:

> . . . it is my power
> To o'erthrow law, and in one self-born hour
> To plant and o'erwhelm custom.[11]

He is alike founder, destroyer, renewer. He cannot (in the agonized words of Lucrece) 'return and make amends'; but, given time and kindly shelter, the seed will yield next year's harvest, and we have but now seen the lost child received into the pastoral refuge.

[10]III, ii, 141.
[11]Prologue to Act IV.

> I turn my glass . . .
> . . . but let Time's news
> Be known when 'tis brought forth.

From now on, growth proceeds underground: things will not be
what they seem; honest characters (Paulina and Camillo) will be involved in a tissue of subterfuge; the truth, if it is told, will be uttered
uncomprehendingly—as when Polixenes tests Perdita with gardeners'
talk of crossing strains, and she maintains that like must mate with like.
One certainty alone holds: in the pastoral world, the promise of the
oracle will be fulfilled as surely as were its threats, and the lost will be
found.

What, then, does this pastoral world signify? Not 'wish-fulfilment'
—a new name for an old misuse of the imagination. *That* requires
obliteration of the boundary which separates the imagined from the
actual. But the world of true pastoral is always known for a country of
the mind, to be attained only by force of the imagination. This, doubtless, holds good for all great imaginative story-telling (whether cast in
narrative or in dramatic form). Pastoral fiction, however, has a distinction of its own to observe, and this may best be indicated in terms of
time and space. Tragedy shakes us with its tremendous *here* and *now*
(no matter how remote its subject). History (Shakespearian history, at
least) makes a sharp impact of *there* and *then*—the sun rising on St.
Crispin's day over the field of Agincourt. But pastoral romance is, and
must always remain, *elsewhere* and *some other time*. Thus, though it is
simply and immediately enjoyable, in a kind and degree beyond that
of other story-telling, it no more invites us to identify ourselves with
its happy people than the rainbow invites us to climb. In its realm,
Shakespearian comedy is free to flourish. Its happy endings are not
flattering fantasies, but tokens of a fulfilment to be imagined only,
not hoped for. In this fulfilment, the partial and piecemeal returns and
renewals which life grants us are capable of completion; not only does
the future stretch before us, with its assured rhythm of the seasons and
the generations—the past itself is no longer irretrievably lost. Not
Perdita alone comes back, but Hermione also.

ISABEL G. MacCAFFREY

Lycidas: Poet in a Landscape

In the pastoral metaphor as Milton explores it in *Lycidas*, something of the life history of the convention is visible, and not only in the many traditional details. Nostalgia has often been the sentiment that produces pastoral; almost since its earliest appearance, an innocent bygone virtue has implied a corrupt present sophistication, acquiring glamor by virtue of the contrast. The pastoral world becomes remote in space or time, or both, retreating to a legendary past or an imaginary country. So Arcadia is born. In *Lycidas*, this remoteness develops before our eyes, as the speaker's lost childhood is re-created in the past tense of memory. Pastoral perfection recedes into a past innocent and unreturning.

In *Lycidas*, too, we can observe the development of a so-called satirical element from the co-presence of harsh reality and benign past. Pastoral innocence provides an ethical measure for judgment and a technical point of departure for analyzing the ruined fallen world of experience. The beginning of such a process may perhaps be seen in Vergil's first eclogue, entitled in one modern translation "The Dispossessed."[1] One of the speakers is taking the rocky road to exile, stripped of his patrimony by a ravenous and unjust state. The other shepherd, Tityrus, has already endured voluntary exile in Rome,

From *The Lyric and Dramatic Milton*, edited by Joseph Summers, pp. 75–92. Published, 1965, by Columbia University Press. Reprinted by permission of the author and the publisher.

[1]E. V. Rieu, *Virgil: The Pastoral Poems* (Penguin Books: London, 1949). The translated passage from the *Eclogues* below is taken from p. 23 of Rieu's edition. The Latin text is that of the Loeb Classical Library: *Virgil* H. R. Fairclough ed., 2 vols., (Cambridge, Mass: 1946).

126

gained a protector, and returned to his farm.[2] Meliboeus' speech to him evokes a changeless peace:

> Time and again, as it has always done, the hedge there . . . will have its willow-blossom rifled by Hyblaean bees and coax you with a gentle humming through the gates of sleep. . . . You will hear the vine-dresser singing to the breezes, while all the time your dear full-throated pigeons will be heard, and the turtle-dove high in the elm will never bring her cooing to an end.

The ceaseless country sounds, the suspension in a friendly element, are rendered by Vergil in words denoting time's recurrence: *nota, semper, nec tamen interea*. Yet the peace is shown to be precarious by the presence of the exile and references to wars in Africa, Scythia, Britain, even at home. Resolution, Vergil implies, is won not simply by retreat but by a prior excursion into and mastery of the "great world" outside. This reading of *Ecologue I* is perhaps an overreading, but it illustrates how readily in pastoral a suggestive contrast develops between a precious but vulnerable rural landscape and a ferocious if sometimes heroic world of history.

Lycidas reenacts, then, both the immemorial journey of the maturing spirit and the development of one of humanity's most resourceful metaphors for that journey. It is a poem "about" poetry *and* "about" human life—about the two in conjunction, man's vision of himself and the mirror of art in which he sees the vision. It can be read as a reassessment of the pastoral mode itself. Innocence is exchanged for bleak experience, in turn to be replaced by a wiser innocence. So "mere" pastoral—both the poetry and the view of the world it implies— is shown as too vulnerable and limited to account for the brutalities of life; but shown, finally, to contain the possibility of deeper, or higher, strains more faithful to "reality."

These intertwined threads of Milton's theme are visible in the details of the landscape picked out by the speaker. All four elements play a part in *Lycidas*, and all an ambivalent part, reflecting their divided allegiance in a fallen world where they may either serve as

---

[2]An apparent allusion to this eclogue in *Epitaphium Damonis* suggests that Milton took an interest in the pattern of exile and return. He speaks of his Italian journey, including the visit to Rome which is no longer "qualem dum viseret olim, Tityrus ipse suas et oves et rura reliquet" (ll. 116–17); even if a reference to Chaucer is intended, behind it is surely Virgil's poem. In the *Epitaphium*, the journey coincides with the death at home of Diodati; it is thus linked with the "discovery" of the rude facts of life and death.

emblems of their Creator or become the playthings of satanic forces. Thus, Air is the "parching wind," the "gust of rugged wings," the figurative wind that bloats the sheep;[3] it is also the breezes in the willows, the "milde whispers" of valley winds. Earth puts forth the vegetation that can either flourish or wither. Fire is represented on, the one hand, by the counterfeit flare of fame's "sudden blaze," the "glistering foil" of worldly reputation; and, on the other, by the lofty light-bearing heavenly bodies: the evening star, and Phoebus who brings dawn and witnesses to the glory of the firmament. "Water imagery" in *Lycidas* has been sufficiently explicated; its doubleness should perhaps be more emphasized.[4] It is at once the monster-harboring, formless ocean that was to symbolize Chaos in *Paradise Lost*, and the fountains, dews, and friendly rivers that mourn for Lycidas in the unsullied pastoral world. In the Alpheus/Arethusa references, the two strands meet but do not merge, and the resurgence of Alpheus from the dark descent beneath ocean's floor bears witness to the ultimate deliverance of creation from the dark forces that hold it enthralled. To look at these elemental patterns in the light of the poem's development is to see mirrored in them the movement of the speaker's mind. He reaches a point where the demonic aspect of creation dominates his consciousness. Experience has supplanted innocence, and the pastoral metaphor of a nature exactly congruent with man's life, responsive to his hopes and fears, has been revealed as inadequate.

In a passage from *Pericles* that was perhaps in Milton's mind when he wrote *Lycidas*, the king speaks to the "scarcely coffin'd" body of his wife and in his grief it seems to him that "th' unfriendly elements/ Forgot thee utterly."[5] We ought not perhaps to go so far as to speak of unfriendly elements in *Lycidas*. "Nature" is always "sympathetic" in the etymological sense, and Miss Tuve has wisely reminded us that

[3]Ruskin's elaboration of ll. 125–27, developing the notion of *spiritus* or "wind" as breath, ought to be recalled: "There are two kinds of breath with which the flock may be filled; God's breath, and man's. The breath of God is health, and life, and peace to them, as the air of heaven is to the flocks on the hills; but man's breath—the word *he* calls spiritual—is disease and contagion to them, as the fog of the fen." Lecture I, *Sesame and Lilies* (New York: 1866), p. 32.

[4]The contrast between sea water and fresh water was noticed by Emerson R. Marks, *Explicator*, IX (1951), Item 44.

[5]III, i, 57–58, ed., J. C. Maxwell (Cambridge: 1956). T. H. Banks observed that a manuscript phrase in *Lycidas*, l. 157—"humming tide" (altered to "whelming")—echoes *Pericles*, III, i, 63: "And humming water must o'erwhelm thy corpse." Pericles' speech powerfully evokes the journey of Thaisa's dead body through the whales' "monstrous" realm. "A Source for *Lycidas*, 154–158," *Modern Language Notes*, LXII (1947), pp. 39–40.

we must beware of importing notions about man's alienation from nature into Renaissance poetry.[6] But just as the Muse can seem thankless, the elements can seem unfriendly to the speaker. They are related to us, we are made of them, yet they are powerless to help, just as "the Muse herself that *Orpheus* bore" was helpless to save him from death at the hands of arbitrary unintelligible forces. But these forces are outside the original economy of nature and cannot be ruled by it, as the speaker ultimately realizes. Of the paragraphs following the passage on "heavy change," one exonerates Nymphs and Muse of responsibility for Lycidas' fate; another speaks in defense of the destructive element itself:

> The Ayr was calm, and on the level brine,
> Sleek *Panope* with all her sisters play'd.

This "level brine" is an innocent extension of pastoral fields, the playground of nymphs. The accusation is diverted to the "fatall and perfidious Bark," belonging to the world of the blind Fury and her shears—a world of fallen, civilized, and unnatural contrivance and of mysterious subnatural hostilities alluded to in the eclipse, which in *Paradise Lost* gives evidence of nature's fall. These progressive exonerations prepare for the final movement of *Lycidas*, into a "nature" hallowed and redeemed, a pastoral mode deepened and reconfirmed.

If nature is excused in *Lycidas*, however, man is not. The passages on Fame and the Church move away from the pastoral foreground into the vicissitudes of history and the consequences of our lost innocence. The embodiment of fallen society is the ominous blind Fury, a Fate rechristened but still as blind as her meaningless power.[7] In this section, as the poet's allusion to a "higher mood" suggests, the style alters; and it can alter decorously because the matter alters. Milton begins in the pastoral present, referring to poetry as the "Shepherds trade." But the action moves immediately into a no-time of eternal verities and questions, and an infinite space where the great antagonists of the major poetry confront each other in the persons of the Fury and Phoebus. It is a metaphorical space inhabited by the august personages of sacred allegory, a world evoked at the opening of the *Nativity* Hymn and of *Comus*, where meek-eyed Peace and the Attendant Spirit make visible things ordinarily invisible to mortal

---

[6]See Rosemond Tuve, *Images and Themes in Five Poems by Milton* (Cambridge, Mass: 1957), p. 95. The present essay is heavily indebted to Miss Tuve's discussion of *Lycidas* in this volume—one of the most expert readings the poem has received.

[7]See Marjorie Nicolson, *John Milton: A Reader's Guide to His Poetry* (New York: 1963), p. 95. on the significance of the eyes of the Furies.

sight. This is, in short, the plane of vision and prophecy, affording a glimpse of final verities ultimately to be affirmed in the poem and in history.

The debate of the speaker with Phoebus defines an aesthetic and moral issue. The lines on Fame, as Miss Tuve has said, use the language of chivalric romance—"guerdon," "foil," "spur," "noble mind."[8] The ambition to win fame by composing the poetry that celebrates earthly glory is shown by Phoebus to be a false direction; this is the same Phoebus, after all, who plucked Vergil's ear and reproved him for writing of "kings and battles" in *Eclogue VI*.[9] This ambition can also be seen as a betrayal of the values embodied in pastoral, which in Christian tradition encompasses both the lowest and the highest subjects. The shepherd singer of the Psalms is one exemplar, another "That Shepherd, who first taught the chosen Seed" (*PL* I.8) in the sacred poetry of Genesis. In *Paradise Regained*, Milton was to contrast Sion's songs with the "swelling Epithetes" of pagan poetry (IV.343). The contrast is confirmed in his rejection of traditional epic in favor of a heroic mode that would treat of virtues at once grander and humbler. The middle realm, the realm of history and its monotonous disasters, is the fallen world in the power of the Fury, recorded in an epic poetry corrupt though brilliant. Perhaps we should not press this point, which depends partly on our knowledge of the author's future, invisible to him in 1637. But the infirmity of ambition rebuked in *Lycidas*, whether poetic or heroic, is conceived in terms inconsistent with the pastoral metaphor.

A second vision of history is developed in the Church passage. As in the one just examined, this section is separated in time and space from the pastoral foreground. We move back or away from the "literal" landscape of rivers—Sicilian or English—and the classical allusions that enforce the pastoral mode, into a development of the convention's *metaphorical* dimensions, principally through the theological associations of "pastor." The figure of St. Peter emerges out of the pastoral world (like the "pastor" metaphor itself); it is continuous with the pageant of witnesses to nature's innocence: the Herald of the Sea, Hippotades, Camus, and then the Galilean Pilot. But the pageant, as it concludes, merges with an envisaged past and the spaces of imagination, and the style of Peter's speech, like that of the Fame

[8]*Images and Themes*, p. 74.

[9]It is interesting that, in the sixth eclogue, Vergil goes on to write, in Silenus' song, of subjects loftier and more permanently significant than battles: Creation, the Deluge, and the shifting shapes of mythological history. This poem, like *Eclogue IV*, provided Milton with a classical precedent for his development of "high pastoral."

meditation, is allusive and oblique, as the two-handed engine and its multitudinous glosses suggest. References to flocks and herdsmen link the speech metaphorically, indeed, with the paragraph early in the poem on the diseased landscape. This later passage sternly explains how that death-pervaded world of experience came into being. The source of contagion in flower and flock is not "innocent nature" but sin-ridden human beings, here monstrously reduced to "blind mouthes." The safe world of the "faithful Herdman" is invaded by their rapacity. Their grating songs contrast with Lycidas' soft lays, their hungry diseased sheep with the flock battened on the "fresh dews" of the water of life. The potent lines on inward contagion recall the "killing" canker that lays waste the shepherd's heart, or "ear." But while at that early stage no consolation beyond Nature's lament could be proposed, the dread voice of the Pilot here speaks in condemnation and prophecy, of the sword's readiness and a heavenly meed.

In the final paragraphs of the song, resolution and consolation are achieved and the validity of the pastoral mode is confirmed. But these certainties, like the other hard-won insights of the swain, emerge only at the end of the process which Milton called elsewhere "the perpetual stumble of conjecture and disturbance in this our dark voyage."[10] *Lycidas* imitates the painful, unsteady effort of imagination which alone, in our mortal state, can lead to vision. The sense of moving forward among the half-lights of the dark voyage is nowhere felt more powerfully than in the poem's last stages. We turn from a minute and loving attention to the details of pastoral landscape in close-up, to the gigantic horizons of distant seascapes, from the bottom of the monstrous world to the heavenly hosts singing in their glory. The sequence embodies those grand shifts of perspective which Milton was to exploit in *Paradise Lost.*[11] It also renders metaphorically the fundamental pattern of Christian literature, a movement through the tragic phase to an ultimately comic vision.

Accompanying this process is a sequence of imagery that supports the movement of insight won, lost again, and rewon. The kinetic and auditory images of Peter's speech are succeeded by the "flower passage," a landscape rich in visual detail. Blind Fury and blind mouths are replaced by a healthier world whose moral value is symbolized by its appeal to the eye, though these quaint enameled flower-eyes do

---

[10]F. A. Patterson, ed., *The Reason of Church Government,* in *The Student's Milton* (New York: 1933), p. 506.

[11]This use of rapidly shifting points of view is discussed and related to Mannerist styles by Roy Daniells, *Milton, Mannerism and Baroque* (Toronto: 1963), p. 41.

not see as far as the "pure eyes" of all-judging Jove, nor is the vision they symbolize finally valid. In these low valleys, the gentle "nature" of the opening sections emerges again: shades, gushing brooks, fresh fields. The "swart Star" reminds us, however, of the flowers' frailty and their melancholy fates—the primrose forsaken, the cowslips wan, even Amaranth shedding his beauty in tribute to Lycidas. Since the mortal sin, this is no plant that grows on mortal soil; it resembles rather the plant of true fame that "lives and spreads aloft." In *Paradise Lost*, Amaranth after the Fall is removed from Eden to Heaven, where it "grows/ And flours aloft shading the Fount of Life" (III.357). Its failure to thrive on earth marks the final failure of unconsecrated pastoral in *Lycidas*, confirmed by the speaker's acknowledgment that the whole vividly evoked scene has been "false surmise," though its falseness to fact need not negate the measure of imaginative consolation it provides.[12] Pastoral as the dream of an actual earthly paradise is about to be finally abandoned, but pastoral as a holy fiction foreshadowing a heavenly meed is about to be confirmed.

The song's conclusion is composed in two movements. The first expresses the poem's deepest terror in a series of sensory impressions that appeal to the dumb, blind responses of the helpless body—not vision, but inhuman sounds and eyeless kinetic forces: "wash," "hurld," "stormy," "whelming." The speaker does not withdraw his earlier assent to Neptune's plea of innocence; he does not accuse, but merely records the facts of Lycidas' condition as they assault the anguished imagination. Then, almost without warning, the perspective shifts again, from the blind depths to "the great vision of guarded Mount," the angel who fixes the sea's boundary and wields a two-handed sword.

In *Paradise Lost*, Michael reveals to Adam the triumph of Chaos in history, symbolized by the Deluge when the sea is allowed to regain its power over the forces of order. Following the vision he unfolds its meaning:

> So willingly doth God remit his Ire,
> Though late repenting him of Man deprav'd,
> Griev'd at his heart, when looking down he saw
> The whole Earth filld with violence, and all flesh
> Corrupting each thir way.

(XI. 885–89)

[12]In the Trinity MS, Milton first wrote "sad thoughts" in line 153. The alteration to "fraile" (one of the crucial words in *Paradise Lost*) introduces the notion of human weakness, in this case perhaps the habit of clinging to consoling fictions which we know to be untrue.

Violence and the corruption of all flesh: these have been revealed, with relentless insistence, to the swain in *Lycidas*. But the rainbow speaks, in the epic, of reestablished order:

> Day and Night,
> Seed time and Harvest, Heat and hoary Frost
> Shall hold thir course, till fire purge all things new,
> Both Heav'n and Earth, wherein the just shall dwell.
>
> (xi. 898–901)

In Books xi and xii, Milton develops on a grand scale the movement from disaster to redemption adumbrated in *Lycidas*. The vision that completes the cycle of history in the epic completes the cycle of meditation in the elegy.

The hinge of the transition from the infernal underworld to the heaven of heavens is the Sun image, the second of the two major similes in *Lycidas*. The ground of the analogy is the circular solar movement, concentric with that of the dead shepherd, from ocean bed to morning sky. This parallel is profoundly reassuring in its context—chiefly, I think, because it denies the most poignant disparity between man and the nonhuman world: for while season, stars, and vegetation move in cyclical patterns, a man's life pursues an unreturning course downward to darkness. This distressing fact is lamented, of course, everywhere in elegiac poetry: in Catullus' reminder that "one ever-during night" awaits us, in Spenser's *November* eclogue, in Castiglione's *Alcon*, where the sun comparison contrasts with that in *Lycidas*:

> Behold, the declining sun now sinking in the heavens is setting, and as it dies, kindles the stars in the sky; still, when it has bathed its chariot in the western waves, it will again revisit the lands with orient light. But when once we have bathed in the black waters of cruel death and the door of that relentless realm has been shut, no way leads ever to the upper light.[13]

But Milton's conclusion reaffirms the congruence between nature's cycle and man's: Lycidas, *like* the daystar, is "sunk low but mounted high." The daystar itself functions in the poem not as a symbol but as an analogue; Milton wishes us to hold apart in imagination the various realms of being—natural, human, supernatural—precisely so that we can admire the marvelous correspondences between them. Therefore he makes the comparison overt, a simile, not an identifying metaphor. The diurnal cycle reminds us that something similar occurs

[13]Harrison, ed., *Pastoral Elegy*, pp. 114–15.

for the youth sunk beneath ocean's floor, as ealier it occurred in the death and resurrection of God himself, who assumed the burdens and necessities of "nature" when he entered our darksome house of mortal clay. The simile, like the rose figure of an earlier section, at once affirms a distinction between ourselves and "nature," and reaffirms its ultimate relationship to us. We are able, owing to the song's last paragraph, to look back to earlier sections, especially the flower passage, and see them in a new light: the pathos and consolation did after all have a "real" basis, the flowers in their annual cycle are after all in harmony with the life of men. In this new perspective of analogy, "nature" is seen to possess a metaphorical relevance to human concerns; its availability for Christian pastoral poetry is implied. But it *becomes* sentient and expressive only in the light of the poet's transforming vision.

The force that accomplishes these metamorphoses is the same that translates Lycidas: "the dear might of him that walk'd the waves." The redemptive power is figured in an image Milton had used earlier; in the *Nativity*, nature's most unruly force is hallowed by the Redeemer's coming, and "Birds of Calm sit brooding on the charmed wave" (Stanza V). The ruling of the waves was heralded in that mythic event when the creative Word ruled Chaos:

> Silence, ye troubl'd waves, and thou Deep, peace.
> (*PL* vii.216)

Christ's walking the waves possesses every kind of aptness in a poem about a drowned youth whose brief life embodied the forces of order implicit in his vocations of poet and priest. In eschatological terms, it defines the relationship between the Redeemer and redeemed Creation that permits the Christian poet to prefigure in his earthly landscapes those "other groves and other streams" of true paradise.

In the poem's temporal scheme, however, the redemption of nature is not final, and the speaker, who has descended and reascended in imagination, must be returned to his native element of life in time, like the Red Cross Knight after his vision of the New Jerusalem, or Calidore when the Graces vanished. The metamorphosis of Lycidas effects this return. He becomes, as Mr. Frye has said, a figure "corresponding to the Attendant Spirit in *Comus*, whose habitation is said to be a world above our own, identified . . . with Spenser's Gardens of Adonis.[14] As the Genius of the shore, he will mediate

[14]*Fables of Identity*, p. 122.

between the still fallen world of the perilous flood and the realm of redeemed nature glimpsed by the speaker in vision. He is the third, and most consoling, of the "heavenly messengers" who descend to the protagonist of *Lycidas*.[15] He will serve as a reminder that the wilderness of the world can be ordered and transcended.

The speaker in *Lycidas* has traveled from a preoccupation with the "melodious tear" of his song as the only possible "meed," to the vision of redemption where there are no tears, where the earthly shepherds weep no more and the song will cease, stilled by the unexpressive heavenly harmonies. The song ceases, but it has not been sung in vain. Its meaning is confirmed in the receding perspective of the coda which offers us, now more distantly but also more distinctly, a figure in a landscape, long familiar but now transfigured, *because* the song has been sung and the vision realized. The pastoral scene is re-created; and now it is informed by the presence of the poets who first made these details into poetry, and by the redeemed imagination that has come gradually to understand their meaning. The ancestor of the coda is Vergil's tenth eclogue, concluding traditionally with a return home and the arrival of the evening star. Line 190 of *Lycidas* echoes the conclusions of two other eclogues, where the sun stretches out the hills:

> et sol crescentis decedens duplicat umbras.[16]

These deliberate allusions to literary tradition underline the function of the stanza as a "return": a return to the pastoral landscape and the poetry based on it, now made potent as a vehicle of human meaning because its patterns are seen to be reproduced in the divine plan of the universe. Like the young shepherds of the poem's third section, this uncouth but more experienced swain has piped through the wheel of a day, from still morn to westering sun. The last line is not to be read only as a personal reference to sea voyaging or a promise of the turn to epic poetry. "Fresh" and "new" surely reaffirm those self-renewing powers of "nature" that legitimately figure our own survival and revival. As for "tomorrow," it marks the return of a world where the future once again exists full of promise, not a long

---

[15]Thomas M. Greene, *The Descent from Heaven* (New Haven: 1963), treats the "heavenly messenger" as a recurrent motif in epic. In *Lycidas*, the three "messengers"— Phoebus, Peter, and the dead shepherd as Genius—enter the poem just at those points where the "old" pastoral idiom is left behind and a new perspective into the heroic finalities of Providence is opened.

[16]*Eclogue II*, l. 67. The other echo, regularly noted by editors, is of *Eclogue I*, l. 83: "maioresque cadunt altis de montibus umbrae."

day's dying, but "such a day tomorrow as today," a process endlessly renewed by the covenant of God himself. In this world will flourish, not eternal boyhood, but a wise innocence that has absorbed and transcended experience. So Spenser's Colin Clout, after the manner of Tasso's shepherd, came home again from court. This new wisdom understands the pastoral world for what it is—a foreshadowing, not an echo. In this peaceful order, "Seed time and Harvest, Heat and hoary Frost/ Shall hold thir course," until the kingdom which the metaphor anticipated is established to succeed the cycles of history.

A decade or so before *Lycidas*, Milton in a Latin poem had celebrated the regular cycles of the universe and affirmed the eternal youth of great Nature, the perpetual flame of bright Phoebus in his strength: "floridus aeternum Phoebus juvenile coruscat." The poem concludes with an anticipation of Michael's revelation:

> Sic denique in aevum
> Ibit cunctarum series justissima rerum.[17]

"The righteous course of all things": it is precisely this sense of control and ultimate rightness that Milton seeks to establish in the final cadences of *Lycidas*. The voice that asserts it is impersonal. Many reasons for Milton's shift to the third person in the coda can be reconstructed by the ingenious critic. Among them is the fact that his subject at this point has transcended the personal. Two others are pertinent to this discussion.

The first concerns the redefinition of pastoral convention. The two similes, as I have suggested, are strategically placed in the fourth and last paragraphs of the song; they record a development in the speaker's treatment of his metaphor, from the naïve assumption that it represents actuality, to the recognition of it as one of man's great symbols for ultimate reality, securely rooted in the imagination's life. This insight is confirmed by the ostensive gesture of the poet in the coda. He can now name the poem's "kind" explicitly: it is a "*Dorick* lay" sung by a swain. In thus specifying its genre, Milton insists that pastoral be taken seriously. Like the swain, we must readjust our notions of what "pastoral" can mean. It is to be recognized as a serious *fiction*, a mode of the imagination, not a self-deluding fancy. The lowest of forms has been demonstrated to be capable of articulating the loftiest insights, embodying that vision of final things from which Milton was to make *Paradise Lost*. This "high pastoral"

[17] *Naturam non pati senium*, ll. 41, 65–66.

is akin to the metamorphosed epic form which Milton later devised for an action more heroic than any known to Homer. In the prologue to Book IX, he was to announce his intention, defining the "Heroic name" of his poem as once he had directed attention to a new meaning of the Doric lay. The habit of transcending and transforming genres is most dazzlingly manifested, in the 1645 volume, in *Lycidas*.

Finally, the coda demonstrates the relevance, not only of the poem's form, but of its theme, to ourselves. As the impersonal voice addresses us, we become co-listeners, and as the foreground recedes into the middle distance we find ourselves paradoxically in a more intimate relation to it. This sensation is effected—I do not say intended—when the poem's frame unexpectedly widens to include the "real" speaker and ourselves, on the same footing because we have heard the same song. The poem's world becomes our world, the song's pattern a paradigm of our experience. In the final lines there is a fusion of worlds created by a confusion of temporal planes, phrased in syntax that unites past and present: "now had stretch'd" "now was dropt." Past and present are one, the song continuing though the singer has ceased. The last line refers ambiguously to the singer's thought, the poet's comment on his future, the author's prospects, and our own hopes.

> To morrow to fresh Woods, and Pastures new.

It is not unmistakably located "in" the mind or spoken by the voice of either the real or the fictive speaker, and can therefore sum up a pattern now possible for all those who, by listening, have participated in the song.

HAROLD E. TOLIVER

Marvell's Pastoral Vision

He hangs in shades the Orange bright,
Like golden Lamps in a green Night.
    ("Bermudas")

Because pastoral often involves opposition between an idealized concept of nature and actual existence, and conflict between the search for simplicity and a complex, pressing society, it is not surprising that Marvell found it a hospitable medium. Overwhelmed by the existent, the pastoral poet frequently retreats from the "red and white" into the "green" world. In poems of pastoral success (as I shall call them—without implying a value judgment), he often consolidates gains, becomes reoriented toward the world, and finally reenters society. The general pattern varies from poet to poet and from poem to poem, but is remarkably persistent. Of all Marvell's poems, "The Garden" perhaps most obviously falls into it. Though the poet does not emerge from the *hortus conclusus* where fair Quiet and Innocence dwell, he nevertheless endorses the processes of time that have threatened the contemplative life: "How could such sweet and wholsome Hours / Be reckon'd but with herbs and flow'rs!" "Upon Appleton House," too, works within the same general framework, with the threat greater and the withdrawal more enigmatic. Whatever he learns from the grove, the poet leaves its contemplative sanctuary having gained a new capacity to deal with the active world. The order and harmony of the forest is suffused through art and the moral life: the scorching sun in the warlike meadow is metamorphosed into the *"tuned* Fires" of the birds and only the "equal Flames" of the stock-doves "burn." Hence, after leaving the protective shades, Marvell

From *Marvell's Ironic Vision*, by Harold E. Toliver, pp. 88–103, 138, 151. Copyright © 1960 by Yale University Press. Reprinted by permission of Yale University Press.

finds the world to be no longer "a rude heap together hurl'd," a "putrid Earth," but a cosmos "vitrifi'd" by a "flame" tried in heaven. The forest sanctuary is in a sense an instrument of immanence brought into action by the symbols the poet finds there, symbols which enable art to reorder, "tune," and "straighten" nature.

This pattern of retreat, discovery of creative capacity, and resurgent control over nature, then, we discover in much pastoral poetry as in seventeenth-century Puritan-Platonism. Distraction, motion, and diversity are frozen, and in a quiet moment of meditation or song, the shepherd relocates himself. In so doing, he may re-examine the function of poetry itself, that is to say, relate self-creation to artistic creation. The soul-artist in "The Garden," singing and waving in its plumes the various light, fuses the creative power of the mind with the body's vegetative functions. It reflects physical nature but transforms, *idea*lizes it. When the antagonism between the self and what exists, or between art and nature, is found to be resolvable like this, the effect is usually one of release—the prophetic poet goes off to "fresh woods and pastures new" or simply enjoys in a kind of primitive, spontaneous way the "fruits and flow'rs."

Thus successful pastoral ordinarily discovers an elementary link "of man with all beings as beings, vague as to its special content, but far-embracing and generalising"[1]—elementary because the diurnal course of rocks, stones, and trees is part of pastoral, but also because what is necessary to well-being tends to be estimated differently in rustic surroundings. Freedom from constricting forms, social torments, and perhaps psychic distortions results in simplified manners and decorum. To be sure, a great deal may be excluded which might tend to destroy the links with "all beings as beings." (Keats' "Ode to Psyche" is an extreme case. Only "Some untrodden region" of the mind will serve for the "rosy sanctuary" of the imagination—in the heart of "the wild-ridged mountains steep by steep" the working brain secludes itself, and only at night and only through a small casement lets "the warm love in.") But we can usually expect at least a symbolic recognition of the real world of passion, death, and poverty.

In contrast to this discovery of elemental being, anti-pastoral poems, or poems of pastoral failure, to give them a convenient name, describe an inability to stay inside the protected world where "letting things be" is possible. Keats' nightingale is eventually "buried deep / In the next

---

[1]Werner Brock, to Martin Heidegger's *Existence and Being*, Introduction (London: 1949), p. 174.

valley-glades," leaving the poet in a state of bewilderment, alone in the unsatisfactory company of his "sole self." Juliana causes the Mower himself to lose himself, never to find his "home." A corrupted idea of art undermines nature and turns the Mower himself into a destroyer, a "Mower *against* Gardens." The "wanton Troopers" violate the sanctified shelter of the nymph. The mowers of "Upon Appleton House" needlessly slaughter the quail. In addition, the artist's difficulty in transforming landscape to symbol may be involved. If the link with nature is broken, hopes of achieving order and meaning fail, or, in the special jargon of the pastoral, the "greenness of the Grass" is destroyed, as Juliana destroys the Mower, the keeper of the meadow: "She / What I do to the grass, does to my Thoughts and me." Instead of achieving rapport with nature, the Mower acknowledges the descent of chaos— "And Flow'rs, and Grass, and I and all/Will in one common Ruine fall"—just as Spenser's Colin falls in ruin as lover, religious reformer, and artist in the December eclogue. And so in "A Dialogue between Thrysis and Dorinda," Elysium lies only in "yonder Skie" where all shepherds are equal; in this world, shepherds are "sick and fain would dye." The artist's instruments are of no avail here; and in heaven, where "thine Ears / May feast with Musick of the Spheres" without the help of artists, they have no use.

Both patterns—the successful reintegration and the severance of the ideal and the real—are prominent, of course, not only in Marvell but in classical and modern writers as well. Rilke's "Eingang," for example, is a modern variation of the reintegration pattern:

> Whoever you are, go out into the evening,
> leaving your room, of which you know each bit;
> your house is the last before the infinite,
> whoever you are.
> Then with your eyes that wearily
> scarce lift themselves from the worn-out door-stone
> slowly you raise a shadowy black tree
> and fix it on the sky: slender, alone.
> And you have made the world (and it shall grow
> and ripen as a word, unspoken, still).
> When you have grasped its meaning with your will,
> then tenderly your eyes will let it go . . .[2]

If Pan is the dread opener of mysterious doors for Keats, the "shadowy black tree" performs the same function for Rilke: the release of a journey

[2]*Selected Poems*, trans., C. F. MacIntyre (Berkeley, University of California Press: 1958), p. 21.

from a town where everything is known to a country on the edge of the
infinite is telescoped in the act of crossing the threshold of the room and
observing the tree, a *locus amoenus* of sorts.[3] One "makes" the world in
that act, which is also an act of the imagination analogous to a word
rising in the consciousness—"und sie ist gross / und wie ein Wort,
das noch in Schweigen reist." When the imagination has done its work,
the will may incorporate its vision; then tenderly the landscape may
be released: the opposition between a stale and limited environment
and an imaginative and infinite one is resolved. "Whoever" the reader
may be, he can perform the ceremony and then return to the well-
known room.

Traditionally, art and the tree are intimately connected in this
way. The protection of the "green shade" where the familiar world can
be both shut out and let in under control is essential to "green thought."
Shepherds meet in the shade to resolve their troubles or at least express
them in dialogue and in singing contests. They forsake the world of
labor and common sense in order to seek an uncommon harmony.
Despite these mythic and romantic aspects of the form, however, the
susccessful pastoral figures in Marvell do not ordinarily sustain themselves in thought alone, even green thought. Marvell discovers sensuous,
concrete links with elemental life—grass, melons, curious peaches,
and so on—and through them seeks a strategy for dealing with
history. Neither the success nor the failure pattern is fully explicable in
terms of otherworldly motives. Marvell generally balances the ideal and
the real carefully instead of absorbing one into the other, though their
reconciliation is not quite as equals: if Adonis is dead and bleeding,
"the blood and tears become flowers upon the ground," as Bion's
"Lament for Adonis" puts it; "of the blood comes the rose, and of the
tears the windflower." However, the green world is violently disturbed
at times. The contemplative life is pursued within a context of struggle,
as in the civil wars and military achievements of Fairfax in "Appleton
House," the love chase of "The Garden," the shattered frame of "The
Coronet," the slaying of the fawn in "A Nymph," and the benevolent
but potentially dangerous tyranny of little T. C. The context of disturbance is traditional in pastoral also, but suffering in traditional love
lyrics and even in the elegy are typically more stylized than the violence
of Marvell's retreats. Nature in Marvell is not "Unerring Nature, still
divinely bright, / One clear, unchanged, and universal light" which art

[3] See Ernst Robert Curtius, *European Literature and the Latin Middle Ages*, trans.,
Willard R. Trask (New York: 1953), pp. 195 ff.

need only imitate. Rather, nature stimulates ambiguously the impulse to maim, and the impulse to be absorbed into it and to absorb it in return.

Though Marvell's primitivism has little in common with romantic primitivism of the eighteenth and early nineteenth centuries, in thus emphasizing the *threats* to pastoral ceremony he looks forward to Blake, Keats, and one strain of post-Darwinian pastoral. For the "Song of the Happy Shepherd" in later times, of course, is not to be, ordinarily, a happy song at all:

> The woods of Arcady are dead,
> And over is their antique joy;
> Of old the world on dreaming fed;
> Grey truth is now her painted toy.[4]

As in T. S. Eliot's "Burnt Norton," the pastoral ideal serves primarily as a reminder of what might have been:

> Footfalls echo in the memory
> Down the passage which we did not take
> Towards the door we never opened
> Into the rose-garden.

When Yeats heard a voice from the past, it was a

> voice of lamentation out of the Golden Age. It told me that we are imperfect, incomplete, and no more like a beautiful woven web, but like a bundle of cords knotted together and flung into a corner. It said that the world was once all perfect and kindly, and that still the kindly and perfect world existed, but buried like a mass of roses under many spadefuls of earth. The faeries and the more innocent of the spirits dwelt within it, and lamented over our fallen world in the lamentation of the wind-tossed reeds, in the song of the birds, in the moan of the waves, and in the sweet cry of the fiddle. It said that . . . the best of our moments are marred by a little vulgarity, or by a needle-prick out of sad recollection, and that the fiddle must ever lament it all. It said that if only they who live in the Golden Age could die we might be happy, for the sad voices would be still; but they must sing and we must weep until the eternal gates swing open.[5]

Modern pastoral, in Edwin Muir's phrase, thus has but "one foot in Eden." The old theme by and large has been inverted: "even in the land of death, I, Arcadia, dwell."[6] Or the poet may discover that

---

[4]W. B. Yeats, *Collected Poems* (New York: The Macmillan Company, 1954), p. 7.

[5]*The Celtic Twilight*, in *Mythologies* (London: Macmillan, 1959), pp. 104–05.

[6]See Erwin Panofsky's essay on this theme in the Renaissance and later, "*Et in Arcadia ego:* On the Conception of Transience in Poussin and Watteau," in *Philosophy and History, Essays Presented to Ernst Cassirer*, eds. R. Klibansky and H. J. Paton (Oxford:

Eden is lost altogether. The Darwinian-minded speaker of Rupert Brooke's "Town and Country," for example, discovers the city to be a protection against a ruthless and indifferent cosmos, a far more formidable enemy than traditional frigid nymphs: "We've found love in little hidden places," he says, "Under great shades, between the mist and mire," but in nature

> Our unwalled loves thin out on vacuous air,
>
> And suddenly there's no meaning in our kiss,
> And your lit upward face grows, where we lie,
> Lonelier and dreadfuller than sunlight is,
> And dumb and mad and eyeless like the sky.

He has an obvious kinship with the man with the double axe in Frost's "New Hampshire" who

> . . . went alone against a grove of trees;
> But his heart failing him, he dropped the axe
> And ran for shelter quoting Mattew Arnold:
> 'Nature is cruel, man is sick of blood; . . .'
> He had a special terror of the flux
> That showed itself in dendrophobia.

Marvell's forests and gardens reflect a "terror of the flux" also; Marvell did not share the dendro-eudaemonia of a later poet who held that "One impulse from a vernal wood/May teach you more of man,/ Of moral evil and of good, / Than all the sages can." Unlike Frost's New York alec, however, he found nature meaningful as well as threatening. In the poems I shall examine in this chapter, he either discovers a principle of compromise between art and nature, the active and contemplative lives, and thus an integration of nature and the supernatural, or he examines obstacles to such integration. The chief patterns are (1) withdrawal, to purgative, masochistic pain or perhaps pleasure, to enlightenment, and finally to symbolic or actual emergence and (2) withdrawal, to constriction, to symbolic self-annihilation.

In "The Coronet," once the kind of pastoral that looks for atonement in the beauty and innocence of nature is rejected, the poet finds a valid use for another kind. If the coronet is spoiled as a crown for the head of "the king of Glory," it may still crown his feet—in fact, the act

1936), pp. 223–54; also in *Meaning in the Visual Arts* (New York: 1957), pp. 295–320. For other useful commentaries on pastoral see Calvin Truesdale's unpublished dissertation "English Pastoral Verse from Spenser to Marvell," University of Washington (1956); Walter W. Greg's standard work, *Pastoral Poetry and Pastoral Drama;* and William Empson, *Some Versions of Pastoral* (London: 1950).

of writing the poem, symbolized in the gathering and weaving of the flowers, shows the natural man to be compatible with the religious man. The pastoral garland, violently shattered at Christ's feet, thus becomes the spoils of victory as well as a spoiled wreath. The poem is a forceful and unique version of the traditional pastoral reconciliation of art, nature, and the supernatural:

> When for the Thorns with which I long, too long,
>> With many a piercing wound,
>> My Saviours head have crown'd,
> I seek with Garlands to redress that Wrong:
>> Through every Garden, every Mead,
> I gather flow'rs (my fruits are only flow'rs)
>> Dismantling all the fragrant Towers
> That once adorn'd my Shepherdesses head.
> And now when I have summ'd up all my store,
>> Thinking (so I my self deceive)
>> So rich a Chaplet thence to weave
> As never yet the king of Glory wore:
>> Alas I find the Serpent old
>> That, twining in his speckled breast,
>> About the flow'rs disguis'd does fold,
>> With wreaths of Fame and Interest.
> Ah, foolish Man, that would'st debase with them,
> And mortal Glory, Heavens Diadem!
> But thou who only could'st the Serpent tame,
> Either his slipp'ry knots at once untie,
> And disintangle all his winding Snare:
> Or shatter too with him my curious frame:
> And let these wither, so that he may die,
> Though set with Skill and chosen out with Care.
> That they, while Thou on both their Spoils dost tread,
> May crown thy Feet, that could not crown thy Head.

The final lines, in which the offering, ruined by Satan, becomes the spoils of the second Adam's feet, may refer to the phophecy of Genesis 3:15: "I will put enmity between thee and the woman and between thy seed and her seed; it shall bruise thy head and thou shalt bruise his heel."[7] St. Gregory had found the mystery of the Incarnation symbolized by Christ's feet, by which divinity touched earth.[8] And so the coronet of

[7]Quoted by Walafred Strabo, *Glossa ordinaria* in Migne, 113:95; cf. John Diodati, *Pious Annotations* (London: 1648), p. 4; Sir Henry Vane, *The Retired Man's Meditations* (London: 1655), p. 402.

[8]Potest quoque per pedes ipsum mysterium in carnationis eius intelligi, quo divinitas terrum tetigit, quia carnem sumpsit," *Homiliarum in evangelia,* lib. II, Migne, 76:1242. On the concept of sacrifice, see Ernst Cassirer, *The Philosophy of Symbolic Forms* (New Haven: 1955), pp. 2, 226–30.

flowers, like Mary in Vaughan's "St. Mary Magdalen," finds its place at that point where the natural and supernatural meet:

> Why art thou humbled thus, and low
> As earth, thy lovely head dost bow?
> Dear Soul! thou knew'st, flowers here on earth
> At their Lords foot-stool have their birth;
> Therefore thy wither'd self in haste
> Beneath his blest feet thou didst cast,
> That at the root of this green tree
> Thy great decays restor'd might be.

The flowers of the gardens and meads are thus not entirely useless. If they cannot be salvaged in any other way, they may at least serve a sacrificial function, like the slain shepherd of the pastoral elegy, whose death results in renewed ceremonies and new life. The impulse to create something of value out of nature is neither pure nor impure, the coronet neither complete gain nor complete loss. But only after gathering and weaving the flowers, "set with Skill and chosen out with Care," can one arrive at self-recognition and awareness of the gulf that separates nature and grace. Fame and interest shatter the pastoral daydream, but the pastoral artist discovers a valid use for his art.

For this reason lavishing skill and care on a poem offered for destruction is no contradiction. As part of the poem's strategy, Marvell weaves the curious frame as tightly as he can. The opening quatrains, equivalent to the composition of place in a three-part meditation, present the problem and the poet's reaction to it. One couplet completes the self-recognition hinted earlier and turns the artist in the right direction ("Ah, foolish Man . . ."), followed by a colloquy with a more complex interweaving of rhyme (klmklm) but with regularized, pentameter lines, as the poet sees his involvement in the winding snare in the light of Christ's relationship with nature. "Though set with Skill . . ." thus concludes a six-line section of intricate interweaving on a curiously ambivalent and lamenting note. Marvell places the qualifying clause in a climactic position and calls attention to it as a parting gesture before throwing the "curious frame" as Christ's feet. The sacrifice, he indicates, is as intricate as one might expect from a previous maker of "Towers" for shepherdesses' heads; it is the tribute of a fabricator whose lavish expenditure only makes for greater "spoils." The poem ends, in the circular manner of a coronet, with the original idea of crowning, but the difference between the final sacrifice, with its mixture of reluctance, wit, and resignation, and the original industry only points up the contrast between naive hopes for nature and art and the Christian poet's recognition of their sacrificial use.

However, though "The Coronet" (like "Lycidas") progresses from innocent ceremony to realization of corruption to a kind of release through sacrifice, its peculiar integration of nature, art, and grace does not leave the poet free to seek new ceremonies in "fresh woods." If it were the only poem on the subject among Marvell's lyrics, its proper place would be at the end, as a kind of palinode: making other frames only to have them shattered would be fruitless. (The suggestion that Christ disentangled the serpent without destroying the garland is not made very hopefully.) In "Clorinda and Damon," on the other hand, though Damon begins by thinking of nature strictly as a temptation comprising a banquet of pleasure like that rejected by the Resolved Soul, the poem eventually finds the fountain's liquid bell to be in harmony with the song of great Pan (Christ). Only by comparison with that song do natural things appear to Damon to be spoiled by sensuality, the cave of love to be a cave of iniquity.[9]

It first appears, however, that the sun from which the pastoral retreat is meant to offer protection, "Heaven's Eye" (*sol justitiae*), exposes the sheltered darkness to hostile scrutiny. No retreat is quite safe. Nor is the pagan fountain baptismal, a place where the soul might bathe and "slake its Drought." The opening lines suggest that the process of reading clearly and purely the signs on the grassy "Scutcheon" was lost when the flock went astray, when, in shepherd dialogue, Adam's golden world lost its integrity. It is this fall from innocence that has made nature dangerous and taught Damon to expect death in Arcadia:

> C. I have a grassy Scutcheon spy'd,
>   Where *Flora* blazons all her pride.
>   The Grass I aim to feast thy Sheep:
>   The Flow'rs I for thy Temples keep.
> D. Grass withers; and the Flow'rs too fade.

The flowers are thus undermined by the fall, and their beauty, though having splendor as Clorinda sees them, will not satisfy the Christian shepherd. Reading nature in the way the divine *allegoria* of the Canticles was read, however, offers a way to sublimate one's attraction to nature. The limitations inherent in the signs on nature's "Scutcheon" (about

[9]John D. Rosenberg's perceptive article "Marvell and the Christian Idiom," *Boston University Studies in English, 4* (1960), 152–61, approaches "Clorinda and Damon" from approximately the same direction.

which "poor Shepherds" sing) are overcome by the transcending song of Pan:

> C. What did great *Pan* say?
> D. Words that transcend poor Shepherds skill,
>   But He ere since my Songs does fill:
>   And his Name swells my slender Oate.

The "Name" supersedes the design of Flora's "Scutcheon," but an enlightened shepherd like Damon may incorporate nature in his song, which is composed of harmonic parts and precisely those images from nature just rejected:

> *Chorus.*
> Of *Pan* the flowry Pastures sing,
> Caves eccho, and the Fountains ring.
> Sing then while he doth us inspire;
> For all the World is our *Pan's* Quire.

Nature's various forms as divine *vestigia*, then, are allowed a function;[10] though they "swell" the shepherd's pagan "Oate," they do not make it an altogether different instrument. The world becomes "Our Pan's Quire" by means of its echoing capacity. A Miltonic hierarchy reclaims all forms of life from lowest to highest: Damon is for Pan, Clorinda for Pan through Damon ("Sweet must *Pan* sound in *Damons* Note"), and the rest of creation for Pan through their combined song. No withdrawal is possible, but none is necessary if the temptress herself is rendered harmless. Guilt and rejection are transformed to divine eros and eulogy.

This manner of bringing together pagan and Hebraic pastoral and thus healing the broad fissure of nature and grace, though seldom so succinctly expressed, is not uncommon in renaissance pastoral. For example, Herman Hugo, in a popularized version of a commentary by Honorius on the Canticles, suggests that a tree's protective shadow "is the traveller's covert from heat, his protection from the storm," because it is "The Tree of Life, to wit, the Apple Tree." It is "the holy cross, its fruit is Christ, its shadow the refreshment and defense of

---

[10]Cf. St. Bonaventura, *The Mind's Road to God*, trans. George Boas (New York: 1953), pp. 8–11; Etienne Gilson, *The Philosophy of St. Bonaventure* (New York: 1938), p. 230; Ruth Wallerstein, *Studies in Seventeenth-Century Poetic* (Madison: 1950), p. 194; Bellarmine, *The Mind's Ascent to God* (1615), trans. Monialis (Oxford: 1925), pp. 36, 110, 117.

mankind."[11] This is to say simply that the shadow cast by the Incarnation sanctifies the forest. The crucifixion "tree" blesses the fruit and makes spiritually beneficial the trees in actual groves encountered by the pilgrim on his simultaneously horizontal journey through time and his vertical *itinerarium mentis in deum*.[12]

Marvell returns to this theme on several occasions, most explicitly in "Bermudas," which in the compact precision of his best style suggests that the two journeys can be made to coincide, that a classical concern with nature-as-such and the Christian book of emblems are not entirely incompatible. Captain John Smith's account of the Summer Isles in *The Generall History of Virginia* (1624) and the experiences of John Oxenbridge may have provided suggestions for the compromise, but more important would seem to be the fact that the Bermudas could be considered mythic without contradicting geography. The myth of the eternal return was not entirely myth:[13] in the climate of the Bermudas was a hint of what had been before the fall, an embodiment of what history, redeemed by providence, could be at any time, and the promise of a future Eden. The remote past and the future are thus brought together in a natural shrine whose message is a "gospel" transmitted to the listening winds. The impulse to retreat is transformed to an exploratory motive and purged of its masochism and symbolic annihilation.

Even so, the poem has its own kind of intensity. The pilgrims in their small boat hover on the edge between their old, unstable world and this "far kinder" one. The "watry Maze" leads back to a place now "long unknown" that they find rising above the storms of their journey:

> What should we do but sing his Praise
> That led us through the watry Maze,
> Unto an Isle so long unknown,
> And yet far kinder than our own?
> Where he the huge Sea-Monsters wracks,
> That lift the Deep upon their Backs.
> He lands us on a grassy Stage;
> Safe from the Storms, and Prelat's rage.

[11]*Pia Desideria*, trans., E. Arwaker (London: 1690), p. 149. On the traditional associations of cross and tree see C. G. Jung, *Symbols of Transformation*, trans., R. F. C. Hull (New York: 1956), pp. 271 ff.

[12]Cf. Bernard Clairvaux, *Vita et res gestae*, I, 4 (Migne, 185:240) and *Tractatus Ascetici* (Migne, 184: 251 ff.); Cf. Boethius, *Consolations of Philosophy* VII, 8.

[13]See Mircea Eliade, *The Myth of the Eternal Return*, trans., Willard Trask (New York: 1954).

> He gave us this eternal Spring,
> Which here enamells every thing;

By wracking sea monsters, pruning nature, and regulating time, providential art resolves a tension between tameness and wildness, nature as a threat and nature as a harbor and shrine. Even while things change and grow, spring is eternal and enameled (that is, surpassing in adornment). The islands are a "grassy Stage" combining the fullest potential of art and nature. Fowl visit daily in harmony with cosmic purposes, while providence itself

> ... hangs in shades the Orange bright,
> Like golden Lamps in a green Night.

The fruit hangs for both beauty and guidance, set like divine light brilliantly against a threatening background. From their side of the line, rowing simply "along" in their small boat and singing, the pilgrims give thanks for this presence of grace in nature: God "in these Rocks for us did frame / A Temple, where to sound his Name." The song from their Protestant English craft may not pierce directly to Spanish and Catholic "Mexique Bay," but if they sing loudly enough it may perhaps get there rebounded from "Heavens Vault."[14] Meanwhile, the temporal task of rowing the small boat is perfectly synchronized with, and regulated by, their religious "chime." The song is "An holy and a chearful Note" because of that divine-human congruity that gets their boat to its goal. Its holiness is natural, its naturalness holy; essence and existence, art and nature, are perfectly fused.

The mower poems, taken as a group, are concerned with the loss of that congruity. Man's fall occasions nature's, and so the integrity of the self and the integrity of garden and meadow are lost together.[15] Love, along with death the shepherd's traditional spoiler, causes the Mower to turn the instrument of his trade against himself and to bring chaos to the meadow. In the Mower's accident, the fall is re-enacted, bringing death once again to Arcadia:

[14]Cf. Rosalie L. Colie, "Marvell's 'Bermudas' and the Puritan Paradise," *Renaissance News, 10* (1957), 75–79.

[15]See Lawrence Hyman on the androgynous Adam theme, "Marvell's 'Garden,'" *ELH*, 25 (1958), 13–22 and Maren-Sofie Røstvig, "Andrew Marvell's 'The Garden,' a Hermetic Poem," *English Studies, 40* (1959), 65–76. For useful commentaries on nature in the mower poems and in the renaissance in general see Joseph Summers, "Marvell's Nature," *ELH, 20* (1953), 121–35; Truesdale, "English Pastoral Verse," pp. 223–24; Jim Corder, "Marvell and Nature," *N&Q, 6* (1959), 58–61; Harold S. Wilson, "Meaning of 'Nature' in Renaissance Literature," *JHI, 2* (1941), 430–48.

> Only for him no Cure is found
> Whom Julianas Eyes do wound.
> Tis death alone that this must do:
> For death thou art a Mower too.

Death as mower will thus ransack nature where the Mower has kept order, and the Mower who has mowed himself awaits it as cure for the wound heterosexual love has given him.

"The Garden" goes beyond these poems in bringing together similar elements of Marvell's sensibility. It combines pastoral themes with the modes of religious meditation, satire, and the philosophical lyric, and in doing so undertakes formal difficulties that seem imposing from any angle we approach them. The mood of "Gestimmtheit" or "letting things be," in Heidegger's phrase, has to prevail through difficult philosophical distinctions, through awareness of the absurdities of man's chase after nymphs and social position, and above all, through awareness of the "fall," the effects of which permeate every moment and activity of the garden.

. . .

One's limited time is thus made fruitful in the garden, which is neither primitive nor excessively trained. Far from destroying the soul, created plenitude is found to enrich it. Higher and lower principles (the Apollo-like sun *in* the flowers), time and eternity are reconciled: the impregnating sun creates the "tyme" in which the bee works. As the sacred plants of innocence and quiet, if below, are harbored in the grosser plants, the *rationes* of a man-made dial are like those of the greater circle of the zodiac. (As Ficino writes concerning human art, man is very much like God: "who could deny that man could somehow also make the heavens, could he only obtain the instruments and the heavenly material, since even now he makes them, though of different material, but still with a very similar order?"[16]) The metamorphosis of the sensual "chase" into a creative, pastoral industry redeems history, transforming time and the "Lucious Clusters" into soul-food, energy for the longer flight. What is "at hand" through the reckoning of the artist is integral to the soul's "being-in-the-world," its *Da-sein*, and thus to its eventual being out of it, which satisfies Marvell as Christian, Neoplatonist, and pastoralist.

[16]*JHI*, 5 (1944), 235, from *Theologia Platonica*, XII, 3.

EARL WASSERMAN

Windsor Forest

In opening *Windsor Forest*—a poem published to celebrate the Tory Peace of Utrecht—with the description of the royal forest as the ideal microcosm, where there is no mere warring of the elements but where the elements are "harmoniously confus'd" and where even "tho' all things differ, all agree," Pope was not only defining the cosmic plan but also expressing in its most inclusive terms a doctrine that, in the context of the Peace, could be read as an especially Tory thesis. For the faith in the harmonious tension of the conflicting political groups at home is also the ground for defending the Tory eagerness for a somewhat arbitrative peace with France—a *concordia discors* between nations—especially in view of the opposing desire of the Whigs to press on the "*Chaos*-like" crushing and bruising of war to undisputed victory. "And where, tho' all things differ, all agree" can be read as "All Nature's diff'rence keeps all Nature's peace" and then applied to the terms of peace that ended the Wars of the Spanish Succession.

.   .   .

But, coherently dominant though the political theme is throughout, it would be quite wrong to read the poem as a mere configuration of allegorical equivalents for the Peace of Utrecht and the political situations surrounding it. Pope's tightly integrated world-view taught that "the first Almighty Cause/Acts not by partial, but by gen'ral laws" (*Essay on Man*, i, 145–46) and that

> All are but parts of one stupendous whole,
> Whose body Nature is, and God the soul;
> . . . chang'd thro' all, and yet in all the same.
>
> (i, 267–69)

From *The Subtler Language*, by Earl Wasserman, pp. 108–13, 129–33, 143–45, 148–57. Copyright © 1959 by the Johns Hopkins Press, Baltimore. Reprinted by permission of the Johns Hopkins Press.

In such a unitary conception of reality, human affairs are not significant in a merely temporal context, drawing their worth only from their causes and consequences, nor can they be autonomous fragments of reality with independent meanings. All events are but variant expressions of one fixed master plan, and meaning and value must derive from that plan, which the age loosely called the Law of Nature and which in *Windsor Forest* takes the form of *concordia discors*. A merely allegorical presentation of the Peace of Utrecht would therefore falsify it and deprive it of meaning by isolating it from the universal context in which all things exist. On the other hand, a poetic system of simultaneous references whereby the immediate occasion, the Peace, is seen in the context of, and in conformity with, the whole pattern of human life, and whereby the conduct of human life is evaluated in terms of Nature's all-embracing law, not only creates the proper philosophic view but also is the necessary means of validating the special event. Therefore, the poem is simultaneously general and particular—the Peace is but a special application of the universal and eternal Law of Nature; and it is simultaneously ethical and political—politics is but a special form of ethics. By presenting the various modes of human conduct and evaluating them in terms of the doctrine of *concordia discors* the poet can also subsume under these general forms of conduct the particular aspects of the Peace. And through the means of these simultaneously operative areas of reference the Peace gains its validity by being an expression of the universal law; the universal law stamps value upon the Peace.

What allows Pope to exploit this law as the ground for the Peace is the double role he assigns to Windsor Forest. For the Forest is both a principle and a place. . . . The essence of this "Eden" is the cosmic principle of harmonious confusion, or ordered variety; and the opening paragraphs are devoted to giving the Forest this symbolic value. The complaints of critics like William Lisle Bowles that the description of the Forest forms no picture arise from irrelevant standards, which ask that the poem accomplish something it never intends. The description is not scenic, but thematic; we are not to see things, but to realize the principle of *concordia discors*. Having embraced the whole cosmic order as that in which "tho' all things differ, all agree," and having intellectually grasped this as perfection, Pope now offers it to us in substantial form. Consequently the entire description is organized around the natural harmonizing of contraries: here are both hills and vales, woods and plains, earth and water; here trees partly admit and partly exclude the light. "Here in full Light the russet Plains extend;/ There wrapt in Clouds the blueish Hills ascend" (23–24); and in this couplet each factor in one line—place, condition, color, form, direction—is counterbalanced in the other, so that the blending of these parallel but contrary lines by the rhyme of the precisely antithetical "extend" and "ascend" is itself the artistic realization of *concordia discors*. Even the wild heath is rich with "Purple Dies," and fruitful fields arise in the midst of wastes (a passage reminiscent of Denham's expression of the same cosmic theme: the Thames "Cities in deserts, woods in Cities plants"). The tension of coexisting contrarieties that is the heart of the theme is most completely captured in the description of the trees that, shading, "shun each others Shades" (22) and in the comparison of the checkered grove to a coy nymph tensely suspended between indulging and repressing her lover's addresses (17–20). By manifesting in perfect form the harmonizing of contraries, Windsor Forest is the Law of Nature.

But the Forest is also, in two senses, a place. It is "as the World," and therefore it *is* the world. It is, in other words, the locale of all human actions. Any other forest or park or estate would have served equally well as a "paradise" to symbolize Nature's law, but few could have served as well as a world-place, a theater for the entire drama of human affairs. Here is the home of the monarch; here monarchs have been born and lie buried; here poets have lived and have written of the Forest-world; here men can hunt or retire from an active life to meditate; here is an Arcadia with mythic possibilities; and here flows the great artery of England's commerce. As the Law of Nature, Windsor Forest is apart from man—it is notable that in the formulation of the Forest as the principle of harmonious confusion no human agent appears, but only the objects of external nature. But as a world-place, the Forest will be a scene for all the modes of human action: despoiling, hunting, poetizing, meditating, ruling, living, and dying. The meaning of the poem, then, will arise from the interaction of the Forest's function as place with its function as principle. The latter, having been established at the opening, persists as the setting throughout the poem; the shifting and seemingly disparate place-aspects involve the varieties of human actions (or are symbolic of them) that are to be tested and evaluated against this setting.

However, at the same time that the Forest is the world it is also England in little, and therefore it *is* England. The Peace that Anne has brought about is but a special human action, and the double place-function of the Forest as both England and the world demands an evaluation of the Peace by the only possible valid standard, the standard of universal human conduct, which in turn is fixed by the law of *concordia discors* that the Forest symbolizes.

.   .   .

Consequently in the next phase of the poem (93–158) the figure of the hunt represents the dynamic principle in man, the energy without which he would stagnate, but which, uncontrolled, produces chaos, just as William's overzealous hunting impulse made a chaos of the cosmic Windsor Forest. Since all "subsists by elemental strife," since "every natural action . . . is nothing else but a hunting," hunting can symbolize the proper expenditure of what otherwise would be a chaotic warring energy. Indeed, in the introductory couplet of this section Pope makes fairly explicit the metaphoric function that the image of the hunt is expected to perform:

> Ye vig'rous Swains! while Youth ferments your Blood,
> And purer Spirits swell the sprightly Flood,
> Now range the Hills. . . .

.   .   .

But if the poet here recommends the hunt and grows ardent in his description of war, he also inveighs against both. For the function of this section of the poem is to use the hunt (and its extension, war) as a metaphor for the recommended norm of human activity, in contrast to the excessive and uncontrolled activity of William. And human norms can be only ambiguous. If man must be "Virtuous and vicious," if he is "Created half to rise, and half to fall," then the norm of human actions is not to be ascertained by a moral discrimination of an absolute good from an absolute bad, but by the distinction between conformity and nonconformity with the objective standard of the Law of Nature; and the result is that the "right," or "natural," actions of that ambiguity, man, must necessarily, in moral terms, be simultaneously good and bad. Consequently in one of the organizational patterns of this movement there are three nearly equal units: the first (93–110) and the last (135–58) present the hunt as good; the unit between these (111–34) presents it as bad. . . .

Yet, despite the ambivalences with which Pope clothes this description of the hunt (indeed, because of them) the section is to be taken as prescriptive of human conduct, for the creature of a "middle state" whose motivating principle is the good-bad hunting-warring force is here in accord with Nature. Coextensive with the organization already

mentioned is the arrangement of the section in terms of the four successive seasons—the "various seasons of the rolling year"—whose multi-
plicity is the variety that characterizes God's works and whose com-
plementary natures and regular recurrence are the harmony whereby
God creates "Order in Variety." Instead of resisting, like William, this
pattern of ordered variety, man now conforms to it: with the changes
of the harmoniously varied seasons he pursues the corresponding seasonal sports in each of the elements, air, earth, and water.[1] We see the
chase alternately from the point of view of the hunter and the hunted;
the hunter both in his eager haste and in his patient intentness; and
even the world of the hunted in the rich diversity of the "Scaly Breed,"
a "various Race." In this ordered variety the hunt is a "well accorded
strife" because man is observing Nature's plan. Under the tyranny of
William's hunting "In vain kind Seasons swell'd the teeming Grain";
but now the "sandy Wilds" are overspread with "yellow Harvests,"
the woods are "gameful," and the streams "plenteous." Because man
is in accord with Nature, Nature is in accord with him.

.   .   .

Thus far we have considered the first movement of the poem as
though all three episodes were governed by the hunting metaphor alone
and that therefore they are concerned exclusively with the active life
and its political correspondent, war. However, the myth of Lodona
involves not only war but also peace, not only the region of chaos but
also a return to the cosmic Forest, not only the zealous huntress but also
the reflecting river. Along with Lodona's metamorphosis the hunting
metaphor has been transmuted into the river metaphor; and one set of
values has been transformed into their opposites. No longer impetuous
in the natural scene, Lodona, now "lingring" (215), has become the
traditional "Loddon slow"; and, being slow, she clearly mirrors the
entire range of nature, its mountains, forests, and flocks, as a tumul-
tuous river could not. But the total scene being reflected in the waters
is, of course, Windsor Forest, the cosmic world; and therefore the
formerly chaotic Lodona now reflects in her gentle placidity the
world-harmony. Moreover, the human figure who now appears on
this scene of peace is not the active and warring huntsman, but the
peaceful and meditative "musing" shepherd who sees in the glass of
the river not the fragmented parts of nature but the harmony of the

---

[1]Cf. the opening chapter of Walton's *Complete Angler*, where the followers of each of
the three forms of sport, hunting, fishing, and fowling, in turn praise each of the corresponding elements.

total representation. In terms of human conduct the distinction between Lodona the huntress and Lodona the river is the distinction
between the active and the retired, or meditative, lives—the *vita activa*
and the *vita contemplativa*.

It is the necessary corollary of the doctrine of concordant discord—
the doctrine that in this world everything has its contrary and that
vital harmony consists in the blending of the two—that human life
must be a proper mingling of public action and private meditation.
If dynamic passion and restraining reason must come to terms, if man
is both beast and angel, life must be both outward and inward, active
and passive, deed and thought. One of Wycherley's poems that Pope
corrected and to which he contributed a long original passage is
entitled "The Various Mix'd Life, against the Constant Publick or
Private Life." Obviously Pope subscribed to this poem's widely accepted thesis that "Action and Thought should then successive reign,"[2]
for he published in 1712 a paper repeating its substance:

> Methinks most of the Philosophers and Moralists have run too
> much into Extremes in praising entirely either Solitude or
> publick Life; in the former Men generally grow useless by too
> much Rest, and in the latter are destroy'd by too much Pre-
> cipitation. . . . Those who . . . can make themselves useful to
> all States, should be like gentle Streams, that not only glide
> through lonely Vales and Forests amidst the Flocks and Shep-
> herds, but visit populous Towns in their Course, and are at once
> of Ornament and Service to them.[3]

Lodona's plea, "Let me, O let me, to the Shades repair" (199), therefore has a special relevance, for it will be echoed when the poet himself

[2]The literature on this theme is very extensive, but it is instructive to observe the
presentation of it by Pope's friend Bishop Atterbury in a sermon "Of Religious Retirement" (1705): "It hath been disputed, which is a State of greater Perfection, the Social,
or the Solitary; whereas, in Truth, neither of these Estates is complete without the
Other; as the Example of our Blessed Lord (the Unerring Test and Measure of Perfection) informs us. His Life (which ought to be the Pattern of Ours), was a Mixture of
Contemplation and Action, of Austerity and Freedom: We find him often, where the
greatest Concourse was, in the Market-Places, in the Synagogues, and at Festival
Entertainments; and we find him also retiring from the Crowd into a Desert, or a
Garden, and there employing himself in all kinds of Religious Exercise, and Inter-
course with God, in Fasting, Meditation, and Prayer. . . . The Retreat therefore which
I am speaking of is not that of Monks and Hermits, but of Men living in the World,
and going out of it for a time, in order to return into it; it is a Temporary, not a Total
Retreat . . .; such, as is consistent with all the Business, and even with the Innocent
Pleasures of Life; and is so far from interfering with the Duties of our Publick Offices
and Stations, that it disposes and enables us for the better Discharge of them."
(*Sermons and Discourses* [1740, fifth ed.], I, 347 ff.)

[3]*Prose Works*, N. Ault, ed., I, 42; see also Pope's letter to Steele, 18 June 1712.

begs to withdraw into the cloistered world of Windsor, "Bear me, oh bear me to *sequester'd* Scenes/Of *Bow'ry* Mazes and *surrounding* Greens" (259–60; italics mine), and is directly related to the description of Trumbull as one "who to these Shades retires" (235) to enjoy "home-felt Quiet." In the total structure of the poem, then, the Lodona episode is transitional, and Lodona's two roles as huntress and as river bring together two of the main themes. The huntress Lodona's flight into the outer world of chaos brings to a conclusion the theme of the active life, expressed by the three hunts; her return to the guardian world in the form of a tranquil river reflecting Nature's harmony and therefore serving as the proper object of the meditative shepherd's musings introduces the subsequent theme of the retired and meditative life.

. . .

It is, then, especially appropriate that the metaphor for man's highest animal life be the hunt, his association with the beasts, and that in his abuses of this life he become wholly the beast, the pursuer pursued. Since man is both angel and beast, it would be interesting, Pope once speculated, to consider into which beasts tyrants might be transmuted.[4] On the other hand, in view of the double nature of man, it is especially appropriate that in the two sections on man's retirement and exercise of his mind, or soul, the recurrent theme be heaven and the sacred: "Ye sacred Nine! that all my Soul possess" (257), "Visions bless" (258), "eternal Wreaths" (263), "consecrated Walks" (265), "By God-like Poets Venerable made" (268), "Heav'nly Voice" (275), "Immortal Greens" (284), "nearer to the Skies" (286), "sacred Rage" (289), "heav'nly *Myra*" (296). And Trumbull

> . . . looks on Heav'n with more than mortal Eyes,
> Bids his free Soul expatiate in the Skies,
> Amidst her Kindred Stars familiar roam,
> Survey the Region, and confess her Home!
>
> (251–54)

Finally, if life must be both active and meditative, and if man is both sentient animal and soul, his mental processes correspondingly combine the sense data contributed by means of the animal spirits and the ratiocination by the mental powers of the soul. In terms of the empirical psychology, the complement to the sentient experience of reality is reflection, the contemplation of the experienced image as it is represented in the form of mental idea.

. . .

[4] *Spectator* 408.

The theme of retirement . . . is expressed not only by the transformation and return of Lodona and by the meditations of Trumbull but also by the accomplishments of the poets. The integration of these sections is effected by the parallelism of Lodona's plea to Diana-Anne that she be returned to the Forest's shades (199) and the poet's calling upon those other divinities, the "sacred Nine," to bear him to the "sequester'd Scenes" of the Forest (257–59). However, Lodona was returned not to live actively in the Forest but to reflect it for the musings of the shepherd; Trumbull retired to do his travelling over "figur'd Worlds," to live past ages by reading, and to reflect on his spiritual existence. Correspondingly, the poet begs to be borne, not simply to the material Forest, but to the Forest as it is ideally represented in the form of art; not merely to the physical scene, but to *la belle nature*, that perfection that exists in no one place and yet is inherent everywhere, and that the poet can capture by reflecting the particular in the idealizing and heightening mirror of art. For he is to be conveyed there, not in person, but by the representative act of the Muses.

. . .

That poetry is a "mirror" of Nature is, of course, an established trope in classical and neoclassical critical theory.[5] Although Plato introduced this metaphor to prove that art reflects only appearances, not the transcendent Ideas, nevertheless the Platonic mirror ultimately became associated with the Aristotelian concept of art as mimetic of a norm in Nature. In the extension of Aristotelian esthetics the mirror of poetry was understood to reflect *la belle nature*, which Batteux defined as not *"le vrai qui est; mais le vrai qui peut être, le beau vrai, qui est représenté comme s'il existoit réelement, et avec toutes les perfections qu'il peut recevoir."*[6] When "fantasy" had lost its pejorative Platonic sense as the faculty producing appearances instead of Ideas, and when the critics began to defend fantasy and its product, poetry, as a significant way of knowing the essence of reality, the mirror remained the metaphor for this faculty. George Puttenham, for example, granted that the fantasy may be deranged and produce monsters, but he insisted that when it is properly disposed, "by it, as by a glasse or mirrour, are represented unto the soule all maner of bewtifull visions, whereby the inventive parte of the mynde is so much holpen as without it no man could devise any new or rare thing." True, he adds, the mirrors of fantasy may be false glasses "and shew things otherwise than they be in deede,

[5]See Meyer Abrams, *The Mirror and the Lamp* (New York: 1953).
[6]Charles Batteux, *Les Beaux Arts* (Paris: 1747), pp. 27–28.

and others right as they be in deede, neither fairer nor fouler, nor greater nor smaller." But there are other mirroring fantasies that "shew thinges exceeding faire and comely. . . . Even so is the phantasticall part of man (if it be not disordered) a representer of the best, most comely, and bewtifull images or appearances of thinges to the soule and according to their very truth."[7] This "very truth" of things is "*le vrai qui peut être*" with all the perfections that it can receive; and therefore it is attained by two means: by representing the entire range of things collectively, since the sum of Nature equals the essence of Nature; and by heightening or perfecting through reflection the beauty of what is being reflected. Because a mirror collects much in little it had long been accepted as the metaphor for a microcosm, and *speculum* was one of the favorite titles for encyclopaedias, the whole world of learning reflected in a glass. But because the mirror also softens the image it reflects, it also came to be a metaphor for the idea, or form, inherent in the image. Dr. Johnson, for example, defined *mirror* as "pattern; . . . that on which the eye ought to be fixed; an exemplar; an archetype," and offered as evidence this sentence from Hooker: "The works of nature are no less exact, than if she did both behold and study how to express some absolute shape or mirror always present before her." Both of these senses come together in the esthetic formulations of the mirror metaphor, as can be seen in Warburton's explanation of a passage in Pope's *Essay on Criticism:* though Virgil "scorned to stoop at anything short of nature, when he understood that Nature and Homer are the same he "had the prudence to contemplate nature in the place where she was seen to most advantage, collected in all her charms in the clear mirror of Homer."[8] The mirror of art is not merely

[7] *The Arte of English Poesie* (1588), i, viii.

[8] *Works of Pope*, ed., Elwin-Courthope, ii, 90. In his *Nosce Teipsum* Sir John Davies defined "fantasy" as "Wit's Looking-Glass," the mirror "Where all the Gath'rings of the Senses are."

The same conception of poetry as mirroring *la belle nature* appears in Francis Knapp's commendatory poem "To Mr. Pope on his Windsor-Forest," published with the 1720 edition of Pope's poem, and reveals that Knapp understood the transformation of Lodona in the sense in which it has been interpreted above:

> The pompous scenes in all their pride appear,
> Fresh in the page, as in the groves they were.
> Not half so true the fair *Lodona* shows
> The sylvan state that on her border grows,
> While she the wondring shepherd entertains
> With a new *Windsor* in her watry plains:
> Thy juster lays the lucid wave surpass;
> The living scene is in the Muse's glass.

repetitive; by collecting Nature and showing her "to most advantage" and "in all her charms" it reveals what Hooker called her "absolute shape."

.   .   .

All three of the retirement passages, then, have been dominated by the mirror image and its significances. The reckless Lodona has been transformed into a tranquil river in whose "Glass" the shepherd sees Nature collected: skies, mountains, woods, and flocks. And it is telling that this mirror is viewed by a shepherd, the very role in which the poet of the poem casts himself as author of a georgic. Trumbull, too, looks on representations of the world and life and reflects within himself to attain an analogous but higher Nature, the soul instead of the essence of things. He studies truth as it is seen in that glass which Pope later was to call "the clear, still Mirrour of Retreat" (*Epilogue to the Satires*, ii, 78). And finally, the poets, inpelled by a "sacred" force and reflecting physical nature in their poetry, reveal an "eternal" Nature of "Immortal Greens" and lift that Nature "nearer to the Skies." The miraculous metamorphosis effected by the divine Anne-Cynthia, therefore, is nearly identical with the mirroring transformation brought about by the equally "God-like" poets; and both acts are related to Trumbull's "reflections" that carry his soul towards God. Anne's act of transforming war into peace—of metamorphosing the extravagant spirit of Lodona into a mirror reflecting the harmony of Nature's essence—is the political and moral analogue of the poet's act of reflecting physical nature to show its "very truth."

The poem has indeed been devoted to Windsor, as the opening proposition announced, as "At once the Monarch's and the Muse's Seats," since the two are almost interchangeable terms. To produce peace and poetry involves a metamorphosis of experiential reality into its essence, the Law of Nature, and this essence is analogous to and directly related to the final essence that is heaven. Such acts can be effected only by "earthly Gods" like Anne, by "God-like Poets," and by man in his highest spiritual exercises. Hence the perfect propriety of Pope's casting the account of Anne's establishment of the Peace into the form of an Ovidian myth. And not merely because Ovid's poem is the archetype of metamorphoses or because myth is "the poetic story" and therefore identifies Anne's political act and the creation of poetry. The very myth upon which Pope built helps identify Anne's creation of peace with the poetic act. In Ovid the prototype of all the subsequent metamorphoses is the transformation of chaos into the harmony of the world; but in addition, in Pope's immediate model, the myth of Pan and Syrinx, the nymph is transformed into Pan's pipes, or, as Bacon wrote, "the harmony and consent of things." Undoubtedly Pope's Lodona, by the sheer parallelism of the two myths and by her act of reflecting Nature, retains much of this significance of harmony and art, peace and poetry.

Pope has considered retirement in its political, human, and esthetic modes; and their expressions are peace, spiritual meditation, and poetry—and all of these are ultimately the Same.

MILTON WILSON

Adonais

The purpose of *Hellas* limits the stretch of Shelley's imagination, the form of *Adonais* extends it. Or, if this seems overstated, the form of the pastoral elegy (without demanding it) at least assists Shelley to take up a more uncompromising position than he might otherwise have chosen for himself. Granted the Platonic and apocalyptic echoes of the "name of death" in Shelley's mind, and the opportunities provided by the genre, the end of *Adonais* seems predictable.

Predictable, but not inevitable. One opportunity Shelley certainly missed, blinded perhaps by the absence of any historical and social content in his material, as well as by his apocalyptic vision of death. The end of an elegy (since Christianity, at any rate) seeks two things: first, to make the death of the person elegized seem victory not defeat; second, to revive the mourners, to show the new life that is possible for them, the direction and achievement that remain for them here and now. (The pastoral convention, when employed, and the consequent emphasis on the natural year, ensure that these elegiac goals will be seen in relation to the cyclic pattern of death and rebirth.) Obviously here is an opportunity for Shelley to distinguish between and relate his Platonic and radical goals: the apocalypse and the millennium. One could be the immediate goal of Adonais, the other, of the mourners. But once he is convinced that the center of the poem is simply the swallowing up of death in victory, this opportunity is lost. The two elegiac goals become the same goal, and the survivors no less than the victim are mainly concerned with the pursuit of death.

But the poem reaches its end only after a good many preparations and even false scents. The loss of Adonais must be made to seem im-

From *Shelley's Later Poetry*, by Milton Wilson, pp. 236–44, 248–49, 253–55, 315. Published, 1957, by Columbia University Press, New York. Copyright ⓒ by Columbia University Press. Reprinted by permission of the publisher.

portant; the mourners must exhibit their sorrow; and, in particular, the chief mourner must appear and reveal her relation to the death of Adonais, so that, having recognized her, we may move on.

. . .

The Venus and Adonis story, cyclic in its assumptions, is inadequate to express what Shelley says in the last stanzas of the poem. In fact, its inadequacy is a major theme.

Adonais has died, as all things must, however admirable:

> he is gone where all things wise and fair
> Descend; oh, dream not that the amorous Deep
> Will yet restore him to the vital air;
> Death feeds on his mute voice, and laughs at our despair.
>
> (III)

Indeed, Adonais, as a human being, is at a special disadvantage in the natural world. Man's life is linear, and death comes as the end of the line. The rest of nature, bound to the wheel of death and rebirth, can say: "If Winter comes, can Spring be far behind?" Man as an individual can only contrast the productive death of the natural cycle with the finality of his own death. This pessimistic contrast is a recurrent theme of the pastoral elegy, as George Norlin has pointed out;[1] an early stage through which it often moves. The theme has been most common since the Renaissance, but it already found unequivocal expression in Moschus' *Lament for Bion*:

> Alas, when the mallows perish in the garden, and the green celery, and the luxuriant, curling dill, they later come to life again and grow in another year; but we, the great, the mighty, the wise men, when once we die, unhearing we sleep in the hollow earth, a right long sleep without end or awaking.[2]

In "November" of the *Shepheardes Calendar* the death of Dido leads to similar reflections:

> Whence is it, that the flouret of the field doth fade,
> And lyeth buried long in winters bale:
> Yet soon as spring his mantle doth displaye,
> It floureth fresh, as it should never fayle?
> But thing on earth that is of most availe,
> As virtues braunch and beauties budde,
> Reliven not for any good.

This contrast is most likely to be strong when the author's frame of

---

[1]Norlin, "The Conventions of Pastoral Elegy," *American Journal of Philology*, XXXII (1911), 307–9. Mr. Norlin provides some of my examples, below.

[2]*The Pastoral Elegy*, ed., Harrison, p. 39.

reference allows very little commerce between the natural and human (or natural and divine) levels. The Christian humanist, for whom the rebirth of nature must figure forth (even if imperfectly and without an ethical imperative) the rebirth of man, will not take it too much to heart, and in *Lycidas* it is suggested only to be repudiated. The "false surmise" (153) that the flowers strewn on the corpse of Lycidas prefigure his destiny turns out not to be false. Nineteenth-century naturalism may also work against the contrast. The second section of *In Memoriam* suggests it in passing, but Tennyson's main problems are different. Nature, seen from a sufficient distance, may not be cyclic at all. Evolution is linear. The death of the species denies the ultimate reality of rebirth. The danger, therefore, is not man's separation from the pattern of nature, but his conformity to it. The cyclic foreground of nature is an illusion; in the background, for man as well as beast, is the void. But for Cowper, a Calvanistic Evangelical certain of damnation, the contrast between the cyclic history of nature and the linear history of man is tragic and almost inescapable. His great new year's letter to Newton of January 13, 1784, is a kind of pastoral elegy *manqué*:

> It is an alleviation of the woes even of an enlightened man, that he can wish for death, and indulge a hope, at least, that in death he shall find deliverance. But, loaded as my life is with despair, I have no such comfort as would result from a supposed probability of better things to come, were it once ended. . . . The weather is an exact emblem of my mind in its present state. A thick fog envelops everything, and at the same time it freezes intensely. You will tell me that this cold gloom will be succeeded by a cheerful spring, and endeavour to encourage me to hope for a spiritual change resembling it;—but it will be lost labour. Nature revives again; but a soul once slain lives no more. The hedge that has been apparently dead, is not so; it will burst into leaf and blossom at the appointed time; but no such time is appointed for the stake that stands in it. It is as dead as it seems, and will prove itself no dissembler. The latter end of next month will complete a period of eleven years in which I have spoken no other language. It is a long time for a man, whose eyes were once opened, to spend in darkness; long enough to make despair an inveterate habit; and such it is in me.[3]

Cowper, of course, is recalling the lament of Job:

> For there is hope of a tree, if it be cut down, that it will sprout

---

[3] *The Correspondence of William Cowper*, ed., Wright, II, 146–47. I have corrected "when" to "were" in my fifth line.

again, and that the tender branch thereof will not cease. Though
the root thereof wax old in the earth, and the stock thereof die
in the ground; yet through the scent of water it will bud, and
bring forth boughs like a plant. But man dieth, and wasteth away;
yea, man giveth up the ghost, and where is he?[4]

If nature is reborn and man is not, then for the sensitive man "April
is the cruellest month" (as a modern pastoral elegy puts it), or, as we
learn from *Adonais*, "grief returns with the revolving year." Such an
elegy will not find any consolation in nature's "high requiem" over the
human "sod" or be tempted into idealizing nature's cyclical permanence ("Thou wast not born for death, immortal bird!").

Shelley develops his version of the theme in some of the finest
stanzas of the poem:

> Ah woe is me! Winter is come and gone,
> But grief returns with the revolving year;
> The airs and streams renew their joyous tone;
> The ants, the bees, the swallows reappear;
> Fresh leaves and flowers deck the dead Seasons' bier;
> The amorous birds now pair in every brake,
> And build their mossy homes in field and brere;
> And the green lizard, and the golden snake,
> Like unimprisoned flames, out of their trance awake.
>
> Through wood and stream and field and hill and Ocean,
> A quickening life from the Earth's heart has burst
> As it has ever done, with change and motion,
> From the great morning of the world when first
> God dawned on Chaos; in its stream immersed
> The lamps of Heaven flash with a softer light;
> All baser things pant with life's sacred thirst;
> Diffuse themselves; and spend in love's delight,
> The beauty and the joy of their renewed might.
>
> (XVIII, XIX)

So much for "baser things." But the organic life of spring seems to
affect even the mortal remains of Adonais. "Touched by this spirit
tender," the corpse

> Exhales itself in flowers of gentle breath;
> Like incarnations of the stars, when splendour
> Is changed to fragrance,
>
> (XX)

these "flowers" mock and deny the reality of death. But the mockery
is ironic. In fact, man is no more than an atom intensified into momen-

[4]Job 14: 7–10.

tary life, and his doom is to be quenched and chilled into the repose of mere lifelessness.

> Nought we know, dies. Shall that alone which knows
> Be as a sword consumed before the sheath
> By sightless lightning?—th' intense atom glows
> A moment, then is quesched in a most cold repose.
>
> (xx)

Observe the metaphysical terminology (as well as the images) in which Shelley states this tragic contrast. The objects of Thought are apparently indestructible; only the Thought which comprehends them is consumed. The sheath remains, the sword passes, destroyed by a blind, irrational force. And all the cycles of nature seem to do for man is to increase his sense of the inescapable monotony of human loss.

> Great and mean
> Meet massed in death, who lends what life must borrow.
> As long as skies are blue, and fields are green,
> Evening must usher night, night urge the morrow,
> Month follow month with woe, and year wake year to sorrow.
>
> (xxi)

Or, in the bare statement of Cowper, "I should rejoice indeed that the old year is over and gone, if I had not every reason to prophesy a new one similar to it."[5]

But a funeral elegist (even, to some extent, Bion and Moschus) will concern himself with possible consolations or compensations as well as with the loss itself. Even on the earthly level there are ways in which a man's death is not the end of him, and the elegy can test such compensations and the sort of perpetuation which they offer. Of these the most commonly invoked are survival in memory, survival in creations, (institutions, works of art, children) and material survival in nature. The first two are often combined, and (excluding children) we may put them both under the broad heading of fame, a subject about which elegies have traditionally had a good deal to say.

If by fame we mean no more than survival in the grief-stricken memory of the mourners, Shelley has little consolation to offer.

> Alas! that all we loved of him should be,
> But for our grief, as if it had not been,
> And grief itself be mortal!
>
> (xxi)

---

[5]*Correspondence of Cowper*, II, 146.

But temporal fame of a less immediate and personal kind is certainly possible, as we learn in an earlier stanza. In the first stanza of the poem Shelley asks the Hour of Adonais' death to rouse the Hours of the Future and teach them to preserve "his fate and fame" until eternity. Later he claims that Milton reigns "the third among the sons of light" (IV). But such fame is subject to the chances and vicissitudes of temporal existence, and an inglorious Milton may fail to rise, or may set prematurely, like Keats.

> Not all to that bright station dared to climb;
> And happier they their happiness who knew,
> Whose tapers yet burn through that night of time
> In which suns perished; others more sublime,
> Struck by the envious wrath of man or God,
> Have sunk, extinct in their refulgent prime;
> And some yet live, treading the thorny road,
> Which leads, through toil and hate, to Fame's serene abode.
>
> (V)

Shelley, no more than Milton, is satisfied with Fame as a "plant which grows on mortal soil," although he would like the Future to bestow it on Keats. The "night of time" is an inadequate medium for the "sons of light."

But inadequate earthly consolations are not what Shelley intends to offer Adonais. As all critics have observed, the transcendental side of Shelley's Platonic dualism suddenly takes over the direction of the poem in stanza thirty-eight and remains dominant until the end. The only significant consolations are otherworldly, and death is the gateway to them. It is not death that deserves to be regretted, but "the eclipsing curse / Of birth" (LIV) and the life which stains and masks with its sordid and unreal shadows the "pure spirit" issuing from the "burning fountain" (XXXVIII). It is we who decay, not Adonais, who has "outsoared the shadow of our night" (XL). He has left our living death behind and through death has rejoined the life of Eternity.

> Peace, peace! he is not dead, he doth not sleep—
> He hath awakened from the dream of life—
>   .   .   .
> He lives, he wakes—'tis Death is dead, not he;
> Mourn not for Adonais.
>
> (XXXIX, XL, XLI)

This is a Platonic opposition of the most uncompromising sort. To be born is to be degraded, and a "portion of the Eternal" (XXXVIII) fulfills its destiny only by returning to the fountain which it would have been better never to have left.

We might expect such a repudiation of time to be characteristic of the pastoral elegy. Presumably the consolations of an elegy will emphasize the advantages of death and the disadvantages of life. But, in fact, although the former are almost inescapable (if consolation is attempted at all), the latter are surprisingly infrequent. We do not find them, for example, at the end of *Lycidas* or *Thyrsis*. Moreover, Shelley differs strikingly in praising death not merely for the sake of Adonais, but for the sake of the mourners as well, including the poet himself. "What Adonais is, why fear we to become?"

> The One remains, the many change and pass;
> Heaven's light forever shines, Earth's shadows fly;
> Life, like a dome of many-coloured glass,
> Stains the white radiance of Eternity,
> Until Death tramples it to fragments.—Die,
> If thou wouldst be with that which thou dost seek!
>
>   .   .   .
>
> 'Tis Adonais calls! oh, hasten thither,
> No more let life divide what Death can join together.
>
>   (LI, LII, LIII)

Since Virgil's Tenth Eclogue, one of the most common ends for the pastoral elegy and its relatives is a return to the necessities of daily life, in particular, to the attending of the flocks. "But now the sun is driving his horses down from the height of the firmament, urging us to offer the river's water to our flocks."[6] "Tomorrow to fresh woods and pastures new." *In Memorian* ends with an epithalamium and an anticipation of the child of the future. But *Adonais* ends as "The massy earth and sphered skies are riven!" (LV), and no return is possible or desirable.

                .   .   .

An earthly consolation which we mentioned earlier but were unable to illustrate from the first thirty-seven stanzas of *Adonais* is material survival in Nature (a pretty thin consolation, but among the few available to a Swinburne or a Meredith). There is, nevertheless, some evidence of it in *Adonais* (however transformed) among the heavenly consolations. For, although Time may be at an end for Adonais, the One to which he returns is still involved in Time.

                .   .   .

But Adonais, in addition to Immortality in the One and participation in its difficult work on the dull or polished mirrors of Time (some-

[6]Nemesian, *Eclogue I*, in *The Pastoral Elegy*, ed., Harrison, p. 54.

thing which he shares with any other "portion of the Eternal") is also given another kind of earthly continuance in the images of Nature. A poet participates in such images in a way that has very little to do with Death and Immortality at all. If the voice of Keats is heard in the "song of night's sweet bird," it is presumably because he wrote the *Ode to a Nightingale* and thereby transformed Nature for the receptive reader. Nature imitates Art. In two senses Keats is

> a portion of the loveliness
> Which once he made more lovely.

 . . . In Shelley's Platonic framework the far goal of each man is death and reunion with the One, and the far goal of Time should be the destruction of Time: the apocalypse. The clogs should finally disappear and the Pavilion of Thought shine out in stainless perfection. I say "should," because, whereas the conception of an individual conquest of Time is omnipresent in Shelley's poetry, the conception of a final destruction of this enemy (more than simply a series of individual victories) is much less apparent.

.   .   .

This far goal of Time remains around the corner. When Adonais beckons to the mourners from his seat in Eternity, Shelley fancies himself embarking on the ocean, as "The massy earth and sphered skies are riven!" The voyage is his own, but the splitting of earth and sky is a foreshadowing of something beyond a private voyage, something which Shelley invokes rather hopelessly after the cyclical pessimism of Hellas has reached its climax:

> The world is weary of the past,
> O might it die or rest at last!

(1100–1)

But the death or rest of this world is never finally imagined in Shelley's poetry, if indeed it is "imaginable" at all in his terms. In Act Four of *Prometheus Unbound*, the Prometheans hack away at the depredations of Chaos and Time, but again the victory is piecemeal, and Demogorgon is still needed to warn as well as encourage. Man, who was once "a decay, / A traveller from the cradle to the grave" (IV. 550–51), has not said an irrevocable farewell to the journey.

At the end of *Adonais* we can imagine the mourners, headed by Shelley, waiting in single file for their own private apocalypses, but we do not see anything like the giant Albion awakening in Blake's *Jerusalem* when "Time was Finished,"[7] or the "sundering ultimate

[7] *Jerusalem*, Plate 94.

kingdom" into which the world of Dylan Thomas is consumed:

> Into the organpipes and steeples
> Of the luminous cathedrals,
> Into the weathercocks' molten mouths
> Rippling in twelve-winded circles,
> Into the dead clock burning the hour
> Over the urn of sabbaths
> Over the whirling ditch of daybreak
> Over the sun's hovel and the slum of fire
> And the golden pavements laid in requiems,
> Into the bread in a wheatfield of flames,
> Into the wine burning like brandy,
> The masses of the sea
> The masses of the sea under
> The masses of the infant-bearing sea
> Erupt, fountain, and enter to utter for ever
> Glory glory glory
> The sundering ultimate kingdom of genesis' thunder.[8]

[8]"Ceremony after a Fire Raid," in *Collected Poems, 1934–1952*, p. 131.

JOHN W. STEVENSON

The Pastoral Setting in the
Poetry of A. E. Housman*

An obvious comment on Housman is that he wrote in a
pastoral vein; it is more difficult to define the nature of his pastoralism
and its contribution to the peculiar and singular achievement of his
poetry. Critics have found it hard to explain the quality and texture of
his verse, praising him rather for his classical smoothness and restraint,
his clarity and succinctness, and his polish and lightness. None has
adequately explained the reason for his poetic success or defined the
quality which makes his poetry work. A great deal of his success seems
to lie in the manner in which he approached his subject matter, and
that manner most frequently was a studied pastoralism, a view of the
universe set in the English countryside.

While Housman's contemporaries were lamenting the plight of the
poet in society and expressing their frustration and their overrefined
theories of art in the precocious pages of *The Yellow Book,* his slim
volume of verse appeared (1896), revealing his brand of philosophic
pessimism; instead of a morbid and self-conscious nihilism or a highly
sophisticated cry of despair, he became Terence, the Shropshire lad,
and revealed his theme through the innocence of a convention long
out of use. The classical shepherds emerged as the lightfoot lads;
Phyllis and Corinna became the rose-lipt maidens. His own sophistication, his position as A. E. Housman, classical scholar, was submerged
and yet highly pointed in the guise of rustic innocence. Housman as a
modern pastoral poet adopted a highly artificial convention, a device

From *The South Atlantic Quarterly,* Vol. 55, 487–90, 492–500. Published, 1956, by
the Duke University Press. Reprinted by permission of the author and the publisher.

*The quotations are by permission from *The Collected Poems of A. E. Housman.*
New York: Holt, Rinehart & Winston, Inc., 1940.

that made his poetry successful where that of his equally sophisticated contemporaries failed. Thus there is a quality in Housman's poetry which has not hitherto been adequately analyzed or defined.

. . .

In so far as I can discover, Housman himself never said anything about the nature or function of the pastoral convention in the few writings he has left; but in the small published essay, *The Name and Nature of Poetry*, which he had previously given as the Leslie Stephen Lecture in May, 1933, he said two things about poetry which bear on a basic attitude in his pastoralism. In one place he writes, "Poetry is not the thing said but a way of saying it." Again, "Poetry indeed seems to me more physical than intellectual." I am not quite sure what Housman fully means by these two statements, but they indicate that language and setting are paramount requisites to poetry; they indicate also that there is an emotional response necessary in poetry at the expense of the rational.

Mr. Cleanth Brooks has noted that a reading of Housman's poetry reveals a not too ambitious or passionately held world view. "Intellectually," he writes, "he has not moved far past an austere scepticism; emotionally, one feels that he has a special and 'literary' interest" in the pageant of life. The result, Brooks adds, is that "the intellectual fabric is so slight that one feels that his impulse borders on the literary and his performance occasionally hovers on the verge of the sentimental." But this is to overstate the case, for it is in just this literary approach that Housman avoids sentimentality by relying on a setting outside of himself. There is a suggested analogy here to the same thing that Mr. Ransom found in Milton's adoption of the pastoral form: ". . . Milton as a Greek shepherd was delivered from being Milton the scrivener's son, the Master of Arts from Cambridge, the handsome and finicky young man. . . ." He adds that "performance is not rated by the rending of garments, heartbreak, verisimilitude of desolation. After all, an artist is standing before the public, and bears the character of a qualified spokesman, and a male. Let him somewhat loudly sweep the strings, even the tender human ones, but not without being almost military and superficial in his restraint. . . ." Whether or not Housman consciously adopted the pastoral form I do not know, but he did become Terence, an English rustic from Shropshire; as such he stood before his public as a qualified spokesman. Only in this way could his piercing intellect probe the superficiality and the unctuous morality of the waning Victorian age. The pastoral setting became then the basis of a studied irony, which became almost too painful when revealed by a country lad, but which would have become sentimental or overstated if revealed by a Cambridge don.

· · ·

The key word for pastoral is "simple." Empson defines it in one place as "simple people expressing strong feelings in learned and fashionable language"; in another, as "the praise of simplicity"; in a third, as "putting the complex into the simple." He defines the paradoxical essence of pastoral by suggesting that "the refined thing must be judged by the fundamental thing; strength must be learnt in weakness and sociability in isolation, the best manners are learnt in simple life." And in another place he writes: "If you choose an important member of a class the result is heroic; if you choose an unimportant one it is pastoral."

A complex of attitudes is implied here, but the essential meaning is a shift of emphasis, and the achievement is a tone of humility. Actually, the trick of the pastoral is a trick of irony; perhaps a better phrase is ironic revelation. Put in another way, it says: I see a man hanged, or a young man killed in war, or a lover deceived, or the indifference of time and the inexorableness of change, and I realize that society is basically vain and cruel, or that happiness is elusive, or that man is not really free, either from nature or from systems, and as a poet I must interpret and see into the crux of existence. How shall I say it? How shall I write it! Unfortunately, there are no final answers, but one answer seems to lie in adopting the pastoral mode; here there is an escape from the complex to the simple, and ironically the naïve man utters a naked truth which the complex man can only surround with a complicated dialectic or a high-sounding moral platitude. There is this further note of irony: the country lad probably does not realize his discovery, is really not interested in it and accepts it as the obvious. Thus, the poet achieves the tone of humility which is a quality of the pastoral; he imagines the feelings of the simple man, and the refined thing is judged by fundamentals; strength is learned in weakness. In a sense, then, the pastoral convention becomes a means for criticism, and the poet himself is able to stand apart; the poetry does the work, and that is the important thing.

I am quite sure that I have not defined pastoral, but something of what has been said applies to the poetry of Housman, and his poetry takes on new meaning when read in the light of this approach.

Empson makes a further observation which applies particularly to

Housman and in which the poet is able to reveal his basic theme through what Empson calls a "realistic sort of pastoral." The realistic pastoral, he writes, "gives a natural expression for a sense of social injustice. So far as the person described is outside society because too poor for its benefits he is independent, as the artist claims to be, and can be a critic of society; so far as he is forced by this into crime he is the judge of the society that judges him." To a degree, Empson suggests, he can stand as a symbol of Christ as the scapegoat and Christ as the sacrificial tragic hero.

The juxtaposition of the dual responsibility reveals here the essential irony that exists in the pastoral. It is perhaps through this convention that Housman reveals the unique paradox of history, the paradox of the Incarnation: the discovery of a spiritual truth in a physical form. Mr. Allen Tate, in his essay "The Symbolic Imagination," remarks that "all proximate incarnations of the Word are shocking. . . ." It was T. S. Eliot, he writes, who made available again to an ignorant generation the common Christian insight that people cannot bear very much reality, which he takes to mean "that only persons of extraordinary courage, and perhaps even genius, can face the spiritual truth in its physical body." That may be why, as Tate suggests, the artist, along with the soldier and the priest, faces death every day. I do not claim that all pastoral poetry does this; but Housman achieves this reality in a few of his poems, and part of the achievement lies in the manner with which he approached his subject matter. He said: "Poetry is not the thing said but a way of saying it." Let us see how he says it.

One reads Housman's poetry with a sense of discovery; it is more than an intellectual discovery. There is a physical meaning as well, and this is partly achieved by the simplicity of setting and the simplicity of language; the result is an aesthetic awareness that is only subtly revealed by a sort of delayed tension. As in Frost's poetry, there is a deceptive simplicity, and the irony, when realized, is pointed and real. This response grows out of the pastoral background which interfuses most of the poetry.

Perhaps the best example is the poem that stands next to last in *The Shropshire Lad* (LXII) and is sometimes given the title "Epilogue." The poem reflects Housman's own attitude towards poetry and illustrates his use of the pastoral. He addresses his remarks to Terence, a name which carries strong allusions to the traditional pastoral names, but which would hardly be associated with a simple Shropshire lad.

Housman usually names his rustics Dick or Fred or Ned, but in this instance the more classical name of Terence seems to be an identification of Housman himself. With this mask to hide behind, he achieves a double perspective; he can pretend to be something else and through a comic understatement reveal, almost with bitterness, the seriousness of his theme. Though Housman is concerned in the poem with the nature and function of poetry, he begins by affecting a boorish and ignorant attitude: "Terence, this is stupid stuff. . . ." As the poem progresses, we find that poetry is "not so brisk a brew as ale," for its intoxication brings another kind of "after-effect," one that is more permanent; instead of the hoped-for escape out of the world, it becomes an escape into the world, into the real:

> Ale, man, ale's the stuff to drink
> For fellows whom it hurts to think:
> Look into the pewter pot
> To see the world as the world's not . . .
> And down in lovely muck I've lain,
> Happy till I woke again.
> Then I saw the morning sky:
> Heigho, the tale was all a lie;
> I was I, my things were wet,
> And nothing now remained to do
> But begin the game anew.

This attitude is carried into the third stanza, where the language, although still simple and informal, changes in tone from one of comic bitterness to a more contemplative, wry humor:

> Therefore, since the world has still
> Much good, but much less good than ill,
> And while the sun and moon endure
> Luck's a chance, but trouble's sure,
> I'd face it as a wise man would,
> And train for ill and not for good.
> 'Tis true, the stuff I bring for sale
> Is not so brisk a brew as ale:
> Out of a stem that scored the hand
> I wrung it in a weary land.
> But take it: if the smack is sour,
> The better for the embittered hour;
> It should do good to heart and head
> When your soul is in my soul's stead;
> And I will friend you, if I may,
> In the dark and cloudy day.

In the passages quoted, Housman does two things intimately related to the pastoral setting: (1) he makes a unique analogy; that is, through the metaphor of ale he reveals two levels of physical awareness, both realistic, the one sensuous and the other spiritual; and (2) he seems to use a colloquial language, colloquial in the sense that the complex is made simple and the refined is judged by the fundamental; the real becomes felt through the wit of the Unconscious. The result is almost parody, for there results a clash between style and theme, but Housman saves himself from this charge by hiding behind Terence and thus gives the effect of not being conscious of what he is doing.

The poem would seem to say that intoxication is found in two ways: a man can be drunk on poetry, and he can be drunk on ale; Housman sees in the comparison a homely way to define a profound experience. There is a very neat relationship here; the man who comes under the effects of ale expands; he relaxes and becomes frank and easy, throwing off acquired poses, social restrictions, and the stiffness of propriety. In brief, he becomes himself; for once he is real and honest, and, paradoxically, the escape from what he thinks of as reality leads him to discover the real. Now, in a sense, the poet experiences the same elation; the intoxication of insight, or of aesthetic discovery, suspends him into the same realm of frankness and freedom of expression. He suddenly perceives reality and must disclose it to the discomfiture of some and to the delight of others. Both conditions produce a temporary madness, or what some might call simplemindedness; that is, the discovery of reality is sometimes so harsh and unpleasant, revealing as it often does man's vanity, avarice, and pride, that we refuse to listen to the drunk man or the poet, calling the one "fool" and the other "madman," laughing at both. Here the analogy stops, for the elation of the drunk man is produced from the outside and is irresponsible, leaving his "necktie God knows where" and only happy till he wakes again; but the poet's elation, coming from inside, has permanence; if you allow him, he can, when your soul is in his soul's stead, friend you "In the dark and cloudy day." For this reason poetry is harder to take; it demands suffering and moral courage; hence, in the purely sensual world it is only "stupid stuff," and ale is the "stuff" to drink, not the waters of Helicon, "For fellows whom it hurts to think."

Poetry, then, for Housman would seem to have the function of revelation, but man can perceive such an insight first by a physical response. Housman must have meant something like this because of the analogy between the two kinds of intoxication. He achieves it through his setting and language. The rustic responds always by his senses to experience; he is close to nature and is not deceived by a purely abstract refinement of what he lives closely with. Moreover, his language is simple and uncomplicated, not polished and rhetorical; he drinks ale or beer, not fine wines or bonded whiskey. Which is to say, that Housman is able through a pastoral setting and character to achieve a sort of synthesis of both levity and seriousness. This effect can be found in a number of his poems, such as

> Could man be drunk for ever
>   With liquor, love, or fights,
> Lief should I rouse at morning
>   And lief lie down of nights.
>
> But men at whiles are sober
>   And think by fits and starts,
> And if they think, they fasten
>   Their hands upon their hearts.
>
> *(Last Poems, X)*

or, in a more guarded context:

> Ho, everyone that thirsteth,
>   And hath the price to give,
> Come to the stolen waters,
>   Drink and your soul shall live.
>
> Come to the stolen waters,
>   And leap the guarded pale,
> And pull the flower in season
>   Before desire shall fail.
>
> It shall not last for ever,
>   No more than earth and skies;
> But he that drinks in season
>   Shall live before he dies.
>
> June suns, you cannot store them
>   To warm the winter's cold,
> The lad that hopes for heaven
>   Shall fill his mouth with mould.
>
> *(More Poems, XXII)*

Here again is the contrast between the sensual and what I call the poetical. The comic and the serious become blended in an ironic revelation. Perhaps a great deal of the success of this synthesis, or juxtaposition of two attitudes, lies in Housman's versification. On the surface, it is simple and rhythmical, easy to recall and memorize; but it is just this simplicity that deceives, for the ballad-like stanza or the rhymed couplets reveal, instead of a light-hearted gaiety or a lilting manner, a grim and sardonic humor. Herrick or Suckling or one of the Cavalier poets can write of love in a conventional and not too serious manner, using conventional forms and meters, such as in

> Gather ye rose buds while ye may,
>   Old time is still a-flying,
> And this same flower that smiles to-day,
>   To-morrow will be dying.

or,

> Out upon it! I have loved
>   Three whole days together;
> And am like to love three more,
>   If it prove fair weather.

And the result is sophisticated and light; we admire tremendously their restraint and pastoral masquerading. The rhythms are easy and smooth, the rhymes simple and uncomplicated. But Housman's wit is more searching in the pastoral vein, and his lovers are more conscious of reality:

> The half-moon westers low, my love,
>   And the wind brings up the rain;
> And wide apart lie we, my love,
>   And seas between the twain.
>
> I know not if it rains, my love
>   In the land where you do lie;
> And oh, so sound you sleep, my love,
>   You know no more than I.
>
> (Last Poems, XXVI)

Here is a rather grim irony, and I suspect that Housman resorts to the pastoral form, not essentially as a city man merely escaping into the country in search of an idyllic setting; rather, he resorts to the form as an escape from the conventional to the real. That is, the language and the setting, unaffected and unsophisticated, produce the physical effect that the poetic revelations sense. Housman's shepherds (lads), and therefore Housman himself, insist upon a basic honesty that is naïve and "generous because free from hypocrisy," as Empson contends, as one of the assumptions of pastoral; this is the effect found in

Oh stay at home, my lad, and plough
  The land and not the sea,
And leave the soldiers at their drill,
And all about the idle hill
  Shepherd your sheep with me.

Oh stay with company and mirth
  And daylight and the air;
Too full already is the grave
Of fellows that were good and brave
  And died because they were.

               (*Last Poems*, XXXVIII)

Almost, then, Housman's manner of expressing his theme becomes the thing by which we are made to feel the paradox which hurts the heart. Ironically, the pastoral form is made to stand for a criticism of life, for, even though we know that "Dick would hate the cold," we know that he would accept it with endurance and that suffering is the only condition for salvation:

The night is freezing fast,
  Tomorrow comes December;
    And winterfalls of old
Are with me from the past;
  And chiefly I remember
    How Dick would hate the cold.

Fall, winter, fall; for he,
  Prompt hand and headpiece clever,
    Has woven a winter robe,
And made of earth and sea
  His overcoat for ever,
    And wears the turning globe.

               (*Last Poems*, XX)

It might be added that Housman's poetry wears the turning globe; it reflects an aesthetic and a physical reaction to a world of reality, which he observes critically, and for which he feels a tough sympathy. Like a rough tweed, he gathers about him "his mantle blue" and sets his poetry in a realistic pastoral. Certainly there is no vision of "fresh woods, and pastures new," but his world view is compounded of a clash between style and theme in which the complex world is viewed from the simple world. Part of his success in writing poetry lies in the manner in which he approached his subject matter, and he seems to have found in the Shropshire countryside a setting and a character which gave meaning and irony to his rather grim combination of levity and seriousness. But Housman's people are not court people masquerading as rustics; they are rustics commenting with honesty and without fear on the transitory nature of man's three score years and ten. In this lies the difference: whereas on the surface a conventional form seems to be used, there is nothing artificial here. An affected and disciplined simplicity results in a modern pastoral which becomes more real and more subtle than the earlier practice. It is the basis of Housman's success, the basis on which almost all of his poetry is built.

JOHN F. LYNEN

New Hampshire and Arcadia

The claim that Frost is a pastoral poet may not appear surprising to many readers, for since the beginning of his literary career commentators have spoken of his verse in terms of pastoralism. In an important early review Lascelles Abercrombie wrote:

> Poetry in Mr. Frost exhibits almost the identical desires and impulses we see in the "bucolic" poems of Theocritus. Nothing so futile as a comparison of personal talents is meant by this; but for general motives, the comparison is true and very suggestive. Poetry, in this book [*North of Boston*], seems determined, once more, just as it was in Alexandria, to invigorate itself by utilizing the traits and necessities of common life, the habits of common speech, the minds and hearts of common folk.[1]

The same idea has often been echoed by other writers, and it is now not unusual to hear Frost casually referred to as a pastoral poet and his poems likened to eclogues.

·   ·   ·

That Frost's dominant mode is pastoral may at first seem doubtful, because the conventions so characteristic of this genre are not to be found in his verse. The unhappy shepherd, the fair shepherdess, the wandering flock, the daisies and violets, the greensward dance, the flowery wreath and oaten pipe represent a cluster of motifs which can be traced in the tradition from Theocritus to Pope and beyond into the nineteenth century. So prominent are the conventions that one may suppose they are an essential element of pastoral form. Part of the pleasure which the old pastorals offer is that of recognizing the familiar images as they appear, just as another part consists in noting how

From *Ths Pastoral Art of Robert Frost*, by John F. Lynen, pp. 8, 13–14, 17–23, 58–61, 64–66, 77. Published, 1960, by Yale University Press. Copyright © 1960 by Yale University Press. Reprinted by permission of the publisher.

[1]Review of *North of Boston*, in *Recognition of Robert Frost*, Richard Thornton, ed. (New York: Holt, Rinehart & Winston, Inc., 1937), p. 28.

skillfully the poet handles the traditional devices of dialogue, singing contest, and lament.

Frost stands outside of this tradition, and to understand his pastoralism we must recognize that the conventions, while typical of the genre, are not a necessary part of its poetic structure. Pastoralism, as the term is generally used, signifies two related but not identical things. It refers to a particular group of poems forming a distinct tradition and also to a kind of poetry possessing a certain fundamental form. The two meanings are inextricably bound together in the public mind, because it is assumed that only the works in line of descent from Theocritus are true instances of the genre. This identifying of the genre with the tradition results from the belief that the conventions are the very core of pastoral. A moment's reflection, however, will show us that this is not so. Consider the many poems which make use of the conventional machinery but are quite different from pastoral. Wordsworth's "Immortality Ode" and Arnold's "Thyrsis" are two clear instances. In the great ode Wordsworth does no more than suggest a parallel with pastoral, while his "Michael," which (beyond the protagonist's occupation as a shepherd) contains nothing conventional, is a genuine eclogue. The pastoral images of "Thyrsis" seem curios brought home from a literary excursion, and although Arnold often reverts to them as if by an effort of will, their main function is to serve as points of departure into lush passages of nature poetry. The conventions are not the true basis of pastoral, but an outgrowth of something deeper and more fundamental. Pastoralism requires an established myth of the rural world, and the conventions gradually developed through tradition belong to the myth of Arcadia. They are formalized symbols whose function is to evoke an imaginative vision of this world. But Arcadia is not the only version of rural life, and it is possible for a poet to write true pastorals within the context of some other mythic rural world.

.   .   .

In studying Frost's pastoralism we must recognize that it is an art which did not and could not have developed within the old framework.[2]

[2]It is true that Frost has on several occasions made use of the conventions of traditional pastoralism. The parallel between "Build Soil—A Political Pastoral" and Virgil's first eclogue and the probable influence of Virgil's eclogues upon Frost are treated in Chapter IV, p. 127. A little lyric reminiscent of the cavalier poets is entitled "The Peaceful Shepherd," and "Beech," which stands as the epigraph to *A Witness Tree*, is signed "The Moodie Forester," apparently in imitation of pastoral ballads of the Renaissance. On one occasion, Frost showed me a large, illustrated edition of Herrick, which he said was a favorite book of his during childhood. Here and there one suspects the influence of Herrick, especially in little poems about flowers such as "The Telephone."

As a matter of fact, one of Frost's earliest poems shows very clearly how remote the conventions of pastoral were from his own interest. In "Pan with Us" he uses the imagery of Arcadia to symbolize all the genteel poetic styles which were dying out during the period of his literary apprenticeship. In despair, Pan throws away his oaten pipes:

> They were pipes of pagan mirth,
> And the world had found new terms of worth.
> He laid him down on the sun-burned earth
>   And raveled a flower and looked away—
>   Play? Play?—What should he play?

The question posed in these lines is directly relevant to his own verse. If the pastoral tradition had long since lost its validity, how was he to write a poetry essentially pastoral? The answer to this question becomes apparent when one recalls the distinction between pastoralism as a kind of poetic structure and pastoralism in the narrower sense of a particular tradition. It was the tradition that had withered; the fundamental form remained as a potential. Occasionally this potential was realized, notably in the work of Burns, and in Wordsworth's "Michael" and a few of his short lyrics. Frost's achievement as a pastoral poet, like Burns' and Wordsworth's, is a distinctly individual triumph. It has resulted from his discovery of a new and realistic basis for examining the rural scene within the structure of pastoral.

To say this is to say that Frost discovered a new myth of rural life. When he wrote the lines quoted above he had not yet arrived at this; and I do not mean to suggest that the discovery was a conscious, reasoned one. As a poet Frost matured late; his early verse reveals a constant searching for an idiom and a subject. From the beginning his instincts drew him towards rural subjects, but in the long period of experiment we find him writing of these in an elegant manner reminiscent of late Victorian nature poetry. Only when he learned to adopt the perspective of pastoral and wrote from the point of view of an actual New England farmer did he come into his own as an artist. The change was a sudden one; it occurred when his imagination grasped the poetic possibilities of the region he knew so well, when, by leaving home for a brief sojourn in old England, he came to see in the life of rural New England a remote, ideal world which could serve the same function as Arcadia. . . .

Frost, like the writers of old pastoral, draws upon our feeling that the rural world is representative of human life in general. By working from this nodal idea he is able to develop in his poems a very broad range of reference without ever seeming to depart from particular matters of fact. . . . If the country is to become the microcosm of the great world it must be pictured as a little world in itself, one which is separate from the realm of ordinary experience even though, in another sense, it displays the familiar reality. It is, then, by making his Arcadia remote that the pastoral poet transforms it into a symbolic world. And since the rustic scene in its entirety is taken as representative of all other levels of being, the things that belong to it—the shepherds and farmers, their tasks, amusements, and concerns, the simple objects familiar to them and the scenic aspects of their surroundings—are all infused with symbolic suggestions.

It is just such a perspective and such a method of pastoral contrast that gives the simple scenes and episodes Frost describes their extraordinary breadth of reference. When one considers his Yankee poems, one begins to notice a number of fundamental similarities between them and the old pastorals. His New England, like Arcadia, is a distinct plane of existence portrayed in such a way that a comparison with the outer world is always strongly implied. It is isolated from ordinary experience, a society with its own folkways, customs, and ideals, a locality with its own distinctive landscape. Like the old pastoralists, he emphasizes the uniqueness of his rural world. It is an agrarian society isolated within an urbanized world, and its country folk are separated from the modern reading public by a gulf of social, cultural, and economic differences nearly as broad as that dividing the swain of the old pastoral from the courtly reader. . . .

Frost's method as pastoral poet is nicely illustrated by one of his most familiar lyrics, "The Pasture." This poem is of particular interest in that the poet has for many years used it as the epigraph for editions of his collected verse, a fact which suggests that he regards it as a symbol of the kind of poetry he writes. "The Pasture" may at first appear very simple indeed, since the materials of which it is composed are so slight. It seems merely to describe a few casual details of farm life which the poet sees in going about his tasks. But as in "Stopping by Woods," the bits of description somehow cohere to form a pattern which expresses a much broader meaning than is overtly stated. It is important to note that the poem is an invitation: the poet invites someone, perhaps a person he loves, perhaps just a friend, to come with him and see the glimpses of delicate beauty to be found in the pasture. The implication is that the person invited knows little of such things. More important, he will have to be initiated into the special way of looking at them which makes them precious and meaningful. The leaves floating in the pasture spring, the little calf, so young it totters when its mother licks it, have the simplicity and innocence of pristine reality, and the poem implies that the average person, like the person invited, could not see the beauty in such natural, everyday things without the poet as guide. To appreciate these, he will have to abandon knowledge as the great world understands it and learn to adopt the poet's special way of seeing.

The poet's invitation is really to a kind of vision, and this vision is to be understood through its implicit difference from the common view of reality. But the invitation is also to a place, the pasture itself, for only within the humble, out-of-the-way rural world is this special mode of perception possible. The pasture, then, is both the subject of the vision and its perspective; the mode of perception is embodied in the images themselves. For all its sweetness the poem is not tainted by sentimentality, because while it describes the charming aspects of the pasture, it is concerned less with beauty for its own sake than with the organic wholeness which makes this beauty meaningful. Frost's theme here is the coherence of the rural scene, the unity between the things observed and the way of seeing, between objects and thought, between man's work—the speaker of the poem must clean the spring and fetch the young calf—and his aesthetic experience. This unity raises the world of the pasture above other realms of human life by showing it as an ordered world where the significance of things is simple and apparent. This is manifest in the symbols themselves: the spring and the calf represent the source, the simple, pure, innocent beginnings of things.

Yet the special value of this world is paradoxical in that the pasture embodies a humble and naïve level of being. The reader is to admire the pasture as a world better than his own because it is more natural, more neatly organized, and more meaningful, but he is also aware that it is a plane of existence inferior in many respects to that on which he lives. The contrast between the country and the town which we have noted in pastoral is clearly the essential element in the design of this poem. By making the rural scene remote from ordinary life and by implying that to understand it we must learn to adopt its special perspective, Frost establishes a comparison between the pasture and the outside world. It is from this implied comparison that the poem's elusive symbolism grows. The calf and the pasture spring emerge as symbols because they exist within a world which is viewed in its relation to other places and other modes of experience.

. . .

The same fundamental contrast underlies both regionalism and pastoral, but regional art only becomes pastoral when the contrast is properly exploited. Not many writers have succeeded in turning local materials to the purpose of pastoral; Burns, Wordsworth, Hardy, and Faulkner are the most notable exceptions. The great bulk of regional writing is second or third rate, because it consists only in a sentimental picturing of local color. Instead of taking the contrast seriously, instead of projecting themselves into the local scene and viewing experience through the eyes of the swain, most regionalists look down from above—from Lowell's comfortable study, for instance—and from there local differences only seem charming, comic, and peculiar. Such writers are concerned merely with the difference between the local and the cosmopolitan, and this, in itself, has little interest or meaning.

Frost, on the other hand, does take the contrast at full value, because he has discovered what the local colorists missed, *that differences can be used as a means of revealing similarities.* He has learned that to make a picture of regional life true, in the deepest sense, one must not seek the unique traits of a place for their own sake, but must use these traits in such a way that they become symbols of what is universal. The aim is not to picture an unusual place, but to develop the image of the region as a world which somehow represents all other places. The basis of his achievement as a regional poet is this: that the very things which seem most unique to New England are the materials with which he suggests realities present on every level of experience.

The process is paradoxical. The more he emphasizes local differences, the more he isolates New England, sets it apart, as it were, from the rest of the universe. Yet it is this isolation which makes his New England symbolic. Only because it *is* set apart does the region cease to be merely a place, one of many places, and become a microcosm within which the great world beyond is mirrored. By constantly showing that the Yankee farmers who inhabit it think in a different and more subtle way, live by a different and more admirable ethic, Frost directs the reader's mind to compare this world with our own, to look for parallels, to see in the images presented veiled references to other things.

Clearly, the success of this method depends upon the poet's skill in discriminating. It is not just a matter of making the regional world as different as possible. Not every local trait, however typical, will serve his purposes. As a matter of fact, Frost has quite rightly rejected much of popular Yankee lore. Nothing would have been more damaging to his poetry than sentimentalized Christmas card scenery and the bric-a-brac of antique shops. The local materials must be so selected that they blend into a unified picture; they must seem to be parts of a single world.

There is, then, a high decorum controlling Frost's choice. This is something very elusive, since it is not based upon any set of conscious principles, but consists, rather, in a sense of fitness, a feeling on the poet's part for harmony between certain visual images, actions, traits of character, attitudes, and the voice tones that express them. Decorum is always hard to explain, but we can get some understanding of Frost's by noting two dominant ideas which seem to be constantly at the back of his mind. The first is that of a strong connection between the individual mind and the land itself. This is the aspect of his poetry which derives most directly from the Romantics. It is from them—most especially from Wordsworth—that he learned the technique of associating aspects of landscape and psychological traits. The clear, frank gaze of the Yankee *persona* is related to the chill air of New England and his strength of mind to its rugged terrain in the same subtle way that Michael's courage and dignity are related to the grandeur of the Lake Country mountains.

The second dominant idea is related to this. Since the Yankee mind reflects the landscape, the whole sense of values which forms the center of this mentality seems to have an organic relation to the land. This sense of values is present in every one of Frost's Yankee characters. It is something above their individuality, something which transcends personal traits while never veiling them. For lack of a better term, I shall call it a regional ethic. Nothing so simple as "morals" is meant. The regional ethic includes a code, but it also includes certain ways of thinking and a set of ideals which are more philosophic than moral— for example a special respect for the individual's rights, or particular attitudes towards work. To describe this ethic in terms of the familiar names for virtue—honesty, sincerity, industry, and the rest—is not helpful, since this only isolates the elements, whereas the ethic's validity and interest result from its inclusiveness, from the way it synthesizes the moral with the intellectual, the practical with the ideal, the human and psychological with the natural and physical. And this, after all, is one of the main objectives of Frost's regionalism. It presents values as an integral part of a way of life—not as abstractions, but as extensions into the mind of physical necessities.

.   .   .

The way in which he has shaped New England as a pastoral myth is shown most clearly in "New Hampshire." . . . New Hampshire, as everyone knows, is a poor state without natural resources, economic power, or political influence, so that Frost must somehow circumvent the danger—and it is a real one for every regionalist—that his humble subject will seem only humble and so dispose the reader to take a patronizing attitude quite hostile to the poem's purposes. Thus the theme of the spiritual superiority which results from poverty comes readily to his hand. He can seem to ridicule New Hampshire while actually ennobling it through comparison with the absurd materialism of other regions. There is, then, a serious intent in these comic sketches. Playfully and casually, he develops the image of New Hampshire as a world set apart from ordinary experience, a place where men live by a higher sense of values.

What starts as merely comic implication soon expands to a definition of the New England spirit. One senses that New Hampshire, by its very barrenness, offers a purer way of life and fosters a finer response to experience. . . . What Frost is doing here, of course, is to transform New Hampshire into a realm of ideals. He presents it as a rarefied level of existence where, in place of a confusing plenty, there is an order of representative things, spare and almost insubstantial. . . . We are made to see New Hampshire as a place where everything is somewhat typical. The lack of material wealth serves to reveal the essential nature of things and suggests the interdependence of substance and form. In this world—just because it is poor and remote from the materialism of modern life—objects become the prototypes of ideas.

.   .   .

"Me for the hills," far from being an anguished call to retreat, is the option for a more penetrating exploration of reality. Of course, there is implicit in it too the idea of withdrawal. At the end Frost is more than a little complacent at the thought that in New Hampshire the poet's mind is freed from the distractions of a more complicated world. It is, as he says, "a most restful state." But one should remember that he is playing upon a major theme of pastoral, present in the classical eclogues and reinforced in the Renaissance by the authority of Christian asceticism: the idea that retreat to the rural world purifies the mind and thus brings it closer to ultimate truth. And indeed, the very form of the poem embodies this theme. The poet casts himself as the folksy rural sage, just as the courtier in the old pastoral took on the guise of the shepherd. His casual speaking manner, which digresses at every turning into anecdote and whimsical speculation, creates the illusion that the poem is just a specimen of back-parlor conversation. But as it turns out, his random comments prove to be the medium for dealing with matters which are very serious indeed. . . .

ERICH AUERBACH

The Knight Sets Forth

Near the beginning of Chrétien de Troyes' *Yvain*, a courtly
romance of the second half of the twelfth century, one of the knights of
King Arthur's court relates an adventure which once befell him.

.   .   .

Calogrenant tells King Arthur's Round Table that, seven years
earlier, he had ridden away alone in quest of adventure, armed as
befits a knight, and he had come upon a road leading to the right,
straight through a dense forest. Here we stop and wonder. To the
right? That is a strange indication of locality when, as in this case, it
is used absolutely. In terms of terrestrial topography it makes sense
only when used relatively. Hence it must here have an ethical signi-
fication. Apparently it is the "right way" which Calogrenant discovered. And that is confirmed immediately, for the road is arduous,
as right ways are wont to be; all day long it leads through a dense
forest full of brambles and thickets, and at night it reaches the right
goal: a castle where Calogrenant is received with delight, as though he
were a long-awaited guest. It is only at night, it seems, as he rides out
of the forest, that he discovers where he is: on a heath in Broceliande.
Broceliande in Armorica, on the continent, is a fairyland well known
in Breton legend, with a magic spring and an enchanted forest. How
Calogrenant—who presumably started out from King Arthur's court on
the Island of Britain—managed to get to continental Brittany is not
explained. We hear nothing of a crossing of the sea, as we hear nothing
of it later (ll. 760ff.) in Yvain's case, who in turn undoubtedly sets out
from Carduel in Wales although his journey to the "right road" in
Broceliande is described in vague and legendary terms. No sooner does

Calogrenant discover where he is, than he sees a hospitable castle. On the bridge stands the lord of the castle, with a hunting falcon on his fist, welcoming him with a delight which goes far beyond the expression of ready hospitality, and which once again assures us that we have been hearing about a "right way": *et il me dist tot maintenant plus de çant fois an un tenant, que beneoite fust la voie, par ou leanz venuz estoie.* The subsequent phases of his welcome follow the knightly ceremonial whose graceful forms seem to have long been established; striking three times upon a copper plate, the host summons his servants; the traveler's horse is led away; a beautiful maiden appears, who is the daughter of the lord of the castle; it is her duty to relieve the guest of his armor, to replace it by a comfortable and beautiful coat, and then, alone with him in a charming garden, to keep him pleasant company until supper is ready. After the meal the lord of the castle informs his guest that he has been receiving knights errant in pursuit of adventure for a very long time; he urges him to visit the castle again on his way back; strangely enough he tells him nothing about the adventure of the spring, although he knows about it and although he is well aware that the dangers which await his guest there will in all probability prevent his contemplated return. But that seems to be quite as it should be; at any rate it in no wise reduces the meed of praise which Calogrenant and, later, Yvain bestow upon their host's hospitality and knightly virtues. So Calogrenant rides away in the morning, and it is not until he meets the satyrlike *vilain* that he hears of the magic spring. This *vilain* of course has no idea of what *avanture* is—how could he, not being a knight?—but he knows the magic qualities of the spring, and he makes no secret of his knowledge.

Obviously we are now deep in fairy tale and magic. The right road through the forest full of brambles, the castle which seems to have sprung out of the ground, the nature of the hero's reception, the beautiful maiden, the strange silence of the lord of the castle, the satyr, the magic spring—it is all in the atmosphere of fairy tale. And the indications of time are as reminiscent of fairy tale as the indications of place. Calogrenant has kept quiet about his adventure for seven years. Seven is a fairy-tale number, and the seven years mentioned at the beginning of the *Chanson de Roland* likewise impart a touch of the legendary: seven years—*set anz tuz plerins*—is the time the Emperor Charles had spent in Spain. However, in the *Chanson de Roland* they are really "full" years; they are *tuz pleins*, because the Emperor used them to subdue the entire land down to the sea and to take all its castles and cities except Saragossa. In the seven years between Calogrenant's adventure at the spring and the time of his narration, on the other hand, nothing seems to have happened or at least we are told nothing about it. When Yvain sets off on the same adventure he finds everything exactly as Calogrenant had described it: the lord of the castle, the maiden, the bulls with their horribly ugly giant of a herdsman, the magic spring, and the knight who defends it. Nothing has changed; the seven years have passed without leaving a trace, just as time usually does in a fairy tale. The landscape is the enchanted landscape of fairy tale; we are surrounded by mystery, by secret murmurings and whispers. All the numerous castles and palaces, the battles and adventures, of the courtly romances—especially of the Breton cycle—are things of fairyland: each time they appear before us as though sprung from the ground; their geographical relation to the known world, their sociological and economic foundations, remain unexplained. Even their ethical or symbolic significance can rarely be ascertained with anything approaching certainty. Has the adventure at the spring any hidden meaning? It is evidently one of those which the Knights of the Round Table are bound to undergo, yet an ethical justification for the combat with the knight of the magic spring is nowhere given. In other episodes of the courtly romances it is sometimes possible to make out symbolic, mythological, or religious motifs; for instance, the journey to the underworld in *Lancelot*, the motif of liberation and redemption in numerous instances, and especially the theme of Christian grace in the Grail legend—but it is rarely possible to define the meaning precisely, at least so long as the courtly romance remains true to type. It is from Breton folklore that the courtly romance took its elements of mystery, of something sprung from the soil, concealing its roots, and inaccessible to rational explanation; it incorporated them and made use of them in its elaboration of the knightly ideal; the *matière de Bretagne* apparently proved to be the most suitable medium for the cultivation of that ideal—more suitable even than the stuff of antiquity, which was taken up at about the same time but which soon lost ground.

A self-portrayal of feudal knighthood with its mores and ideals is the fundamental purpose of the courtly romance. Nor are its exterior forms of life neglected—they are portrayed in leisurely fashion, and on these occasions the portrayal abandons the nebulous distance of fairy tale and gives salient pictures of contemporary conditions. Other episodes in courtly romance convey much more colorful and detailed pictures of this sort than our passage does; but even our passage permits us to observe the essential features which indicate its realistic character. The lord of the castle with his falcon; the summoning of the servants by striking a copper plate; the beautiful young mistress of the castle, relieving the visitor of his armor, wrapping him in a comfortable cloak, and entertaining him most pleasantly until supper is served—all these are graceful vignettes of established custom, one might say of a ritual which shows us courtly society in its setting of highly developed conventionality. The setting is as fixed and isolating, as distinct from the mores of other strata of society, as is that of the *chanson de geste*, but it is much more refined and elegant. Women play an important part in it; the mannerly ease and comfort of the social life of a cultured class have been attained. And indeed it has assumed a nature which is long to remain one of the most distinctive characteristics of French taste: graceful amenity with almost an excess of subtlety. The scene with the young lady of the castle—her appearance, his way of looking at her, the removal of his armor, the conversation in the meadow— though it is not a particularly developed example, yet sufficiently conveys the impression of that delicately graceful, limpid and smiling, fresh and elegantly naïve coquetry of which Chrétien in particular is a past master. Genre scenes of this sort are found in French literature very early—in the *chansons de toile* and once even in the *Chanson de Roland*, in the laisse which tells of Margariz of Seville (ll. 955ff.); but their full development was a contribution of courtly society, and Chétien's great charm especially is in no small measure due to his gift for carrying on this tone in the most varied fashion. We find the style in its greatest brilliance where the subject matter is the dalliance of true love. Between these scenes of dalliance come antithetical reasonings over the emotions involved, seemingly naïve yet of accomplished artistry and grace. The most celebrated example occurs at the beginning of the *Cligès*, where the budding love between Alixandre and Soredamors—with its initial reticence and mutual hide-and-seek and the ultimate welling up of emotions—is represented in a series of enchanting scenes and analytical soliloquies.

The grace and attractiveness of this style—whose charm is freshness and whose danger is silly coquetry, trifling, and coldness—can hardly be found in such purity anywhere in the literature of antiquity. Chrétien did not learn it from Ovid; it is a creation of the French Middle Ages. It must be noted, furthermore, that this style is by no means restricted to love episodes. In Chrétien, and also in the later romance of adventure and the shorter verse narrative, the entire portrayal of life within feudal society is tuned to the same note, not only in the twelfth but also in the thirteenth century. In charmingly graceful, delicately painted, and crystalline verses, knightly society offers its own presentment; thousands of little scenes and pictures describe its habits, its views, and its social tone for us. There is a great deal of brilliance, of realistic flavor, of psychological refinement, and also a great deal of humor in these pictures. It is a much richer, more varied, and more comprehensive world than the world of the *chansons de geste*, although it too is only the world of a single class. At times indeed Chrétien seems to break through this class confinement, as in the workroom of the three hundred women in the Chastel de Pesme Avanture (*Yvain*, 5107ff.) or in the description of the wealthy town whose citizens (*quemune*) attempt to storm the castle where Gauvain is quartered (*Perceval*, 5710ff.)—but such episodes are after all only a colorful setting for the life of the knight. Courtly realism offers a very rich and pungent picture of the life of a single class, a social stratum which remains aloof from the other strata of contemporary society, allowing them to appear as accessories, sometimes colorful but more usually comic or grotesque; so that the distinction in terms of class between the important, the meaningful, and the sublime on the one hand and the low-grotesque-comic on the other, remains strictly intact in regard to subject matter. The former realm is open only to members of the feudal class. Yet a real separation of styles is not in question here, for the simple reason that the courtly romance does not know an "elevated style," that is, a distinction between levels of expression. The easy-going, adroit, and elastic rhymed octosyllable effortlessly adapts itself to any subject and any level of emotion or thought. Did it not elsewhere serve the most varied ends, from farce to saint's legend? When it treats very serious or terrible themes, it is apt— at least to our way of feeling—to fall into a certain touching naïveté and childishness. And indeed, there is the courage of a child in the freshness of outlook which undertook—with the sole tool of a literary language so young that it had no ballast of theory, had not yet emerged from the confusion of dialectical forms—to master a life which had, after all, attained a considerable degree of differentiation. The problem of levels of style is not consciously conceived in the vernaculars until much later, that is, from the time of Dante.

But an even stronger limitation than that in terms of class results for the realism of the courtly romance from its legendary, fairy-tale atmosphere. It is this which makes all the colorful and vivid pictures of contemporary reality seem, as it were, to have sprung from the ground : the ground of legend and fairy tale, so that—as we said before—they are entirely without any basis in political reality. The geographical, economic, and social conditions on which they depend are never explained. They descend directly from fairy tale and adventure. The strikingly realistic workroom in *Yvain,* which I mentioned earlier, and in which we even find discussions of such things as working conditions and workers' compensation, was not established because of concrete economic conditions but because the young king of the Island of Maidens had fallen into the hands of two evil gnomelike brothers and ransomed himself by promising that once a year he would deliver to them thirty of his maidens to perform labor. The fairy-tale atmosphere is the true element of the courtly romance, which after all is not only interested in portraying external living conditions in the feudal society of the closing years of the twelfth century but also and especially in expressing its ideals. And with that we reach the very core of courtly romance, insofar as its particular ethos came to be important in the history of the literary treatment of reality.

Calogrenant sets out without mission or office; he seeks adventure, that is, perilous encounters by which he can prove his mettle. There is nothing like this in the *chanson de geste.* There a knight who sets off has an office and a place in a politico-historical context. It is doubtless simplified and distorted in the manner of legend, but it is maintained insofar as the characters who take part in the action have a function in the real world—for instance, the defense of Charles's realm against the infidels, their conquest and conversion, and so forth. Such are the political and historical purposes served by the feudal ethos, the warriors' ethos which the knights profess. Calogrenant, on the other hand, has no political or historical task, nor has any other knight of Arthur's court. Here the feudal ethos serves no political function; it serves no practical reality at all; it has become absolute. It no longer has any purpose but that of self-realization. This changes its nature completely. Even the term which we find for it in the *Chanson de Roland* most frequently and in the most general acceptation—the term *vasselage*—seems gradually to drop out of fashion. Chrétien uses it three times in *Erec,* in *Cligès* and *Lancelot* it occurs in one passage each, and after that not at all. The new term which he now prefers is *corteisie,* a word whose long and significant history supplies the most complete interpretation of the ideal concept of class and man in Europe. In the *Chanson de Roland* this word does not yet occur. Only the adjective *curteis* appears three times, twice in reference to Olivier in the combination *li proz e li courteis*. It would seem that *corteisie* achieved its synthetic meaning only in the age of chivalry or courtly culture, which indeed derives the latter name from it. The values expressed in it—refinement of the laws of combat, courteous social intercourse, service of women— have undergone a striking process of change and sublimation in comparison with the *chanson de geste* and are all directed toward a personal and absolute ideal—absolute both in reference to ideal realization and in reference to the absence of any earthly and practical purpose. The personal element in the courtly virtues is not simply a gift of nature; nor is it acquired by birth; to implant them now requires, besides birth, proper training too, as preserving them requires the unforced will to renew them by constant and tireless practice and proving.

The means by which they are proved and preserved is adventure, *avanture*, a very characteristic form of activity developed by courtly culture. Of course, fanciful depiction of the miracles and dangers awaiting those whom their destiny takes beyond the confines of the familiar world into distant and unexplored regions had long been known, as well as no less imaginative ideas and narratives about the mysterious perils which also threaten man within the geographically familiar world, from the influence of gods, spirits, demons, and other magic powers; so too the fearless hero who, by strength, virture, cunning, and the help of God, overcomes such dangers and frees others from them was known long before the age of courtly culture. But that an entire class, in the heyday of its contemporary flowering, should regard the surmounting of such perils as its true mission—in the ideal conception of things as its exclusive mission; that the most various legendary traditions, especially but not only those of the Breton cycle, are taken over by it for the purpose of producing a chivalrous world of magic especially designed for the purpose, in which fantastic encounters and perils present themselves to the knight as if from the end of an assembly-line—this state of affairs is a new creation of the courtly romance. Although these perilous encounters called *avantures* now have no experiential basis whatever, although it is impossible to fit them into any actual or practically conceivable political system, although they commonly crop up without any rational connection, one after the other, in a long series, we must be careful not to be misled by the modern value of the term adventure, to think of them as purely "accidental." When we moderns speak of adventure, we mean something unstable, peripheral, disordered, or, as Simmel once put it, a something that stands outside the real meaning of existence. All this is precisely what the word does not mean in the courtly romance. On the contrary, trial through adventure is the real meaning of the knight's ideal existence. That the very essence of the knight's ideal of manhood is called forth by adventure, E. Eberwein undertook to show some years since with reference to the *Lais* of Marie de France[1] It can also be demonstrated on the basis of the courtly romance.

.   .   .

The world of knightly proving is a world of adventure. It not only contains a practically uninterrupted series of adventures; more specifically, it contains nothing but the requisites of adventure. Nothing is found in it which is not either accessory or preparatory to an adventure. It is a world specifically created and designed to give the knight opportunity to prove himself. The scene of Calogrenant's departure shows this most clearly. He rides on all day and encounters nothing but the castle prepared to receive him. Nothing is said about all the practical conditions and circumstances necessary to render the existence of such a castle in absolute solitude both possible and compatible with ordinary experience. Such idealization takes us very far from the imitation of reality. In the courtly romance the functional, the historically real aspects of class are passed over. Though it offers a great many culturally significant details concerning the customs of social intercourse and external social forms and conventions in general, we can get no penetrating view of contemporary reality from it, even in respect to the knightly class. Where it depicts reality, it depicts merely the colorful surface, and where it is not superficial, it has other subjects and other ends than contemporary reality. Yet it does contain a class ethics which as such claimed and indeed attained acceptance and validity in this real and earthly world. For it has a great power of attraction which, if I mistake not, is due especially to two characteristics which distinguish it: it is absolute, raised above all earthly contingencies, and it gives those who submit to its dictates the feeling that they belong to a community of the elect, a circle of solidarity (the term comes from Hellmut Ritter, the Orientalist) set apart from the common herd. The ethics of feudalism, the ideal conception of the perfect knight, thus attained a very considerable and very long-lived influence. Concepts associated with it—courage, honor, loyalty, mutual respect, refined manners, service to women—continued to cast their spell on the contemporaries of completely changed cultural

[1] *Zur Deutung mittelalterlicher Existenz* (Bonn and Cologne: 1933), pp. 27ff.

periods. Social strata of later urban and bourgeois provenance adopted this ideal, although it is not only class-conditioned and exclusive but also completely devoid of reality. As soon as it transcends the sphere of mere conventions of intercourse and has to do with the practical business of the world, it proves inadequate and needs to be supplemented, often in a manner most unpleasantly in contrast to it. But precisely because it is so removed from reality, it could—as an ideal—adapt itself to any and every situation, at least as long as there were ruling classes at all.

So it came to pass that the knightly ideal survived all the catastrophes which befell feudalism in the course of the centuries. It survived even Cervantes' *Don Quixote*, in which the problem was interpreted in the most thorough manner. Don Quixote's first setting forth, with his arrival at nightfall at an inn which he takes to be a castle, is a perfect parody of Calogrenant's journey—precisely because the world which Don Quixote encounters is not one especially prepared for the proving of a knight but is a random, everyday, real world. By his detailed description of the circumstances of his hero's life, Cervantes makes it perfectly clear, at the very beginning of his book, where the root of Don Quixote's confusion lies: he is the victim of a social order in which he belongs to a class that has no function. He belongs to this class; he cannot emancipate himself from it; but as a mere member of it, without wealth and without high connections, he has no role and no mission. He feels his life running meaninglessly out, as though he were paralyzed. Only upon such a man, whose life is hardly better than a peasant's but who is educated and who is neither able nor permitted to labor as a peasant does, could romances of chivalry have such an unbalancing effect. His setting forth is a flight from a situation which is unbearable and which he has borne far too long. He wants to enforce his claim to the function proper to the class to which he belongs. It goes without saying that, three and a half centuries earlier, and in France, the situation is completely different. Feudal knighthood is still of crucial importance in military matters. The growth of an urban bourgeoisie and the growth of absolutism with its trend toward centralization are still in their earliest stages. But if Calogrenant had really set off on his quest as he describes it, he would even then have encountered things very different from those he reports. At the time of the second and third crusades, in the world of Henry II or Louis VII or Philip Augustus, things were hardly managed as they are in courtly romances. The courtly romance is not reality shaped and set forth by art, but an escape into fable and fairy tale. From the very beginning, at the height of its cultural florescence, this ruling class adopted an ethos and an ideal which concealed its real function. And it proceeded to describe its own life in extrahistorical terms, as an absolute aesthetic configuration without practical purpose. Certainly, one explanation of so strange a phenomenon lies in the surging imagination of that great century, in its spontaneous and soaring flight beyond reality into the absolute. But this explanation is too general to be adequate, especially since the courtly epic offers not only adventure and absolute idealization but also graceful manners and pompous ceremonies. One feels tempted to suggest that the long functional crisis of the feudal class had already begun to make itself felt—even at the time of the flowering of courtly literature. Chrétien de Troyes, who lived first in Champagne where, precisely during his lifetime, the great commerical fairs began to assume outstanding continental importance, then in Flanders where the burghers attained economic and political significance earlier than elsewhere north of the Alps, may well have begun to sense that the feudal class was no longer the only ruling class.

The widespread and longer-enduring flowering of the courtly-chivalric romance exerted a significant and, more precisely, a restrictive influence upon literary realism, even before the antique doctrine of different levels of style began to be influential in the same restrictive direction. Finally the two were merged in the idea of an elevated style, as it gradually developed during the Renaissance. . . . An elevated style of poetic expression had not yet been produced by the courtly epic. On the contrary, it did not even employ the elements of sublimity present in the paratactic form of the heroic epic. Its style is rather pleasantly narrative than sublime; it is suitable for any kind of subject matter. The later trend toward a linguistic separation of styles goes back entirely to the influence of antiquity, and not to that of courtly chivalry. Restrictions in terms of subject matter, however, are all the stronger.

They are class-determined. Only members of the chivalric-courtly society are worthy of adventure, hence they alone can undergo serious and significant experiences. Those outside this class cannot appear except as accessories, and even then generally in merely comic, grotesque, or despicable roles. This state of affairs is less apparent in antiquity and in the older heroic epic than here, where we are dealing with a conscious exclusiveness within a group characterized by class solidarity. Now it is true that before very long there were tendencies at work which sought to base the solidarity of the group not on descent but on personal factors, on noble behavior and refined manners. The beginning of this can already be discerned in the most important examples of the courtly epic itself, for in them the picture of the knightly individual, with increasing emphasis on inner values, is based on personal election and personal formation. Later, when—in Italy especially—social strata of urban background took over the courtly ideal and refashioned it, the concept of nobility became ever more personal, and as such it was actually often contrasted polemically with the other concept of nobility based soleley on lineage. But all this did not render the ideal less exclusive. It continued to apply to a class of the elect, which at times indeed seemed to constitute a secret society. In the process, social, political, educational, mystical, and class motifs were interwoven in the most varied way. But the most important point is that this emphasis on inner values by no means brought a closer approach to earthly realities. On the contrary: in part at least it was precisely the emphasis laid on the inner values of the knightly ideal which caused the connection with the real things of this earth to become ever more fictitious and devoid of practical purpose. The relation of the courtly ideal to reality is determined by the fictitiousness and lack of practical purpose which, as we hope we have sufficiently shown, characterize it from the very first. Courtly culture gives rise to the idea, which long remained a factor of considerable importance in Europe, that nobility, greatness, and intrinsic values have nothing in common with everyday reality—an attitude of much greater emotional power and of much stronger hold on the minds of men than the classical forms of a turning away from reality, as we find them for example in the ethics of Stoicism. To be sure, antiquity offers one form of turning away from reality even more compelling in its hold on men's minds, and that is Platonism. There have been repeated attempts to show that Platonic elements were a contributing factor in the development of the courtly ideal. In later times Platonism and the courtly ideal complemented each other perfectly. The most famous illustration of this is probably Count Castiglione's *Il Cortegiano*. Yet the specific form which turning away from reality received from courtly culture—with the characteristic establishment of an illusory world of class (or half class, half personal) tests and ordeals—is still, despite its superficial Platonic varnish, a highly autonomous and essentially a medieval phenomenon.

.   .   .

So the result of our interpretation and the considerations which have accompanied it is that courtly culture was decidedly unfavorable to the development of a literary art which should apprehend reality in its full breadth and depth. . . .

J. R. R. TOLKIEN

Fantasy

The human mind is capable of forming mental images of things not actually present. The faculty of conceiving the images is (or was) naturally called Imagination. But in recent times, in technical not normal language, Imagination has often been held to be something higher than the mere image-making, ascribed to the operations of Fancy (a reduced and depreciatory form of the older word Fantasy); an attempt is thus made to restrict, I should say misapply, Imagination to 'the power of giving to ideal creations the inner consistency of reality'.

Ridiculous though it may be for one so ill-instructed to have an opinion on this critical matter, I venture to think the verbal distinction philologically inappropriate, and the analysis inaccurate. The mental power of image-making is one thing, or aspect; and it should appropriately be called Imagination. The perception of the image, the grasp of its implications, and the control, which are necessary to a successful expression, may vary in vividness and strength: but this is a difference of degree in Imagination, not a difference in kind. The achievement of the expression, which gives (or seems to give) 'the inner consistency of reality',[1] is indeed another thing, or aspect, needing another name: Art, the operative link between Imagination and the final result, Sub-creation. For my present purpose I require a word which shall embrace both the Sub-creative Art in itself and a quality of strangeness and wonder in the Expression, derived from the Image: a quality essential to fairy-story. I propose, therefore, to arrogate to myself the powers of Humpty-Dumpty, and to use Fantasy for this

From *Tree and Leaf*, by J. R. R. Tolkien, pp. 43–45, 50–52, 60–63. Published, 1964, George Allen and Unwin Ltd. Reprinted by permission of George Allen and Unwin Ltd. and Houghton Mifflin Company.

[1]That is: which commands or induces Secondary Belief.

purpose: in a sense, that is, which combines with its older and higher use as an equivalent of Imagination the derived notions of 'unreality' (that is, of unlikeness to the Primary World), of freedom from the domination of observed 'fact', in short of the fantastic. I am thus not only aware but glad of the etymological and semantic connexions of *fantasy* with *fantastic*: with images of things that are not only 'not actually present', but which are indeed not to be found in our primary world at all, or are generally believed not to be found there. But while admitting that, I do not assent to the depreciative tone. That the images are of things not in the primary world (if that indeed is possible) is a virtue not a vice. Fantasy (in this sense) is, I think, not a lower but a higher form of Art, indeed the most nearly pure form, and so (when achieved) the most potent.

Fantasy, of course, starts out with an advantage: arresting strangeness. But that advantage has been turned against it, and has contributed to its disrepute. Many people dislike being 'arrested.' They dislike any meddling with the Primary World, or such small glimpses of it as are familiar to them. They, therefore, stupidly and even maliciously confound Fantasy with Dreaming, in which there is no Art;[2] and with mental disorders, in which there is not even control: with delusion and hallucination.

But the error or malice, engendered by disquiet and consequent dislike, is not the only cause of this confusion. Fantasy has also an essential drawback: it is difficult to achieve. Fantasy may be, as I think, not less but more sub-creative; but at any rate it is found in practice that 'the inner consistency of reality' is more difficult to produce, the more unlike are the images and the rearrangements of primary material to the actual arrangements of the Primary World. It is easier to produce this kind of 'reality' with more 'sober' material. Fantasy thus, too often, remains undeveloped; it is and has been used frivolously, or only half-seriously, or merely for decoration: it remains merely 'fanciful'. Anyone inheriting the fantastic device of human language can say *the green sun*. Many can then imagine or picture it. But that is not enough—though it may already be a more potent thing than many a 'thumbnail sketch' or 'transcript of life' that receives literary praise.

To make a Secondary World inside which the green sun will be credible, commanding Secondary Belief, will probably require labour

---

[2]This is not true of all dreams. In some Fantasy seems to take a part. But this is exceptional. Fantasy is a rational not an irrational activity.

and thought, and will certainly demand a special skill, a kind of elvish craft. Few attempt such difficult tasks. But when they are attempted and in any degree accomplished then we have a rare achievement of Art: indeed narrative art, story-making in its primary and most potent mode.

·   ·   ·

Fantasy is a natural human activity. It certainly does not destroy or even insult Reason; and it does not either blunt the appetite for, nor obscure the perception of, scientific verity. On the contrary. The keener and the clearer is the reason, the better fantasy will it make. If men were ever in a state in which they did not want to know or could not perceive truth (facts or evidence), then Fantasy would languish until they were cured. If they ever get into that state (it would not seem at all impossible), Fantasy will perish, and become Morbid Delusion.

For creative Fantasy is founded upon the hard recognition that things are so in the world as it appears under the sun; on a recognition of fact, but not a slavery to it. So upon logic was founded the nonsense that displays itself in the tales and rhymes of Lewis Carroll. If men really could not distinguish between frogs and men, fairy-stories about frog-kings would not have arisen.

Fantasy can, of course, be carried to excess. It can be ill done. It can be put to evil uses. It may even delude the minds out of which it came. But of what human thing in this fallen world is that not true? Men have conceived not only of elves, but they have imagined gods, and worshipped them, even worshipped those most deformed by their authors' own evil. But they have made false gods out of other materials: their notions, their banners, their monies; even their sciences and their social and economic theories have demanded human sacrifice. *Abusus non tollit usum*. Fantasy remains a human right: we make in our measure and in our derivative mode, because we are made: and not only made, but made in the image and likeness of a Maker.

·   ·   ·

We do not, or need not, despair of drawing because all lines must be either curved or straight, nor of painting because there are only three 'primary' colours. We may indeed be older now, in so far as we are heirs in enjoyment or in practice of many generations of ancestors in the arts. In this inheritance of wealth there may be a danger of boredom or of anxiety to be original, and that may lead to a distaste for fine drawing, delicate pattern, and 'pretty' colours, or else to mere manipulation and over-elaboration of old material, clever and heartless. But the true road of escape from such weariness is not to be found in the wilfully awkward, clumsy, or misshapen, not in making all things dark or unremittingly violent; nor in the mixing of colours on through subtlety to drabness, and the fantastical complication of shapes to the point of silliness and on towards delirium. Before we reach such states we need recovery. We should look at green again, and be startled anew (but not blinded) by blue and yellow and red. We should meet the centaur and the dragon, and then perhaps suddenly behold, like the ancient shepherds, sheep, and dogs, and horses—and wolves. This recovery fairy-stories help us to make. In that sense only a taste for them may make us, or keep us, childish.

Recovery (which includes return and renewal of health) is a re-gaining—regaining of a clear view. I do not say 'seeing things as they are' and involve myself with the philosophers, though I might venture to say 'seeing things as we are (or were) meant to see them'— as things apart from ourselves. We need, in any case, to clean our windows; so that the things seen clearly may be freed from the drab blur of triteness or familiarity—from possessiveness. Of all faces those of our *familiares* are the ones both most difficult to play fantastic tricks with, and most difficult really to see with fresh attention, perceiving their likeness and unlikeness: that they are faces, and yet unique faces. This triteness is really the penalty of 'appropriation': the things that are trite, or (in a bad sense) familiar, are the things that we have appropriated, legally or mentally. We say we know them. They have become like the things which once attracted us by their glitter, or their colour, or their shape, and we laid hands on them, and then locked them in our hoard, acquired them, and acquiring ceased to look at them.

.   .   .

The consolation of fairy-stories, the joy of the happy ending: or more correctly of the good catastrophe, the sudden joyous 'turn' (for there is no true end to any fairy-tale): this joy, which is one of the things which fairy-stories can produce supremely well, is not essenti-ally 'escapist', nor 'fugitive'. In its fairy-tale—or otherworld—setting, it is a sudden and miraculous grace: never to be counted on to recur. It does not deny the existence of *dyscatastrophe*, of sorrow and failure: the possibility of these is necessary to the joy of deliverance;

it denies (in the face of much evidence, if you will) universal final defeat and in so far is *evangelium,* giving a fleeting glimpse of Joy, Joy beyond the walls of the world, poignant as grief.

It is the mark of a good fairy-story, of the higher or more complete kind, that however wild its events, however fantastic or terrible the adventures, it can give to child or man that hears it, when the 'turn' comes, a catch of the breath, a beat and lifting of the heart, near to (or indeed accompanied by) tears, as keen as that given by any form of literary art, and having a peculiar quality.

Even modern fairy-stories can produce this effect sometimes. It is not an easy thing to do; it depends on the whole story which is the setting of the turn, and yet it reflects a glory backwards. A tale that in any measure succeeds in this point has not wholly failed, whatever flaws it may possess, and whatever mixture or confusion of purpose. . . .

Far more powerful and poignant is the effect in a serious tale of Faërie. In such stories when the sudden 'turn' comes we get a piercing glimpse of joy, and heart's desire, that for a moment passes outside the frame, rends indeed the very web of story, and lets a gleam come through.

> Seven long years I served for thee,
> The glassy hill I clamb for thee,
> The bluidy shirt I wrang for thee,
> And wilt thou not wauken and turn to me?
>
> *He heard and turned to her.*[3]

This 'joy' which I have selected as the mark of the true fairy-story (or romance), or as the seal upon it, merits more consideration. Probably every writer making a secondary world, a fantasy, every sub-creator, wishes in some measure to be a real maker, or hopes that he is drawing on reality: hopes that the peculiar quality of this secondary world (if not all the details)[4] are derived from Reality, or are flowing into it. If he indeed achieves a quality that can fairly be described by the dictionary definition: 'inner consistency of reality', it is difficult to conceive how this can be, if the work does not in some way partake of reality. The peculiar quality of the 'joy' in successful Fantasy can thus be explained as a sudden glimpse of the underlying reality or truth. It is not only a 'consolation' for the sorrow of this world, but a

[3] *The Black Bull of Norroway.*
[4] For all the details may not be 'true': it is seldom that the 'inspiration' is so strong and lasting that it leavens all the lump, and does not leave much that is mere uninspired 'invention'.

satisfaction, and an answer to that question, 'Is it true?' The answer to this question that I gave at first was (quite rightly): 'If you have built your little world well, yes: it is true in that world.' That is enough for the artist (or the artist part of the artist). But in the 'eucatastrophe' we see in a brief vision that the answer may be greater—it may be a far-off gleam or echo of *evangelium* in the real world. The use of this word gives a hint of my epilogue. It is a serious and dangerous matter. It is presumptuous of me to touch upon such a theme; but if by grace what I say has in any respect any validity, it is, of course, only one facet of a truth incalculably rich: finite only because the capacity of Man for whom this was done is finite.

I would venture to say that approaching the Christian Story from this direction, it has long been my feeling (a joyous feeling) that God redeemed the corrupt making-creatures, men, in a way fitting to this aspect, as to others, of their strange nature. The Gospels contain a fairy-story, or a story of a larger kind which embraces all the essence of fairy-stories. They contain many marvels—peculiarly artistic,[5] beautiful, and moving: 'mythical' in their perfect, self-contained significance; and among the marvels is the greatest and most complete conceivable eucatastrophe. But this story has entered History and the primary world; the desire and aspiration of sub-creation has been raised to the fulfilment of Creation. The Birth of Christ is the eucatastrophe of Man's history. The Resurrection is the eucatastrophe of the story of the Incarnation. This story begins and ends in joy. It has pre-eminently the 'inner consistency of reality'. There is no tale ever told that men would rather find was true, and none which so many sceptical men have accepted as true on its own merits. For the Art of it has the supremely convincing tone of Primary Art, that is, of Creation. To reject it leads either to sadness or to wrath.

[5]The Art is here in the story itself rather than in the telling; for the Author of the story was not the evangelists.

NORTHROP FRYE

The Mythos of Summer: Romance

The romance is nearest of all literary forms to the wish-fulfilment dream, and for that reason it has socially a curiously paradoxical role. In every age the ruling social or intellectual class tends to project its ideals in some form of romance, where the virtuous heroes and beautiful heroines represent the ideals and the villains the threats to their ascendancy. This is the general character of chivalric romance in the Middle Ages, aristocratic romance in the Renaissance, bourgeois romance since the eighteenth century, and revolutionary romance in contemporary Russia. Yet there is a genuinely "proletarian" element in romance too which is never satisfied with its various incarnations, and in fact the incarnations themselves indicate that no matter how great a change may take place in society, romance will turn up again, as hungry as ever, looking for new hopes and desires to feed on. The perennially childlike quality of romance is marked by its extraordinarily persistent nostalgia, its search for some kind of imaginative golden age in time or space. There has never to my knowledge been any period of Gothic English literature, but the list of Gothic revivalists stretches completely across its entire history, from the *Beowulf* poet to writers of our own day.

The essential element of plot in romance is adventure, which means that romance is naturally a sequential and processional form, hence we know it better from fiction than from drama. At its most naïve it is an endless form in which a central character who never develops or ages goes through one adventure after another until the author himself collapses. We see this form in comic strips, where the central characters persist for years in a state of refrigerated deathlessness. However, no book can rival the continuity of the newspaper, and as soon as romance achieves a literary form, it tends to limit itself to a sequence of minor adventures leading up to a major or climacteric adventure, usually announced from the beginning, the completion of which rounds off the story. We may call this major adventure, the element that gives literary form to the romance, the quest.

The complete form of the romance is clearly the successful quest, and such a completed form has three main stages: the stage of the perilous journey and the preliminary minor adventures; the crucial struggle, usually some kind of battle in which either the hero or his foe, or both, must die; and the exaltation of the hero. We may call these three stages respectively, using Greek terms, the *agon* or conflict, the *pathos* or death-struggle, and the *anagnorisis* or discovery, the recognition of the hero, who has clearly proved himself to be a hero even if he does not survive the conflict. Thus the romance expresses more clearly the passage from struggle through a point of ritual death to a recognition scene that we discovered in comedy. A threefold structure is repeated in many features of romance—in the frequency, for instance, with which the successful hero is a third son, or the third to undertake the quest, or successful on his third attempt. It is shown more directly in the three-day rhythm of death, disappearance and revival which is found in the myth of Attis and other dying gods, and has been incorporated in our Easter.

A quest involving conflict assumes two main characters, a protagonist or hero, and an antagonist or enemy. (No doubt I should add, for the benfit of some readers, that I have read the article "Protagonist" in Fowler's *Modern English Usage*.) The enemy may be an ordinary human being, but the nearer the romance is to myth, the more attributes of divinity will cling to the hero and the more the enemy will take on demonic mythical qualities. The central form of romance is dialectical: everything is focussed on a conflict between the hero and his enemy, and all the reader's values are bound up with the hero. Hence the hero of romance is analogous to the mythical Messiah or deliverer who comes from an upper world, and his enemy is analogous to the demonic powers of a lower world. The conflict however takes place in, or at any rate primarily concerns, *our* world, which is in the middle, and which is characterized by the cyclical movement of nature. Hence the opposite poles of the cycles of nature are assimilated to the opposition of the hero and his enemy. The enemy is associated with winter, darkness, confusion, sterility, moribund life, and old age, and the hero with spring, dawn, order, fertility, vigor, and youth. As all the cyclical phenomena can be readily associated or identified, it follows that any attempt to prove that a romantic story does or does not resemble, say, a solar myth, or that its hero does or does not resemble a sun-god, is likely to be a waste of time. If it is a story within this general area, cyclical imagery is likely to be present, and solar imagery is normally prominent among cyclical images. If the hero of a romance returns from a quest disguised, flings off his beggar's rags, and stands forth in the resplendent scarlet cloak of the prince, we do not have a theme which has necessarily descended from a solar myth; we have the literary device of displacement. The hero does something which we may or may not, as we like, associate with the myth of the sun returning at dawn. If we are reading the story as critics, with an eye to structural principles, we shall make the association, because the solar analogy explains why the hero's act is an effective and conventional incident. If we are reading the story for fun, we need not bother: that is, some murky "subconscious" factor in our response will take care of the association.

We have distinguished myth from romance by the hero's power of action: in the myth proper he is divine, in the romance proper he is human. This distinction is much sharper theologically than it is poetically, and myth and romance both belong in the general category of mythopoeic literature. The attributing of divinity to the chief characters of myth, however, tends to give myth a further distinction, already referred to, of occupying a central *canonical* position. Most cultures regard certain stories with more reverence than others, either because they are thought of as historically true or because they have come to bear a heavier weight of conceptual meaning. The story of Adam and Eve in Eden has thus a canonical position for poets in our tradition whether they believe in its historicity or not. The reason for the greater profundity of canonical myth is not solely tradition, but the result of the greater degree of metaphorical identification that is possible in myth. In literary criticism the myth is normally the metaphorical key to the displacements of romance, hence the importance of the quest-myth of the Bible in what follows. But because of the tendency to expurgate and moralize in canonical myth, the less inhibited area of legend and folk tale often contains an equally great concentration of mythical meaning.

The central form of quest-romance is the dragon-killing theme exemplified in the stories of St. George and Perseus, already referred to.

A land ruled by a helpless old king is laid waste by a sea-monster, to whom one young person after another is offered to be devoured, until the lot falls on the king's daughter: at that point the hero arrives, kills the dragon, marries the daughter, and succeeds to the kingdom. Again, as with comedy, we have a simple pattern with many complex elements. The ritual analogies of the myth suggest that the monster *is* the sterility of the land itself, and that the sterility of the land is present in the age and impotence of the king, who is sometimes suffering from an incurable malady or wound, like Amfortas in Wagner. His position is that of Adonis overcome by the boar of winter, Adonis's traditional thigh-wound being as close to castration symbolically as it is anatomically.

In the Bible we have a sea-monster usually named leviathan, who is described as the enemy of the Messiah, and whom the Messiah is destined to kill in the "day of the Lord." The leviathan is the source of social sterility, for it is identified with Egypt and Babylon, the oppressors of Israel, and is described in the Book of Job as "king over all the children of pride." It also seems closely associated with the natural sterility of the fallen world, with the blasted world of struggle and poverty and disease into which Job is hurled by Satan and Adam by the serpent in Eden. In the Book of Job God's revelation to Job consists largely of descriptions of the leviathan and a slightly less sinister land cousin named behemoth. These monsters thus apparently represent the fallen order of nature over which Satan has some control. (I am trying to make sense of the meaning of the Book of Job as we now have it, on the assumption that whoever was responsible for its present version had some reason for producing that version. Guesswork about what the poem may originally have been or meant is useless, as it is only the version we know that has had any influence on our literature.) In the Book of Revelation the leviathan, Satan, and the Edenic serpent are all identified. This identification is the basis for an elaborate dragon-killing metaphor in Christian symbolism in which the hero is Christ (often represented in art standing on a prostrate monster), the dragon Satan, the impotent old king Adam, whose son Christ becomes, and the rescued bride the Church.

.   .   .

We have spoken of the Messianic hero as a redeemer of society, but in the secular quest-romances more obvious motives and rewards for the quest are more common. Often the dragon guards a hoard: the quest for buried treasure has been a central theme of romance from the Siegfried cycle to *Nostromo*, and is unlikely to be exhausted yet. Treasure means wealth, which in mythopoeic romance often means wealth in its ideal forms, power and wisdom. The lower world, the world inside or behind the guarding dragon, is often inhabited by a prophetic sybil, and is a place of oracles and secrets, such as Woden was willing to mutilate himself to obtain. Mutilation or physical handicap, which combines the themes of *sparagmos* and ritual death, is often the price of unusual wisdom or power, as it is in the figure of the crippled smith Weyland or Hephaistos, and in the story of the blessing of Jacob. The Arabian Nights are full of stories of what may be called the etiology of mutilation. Again, the reward of the quest usually is or includes a bride. This bride-figure is ambiguous: her psychological connection with the mother in an Oedipus fantasy is more insistent than in comedy. She is often to be found in a perilous, forbidden, or tabooed place, like Brunnhilde's wall of fire or the sleeping beauty's wall of thorns, and she is, of course, often rescued from the unwelcome embraces of another and generally older male, or from giants or bandits or other usurpers. The removal of some stigma from the heroine figures prominently in romance as in comedy, and ranges from the "loathly lady" theme of Chaucer's *Wife of Bath's Tale* to the forgiven harlot of the Book of Hosea. The "black but comely" bride of the Song of Songs belongs in the same complex.

The quest-romance has analogies to both rituals and dreams, and the rituals examined by Frazer and the dreams examined by Jung show the remarkable similarity in form that we should expect of two symbolic structures analogous to the same thing. Translated into dream terms, the quest-romance is the search of the libido or desiring self for a fulfilment that will deliver it from the anxieties of reality but will still contain that reality. The antagonists of the quest are often sinister figures, giants, ogres, witches and magicians, that clearly have a parental origin; and yet redeemed and emancipated paternal figures are involved too, as they are in the psychological quests of both Freud and Jung. Translated into ritual terms, the quest-romance is the victory of fertility over the waste land. Fertility means food and drink, bread and wine, body and blood, the union of male and female. The precious objects brought back from the quest, or seen or obtained as a result of it, sometimes combine the ritual and the psychological associations. The Holy Grail, for instance, is connected with Christian Eucharist symbolism; it is related to or descended from a miraculous food provider like the cornucopia, and, like other cups and hollow vessels, it has female sexual affinities, its masculine counterpart being, we are told, the bleeding lance. The pairing of solid food and liquid refreshment recurs in the edible tree and the water of life in the Biblical apocalypse.

We may take the first book of *The Faerie Queene* as representing perhaps the closest following of the Biblical quest-romance theme in English literature: it is closer even than *The Pilgrim's Progress*, which resembles it because they both resemble the Bible. Attempts to compare Bunyan and Spenser without reference to the Bible, or to trace their similarities to a common origin in *secular* romance, are more or less perverse. In Spenser's account of the quest of St. George, the patron saint of England, the protagonist represents the Christian Church in England, and hence his quest is an imitation of that of Christ. Spenser's Redcross Knight is led by the lady Una (who is veiled in black) to the kingdom of her parents, which is being laid waste by a dragon. The dragon is of somewhat unusual size, at least allegorically. We are told that Una's parents held "all the world" in their control until the dragon "Forwasted all their land, and them expelled." Una's parents are Adam and Eve; their kingdom is Eden or the unfallen world, and the dragon, who is the entire fallen world, is identified with the leviathan, the serpent of Eden, Satan, and the beast of Revelation. Thus St. George's mission, a repetition of that of Christ, is by killing the dragon to raise Eden in the wilderness and restore England to the status of Eden. The association of an ideal England with Eden, assisted by legends of a happy island in the western ocean and by the similarity of the Hesperides story to that of Eden, runs through English literature at least from the end of Greene's *Friar Bacon* to Blake's "Jerusalem" hymn. St. George's wanderings with Una, or without her, are parallel to the wandering of the Israelites in the wilderness, between Egypt and the Promised Land, bearing the veiled ark of the covenant and yet ready to worship a golden calf.

The battle with the dragon lasts, of course, three days: at the end of each of the first two days St. George is beaten back and is strengthened, first by the water of life, then by the tree of life. These represent the two sacraments which the reformed church accepted; they are the two features of the garden of Eden to be restored to man in the apocalypse, and they have also a more general Eucharist connection. St. George's emblem is a red cross on a white ground, which is the flag borne by Christ in traditional iconography when he returns in triumph from the prostrate dragon of hell. The red and white symbolize the two aspects of the risen body, flesh and blood, bread and wine, and in Spenser they have a historical connection with the union of red and white roses in the reigning head of the church. The link between the sacramental and the sexual aspects of the red and white symbolism is indicated in alchemy, with which Spenser was clearly acquainted, in which a crucial phase of the production of the elixir of immortality is known as the union of the red king and the white queen.

The characterization of romance follows its general dialectic structure, which means that subtlety and complexity are not much favored. Characters tend to be either for or against the quest. If they assist it they are idealized as simply gallant or pure; if they obstruct it they are caricatured as simply villainous or cowardly. Hence every typical character in romance tends to have his moral opposite confronting him, like black and white pieces in a chess game. In romance the "white" pieces who strive for the quest correspond to the *eiron* group in comedy, though the word is no longer appropriate, as irony has little place in romance. Romance has a counterpart to the benevolent retreating *eiron* of comedy in its figure of the "old wise man," as Jung calls him, like Prospero, Merlin, or the palmer of Spenser's second quest, often a magician who affects the action he watches over. The Arthur of *The Faerie Queene*, though not an old man, has this function. He has a feminine counterpart in the sybilline wise mother-figure, often a potential bride like Solveig in *Peer Gynt*, who sits quietly at home waiting for the hero to finish his wanderings and come back to her. This latter figure is often the lady for whose sake or at whose bidding the quest is performed: she is represented by the Faerie Queene in Spenser and by Athene in the Perseus story. These are the king and queen of the white pieces, though their power of movement is of course reversed in actual chess. The disadvantage of making the queen-figure the hero's mistress, in anything more than a political sense, is that she spoils his fun with the distressed damsels he meets on his journey, who are often enticingly tied naked to rocks or trees, like Andromeda or Angelica in Ariosto. A polarization may thus be set up between the lady of duty and the lady of pleasure—we have already glanced at a late development of this in the light and dark heroines of Victorian romance. One simple way out is to make the former the latter's mother-in-law: a theme of reconciliation after enmity and jealousy most commonly results, as in the relations of Psyche and Venus in

Apuleius. Where there is no reconciliation, the older female remains sinister, the cruel stepmother of folk tale.

The evil magician and the witch, Spenser's Archimago and Duessa, are the black king and queen. The latter is appropriately called by Jung the "terrible mother," and he associated her with the fear of incest and with such hags as Medusa who seem to have a suggestion of erotic perversion about them. The redeemed figures, apart from the bride, are generally too weak to be strongly characterized. The faithful companion or shadow figure of the hero has his opposite in the traitor, the heroine her opposite in the siren or beautiful witch, the dragon his opposite in the friendly or helping animals that are so conspicuous in romance, among which the horse who gets the hero to his quest has naturally a central place. The conflict of son and father that we noted in comedy recurs in romance: in the Bible the second Adam comes to the rescue of the first one, and in the Grail cycle the pure son Galahad accomplishes what his impure father Lancelot failed in.

The characters who elude the moral antithesis of heroism and villainy generally are or suggest spirits of nature. They represent partly the moral neutrality of the intermediate world of nature and partly a world of mystery which is glimpsed but never seen, and which retreats when approached. Among female characters of this type are the shy nymphs of Classical legends and the elusive half-wild creatures who might be called daughter-figures, and include Spenser's Florimell, Hawthorne's Pearl, Wagner's Kundry, and Hudson's Rima. Their male counterparts have a little more variety. Kipling's Mowgli is the best known of the wild boys; a green man lurked in the forests of medieval England, appearing as Robin Hood and as the knight of Gawain's adventure; the "salvage man," represented in Spenser by Satyrane, is a Renaissance favorite, and the awkward but faithful giant with unkempt hair has shambled amiably through romance for centuries.

Such characters are, more or less, children of nature, who can be brought to serve the hero, like Crusoe's Friday, but retain the inscrutability of their origin. As servants or friends of the hero, they impart the mysterious rapport with nature that so often marks the central figure of romance. The paradox that many of these children of nature are "supernatural" beings is not as distressing in romance as in logic. The helpful fairy, the grateful dead man, the wonderful servant who has just the abilities the hero needs in a crisis, are all folk tale commonplaces. They are romantic intensifications of the comic tricky slave, the author's *architectus*. In James Thurber's *The Thirteen Clocks* this character type is called the "Golux," and there is no reason why the word should not be adopted as a critical term.

In romance, as in comedy, there seem to be four poles of characterization. The struggle of the hero with his enemy corresponds to the comic contest of *eiron* and *alazon*. In the nature-spirits just referred to we find the parallel in romance to the buffoon or master of ceremonies in comedy: that is, their function is to intensify and provide a focus for the romantic mood. It remains to be seen if there is a character in romance corresponding to the *agroikos* type in comedy, the refuser of festivity or rustic clown.

Such a character would call attention to realistic aspects of life, like fear in the presence of danger, which threaten the unity of the romantic mood. St. George and Una in Spenser are accompanied by a dwarf who carries a bag of "needments." He is not a traitor, like the other bag-carrier Judas Iscariot, but he is "fearful," and urges retreat when the going is difficult. This dwarf with his needments represents, in the dream world of romance, the shrunken and wizened form of practical waking reality: the more realistic the story, the more important such a figure would become, until, when we reach the opposite pole in *Don Quixote*, he achieves his apotheosis as Sancho Panza. In other romances we find fools and jesters who are licensed to show fear or make realistic comments, and who provide a localized safety valve for realism without allowing it to disrupt the conventions of romance. In Malory a similar role is assumed by Sir Dinadan, who, it is carefully explained, is really a gallant knight as well as a jester: hence when he makes jokes "the king and Launcelot laughed that they might not sit"—the suggestion of excessive and hysterical laughter being psychologically very much to the point.

Romance, like comedy, has six isolatable phases, and as it moves from the tragic to the comic area, the first three are parallel to the first three phases of tragedy and the second three to the second three phases of comedy, already examined from the comic point of view. The phases form a cyclical sequence in a romantic hero's life.

The first phase is the myth of the birth of the hero, the morphology of which has been studied in some detail in folklore. This myth is often associated with a flood, the regular symbol of the beginning and the end of a cycle. The infant hero is often placed in an ark or chest floating on the sea, as in the story of Perseus; from there he drifts to land, as in the exordium to *Beowulf*, or is rescued from among reeds and bulrushes on a river bank, as in the story of Moses. A landscape of water, boat, and reeds appears at the beginning of Dante's journey up the mount of Purgatory, where there are many suggestions that the soul is in that stage a newborn infant. On dry land the infant may be rescued either from or by an animal, and many heroes are nurtured by animals in a forest during their nonage. When Goethe's Faust begins to look for his Helena, he searches in the reeds of the Peneus, and then finds a centaur who carried her to safety on his back when she was a child.

Psychologically, this image is related to the embryo in the womb, the world of the unborn often being thought of as liquid; anthropologically, it is related to the image of seeds of new life buried in a dead world of snow or swamp. The dragon's treasure hoard is closely linked with this mysterious infant life enclosed in a chest. The fact that the real source of wealth is potential fertility or new life, vegetable or human, has run through romance from ancient myths to Ruskin's *King of the Golden River*, Ruskin's treatment of wealth in his economic works being essentially a commentary on this fairy tale. A similar association of treasure hoard and infant life appears in more plausible guise in *Silas Marner*. The long literary history of the theme of mysterious parentage from Euripides to Dickens has already been mentioned.

In the Bible the end of a historical cycle and the birth of a new one is marked by parallel symbols. First we have a universal deluge and an ark, with the potency of all future life contained in it, floating on the waters; then we have the story of the Egyptian host drowned in the Red Sea and the Israelites set free to carry their ark through the wilderness, an image adopted by Dante as the basis of his purgatorial symbolism. The New Testament begins with an infant in a manger, and the tradition of depicting the world outside as sunk in snow relates the Nativity to the same archetypal phase. Images of returning spring soon follow: the rainbow in the Noah story, the bringing of water out of a rock by Moses, the baptism of Christ, all show the turning of the cycle from the wintry water of death to the reviving waters of life. The providential birds, the raven and dove in the Noah story, the ravens feeding Elijah in the wilderness, the dove hovering over Jesus, belong to the same complex.

Often, too, there is a search for the child, who has to be hidden

away in a secret place. The hero being of mysterious origin, his true
paternity is often concealed, and a false father appears who seeks the
child's death. This is the role of Acrisius in the Perseus story, of
the Cronos of Hesiodic myth who tries to swallow his children, of the
child-killing Pharaoh in the Old Testament, and of Herod in the New.
In later fiction he often modulates to the usurping wicked uncle who
appears several times in Shakespeare. The mother is thus often the
victim of jealousy, persecuted or calumniated like the mother of Perseus
or like Constance in the *Man of Law's Tale*. This version is very close
psychologically to the theme of the rivalry of the son and a hateful
father for possession of the mother. The theme of the calumniated girl
ordered out of the house with her child by a cruel father, generally into
the snow, still drew tears from audiences of Victorian melodramas, and
literary developments of the theme of the hunted mother in the same
period extend from Eliza crossing the ice in *Uncle Tom's Cabin* to
Adam Bede and *Far from the Madding Crowd*. The false mother, the
celebrated cruel stepmother, is also common: her victim is of course
usually female, and the resulting conflict is portrayed in many ballads
and folktales of the Cinderella type. The true father is sometimes
represented by a wise old man or teacher: this is the relation of Prospero to Ferdinand, as well as of Chiron the centaur to Achilles. The
double of the true mother appears in the daughter of Pharaoh who
adopts Moses. In more realistic modes the cruel parent speaks with the
voice of, or takes the form of, a narrow-minded public opinion.

The second phase brings us to the innocent youth of the hero, a
phase most familiar to us from the story of Adam and Eve in Eden
before the Fall. In literature this phase presents a pastoral and Arcadian world, generally a pleasant wooded landscape, full of glades,
shaded valleys, murmuring brooks, the moon, and other images
closely linked with the female or maternal aspect of sexual imagery.
Its heraldic colors are green and gold, traditionally the colors of
vanishing youth: one thinks of Sandburg's poem *Between Two Worlds*.
It is often a world of magic or desirable law, and it tends to center on a
youthful hero, still overshadowed by parents, surrounded by youthful
companions. The archetype of erotic innocence is less commonly
marriage than the kind of "chaste" love that precedes marriage; the
love of brother for sister, or of two boys for each other. Hence, though in
later phases it is often recalled as a lost happy time or Golden Age, the
sense of being close to a moral taboo is very frequent, as it is of course
in the Eden story itself. Johnson's *Rasselas*, Poe's *Eleanora*, and Blake's

Book of Thel introduce us to a kind of prison-Paradise or unborn world from which the central characters long to escape to a lower world, and the same feeling of malaise and longing to enter a world of action recurs in the most exhaustive treatment of the phase in English literature, Keats's *Endymion*.

The theme of the sexual barrier in this phase takes many forms: the serpent of the Eden story recurs in *Green Mansions*, and a barrier of fire separates Amoret in Spenser from her lover Scudamour. At the end of the *Purgatorio* the soul reaches again its unfallen childhood or lost Golden Age, and Dante consequently finds himself in the garden of Eden, separated from the young girl Matelda by the river Lethe. The dividing river recurs in William Morris's curious story *The Sundering Flood*, where an arrow shot over it has to do for the symbol of sexual contact. In *Kubla Khan*, which is closely related both to the Eden story in *Paradise Lost* and to *Rasselas*, a "sacred river" is closely followed by the distant vision of a singing damsel. Melville's *Pierre* opens with a sardonic parody of this phase, the hero still dominated by his mother but calling her his sister. A good deal of the imagery of this world may be found in the sixth book of *The Faerie Queene*, especially in the stories of Tristram and Pastorella.

The third phase is the normal quest theme that we have been discussing, and needs no further comment at this point. The fourth phase corresponds to the fourth phase of comedy, in which the happier society is more or less visible throughout the action instead of emerging only in the last few moments. In romance the central theme of this phase is that of the maintaining of the integrity of the innocent world against the assault of experience. It thus often takes the form of a moral allegory, such as we have in Milton's *Comus*, Bunyan's *Holy War*, and many morality plays, including *The Castell of Perseveraunce*. The much simpler scheme of the *Canterbury Tales*, where the only conflict is to preserve the mood of holiday and festivity against bickering, seems for some reason to be less frequent.

The integrated body to be defended may be individual or social, or both. The individual aspect of it is presented in the allegory of temperance in the second book of *The Faerie Queene*, which forms a natural sequel to the first book, dealing as it does with the more difficult theme of consolidating heroic innocence in this world after the first great quest has been completed. Guyon, the knight of temperance, has as his main antagonists Acrasia, the mistress of the Bower of Bliss, and Mammon. These represent "Beauty and money," in their aspects as instrumental goods perverted into external goals. The temperate mind contains its good within itself, continence being its prerequisite, hence it belongs to what we have called the innocent world. The intemperate mind seeks its good in the external object of the world of experience. Both temperance and intemperance could be called natural, but one belongs to nature as an order and the other to nature as a fallen world. Comus's temptation of the Lady is based on a similar ambiguity in the meaning of nature. A central image in this phase of romance is that of the beleaguered castle, represented in Spenser by the House of Alma, which is described in terms of the economy of the human body.

The social aspect of the same phase is treated in the fifth book of *The Faerie Queene*, the legend of justice, where power is the prerequisite of justice, corresponding to continence in relation to temperance. Here we meet, in the vision of Isis and Osiris, the fourth-phase image of the monster tamed and controlled by the virgin, an image which appears episodically in Book One in connection with Una, who tames satyrs and a lion. The Classical prototype of it is the Gorgon's head on the shield of Athene. The theme of invincible innocence or virginity is associated with similar images in literature from the child leading the beasts of prey in Isaiah to Marina in the brothel in *Pericles*, and it reappears in later fictions in which an unusually truculent hero is brought to heel by the heroine. An ironic parody of the same theme forms the basis of Aristophanes' *Lysistrata*.

The fifth phase corresponds to the fifth phase of comedy, and like it is a reflective, idyllic view of experience from above, in which the movement of the natural cycle has usually a prominent place. It deals with a world very similar to that of the second phase except that the mood is a contemplative withdrawal from or sequel to action rather than a youthful preparation for it. It is, like the second phase, an erotic world, but it presents experience as comprehended and not as a mystery. This is the world of most of Morris's romances, of Hawthorne's *Blithedale Romance*, of the mature innocent wisdom of *The Franklin's Tale*, and of most of the imagery of the third book of *The Faerie Queene*. In this last, as well as in the late Shakespearean romances, notably *Pericles*, and even *The Tempest*, we notice a tendency to the moral stratification of characters. The true lovers are on top of a hierarchy of what might be called erotic imitations, going down through the various grades of lust and passion to perversion (Argante and Oliphant in Spenser; Antiochus and his daughter in *Pericles*). Such an arrangement of characters is consistent with the detached and contemplative view of society taken in this phase.

The sixth or *penseroso* phase is the last phase of romance as of comedy. In comedy it shows the comic society breaking up into small units or individuals; in romance it marks the end of a movement from active to contemplative adventure. A central image of this phase, a favorite of Yeats, is that of the old man in the tower, the lonely hermit absorbed in occult or magical studies. On a more popular and social level it takes in what might be called cuddle fiction: the romance that is physically associated with comfortable beds or chairs around fireplaces or warm and cosy spots generally. A characteristic feature of this phase is the tale in quotation marks, where we have an opening setting with a small group of congenial people, and then the real story told by one of the members. In *The Turn of the Screw* a large party is telling ghost stories in a country house; then some people leave, and a much smaller and more intimate circle gathers around the crucial tale. The opening dismissal of catechumens is thoroughly in the spirit and conventions of this phase. The effect of such devices is to present the story through a relaxed and contemplative haze as something that entertains us without, so to speak, confronting us, as direct tragedy confronts us.

Collections of tales based on a symposium device like the *Decameron* belong here. Morris's *Earthly Paradise* is a very pure example of the same phase: there a number of the great archetypal myths of Greek and Northern culture are personified as a group of old men who forsook the world during the Middle Ages, refusing to be made either kings or gods, and who now interchange their myths in an ineffectual land of dreams. Here the themes of the lonely old men, the intimate group, and the reported tale are linked. The calendar arrangement of the tales links it also with the symbolism of the natural cycle. Another and very concentrated treatment of the phase is Virginia Woolf's *Between the Acts*, where a play representing the history of English life is acted before a group. The history is conceived not only as a progression but as a cycle of which the audience is the end, and, as the last page indicates, the beginning as well.

From Wagner's *Ring* to science fiction, we may notice an increasing popularity of the flood archetype. This usually takes the form of some cosmic disaster destroying the whole fictional society except a small group, which begins life anew in some sheltered spot. The affinities of this theme to that of the cosy group which has managed to shut the rest of the world out are clear enough, and it brings us around again to the image of the mysterious newborn infant floating on the sea.

One important detail in poetic symbolism remains to be considered. This is the symbolic presentation of the point at which the undisplaced apocalyptic world and the cyclical world of nature come into alignment, and which we propose to call the point of epiphany. Its most common settings are the mountain-top, the island, the tower, the lighthouse, and the ladder or staircase. Folk tales and mythologies are full of stories of an original connection between heaven or the sun and earth. We have ladders of arrows, ropes pecked in two by mischievous birds, and the like: such stories are often analogues of the Biblical stories of the Fall, and survive in Jack's beanstalk, Rapunzel's hair, and even the curious bit of floating folklore known as the Indian rope trick. The movement from one world to the other may be symbolized by the golden fire that descends from the sun, as in the mythical basis of the Danae story, and by its human response, the fire kindled on the sacrificial altar. The "gold bug" in Poe's story, which reminds us that the Egyptian scarab was a solar emblem, is dropped from above on the end of a string through the eyehole of a skull on a tree and falls on top of a buried treasure: the archetype here is closely related to the complex of images we are dealing with, especially to some alchemical versions of it.

In the Bible we have Jacob's ladder, which in *Paradise Lost* is associated with Milton's cosmological diagram of a spherical cosmos hanging from heaven with a hole in the top. There are several mountain-top epiphanies in the Bible, the Transfiguration being the most notable, and the mountain vision of Pisgah, the end of the road through the wilderness from which Moses saw the distant promised Land, is typologically linked. As long as poets accepted the Ptolemaic universe, the natural place for the point of epiphany was a mountain-top just under the moon, the lowest heavenly body. Purgatory in Dante is an enormous mountain with a path ascending spirally around it, on top of which, as the pilgrim gradually recovers his lost innocence and casts off his original sin, is the garden of Eden. It is at this point that the prodigious apocalyptic epiphany of the closing cantos of the *Purgatorio* is achieved. The sense of being between an apocalyptic world above and a cyclical world below is present too, as from the garden of Eden all seeds of vegetable life fall back into the world, while human life passes on.

In *The Faerie Queene* there is a Pisgah vision in the first book, when St. George climbs the mountain of contemplation and sees the heavenly city from a distance. As the dragon he has to kill is the fallen world, there is a level of the allegory in which his dragon is the space between himself and the distant city. In the corresponding episode of Ariosto the link between the mountain-top and the sphere of the moon is clearer. But Spenser's fullest treatment of the theme is the brilliant metaphysical comedy known as the *Mutabilitie Cantoes*, where the conflict of being and becoming, Jove and Mutability, order and change, is resolved at the sphere of the moon. Mutability's evidence consists of the cyclical movements of nature, but this evidence is turned against her and proved to be a principle of order in nature instead of mere change. In this poem the relation of the heavenly bodies to the apocalyptic world is not metaphorical identification, as it is, at least as a poetic convention, in Dante's *Paradiso*, but likeness: they are still within nature, and only in the final stanza of the poem does the real apocalyptic world appear.

The distinction of levels here implies that there may be analogous forms of the point of epiphany. For instance, it may be presented in erotic terms as a place of sexual fulfilment, where there is no apocalyptic vision but simply a sense of arriving at the summit of experience in nature. This natural form of the point of epiphany is called in Spenser the Gardens of Adonis. It recurs under that name in Keats's *Endymion* and is the world entered by the lovers at the end of Shelley's *Revolt of Islam*. The Gardens of Adonis, like Eden in Dante, are a place of seed, into which everything subject to the cyclical order of nature enters at death and proceeds from at birth. Milton's early poems are, like the *Mutabilitie Cantoes*, full of the sense of a distinction between nature as a divinely sanctioned order, the nature of the music of the spheres, and nature as a fallen and largely chaotic world. The former is symbolized by the Gardens of Adonis in *Comus*, from whence the attendant spirit descends to watch over the Lady. The central image of this archetype, Venus watching over Adonis, is (to use a modern distinction) the analogue in terms of Eros to the Madonna and Son in the context of Agape.

Milton picks up the theme of the Pisgah vision in *Paradise Regained*, which assumes an elementary principle of Biblical typology in which the events of Christ's life repeat those of the history of Israel. Israel goes to Egypt, brought down by Joseph, escapes a slaughter of innocents, is cut off from Egypt by the Red Sea, organizes into twelve tribes, wanders forty years in the wilderness, receives the law from Sinai, is saved by a brazen serpent on a pole, crosses the Jordan, and enters the Promised Land under "Joshua, whom the Gentiles Jesus call." Jesus goes to Egypt in infancy, led by Joseph, escapes a slaughter of innocents, is baptized and recognized as the Messiah, wanders forty days in the wilderness, gathers twelve followers, preaches the Sermon on the Mount, saves mankind by dying on a pole, and thereby conquers the Promised Land as the real Joshua. In Milton the temptation corresponds to the Pisgah vision of Moses, except that the gaze is turned in the opposite direction. It marks the climax of Jesus' obedience to the law, just before his active redemption of the world begins, and the sequence of temptations consolidates the world, flesh, and devil into the single form of Satan. The point of epiphany is here represented by the pinnacle of the temple, from which Satan falls away as Jesus remains motionless on top of it. The fall of Satan reminds us that the point of epiphany is also the top of the wheel of fortune, the point from which the tragic hero falls. This ironic use of the point of epiphany occurs in the bible in the story of the Tower of Babel.

The Ptolemaic cosmos eventually disappeared, but the point of epiphany did not, though in more recent literature it is often ironically reversed, or brought to terms with greater demands for credibility. Allowing for this, one may still see the same archetype in the final mountain-top scene of Ibsen's *When We Dead Awaken* and in the central image of Virginia Woolf's *To the Lighthouse*. In the later poetry of Yeats and Eliot it becomes a central unifying image. Such titles as *The Tower* and *The Winding Stair* indicate its importance for Yeats, and the lunar symbolism and the apocalyptic imagery of *The Tower* and *Sailing to Byzantium* are both thoroughly consistent. In Eliot it is the flame reached in the fire sermon of *The Waste Land*, in contrast to the natural cycle which is symbolized by water, and it is also the "multifoliate rose" of *The Hollow Men*. *Ash Wednesday* brings us back again to the purgatorial winding stair, and *Little Gidding* to the burning rose, where there is a descending movement of fire symbolized by the Pentecostal tongues of flame and an ascending one symbolized by Hercules' pyre and "shirt of flame."

CHARLES MUSCATINE

Gothic Form and the Knight's Tale

Though Chaucer completed only a quarter of the projected *Canterbury Tales*, he left a very good idea of its form. This form—a collection of stories framed in the account of a pilgrimage, with the pilgrims telling the stories—has no precise, positivistic source in medieval literature. The framed collection as a genre was already three thousand years old, and had a number of other exemplars in the Middle Ages, but the best and most likely model, Boccaccio's *Decameron*, still lacks certain features that would give it absolute claim to parentage. . . . We do not know whether Chaucer had acquaintance with the *Decameron* or not. The form of his work can be approached, certainly, from a number of other directions. It was an age of collections, attended by a scarcity of books and of entertainment generally, by a newly vigorous intellectual culture, especially among laymen, and by a tradition of gathering exempla for moral guidance and for sermons. . . . The larger form of the poem can be substantially defined by a common generalization about Gothic art. "The basic form of Gothic art," says Hauser (following Frey, and doubtless with no thought of Chaucer),

> is juxtaposition. Whether the individual work is made up of several comparatively independent parts or is not analyzable into such parts, whether it is a pictorial or a plastic, an epic or a dramatic representation, it is always the principle of expansion and not of concentration, of co-ordination and not of subordination, of the open sequence and not of the closed geometric form, by which it is dominated. The beholder is, as it were, led through the stages and stations of a journey, and the picture of reality which it reveals is like a panoramic survey, not a one-sided, unified

From *Chaucer and the French Tradition*, by Charles Muscatine, pp. 167–71, 175, 181–82, 185, 187–90. Published, 1957, by the University of California Press. Reprinted by permission of the publisher.

representation, dominated by a single point of view. In painting it is the 'continuous' method which is favoured; the drama strives to make the episodes as complete as possible and prefers, instead of the concentration of the action in a few decisive situations, frequent changes of scene, of the characters and the motifs. . . . Gothic art leads the onlooker from one detail to another and causes him, as has been well said, to 'unravel' the successive parts of the work one after the other. . . .[1]

This Gothic, sequential procession "through the stages and stations of a journey," a deep-seated general form for the ordering of experience, takes on specific symbolic meaning in its particular manifestations. Edith Kern finds in the *Decameron* journey, the stations of which are successive gardens, a progression "away from society with its sufferings and horrors . . . to the very temple of Venus in the heart of Nature . . . ."[2] The procession of the stages in the English mystery cycle, representing the biographical and historical journey of Man from the Creation to the Resurrection, has a more public and self-evident meaning. The dual procession of Chaucer's travelers and their tales is given such specific moral significance by the conception of a religious pilgrimage. If Chaucer knew the road through Greenwich, he also knew the one through the *Divine Comedy*: "Nel mezzo del *cammin* di nostra vita." The metaphor permeated medieval consciousness. Chaucer adapted his early lyric, *An ABC*, from a poem entitled *Le Pèlerinage de vie humaine*. The idea is expressed nobly in his ballade *Truth*:

> Her is non hoom, her nis but wildernesse:
> Forth, pilgrim, forth! Forth, beste, out of thy stal!
> Know thy contree, look up, thank God of al;
> Hold the heye wey, and lat thy gost thee lede;
> And trouthe thee shal delivere, it is no drede.

The two pilgrimages are specifically related in the Parson's prayer for wisdom,

> To shewe you the wey, in this viage,
> Of thilke parfit glorious pilgrymage
> That highte Jerusalem celestial.

(Pars Prol 49)

The coördinateness and linearity of Chaucer's form, his "heye weye" through life, with its various juxtaposed versions of experience,

[1]Arnold Hauser, *The Social History of Art*, I, trans. Stanley Godman (New York: Alfred A. Knopf, Inc., 1952), pp. 272–73; cf. Dagobert Frey, *Gotik und Renaissance* (Augsburg: 1929), p. 38.
[2]Kern, "Gardens in the *Decameron*," *PMLA*, LXVI (1951), 522.

is invested with a second typically Gothic quality, the tension between phenomenal and ideal, mundane and divine, that informs the art and thought of the period. The variety of pilgrims and tales is thus ordered between traditionally opposed values. This has been very widely recognized in Chaucer criticism, though usually expressed in terms of dramatic rather than symbolic contrast. The pilgrimage frame, with the prologue and links that define it, is likewise ambivalent; it is both realistic and symbolic. This ambivalence is in the symbolic conception of life as a pilgrimage alongside the concrete existence of the Canterbury road, in the generally symbolic character of Chaucer's later naturalism next to his "good ear" and his keen reportorial eye. It is also in various conventionalizations of form and style which stand in an artistically effective relationship to this naturalism.

Of the "two factors in the Gothic duality," Charles Morey says that "the ideal one is visible only in its ensembles; the other [i.e., the realistic] is revealed in innumerable details of which these ensembles are composed."[3] While this formula cannot be strictly applied to the poem, it fits closely enough to explain why so much of its character has eluded naturalistic criticism. Fortunately we have two excellent inspections of the "ensemble" of the *General Prologue*. J. V. Cunningham, bringing to it a sophisticated notion of the nature and function of literary tradition,[4] shows that the form of the opening of the *Tales* is a "special realization" of the form of the dream vision. The setting at a given time of year, the seasonal description, the arrival of the Narrator-actor at a special place, the successive portrayals of the company met there, the introduction of a "guide," and the subsequent initiation of the main action, are the elements and the order of the tradition of the *Roman de la Rose*. In the very largest sense, this dream-vision sequence is itself a modification of the universal medieval pilgrimage, be it in quest of human or divine love, but here it is special enough to show how much of Chaucer's seeing still employs the forms of the specifically courtly tradition.

Cunningham has remarked the persistence of the traditional form, but we must go on to investigate its function. It is not a relic; it enters

[3]Charles R. Morey, *Mediaeval Art* (New York: W. W. Norton & Company, Inc., 1942), p. 259.

[4]"The Literary Form of the Prologue to the *Canterbury Tales*," *MP*, XLIX (1952), pp. 173-74: "What a writer finds in real life is to a large extent what his literary tradition enables him to see and to handle. . . . A literary form . . . is a scheme of experience recognized in the tradition. . . . It is, moreover, a scheme that directs the discovery of material and detail and that orders the disposition of the whole."

a meaningful synthesis such as we have seen unfolding through the early poems and the *Troilus*. By means of this synthesis, secular love is set in juxtaposition to divine love and, on the other side, to the various profanenesses supported by Chaucer's naturalism. Arthur Hoffman's recent study of the "two voices" of the *Prologue* makes just this kind of observation, so sensitively that I can give in summary only a partial indication of its content. Hoffman shows how the opening description of spring, with its natural, sexual metaphors of regeneration, and then its progress toward the other motive of spiritual regeneration, at once establishes a "double view" of the pilgrimage. This ambiguity is perpetuated in the series of portraits, both between and within them. Thus between the Knight and the Squire there is a pointed dualism:

> The Knight's love is an achieved devotion, a matter of pledges fulfilled and of values, if not completely realized, yet woven into the fabric of experience (ideals—"trouthe," "honour," "fredom," "curteisie"). The Squire is a lover, a warm and eager lover, paying court to his lady and sleeping no more then the nightingale. In the one, the acquired, tutored, disciplined, elevated, enlarged love, the piety; in the other, the love channelled into an elaborate social ritual, a parody piety, but still emphatically fresh and full of natural impulse. One cannot miss the creation of the Squire in conventional images of nature . . . comparisons that are a kind of re-emergence of the opening lines of the Prologue, the springtime surge of youthful, natural energy . . . the Knight's pilgrimage is more nearly a response to the voice of the saint.[5]

Within the portraits of the Prioress, the Monk, and the Friar there is tension, in various degrees, between the sacred office and the person, the conventional standard and the individual detail. In the Summoner and the Pardoner it lies in a grimly ironic perversion of the "love" which all of the pilgrims variously pursue. Hoffman's most profound observations come when he shows these tensions ultimately resolved: the Squire bent to the service of his father, and thus to his religious goal; the ambiguous motto of the Prioress, in which secular love is encircled by divine; the Parson and the Plowman, brothers, linking the sacred snd the secular in harmony of purpose and relationship. Even the Summoner and Pardoner, who are described last, suggest in their offices, "beyond their appalling personal deficiency . . . the summoning and pardoning, the judgement and grace which in Christian thought embrace and conclude man's pilgrimage. . . ."[6]

[5]"Chaucer's Prologue to Pilgrimage: The Two Voices," *ELH*, XXI (1954), 6.
[6]Hoffman, "Chaucer's Prologue," p. 16.

Chaucer's use of the seasonal description and the portrait series—both of them conventional devices of romance and rhetoric—is part, then, of an artistic synthesis, and has nothing either of mechanical habit or gratuitous invention about it. The formal portrait and its formal arrangement mean—and here I come somewhere between the historical observation of Cunningham and the textual analysis of Hoffman—a formal, *a priori*, ideal ordering of experience, without which the naturalistic detail would have only the barest sociological significance. The portraits of the *Roman de la Rose* and of the fabliaux, as we have seen, are full of such detail. What Chaucer has done to the conventional portrait is to pull the traits out of their formulated, uniplanar arrangement, thus to give them an added dimension. Many of the portraits in the *Roman* come in selected series, as first the Vices painted on the garden wall, then the company of courtly Virtues of the Lord Deduit. Boccaccio has just such a select company in the *Decameron*. Chaucer quite consciously abandons the exclusive classification and the reasoned sequence—"Al have I nat set folk in hir degree"—to produce pairings and contrasts that span virtue and vice, heaven and earth. His modifications of convention both within and between the portraits produce not only the "real life" of naturalistic criticism, but also the tension, detail against form, observed nature against formulated order, that supports his deepest meaning.

. . .

A reasonable sympathy with conventionalism requires our understanding that the experience of the idealizing imagination is no less varied than that of realistic observation, and no less true. If the themes of most of Chaucer's conventional poems seem to converge toward the single point of recognizing supernal values in human affairs, the nature of the pointing differs with each poem. We do not read Chaucer, after all, for his philosophical conclusions, but for his workings-out, his poetry. Similarly, if tradition seems to codify Chaucer's poetry according to a fixed number of general forms in a defined area of style, the particular structure and local style of each poem are unique.

Chaucer's conventionalism should neither be dismissed nor taken for granted. The criticism of the *Knight's Tale* has long suffered from both of these errors.[7] The trouble has been in the kinds of assumptions

[7]The ensuing remarks are adapted and slightly condensed from my "Form, Texture and Meaning in Chaucer's *Knight's Tale*," *PMLA*, LXV (1950), 911–29. For fuller bibliography and more minute documentation the reader is referred thereto. I must also refer here to three essays, published earlier but unknown to me at the time of first writing, which anticipate and are at least partly confirmed by the present inter-

brought to the poem, in an attention to its poor dramatics rather than its rich symbolism, to its surface rather than its structure. The poem is nominally a romance, adapted from Boccaccio's *Teseida*. The plot concerns the rivalry of Palamon and Arcite, Theban knights, who while they are imprisoned by Duke Theseus fall in love with his fair kinswoman, Emilye. Arcite is released from prison and Palamon escapes; they finally fight for Emilye's hand in a tournament. Arcite wins, but as the moment of victory, in a supernaturally inspired accident, he is thrown from his horse and thereafter dies. After a period of mourning, Palamon marries Emilye. This plot has been taken to be the poem's main feature; but unless we wish to attribute to Chaucer an unlikely lapse of skill or taste, it will not sustain very close scrutiny. The "characterization" of Palamon and Arcite has been widely invoked as a key to the poem. In one view the two knights have quasi-allegorical status, respresenting the Active Life versus the Contemplative Life. But there is little agreement upon which knight is actually the more "contemplative" or the more admirable: if Palamon, the ending is poetic justice; if Arcite, it is irony.[8]

.   .   .

The *Knight's Tale* is essentially neither a story nor a static picture, but rather a sort of poetic pageant. Its design expresses the nature of the noble life,

> That is to seyn, trouthe, honour, knyghthede,   (2789)
> Wysdom, humblesse, estaat, and heigh kynrede,
> Fredom, and al that longeth to that art . . . .

The story is immediately concerned with those two noble activities, love and chivalry, but even more important is the general tenor of the noble life, the pomp and ceremony, the dignity and power, and particularly the repose and assurance with which the exponent of nobility invokes order. Order, which characterizes the structure of the poem, is also the heart of its meaning. The society depicted is one in which form is full of significance, in which life is conducted at a dignified, processional pace, and in which life's pattern is itself a reflection, or

pretation: W. H. French, "The Lovers in the *Knight's Tale*," *JEGP*, XLVIII (1949), 320–28; H. S. Wilson, "*The Knight's Tale* and the *Teseida* Again," *UTQ*, XVIII (1949), 131–46; and most important, William Frost, "An Interpretation of Chaucer's Knight's Tale," *RES*, XXV (1949), 289–304.

[8]See, respectively, H. N. Fairchild, "Active Arcite, Contemplative Palamon," *JEGP*, XXVI (1927), 285–93; J. S. P. Tatlock, *The Development and Chronology of Chaucer's Works* (London: 1907), pp. 232–33.

better, a reproduction, of the order of the universe. And what gives this conception of life its perspective, its depth and seriousness, is its constant awareness of a formidably antagonistic element—chaos, disorder—which in life is an ever-threatening possibility, even in the moments of supremest assuredness, and which in the poem falls across the pattern of order, being clearly exemplified in the erratic reversals of the poem's plot, and deeply embedded in the poem's texture.[9]

The descriptive sections of the *Tale* support this interpretation perfectly, not only in the long passages that come immediately to mind, but also in the short flights that interrupt the narrative more than is warranted by what little information they add to the mere story. By contributing to currents that run continuously throughout the poem— currents that make up the main stream of the noble life—these super- ficially "irrelevant" descriptions achieve a secure position in the poem's pattern, and ultimately contribute in an important way to its meaning.

The portraits of Emetrius and Lygurge, for instance, have this kind of poetic relevance although their contribution to the surface narrative is slight. Emetrius has "A mantelet upon his shulder hang- ynge,/Bret-ful of rubyes rede as fyr sparklynge" (2163–64). Lygurge wears

> A wrethe of gold, arm-greet, of huge wighte,   (2145)
> Upon his heed, set ful of stones brighte,
> Of fyne rubyes and of dyamauntz.

Unlike the portraits in the *General Prologue,* here the imagery is orga- nized around no three-dimensional conception of personality; it is conventional, framed in the flat, to express the magnificence that befits nobility. I have noted that after all the description of these two kings they hardly figure in the narrative. The inference, however, is not that the portraits are a waste and an excrescence, "merely decorative," but that they perform a function that is not directly related to the action and is independent of the question of character. They contribute first to the poem's general texture, to the element of richness in the fabric

---

[9]Cf. William Frost, "An Interpretation of Chaucer's Knight's Tale," *RES,* XXV (1949), 293: "Much of the beauty of the Knight's Tale . . . resides in a certain formal regularity of design"; p. 299: "The recurrent occasions of life for people of such con- dition as this are ceremonious, their actions at such times being imbued with the piety of ancient ritual"; p. 300 (quoting *KnT* 2847–49: "This world nys but a thurghfare ful of wo . . ."): "The sentiment is a commonplace . . . it nevertheless has power in the Knight's Tale because that poem, athough its plot is concerned with success in love and its setting pictures aristocratic splendours, presents on the whole such an abiding and various image of 'every worldly soore.'"

of noble life. More specifically, Chaucer solves the problem of describing the rival companies by describing their leaders; not Palamon and Arcite, but their supporting kings.[10] Their varicolored magnificence, like Theseus' banner, makes the whole field glitter up and down— black, white, yellow, red, green, and gold. Their personal attributes— the trumpet voice of Emetrius, the great brawn of Lygurge, their looks, like lion and griffin—give both a martial quality that we are to attribute to the whole company. About the chariot of Lygurge run great, white, muzzled hunting dogs, big as bullocks. Emetrius' pet animals are a white eagle, lions, and leopards. The fact that these animals are tame only makes the comparison with their masters the more impressive. And practically every other detail is a superlative, the quality of which contributes to martial or royal magnificence.

. . .

Theseus' speech on the loves of Palamon and Arcite (1785–1820), for instance, has prompted the suggestion that here Chaucer revolts against the courtly code which the knights represent.[11] First of all, it must be seen that the poet is not here dealing with courtly love *per se*, but only with love, on a par with chivalry, as one of the persistent facts of the noble life. The tournament is held, we remember, "For love and for encrees of chivalrye" (2184). The emphasis, however, is not as in the courtly allegory, where the inner life is explored and where the action revolves about the pursuit and defense of the lady's rose. The lady in the *Knight's Tale* is merely a symbol of the noble man's desires. And the question of love is never in debate here. We take love in this society for granted, and then go on to discover how faithfully experience in love exemplifies the partial blindness of all earthly experience. Love, we find, can create dissension between sworn brothers; can make a man lament his release from prison; make him forsake safety and native land; and, after unending toll of time and strength, it can leave him bloody and desirous of death. Theseus' speech on love, as his speech on Arcite's death, is normative and judicial; and to the noble, the mature mind, the paradoxically impractical quality of love is both laughable and admirable. The rivalry and consequent exploits of Palamon and

[10]Walter Clyde Curry, *Chaucer and the Mediaeval Sciences* (Oxford: 1926), pp. 130–39, shows that the physiognomies of Lygurge and Emetrius, in line with the precise astrological correspondences of the poem, are respectively those of "Saturnalian" and "Martian" men. Curry asserts (p. 120) "that the real conflict behind the surface action of the story is a conflict between the planets Saturn and Mars." But this is to mistake the cosmic symptoms for the disease itself.

[11]Agnes K. Getty, "Chaucer's Changing Conceptions of the Humble Lover," *PMLA*, XLIV (1929), 210–12.

Arcite are so impractical, and yet so much a reflex of their knightly spirits, that there is something to be said on both sides. Theseus' speech, therefore, is a mature appraisal, not an adverse criticism, of courtly love; certainly not a reflection of Chaucer's "strong revolt against the code."

.   .   .

I have already suggested that the poem's speeches, like its descriptions, are largely part of its texture; many of them are less important as pointing to specific psychological characteristics that issue in direct action than as elements in broader organizations, with deeper and more ulterior relevance to what goes on in the poem. Thus we have from Palamon and Arcite a considerable number of lyrics, some of them contributing only to the poem's general background of conventional love and chivalry, and others, more important, in which love lament melts into poetry of a more philosophical kind, and brings us to the heart of the issue. This latter characteristic of the poem's texture supports the view that love, which has been too often regarded as the poem's central theme, is used only as a vehicle of expression, a mode of experience of the noble life, which is itself the subject of the poem and the object of its philosophic questions. Thus, in the magnificent death speech of Arcite the lyric of love merges with the philosophical, the lady addressed becomes part of the speech's descriptive imagery, and the theme of love itself is subsumed in the category of all earthly experience:

> "Naught may the woful spirit in myn herte   (2765)
> Declare o point of alle my sorwes smerte
> To yow, my lady, that I love moost;
> But I biquethe the servyce of my goost
> To yow aboven every creature,
> Syn that my lyf may no lenger dure.
> Allas, the wo! allas, the peynes stronge,
> That I for yow have suffred, and so longe!
> Allas, the deeth! allas, myn Emelye!
> Allas, departynge of oure compaignye!
> Allas, myn hertes queene! allas, my wyf!
> Myn hertes lady, endere of my lyf!
> What is this world? what asketh men to have?
> Now with his love, now in his colde grave
> Allone, withouten any compaignye."

.   .   .

In Theseus' majestic summary there is a final echo, the continuing rhetorical repetition as insistent as fate itself:

> "He moot be deed, the kyng as shal a page;   (3030)
> Som in his bed, som in the depe see,
> Som in the large feeld, as men may see . . . ."

This subsurface insistence on disorder is the poem's crowning complexity, its most compelling claim to maturity. We have here no glittering, romantic fairy-castle world. The impressive, patterned edifice of the noble life, its dignity and richness, its regard for law and decorum, are all bulwarks against the everthreatening forces of chaos, and in constant collision with them. And the crowning nobility, as expressed by this poem, goes beyond a grasp of the forms of social and civil order, beyond magnificence in any earthly sense, to a perception of the order beyond chaos. When the earthly designs suddenly crumble, true nobility is faith in the ultimate order of all things. Saturn, disorder, nothing more nor less, is the agent of Arcite's death, and Theseus, noble in the highest sense, interprets it in the deepest perspective. In contrast is the incomplete perception of the wailing women of Athens:

> "Why woldestow be deed," thise wommen crye,   (2835)
> And haddest gold ynough, and Emelye?"

The history of Thebes had perpetual interest for Chaucer as an example of the struggle between noble designs and chaos. Palamon and Arcite, Thebans, lovers, fighters and sufferers, through whom the pursuit of the noble life is presented, exemplify through their experiences and express through their speeches this central conflict.

W. P. KER

Romance

The eighteenth century is generally supposed to have been
anti-romantic in literature, through the revolution in taste which is
described by Hurd in his *Letters on Chivalry and Romance* (1762):

> Henceforth, the taste of wit and poetry took a new turn, and the
> Muse who had wandered so long in the world of fiction was
> now constrained against her will—
> > To stoop with disenchanted wings to truth,
>
> as Sir John Denham somewhere expresses her present enforced
> state, not unhappily. What we have gotten by this revolution,
> you will say, is a great deal of good sense. What we have lost is
> a world of fine fabling.

It could not be put better than this, the difference between the two
ages—Spenser and Pope. It is an historical judgment that really
describes a real difference, and the judgment is all the more significant
because it is uttered by a man who is living in the middle of what he
describes, who belongs as an eighteenth-century literary man to a
world of good sense—a world which is thus conscious of itself, and able
to describe itself. What Hurd says in the lifetime of Dr. Johnson could
not be improved by anyone writing in a later age with all the opportunities for comparison and revision of judgment that are afforded by
later revolutions in taste. Hurd is one of the chief advocates of the
Faerie Queene in the eighteenth century; one of those who were not quite
satisfied with good sense. His *Letters on Chivalry and Romance* are a protest against the restriction of poetry, a claim for freedom, a justification
of the things which were popularly condemned as Gothic and fanciful.
His protest throughout is delightfully written, and full of good sayings
and good temper. It is not extravagant or effusive; it is all the more

From *Collected Essays II*, by W. P. Ker, pp. 310–26. Published, 1925, Macmillan
& Co. Ltd., London. Reprinted by permission of the publisher.

235

telling as a proof of the literary reaction against common sense. Here is a very reasonable man, no anarchist or revolutionary, writing in elegant language to defend the miraculous things in Ariosto, Tasso and Spenser. "The Fairy tales of Tasso do him more honour than what are called the more natural, that is the classical, parts of his poem. We make a shift to run over the passages he has copied from Virgil. We are all on fire amidst the magical feats of Ismen, and the enchantments of Armida."

Hurd, of course, could not have written as he did if he had been alone in his taste. He was writing on behalf of many unknown readers, who agreed with him. There was a strong romantic tradition in the eighteenth century, though it is not the main influence and does not give its character to the literature of the time. "The fictions of the Gothic romances are not so remote from credibility as is commonly supposed," said Dr. Johnson; he amused himself in Skye by thinking of his long days in the saddle or at sea, as the journey of a knight errant who finds entertainment, at the end of his day, in some gracious gentle house at Raasay or Dunvegan.

Dr. Johnson was fond of old romances, and so no doubt were other people in his time, and many other people who did not share this taste had at one time shared it, had wandered like Milton in the fables of chivalry, had at any rate in the nursery, like Steele's young friend, passed from the fiction of Æsop's Fables to the history of Belianis of Greece and the Seven Champions of Christendom.[1] Wordsworth, like Dr. Johnson, had much more reading than he ever turned to use in his own works, and Wordsworth gives evidence about the vogue of old romances in his own early days. He has nothing but gratitude for them, and he cannot bear to see them displaced by the crude new

[1]"—a great Master of all the Learning on t'other Side Eight Years old. I perceived him a very great Historian in Æsop's Fables: But he frankly declared to me his mind, that he did not delight in that learning, because he did not believe they were true; for which reason I found that he had very much turned his studies for about a twelve-month past into the Lives and Adventures of Don Bellianis of Greece, Guy of War-wick, the Seven Champions, and other historians of that age. . . . He would tell you the mismanagements of John Hickathrift, find fault with the passionate temper in Bevis of Southampton, and loved St. George for being the champion of England; and by this means had his thoughts insensibly moulded into the notions of discretion, virtue, and honour. I was extolling his accomplishments when the mother told me that the little girl who led me in this morning was in her way a better scholar than he: 'Betty' (says she) 'deals chiefly in Fairies and Sprights, and sometimes in a winter night will terrify the maids with her accounts till they are afraid to go up to bed.'" Tatler No. 95 (Steele).

educational substitutes which are provided by modern progress and the
march of intellect:

> Oh! give us once again the wishing cap
> Of Fortunatus, and the invisible coat
> Of Jack the Giant-Killer, Robin Hood,
> And Sabra in the forest with St. George!

Now if one puts together Hurd's remark—"We have lost a world of
fine fabling"—with Wordsworth's complaint against the modern edu-
cator, a rather unexpected result may appear. Hurd means that the
change of taste (we may call it "eighteenth century," though of course
it began before that) expelled romance from poetry, and did harm to
poetry by confining it in range and method. Wordsworth, writing
early in the nineteenth century, finds that whatever may be the fortune of poetry the common prose children of England are being de-
frauded of their inheritance; their allowance of fairy tales is stopped.
The result, when these two statements are put together, is this: that the
eighteenth century, which generally did without romance in its literature, kept up the supply of romance for its children, and at least allowed the reading of romance to its grown men; while the nineteenth
century, coming in with a great romantic revolution in literature,
cuts off the tradition of romance among simpler unliterary people,
takes away the *Seven Champions* from the schoolboy and the ballads
from the country-side—at the same time that motives of romance are
being sought for everywhere by literary artists for their own purposes.

Few revolutions or general changes of habit have been more important than that which cut off the old romantic popular traditions of
folk-lore and ballads in the nineteenth century, and put modern educational text-books in their place. This means a change in the minds of
modern civilised human beings, making them unlike all their ancestors.
They learn nothing now in the way that all generations, including
those of the enlightened eighteenth century, learned their ballads
and fairy stories. These things may come to them by way of books; they
do not come as part of their real life, from the mouth of their nurse or
grandmother; and so the child is taken away from his native earth and
his home, and is turned into an abstract educational product, owing the
contents of his mind to schoolmasters. In the nineteenth century almost
everywhere the old immemorial traditions of popular romance have
withered up. The shepherds of Ettrick and Liddesdale know nothing
of the old ballads, or know them only as any foreigner might know the

Border Minstrelsy, out of books. The Fairy Tales that once were English are known now mostly through Grimm, where they are known at all. Every child knows the *Travelling Companion*, which was Peele's *Old Wives' Tale*, but they know it from Hans Andersen, not from their grandmothers.

The appetite for romance has always been strong, even in the most reasonable and scientific ages. The eighteenth century was fairly well supplied; it had, as Dr. Johnson proves, the old books of chivalry, it had the *Arabian Nights*, it had the *Orlando* and the *Faerie Queene*. The favourite reading of Edward Waverley in his boyhood was that of Charles James Fox through all his life. But the craving was unsatisfied; there were not enough new stories. We know more or less how the fashion changed again; how literary good sense went down in value, how Macpherson's Ossian triumphed and took captive some of the strongest minds in Europe.

Peacock has described the new fashions in the essay which provoked Shelley to his Defence of Poetry:

> Mr. Scott digs up the poachers and cattle-stealers of the ancient border. Lord Byron cruises for thieves and pirates on the shores of the Morea and among the Greek islands. Mr. Southey wades through ponderous volumes of travels and old chronicles, from which he carefully selects all that is false, useless, and absurd, as being essentially poetical; and when he has a commonplace book full of monstrosities, strings them into an epic. Mr. Wordsworth picks up village legends from old women and sextons; and Mr. Coleridge to the valuable information derived from similar sources superadds the dreams of crazy theologians and the mysticisms of German metaphysics, and favours the world with visions in verse in which the quadruple elements of sexton, old woman, Jeremy Taylor, and Emanuel Kant, are harmonised into a delicious poetical compound.

In this revolution one is often amazed at the feebleness of the victors, the disproportion between the trifling interest of the *Castle of Otranto* and its immense success—or between the present value of Macpherson and the praise of Ossian in Goethe's *Werther*. Among the strange things in history is the relation of Monk Lewis and Scott. The tales of Terror and Wonder are mostly trash:

> Not long lived the Baron and none since that time
>   To inhabit the castle presume,
> For chroniclers tell that by order sublime
> There Imogene suffers the pain of her crime
>   And mourns her deplorable doom.

At midnight four times in the year does her sprite,
  When mortals in slumber are bound,
Arrayed in her bridal apparel of white
Appear in the hall with the skeleton-knight,
  And shriek as he whirls her around.

While they drink out of skulls newly torn from the grave,
  Dancing round them pale spectres are seen;
Their liquor is blood, and this horrible stave
They howl: "To the health of Alonzo the brave
  And his consort the False Imogene!"

This verse Coleridge says "has an effect not unlike that of galloping over a paved road in a German stagewaggon without springs." But he thinks *Alonzo and Imogene* worth mentioning.

The appetite was so strong that almost anything with a touch of romance was welcome. "Castle of Wolfenbach, Clermont, Mysterious Warnings, Necromancer of the Black Forest, Midnight Bell, Orphan of the Rhine, and Horrid Mysteries. Those will last us some time." The evidence of Miss Austen is not to be refused.

Those who provided the "horrid mysteries" were often clear enough in their own mind as to their value. Lewis parodies his own romance, and adds to his Tales of Wonder a satirical ballad which, to use "a selection from the language spoken among men," gives the whole thing away. Smedley's Ghost speaks (out of the *Dunciad*):

Ah! knew'st thou in the happier days
  How smooth the way to fame,
That now e'en D—r—n wears the bays,
  E'en Kn—t acquires a name:

Thyself would leave the hackneyed themes
  That Pope, that Dryden tired;
Thyself indulge in German dreams
  By great Goethe inspired.

Loves not Invention ever young
  The Weser's golden strand?
Has not the harp wild genius strung
  In Schiller's magic hand?

O come with foreign fable fraught
  And weave the Runic rhyme,
Drink as I drank the siren draught
  In Thames' congenial slime.

> Though first the nymph thou hast not led
> From Danube's parent shore,
> Still may'st thou to the tuneful dead
> Add one dull Briton more.

The truth seems to be that all romantic revivals are followed by crowds of impostors; sham romance appears to be easy; it has often been profitable. It is found in many different periods, and the explorer who goes back into the Middle Ages to get the genuine thing will too often find only the ancestors of Monk Lewis—mechanical contrivers, professional dealers of more or less ingenuity and various degrees of dullness. Oberon in *Huon of Bordeaux* is a son of Julius Caesar and Fata Morgana, and that is a type of the incongruous things to be found in the old romantic schools. A great philologist has told me how, in his youth, he was drawn to read *William and the Werwolf*; the title was promising. But the result was so disappointing that he gave up romance and took to the study of Middle English. There are similar cases of disappointment to be confessed by those whom Carlyle once led to his German romantic authors.

Where is true romance? Where is it, the *blaue Blume*? Where is the island of Bimini? It is not to be found where the professional agents of the romantic schools have "opened up the country." The fashionable romance of the twelfth century has little more of the true magic than Macpherson or the German work that followed him; the "horrid mysteries" of the Elizabethan drama often fail as grievously as the emphasis of Manfred or Hernani, in comparison with what one knows for the true test of romance, the spell of the *Ancient Mariner* or some of the old ballads, *The Widow's Sons*, *The Milldams of Binnorie*—or let us say, to the due honour of the despised rationalist eighteenth century, the magic of the *Castle of Indolence*:

> Full in the passage of the vale above
> A sable silent solemn forest stood,
> Where nought but shadowy forms were seen to move,
> As Idless fancied in her dreaming mood;
> And up the hills on either side a wood
> Of blackening pines aye waving to and fro
> Sent forth a sleepy horror through the blood,
> And where the valley winded out below,
> The murmuring main was heard and scarcely heard
>   to flow.

Many a reader of romance has fared badly and returned in depression like the gentleman who went in the twelfth century to look for the marvels of the forest of Broceliande:

> A fool I went, a fool I came,
> Folly I sought, and mine the blame.

Is the magic world anywhere to be found? One good rule in this as in other holiday explorations is to do without the organisers of traffic as far as possible. Romance is often near its best with authors who are not thinking about it, or who think other things more important; with Homer, and with Dante, who like Dr. Johnson was a reader of books of chivalry, but did not imitate them directly. The romance that springs up along with the graver intentions of Dante and Milton is often more worth than the deliberate romance of Ovid or Ariosto.

Then, quite at the other side and far away from the great poets, are the anonymous authors of ballads and tellers of folk-lore stories, and along with these I would put some authors who have the gift of bringing back the charm of a winter's tale to stories that have been sophisticated or overdressed by professional literary men. I think particularly of the old Italian writer from whom Tennyson took the *Lady of Shalott*; I think of the beautiful Welsh prose stories of *Peredur* and the *Lady of the Fountain* and *Geraint and Enid*—stories recovered from the French and restored from the verse of the fashionable French poet—admirable in its own way—to a simpler and more effective form.

It would be a great mistake to think of popular folk-lore fairy tales as containing no more than the *matter* of romance—plots and adventures that may serve an ambitious poet and be turned into a noble form of poetry in the *Odyssey*. This no doubt is one of the uses of fairy tales; to be the matter for successive poets, from Homer onwards. But they are not mere material; and one language differs from another in the fashion of its fairy tales. We know how easy it is for tradition to go wrong, to mix and deface and mangle stories. Yet often we find stories surviving unimpaired, with the unities preserved, taking different shapes, all good and sound, in different countries—like that of the *Travelling Companion*, which is better and fresher in a West Irish traditional version, written down in the nineteenth century, than in many of the older medieval literary renderings. It is enough to compare Dr. Hyde's Irish stories or Campbell's *Tales of the West Highlands* with Grimm or with Dasent's *Tales from the Norse*, to see how much variety of style and what admirable form there may be in traditional stories.

I take one example which is the more remarkable because it gives an incident that comes at the beginning of *Percival* and may be compared with *Peredur* and the other versions of that story by those who are interested specially in such things.

This that I am going to quote is not from a variant of *Percival*, though it has some resemblances in detail; it is the opening of the story of *The Knight of the Red Shield* in Campbell of Islay's second volume:

> There was before now a king of Eirinn and he went himself and his people and his warriors and his nobles and his great gentles to the hill of hunting and game. They sat on a hillock coloured green colour, where the sun would rise early and where she would set late. Said the one of swifter mouth than the rest: "Who now in the four brown quarters of the universe would have the heart to put an affront and disgrace on the King of Eirinn, and he in the midst of the people and the warriors, great gentles and nobles of his realm?"
>
> "Are ye not silly," said the king; "he might come, one who should put an affront and disgrace on me, and that ye could not pluck the worst hair in his beard out of it."
>
> It was thus it was. They saw the shadow of a shower coming from the western airt and going to the eastern airt, and the rider of a black filly coming cheerily after it. [Here follows one of the ornamental rhetorical amplifications which are common in the Gaelic; unnecessary for the story.]
>
> Then he spoke to them in the understanding quieting truly wise words of real knowledge; and before there was any more talk between them he put over the fist, and he struck the king between the mouth and the nose, and he drove out three of his teeth, and he caught them in his fist, and he put them in his pouch, and he went away.
>
> "Did not I say to you," said the king, "that one might come who should put an affront and disgrace on me, and that you could not pluck the worst hair in his beard out of it?"

Let me quote another passage of romance from another Gaelic story, the voyage of Mael Duin. Its translator, Mr. Whitley Stokes (many thanks to him for that and many other good gifts to the lovers of stories), has noted this as having the "natural magic" of which Mr. Arnold spoke in his *Lectures on Celtic Literature*:

> Thereafter they voyaged till they found a great silvern column. It had four sides, and the width of each of these sides was two oarstrokes of the boat, so that in its whole circumference there were eight oarstrokes of the boat. And not a single sod of earth was about it, but only the boundless ocean. And they saw not how its base was below nor how its summit was above. Out of its summit came a silvern net far away from it; and the boat went under sail through a mesh of that net.
>
> And then they heard a voice from the summit of yonder pillar, mighty, and clear, and distinct. But they knew not the tongue it spake, nor the words it uttered.

Sometimes one is inclined to think that Romance, like Happiness, is "there where thou art not"; if it were real, would it be romance? Is it not all vague, impalpable—less true to its own nature in the *Rime of the Ancient Mariner*, which is a complete and reasonable thing, than in the music of *Kubla Khan*? It is strange how often it seems to spring up in the most unlikely ground, in burlesque even, like the *Castle of Indolence*, or in satire, like the *Vision of Judgement*. But perhaps one ought not to be led away like this by the magic of the artists who play with shadowy recollections, who show the landscape of romance, as in the *Castle of Indolence*, but never tell the story, who evoke the form of it, as in *Kubla Khan*, and leave the matter, a *caput mortuum*, to be thrown away. Sometimes one is inclined to take *Romance* as a name for the most subtle spirit of imagination, for the quintessence of poetry; and this may be right. But it is too difficult, for the present purpose at any rate, and there are other meanings of the word and other considerations which may be dealt with more familiarly; I come back to plainer ground.

Though it is true that the story-tellers are often disappointing, yet the poor stories, even those ridiculed in *Sir Thopas* and *Don Quixote*, have their value and an important place in history. Many of them seem only fit for puppet-shows, like that of Don Gayferos; but the puppet-shows and chapbooks, the beggar minstrels and reciters, have had a great deal to do with the making of people's minds. The uses of romance —in its ruder form we need not scruple to consider what is the use of it—may be seen most beautifully in the passage of Barbour's *Bruce* where the good King Robert takes the romance of *Ferumbras* to amuse his people on the shore of Loch Lomond, while the slow ferryboat works to and fro bringing the rest of the party across:

> The king the quhilis meryly
> Red to thaim that war him by
> Romanys of worthi Ferambrace
> That worthily our-cummyn was
> Throw the rycht douchty Olywer.
>
> . . .
>
> The gud king upon this maner
> Comfortyt thaim that war him ner;
> And maid thaim gamyn and solace
> Till that his folk all passyt was.

I bought a copy of the same story as a chapbook in Madrid, and think there must be something in it to have lasted so long. In Italy you may still find *I Reali di Francia* on bookstalls, alongside of the realists of France, and you may remember the old story of the man found weeping in an Italian market-place because he had just heard from a reciter the news of the death of Roland. It was from tastes and interests of that sort that the *Orlando* grew to its poetical form with Boiardo and Ariosto; and so the old Italian audiences and the story-tellers of the market-place have their share in Spenser's *Faerie Queene*, together with the family of Sir Thopas, as Warton has shown. In Jusserand's *English Novel in the Time of Shakespeare* we may trace the fortunes of many of the old books of chivalry; Mr. Firth, in his introduction to the *Pilgrim's Progress*, has made out the debt of Bunyan to Sir Bevis of Southampton —one of the pleasantest of demonstrations, in a kind of science which is often horribly abused by dull people, but not on that account to be rejected.

The *Pilgrim's Progress* is one of the results of medieval romance;[2] it has the sort of plan which saves even some of the dull romances from total failure, and is found in some of the best. It is the simplest thing in the world; scarcely to be called a plot—merely a journey with adventures. Yet what more is wanted to give the romancer his opportunity? It is one of the things that never grow old, from Theseus and Jason to Sir Percival, and so on to the *Pilgrim's Progress* and so to modern examples, which anyone may think of for himself. *Rob Roy* has it. The second part of *Rob Roy*, the Highland adventures and Bailie Nicol Jarvie, have generally rather eclipsed the first part, but not so as to spoil the impression of Francis Osbaldistone's journey northward, with the accompaniment of "Mr. Campbell"—surely one of the best things in the whole of Scott for suspense and gradual deepening of interest.

Here I come to perilous ground, and I ask for sympathy. I have known about it all along, and so far I have succeeded in evading that particular risk. But now I come, to use the old ambiguous phrase, "into the danger" of Stevenson's *Essay on Romance*. The danger is twofold; first, when one thinks of what Stevenson has written, it is more difficult than ever to have ideas of one's own; but again he speaks rather slightingly of the art of Scott, and ends not quite generously with a note of depreciation—a mistake, surely, in his own art. Of

[2]"The Scriptures, thought I, what are they? A dead letter, a little ink and paper, of three or four shillings worth. Give me a ballad, a newsbook, George on horseback or Bevis of Southampton, give me some book that teaches curious arts, that tells of old fables; but for the holy Scriptures I cared not."

course Stevenson is very far from the enemies of Scott—from those who see no more in him than Peacock saw, or Mark Twain, with his philosophical proof that all the vanity of Southern chivalry—that is, of the Southern States in America—is attributable to *Ivanhoe*. And it can hardly be said that Stevenson's criticism of the one particular passage in *Guy Mannering* is unreasonable or unjustified, as far as it goes. But it gives a wrong impression, and the conclusion—Scott "an idle child"— is a failure of critical judgment. There is every kind of interest and every variety of art in Scott. There is the machinery of the ordinary historical novel so easily imitated by G. P. R. James and many others in all the tongues of Europe, so hopelessly antiquated now. One remembers the story of Neibuhr; how when he was on his death bed he had Fenimore Cooper recommended to him for diversion, and tried him, and then asked for Josephus instead. And there is the adventure which is of quite a different sort from the antiquarian furniture and the conventional dialogue—adventures like those of which I have spoken in *Rob Roy*—like that of Sir Dugald Dalgetty in his escape from Inverary, or Everard in *Woodstock*, when he is caught in the dark and held down with the sword-point pricking at his throat. I have cause to remember that, because it is the first thing of Scott's that I remember; the book was being read aloud, and it seemed to me that it would be worth looking into. There is the admirable plot of the *Talisman*, a story which does not bring into play any of the comic genius of the author, and so attains a different kind of success from the richer books like *Old Mortality* and the *Heart of Midlothian, Guy Mannering*, and the *Fair Maid of Perth*, where there are interests woven into romance—interests of character and conversation—which are not, properly speaking, romantic at all—the humours of Dandie Dinmont and Cuddie Headrigg.

Quite unlike the diffuse historical manner of much of *Waverley* and *Kenilworth* and *Quentin Durward*, there is the form, or rather many forms, of short story: Wandering Willie's Tale in *Redgauntlet—The Highland Widow—The Two Drovers*: these last bringing in a tragic element of mistake and misunderstanding with more effect than any of the longer novels. And in verse there is the same enormous variety— between the plain straightforward narrative of the *Lady of the Lake* and the lyrical mystery of *County Guy* and some other of the shorter pieces. All which goes to prove what needs no particular proof, that Romance means almost everything—from the two horsemen riding together at the beginning of the historical novel, or from the pasteboard Moors of the puppet-show, to the spell of the enchanted ground, the music of dreams and shadows.

Additional Note

The following passage from the *Citizen of the World* gives a glimpse of a romantic school not now very clearly remembered:

"I was going to expose his mistakes when it was insisted that I had nothing of the true Eastern manner in my delivery. 'This gentleman's conversation,' said one of the ladies who was a great reader, 'is like our own—mere chit-chat and common sense; there is nothing like sense in the true Eastern style, where nothing more is required but sublimity. Oh! for a history of Aboulfaouris the grand voyager, of genii, magicians, rocks, bags of bullets, giants and enchanters, where all is great, obscure, magnificent, and unintelligible.' 'I have written many a sheet of Eastern tale myself,' interrupts the author, 'and I defy the severest critic to say but that I have stuck close to the true manner. I have compared a lady's chin to the snow upon the mountains of Banek; a soldier's sword to the clouds that obscure the face of heaven. If riches are mentioned, I compare them to the flocks that graze the verdant Tefflis; if poverty, to the mists that veil the brow of Mount Baku. I have used *thee* and *thou* upon all occasions; I have described fallen stars and splitting mountains, not forgetting the little houris who make a pretty figure in every description. But you shall hear how I generally begin: "Eben-benbolo who was the son of Ban, was born on the foggy summits of Benderabassi. His beard was whiter than the feathers which veil the breast of the penguin; his eyes were like the eyes of doves when washed by the dews of the morning; his hair, which hung like the willow weeping over the glossy stream, was so beautiful that it seemed to reflect its own brightness, and his feet were as the feet of a wild deer which fleeth to the tops of the mountains." There, there is the true Eastern taste for you; every advance made towards sense is only a deviation from sound. Eastern tales should always be sonorous, lofty, musical, and unmeaning.' " Goldsmith, *Citizen of the World*, Letter XXXIII.

ARTHUR JOHNSTON

Romance Reborn

Give me the works which delighted my youth! Give me the History of St
George, *and the* Seven Champions of Christendom, *which at every
leisure moment I used to hide myself in a corner to read.*
Coleridge, Letters, ed. E. M. Coleridge (*1895*), *i. II n.*

The gradual descent of the romances to the literature of
the nursery, though in one sense an embarrassment to the scholars
who tried to revive interest in them in their original forms, was also an
encouragement to the historically minded antiquary, who could thereby trace an unbroken link with the literature of the middle ages.
Thomas Warton, for example, collected references to the reading of
romances in the sixteenth and seventeenth centuries to show that
'however monstrous and unnatural these compositions may appear to
this age of reason and refinement',[1] they were not only popular reading
in previous ages, but the reading of poets and men of letters whom it
was impossible not to admire. They were the source 'from which
young readers especially, in the age of fiction and fancy, nourished the
SUBLIME'.[2] Since the romances were in his own day the literature of
children, it was natural for Johnson to argue that the ages in which
they were the predominant imaginative literature were ages when
learning was in its infancy.[3] The nation, like the individual, grew out
of such a taste for 'very wild improbable tales' that 'exhibited only the
superficial appearances of action, related the events but omitted the
causes, and were formed for such as delighted in wonders rather than

From *Enchanted Ground* by Arthur Johnston, pp. 32–33, 38–50 *passim*. Copyright
© 1964 by Arthur Johnston. Reprinted by permission of The Athlone Press and
Oxford University Press, Inc.

[1]T. Warton, *Observations on the Faerie Queene* (1762), ii, 267.
[2]*Ibid.*, i, 188.
[3]Johnson, Preface to *The Plays of Shakespeare* (1765), i, xl.

247

in truth'.[4] The revival of interest in them was an attempt to return to sources of inspiration which had been invaluable for Spenser, Shakespeare and Milton, but not an encouragement to 'common Readers', amongst whom, thought Percy, 'it would do hurt'.[5]

For Johnson an understanding of the literary expectations of Shakespeare's audience was to be derived from a study of the romances on which Elizabethan popular taste was built. But he justified such reading by the modern scholar by pointing also to the

> fertility of invention, the beauty of style and expression, the curiosity of seeing with what kind of performance the age and country in which they were written was delighted: for it is to be apprehended, that at the time when very wild and improbable tales were well received, the people were in a barbarous state, and so on the footing of children.[6]

There had always been uneasiness about the reading of romances, whether on literary or moral grounds. The decline of the medieval stories to the lowest level of literacy in the community did not result in the disappearance of the age-old arguments against them. These flourished in application to their descendants, the modern romances and novels.[7]

.   .   .

For the traditionalist . . . the perpetuation into adult life of a vision admittedly valuable in childhood rendered the adult incapable of attending coolly to reality. As Foster explained, in the adult

> the influence of this habit of dwelling on the beautiful fallacious forms of imagination, will accompany the mind into the most serious speculations, or rather musings, on the real world, and what is to be done in it and expected; . . . . The vulgar materials, that constitute the actual economy of the world, will rise up to its sight in fictitious forms, which it cannot disenchant into plain reality, nor will even suspect to be deceptive.[8]

This view was a legacy from the late seventeenth century, when the 'world in imagination' was distrusted. To John Smith, the 'Imagina-

---

[4]*Ibid.*

[5]*Percy-Farmer Correspondence*, p. 7.

[6]Boswell, *Life of Johnson*, ed. G. Birbeck Hill and L. F. Powell (Oxford: 1934–50), iv, 17.

[7]For examples of attacks on the novel see such periodical essays as *The World*, Nos. 19, 25, 79; *The Lounger*, Nos. 20, 74, 92; *The Observer*, No. 27; *The Miniature*, No. 2; Vicesimus Knox, *Essays* (ed. 1823), No. 14; and George Colman's *Polly Honeycombe* (1760).

[8]John Foster, 'On the Application of the Epithet "Romantic"' in *Essays in a Series of Letters to a Friend* (1806) i, 249.

tive Powers . . . will be breathing a gross dew upon the pure Glass of our Understandings'.[9] The romances, whether medieval, Peninsular or modern, were condemned as filling the mind with false notions, hindering 'the *true understanding* and *real notions* of things as they are in the World, which *true histories* set forth'.[10] Even serious thinkers were troubled by false notions of *things*, thought Obadiah Walker, 'wandering and insignificant fancies *in the brain* (Romances in thought)'. How much more troubled were weak-minded people by the romances themselves. As with the novel later, the enemies of romance were almost as numerous as the readers of it. Those who supplied the stories argued that 'Romantick Poetry' had as its end

> 1. Either to attract the Curious and Careless Eyes of such, who can be no otherwayes induc'd to cultivate their wits and inform their Minds; or 2. To Recreate (not without some profit) the overintense Spirits after more serious Reading; or 3. To Reprove Powerful Vice without danger to the Mythologist; or 4. Lastly, to Affect those with Vertue thus set off by Fable, whose Luxuriant Fancies cannot descend to the looking on more plain Morality.[11]

Those who opposed them complained that

> they commonly do more Mischief than Good. For besides misspending of time, giving an ill-Tincture to the Imagination, and stuffing the Head with Rubbish, they paint good Qualities out of Character, give false Images of Life, teach young people to be indiscreet in Friendship and Passions, put them in a Way how to cheat their Parents with more Dexterity, and steal a Misfortune for their Life-Time.[12]

Dr. Johnson, however, was in agreement with Coleridge, Wordsworth, Lamb and Godwin when he pointed out that 'Babies do not want to hear about babies; they like to be told of giants and castles, and of somewhat which can stretch and stimulate their little minds'.[13]

In 1851 Henry Mayhew's penny bookseller was still selling *The Seven Champions*. 'There's plenty of "Henry and Emmas", and . . . "Good Books for Good Boys and Girls"; but when people buys really for their children, they buys the old stories—at least they does of me'.[14]

[9]John Smith, *Discourses* (1673), p. 21.
[10]Obadiah Walker, *Of Education, Especially of Young Gentlemen* (Oxford: 1673), ch. v, §6.
[11]*Arnaldo, or The Injur'd Lover*, Made English by T. S. (1660), Preface, sig. A7.
[12]Jeremy Collier, *Appendix to Morey's Great Historical, Geographical, and Poetical Dictionary* (1721), sig. 602.
[13]Mrs. Piozzi, *Anecdotes*, p. 13.
[14]Henry Mayhew, *London Labour and the London Poor* (1864), i, 324.

In the households of Percy and Scott, to move from the nursery to the study, from the chapbook to the manuscript, must have been no un-usual experience. Once in the study, the scholar's attitude towards the romances was coloured by the recollection that these stories had fired the imaginations of Spenser, Shakespeare and Milton. As they worked, Percy, Warton, Ritson, Scott and Ellis began to give recogniz-able shape to various branches of literary study that we now take for granted. Percy, for example, collected the Peninsular romances in order to illustrate the satirical basis of *Don Quixote*, wrote essays on minstrels, alliterative poetry and the development of the drama, and printed the first bibliography of metrical romances. Ritson and Ellis wrote on the development of the English language in the middle ages, and both followed Warton in mastering some of the medieval French romances in order to assess the dependence of English romances upon them. Warton traced the development of romance and allegory in the middle ages in order to illustrate Spenser's heritage. Scott, in his edition of *Sir Tristrem*, set a pattern for the thorough presentation of medieval texts, providing full notes, glossary, and a discussion of authorship, dating, analogues, and a description of his manuscript source. All their work was discovery—of texts that had probably not been read for centuries.

. . .

The scholars were conscious that the romances were not only cen-tral to a study of the development of English literature, but could be of value in revivifying contemporary poetry. Their scholarly interests were directed to a true understanding of the past, but, by presenting their findings in a form that would appeal to the cultured reader, they sought also to encourage antiquarian studies as a valuable stimulus for the modern poet. Thomas Warton combined the roles of scholar and Poet Laureate, and advocated new forms of poetry, 'Poetry endued with new Manners and Images'.[15] He agreed with Percy that 'the appetite of the public is so palled with all the common forms of poetry', and looked to 'some new Spenser' to revive it[16] Both shared Hurd's belief that 'the manners of romance are better calculated to answer the purposes of pure poetry, to captivate the imagination, and to produce surprise, than the fictions of classical antiquity'.[17] Since they could point to Spenser and Milton for their

[15]Warton to Percy, 4 September, 1762, in *Percy-Warton Correspondence*, p. 47.
[16]*Ibid.*, pp. 44–45.
[17]Warton, *History* (1774), i, 434.

examples, they were confident in their assumptions. The Elizabethan age appeared to them to have possessed the qualities most 'favourable to the purposes of poetry', since it lay in time 'between the rude essays of uncorrected fancy', as exemplified in the romances themselves, and 'the refinements of reason and science'[18] which were the virtues of the literature of their own age. In turning to the romances, they were exploring the immediate background of the Elizabethans, whom Hurd, for example, praises for virtues that derive from the practice of chivalry, 'in their festivities, their exercises, and their poetical fictions'.[19]

Interest in chivalry, romance and feudalism was a byproduct of interest in Shakespeare, Spenser and Milton and to explain these authors, scholarship was brought to the aid of criticism. The scholar-critic began to read the books, especially the imaginative works, which had helped to mould the literary masterpieces of the past. Until Warton's *Observations on the Faerie Queene* in 1754, Johnson could justly complain that no help was borrowed 'from those who lived with them, or before them'.[20] Johnson himself adds little of this type of annotation in his edition of Shakespeare, but what he does witnesses to the prevailing interest in romances. He instances *Guy of Warwick, Morte Darthur*[21] and Caxton's *Recuyel of the Histories of Troy*, and pauses to refute at length Warburton's view that belief in witchcraft was brought to Europe by the Crusaders.[22] Johnson's main interest in this type of scholarship is the light it throws on the critical suppositions of the audience for whom the plays were originally written. Thus he explains the crowding of incidents, the show and bustle, by Shakespeare's need to satisfy an audience whose taste was formed by the romances, which 'invigorated the reader by a giant and a dwarf'. For Thomas Percy, however, minutiae of annotation provided sufficient excitement. He discovered that the words of the Fool in *King Lear* (III, iv, 138–39)

[18]Hurd, *Dialogues* (1798), i, 198.
[19]*Ibid.*, pp. 201–2.
[20]Boswell, *Life of Johnson*, i, 270.
[21]See Mary Lascelles, 'Sir Dagonet in Arthur's Show', *Shakespeare-Jahrbuch*, 96 (1960), 145–54.
[22]In a note on the witches in *Macbeth*, which, like the note on Prospero, draws on Hooker and on King James' *Daemonologie*. Both Johnson and Swift assert that Milton's 'and on their Hinges grate Harsh thunder' (*Paradise Lost*, ii, 881–82) was borrowed from *Don Bellianis*, Part 2, ch. 19 (Johnson's *Shakespeare* [1765], vi, 424–25; H. J. Todd ed., *Poetical Works of Milton* [1852], i, 511 n.). I have not found the phrase in any edition of the romance.

> But rats and mice and such small deer
> Have been Tom's food for seven long year

were adapted from *Bevis*, and that the reference in *King John* to Richard's encounter with a lion was to an episode in the romance of *Richard Coeur de Lion*.[23] These were two strong points in his argument that the romances deserved study.

With the same sense of triumph Thomas Warton and Hurd pointed to Milton's 'predilection for the legends of chivalry', his references to them in *Il Penseroso, Paradise Lost* and *Paradise Regained*, his projected *Arthuriad*, his use of material from Geoffrey of Monmouth in *Comus*, his intended treatise on Geoffrey, and his telling over the materials of the *Historia* in the *History of Britain* 'be it for nothing else but in favour of our English Poets, and Rhetoricians, who by their Art will know, how to use them judiciously'.[24] Chaucer provided an example of an English poet who had actually composed romances, one of which, the *Squire's Tale*, had attracted both Milton and Spenser. The value of romance studies was further vindicated, however, by the realization that Chaucer had also seen the foolishness of romances and in *Sir Thopas* had anticipated Cervantes, exposing 'with infinite humour' 'the leading impertinencies of books of chivalry'.[25] . . . By the 1760's there was a sufficiently large audience for the literature of the Elizabethan and medieval periods. Goldsmith noted in *The Vicar of Wakefield* (1766), 'Dryden and Rowe's manner . . . are quite out of fashion! Our taste has gone back a whole century'. The narrower antiquarianism of the previous century, the scholarship that had concerned itself with non-literary texts, had gradually filtered through to a wider public. Interest was aroused by the publication of evidence that our ancestors had been not merely politically and religiously conscious, but also creators of works of literature. Of course many a scholar and collector of the seventeenth century had been interested in earlier literature. Pepys and Anthony Wood had collected ballads, including many of the Elizabethan age. The collectors of manuscripts had rescued many medieval texts. Nameless men, like the person who compiled Percy's Folio MS, had transcribed texts. Ballads ancient or modern had found ready readers in Dryden and Addison, they had been imi-

[23]*Percy-Farmer Correspondence*, pp. 49–50; *Reliques* (1765), iii, pp. ix-xii; Johnson, *Shakespeare* (1765), viii. Appendix, Notes to vi, 92.

[24]Milton, *History of Britain* (ed. 1695), p. 7. See Warton, *Observations on the Faerie Queene* (1762), ii, sect. vii; Hurd, *Letters on Chivalry* (1762), Letter vii.

[25]Hurd, *Letters on Chivalry* (1762), Letter xi; the account was expanded in the 1765 edition.

tated, and one at least, *Hardyknute*, had been forged. Scott, in his autobiographical fragment, commented that Percy's collection in the *Reliques* was a new departure not so much in the assembling of texts, as in the 'sober research, grave commentary, and apt illustration' with which they were presented.

. . .

Scott's love of all that belonged to chivalry and to legendary story inspired his voluminously annotated series of narrative poems. He aimed to give an imaginative presentation of the past, mingling authentic customs and manners, as the romance-writers of the middle ages did, with a fictitious story. But since the customs and manners which he represented were those of a past age, his annotations proved the authenticity of his picture and gave added entertainment.[26] Scott had, however, been preceded as a commentator by Southey. His *Joan of Arc* and *Thalaba* and later *Madoc*, *The Curse of Kehama* and *Roderick*, are as learnedly annotated as any of Scott's poems. The fashion for poems set either in the past or in an alien civilization produced many imitations—such as *Lalla Rookh* (Thomas Moore), *Theodric*, *Gertrude of Wyoming*, *The Pilgrim of Glencoe* (Campbell), and Byron's *The Bride of Abydos*, *The Corsair* and *Mazeppa*. In these, the notes grow thinner until they disappear altogether. But the narrative poem was firmly re-established, as Keats, Shelley and the succeeding poets prove. By 1809 Malone might well write 'the whole world is to be "bespread with the dust of antiquity"' and what was formerly thought a good subject of ridicule, is now quite the fashion'.[27]

. . .

[26]Later he added notes to the Waverley novels, as well as autobiographical and informative prefaces to novels and poems.

[27]*Percy-Malone Correspondence*, p. 260. It will be remembered that Erasmus Darwin's *Botanic Garden* (1792) was heavily annotated. Selden's notes to Drayton's *Poly-Olbion* (1612–13) were probably not without influence on Southey and Scott.

EDWIN M. EIGNER

The Bad Tradition
and the Romance of Man

No voice protested when F. R. Leavis dismissed Stevenson from respectability in an eloquent footnote to *The Great Tradition*:

> Out of Scott a bad tradition came. It spoiled Fenimore Cooper, who had new and first-hand interests and the makings of a distinguished novelist. And with Stevenson it took on "literary" sophistication and fine writing.[1]

Dr. Leavis's judgment combines the two prejudices that have deprived Robert Louis Stevenson of a critical audience—that he was a mere romantic fabulist, writing in the Scott tradition, and that he composed English prose rather too well. The second of these strictures originated from George Moore, the professional young man. It belongs now to an old debate between manner and matter which few people take seriously anymore. We shall not rehearse it here. The other objection, more basic and more serious, derives largely from our own and Leavis's nursery experiences, for it was in the nursery that most of us last encountered the works of Stevenson. Certainly the time has come for us to do them fuller justice.

. . . .

What we must realize is that English fiction contains two Romantic traditions. Stevenson has a place in both of them, while Scott belongs only to one, to the "bad tradition," as Leavis quite properly calls it. What is valuable in Walter Scott has, by virtue of his Fieldingesque techniques of characterization and his dominant theme of disillusion-

From *Robert Louis Stevenson and Romantic Tradition*, by E. M. Eigner, pp. 4–8, 12–18, 245–46. Reprinted by permission of Princeton University Press. Copyright © 1966 by Princeton University Press.

[1] *The Great Tradition* (New York: 1963), p. 6n.

ment, a firm and lasting place in the history of the realistic novel, which is still a third tradition. But the serious romance in England has little to do with Scott. Its tradition begins long before him, with Richardson, and it includes, besides Stevenson, such figures as William Godwin, Ann Radcliffe, Charles Maturin, Mary Shelley, Bulwer-Lytton, Dickens, Charlotte and Emily Brontë, Meredith, Hardy, Wilde, Conrad, and D. H. Lawrence—important writers, many of whom we have forgotten how to value because they have been disinherited by the notion of a Great Tradition.

The serious romance is well understood and appreciated in the criticism of American literature. Richard Chase, for instance, acknowledges a "justly contemned,"[2] picturesque, American tradition, the legacy of Scott, but he insists equally on the existence of a more serious type of fiction, which is distinct nevertheless from what we have called the realistic novel. Along with a number of other American critics—most notably Harry Levin and Leslie Fiedler—Chase has established the serious romance as the most significant form of American prose fiction. But the dominance of the romance tradition was not always acknowledged. "For a long time," writes Fiedler, "American critics (influenced by Parrington among others) read the history of our novel as a melodrama with a happy denouement in which a virtuous but harried realistic tradition, after resisting the blandishments of fantasy, romance, and allegory, was recognized as the true heir to the patrimony."[3] Nevertheless, today there are probably fewer courses in American literature victoriously entitled "The Rise of Realism" than there were a decade ago.

. . .

The old sensational romances had the worst reputations as teachers of moral virtue. They had been blamed for the madness of Don Quixote and the damnation of Francesca da Rimini. Scott, who despite his admiration for the serious romance, became the chief inheritor of the old, heroic tradition, was eventually held responsible not only for the American Civil War,[4] but for the adulteries of Emma Bovary. But in the late eighteenth and early nineteenth centuries it was believed that the serious romance could be a force for good, a means of instructing the young.

. . .

The great opposing document of English romantic criticism is, of

<hr />

[2] *The American Novel and Its Tradition* (New York: 1957), p. 20.
[3] *Love and Death in the American Novel* (New York: 1960), p. 141.
[4] By Mark Twain in *Life on the Mississippi*, Chapter XLVI.

course, Shelley's *A Defence of Poetry*, and here we find expressed the attitudes towards man and art with which the writers of the serious romance would have felt more in sympathy.[5] For the truths of the romance are usually more mystic, more inspirationally derived, more visionary than those of the novel. The writer of the romance, at least apparently, is more intellectual than the novelist; and rather than striving to go deep by staying on the flesh, he tries to capture an internal vision, never expressed on the surface of the real world or, indeed, in the conscious portion of the writer's mind. Moreover, the romancer believes with Shelley that "when composition begins, inspiration is already on the decline, and the most glorious poetry that has ever been communicated to the world is probably a feeble shadow to the original conception of the poet." He expects to discover no new truths through recollection or in the process of writing.

Always the writer of the romance *begins* with his conception. Those writers we have so far been looking at started oftentimes with a thesis, but more usually the romancer begins with a vision or an overpowering truth which he feels incapable of holding back. Charlotte Brontë, for instance, apologizes for her sister's creation of Heathcliff by stating that "the writer who possesses the creative gift owns something of which he is not always master." And she goes on to say:

> Be the work grim or glorious, dread or divine, you have little choice left but quiescent adoption. As for you—the nominal artist—your share in it has been to work passively under dictates you neither delivered nor could question—that would not be uttered at your prayer, nor suppressed nor changed at your caprice.[6]

And the vividly symbolic, almost surrealistic pictures which Charlotte's Jane Eyre draws seem indeed to have been so inspired and executed. *The Castle of Otronto, Zanoni, Frankenstein*, and the *Strange Case of Dr. Jekyll and Mr. Hyde* are each attempts to recreate visionary and significant dreams which their authors claimed actually to have dreamed. By way of contrast, the realist, if he begins his work with any preconception stronger than a general attitude towards experience, will probably distort the phenomenal world he is trying to portray. He finds the

[5]Of all the great Romantic poets, Shelley owed the largest debt to the romance tradition. In his youth he had read Gothic stories avidly and written them enthusiastically, though inexpertly. Later he became related by marriage to two of the most important Gothic writers, his wife Mary and her father, William Godwin.

[6]"Editor's Preface to the New Edition of Wuthering Heights," *Wuthering Heights* (New York: 1960), p. xxxv.

kernel of truth within his real or imagined experiences, while the writer of romance fabricates experience to illustrate a truth which in his vision or his theory he has already apprehended. Conrad expresses this difference admirably in "Heart of Darkness" when he compares the kind of story Marlow tells with the downright yarns of typical seamen, where "the whole meaning . . . lies within the shell of a cracked nut." To Marlow, on the other hand, "the meaning of an episode was not inside like a kernel; but outside, enveloping the tale which brought it out only as a glow brings out a haze, in the likeness of one of these misty halos that sometimes are made visible by the spectral illumination of moonshine."[7] Marlow himself says that it seems he is trying unsuccessfully to relate a dream.[8]

. . .

Poe called realism "pitiable stuff," the truthful depiction of "decayed cheeses."[9] And Edward Bulwer-Lytton, who, more than most mid-century writers, saw the tide of realism rising, bitterly attacked both the realistic novel and the critics who were its champions:

> The artist of the higher schools must make the broadest distinction between the Real and the True,—in other words, between the imitation of actual life, and the exaltation of Nature into the Ideal. The one . . . is the Dutch School, the other is the Greek. . . . The Dutch is the most in fashion. . . . Our growing poets are all for simplicity and Betty Foy[10] and our critics hold it the highest praise of a work of imagination to say that its characters are exact to common life. . . . People make the adoration of Shakespeare the excuse for attacking everybody else. But then our critics have discovered that Shakespeare is so *real*! Real! The poet who has never once drawn a character to be met with in actual life— who has never once descended to a passion that is false, or a personage who is real![11]

Truth to the writer of romances could mean only one thing: truth to the human heart. He saw realism as an unpleasant modern fashion, which he hoped would pass quietly away. Like Stevenson, "in this age of the particular," he remembered and took comfort in remember-

[7] *Youth* (New York: 1927), p. 48.

[8] *Ibid.*, p. 82.

[9] "Marginalia," *The Works of Edgar Allan Poe*, eds. Edmund Clarence Stedman and George Edward Woodberry (New York: 1914), VII, 426.

[10] A character from Wordsworth, we should note.

[11] "Introduction to *Zanoni*," *The Works of Edward Bulwer-Lytton*, 9 vols. (New York: P. F. Collier, n.d.), VIII, 470. Subsequent references to this edition will be to *Bulwer's Works*.

ing "the ages of the abstract, the great books of the past, the brave men that lived before Shakespeare and before Balzac."[12]

. . .

Many writers of romances require not only strange circumstances and abnormal psychology to portray their visions, but exotic scenery, as well. But their imaginary landscapes provide a way to reality, not an escape from it, and their faraway islands are not discoverable on any map only because, as Melville says, "true places never are."[13] Blake felt that he "must Create a System, or be enslaved by another Man's." Unlike Wordsworth, he and Shelley sought to escape from the world around them, from physical nature, in order that they might free their imaginations. Similarly the serious romancer seeks a never-land where his mind will be released from the common sense of his neighbors and the truths of the sociologists.

. . .

The tendency to regard Stevenson as a lesser Scott may have been all right, for the booksellers at least, in days when serious historians of fiction could write of Scott as the only English novelist "whose work can, without absurdity, be compared to Shakespeare's."[14] But in these times of more demanding tastes, when, to be well regarded, a writer must be not only a sage and a storyteller, but an artist, as well; when Scott himself must fight to stay in the canon and even Shakespeare is forced to concede a few carelessly written plays; then Stevenson's other loyalty, to the more profoundly Romantic tradition, must be emphasized. It must be stressed, moreover, because it is the truer and more serious loyalty. As we saw at the beginning, Stevenson did not base his art on the daydream literature of Scott, but on the artistically and intellectually controlled romances of Victor Hugo, for whom "the moral significance," Stevenson wrote, "is the essence of the romance; it is the organising principle."[15] Finally, this loyalty to the serious romance tradition must be insisted upon because here Stevenson did most certainly bring something new, and here he is far from being a mere afterglow. He enriched romantic prose fiction by informing its conventions with his own particular vision, and by understanding its principles and its past literature as perhaps no other romancer had ever done.

[12]"A Humble Remonstrance," *Works*, XII, 221.
[13]*Moby-Dick* (Boston: 1956), p. 62.
[14]Edward Wagenknecht, *Cavalcade of the English Novel* (New York: 1944), p. 152.
[15]"Victor Hugo's Romances," *Works*, IV, 56.

LOWRY NELSON, JR.

Night Thoughts on the
Gothic Novel

Horror fiction has only a recent history. In the ancient past tyrants like Phalaris and Nero provided fabulists and historians with lurid events unmitigated by the distance of guiltily pleasurable fiction. Such early monsters of the mind as Scylla and Charybdis, Polyphemus, Cerberus, and Procrustes existed only as prisoners of places which could be braved or avoided according to need and daring. At least they could be counted upon not to stalk about at random. The ancients, however much they felt themselves exposed to the delinquent passions of the gods, seem not to have imagined fiendish supermen who at any moment might come to terrorize or kill. Even the two famous haunted houses in antiquity, the one reported in a letter of Pliny the Younger and the entirely specious one in Plautus's *Mostellaria*, were easily exorcised.

In the later eighteenth century a complicated and irregular pullulation began. It would be satisfying to ascribe the rise of the gothic novel to the growing ranks of graveyard enthusiasts and to the relatively new passion for the awesome in secular nature, the "sublime" as distinct from the "beautiful." That may well be too simple, though it is tempting to suppose that once God had been secularized out of the graveyard and the terrifying manifestations of nature, what remained was the primeval horror of demonic violence and bodily decay. When the ancient gods took on human or animal form they generally did no more than rape. At most they punished for some palpable reason. They were not a nameless and unpredictable terror to the general

From *The Yale Review*, Vol. 52, pp. 236–39, 247–57. Published, 1963, Yale University Press. Copyright © Yale University. Reprinted by permission of the editors of *The Yale Review*.

populace: indeed, they were far more ingeniously malicious toward each other. It might seem that once the totemic animal loses its god-head it can become an unpropitiable terror and that degeneration of the fabric of mythology and religion is conducive to gothic terrors, just as, conversely, mythology is often thought to be the safe-making systematizing of the otherwise uncontrollable terrors known as natural phenomena. Whatever the explanation, it remains a fact that on the threshold of the romantic revolution a vigorous new genre got under way, principally in northern countries where Grendels and trolls and werewolves had long stalked through the marshes of folklore.

One might ascribe the origins of the gothic novel to the several revivals in the later eighteenth century: interest in folklore, in the mythified Middle Ages, in the eccentric asocial individual, and in the mysterious Mediterranean world. A cruder ascription would be to the heightened imagination of youth and inexperience. Matthew Lewis and Mary Shelley, though precociously experienced, were hardly twenty when they composed their horror tales; Ann Radcliffe and Emily Brontë were quite limited in their knowledge of the outside world. Charles Maturin, author of *Melmoth the Wanderer*, is perhaps an exception, but he comes toward the end of the efflorescence of pure gothic and can hardly be called a founder though he was one of the best, if not the most original, of the practitioners. But it is hazardous in literature to assign simple causes to complex phenomena. A more secure office would be to define, describe, and judge what we have.

The gothic novel owes much to the popularity of exotic themes and to the emancipation of the novel from overt moral commitment. Perhaps it derives most from the enormous interest around the turn of the century in the solitary eccentric, the misfit, the social outcast, or, to use the handy phrase, the guilt-haunted wanderer. In the romantic transvaluation of values Cain becomes a sympathetic figure, unjustly cursed by a vengeful God and incapable of ever purging his guilt. He looks in vain for human trust and friendship; his "benevolent" impulses are thwarted; at worst he is twisted by circumstances into a monster of inhumanity—a tortured image of his tormentors. We see the rudiments in Byron's play called *Cain: a Mystery*. The hero is a malcontent who blames his parents for their expulsion from Eden and also blames the tyrannical deity who will not readmit them. Even his beloved wife and sister Adah (incest is handily unavoidable) cannot give him the sympathy he craves. Only Lucifer, the voice of independence and illumination, can open to him a vision of proud freedom and fulfilment. After Cain in a frenzy kills Abel at the altar, it is Eve who pronounces the curse of alienation on her son. His faithful Adah insists on accompanying him. At the very end of the play Cain laments his brother's death; but Adah exclaims, "Peace be with him!" while Cain can only query and lament, "But with *me!*—." What might happen later—the wandering and the pangs of nameless guilt—is of course the favorite subject, boasting its Alastors, its Manfreds, its Childe Harolds, and its more natively gothic heroes.

Curiously enough, the fascination for the bizarre, the individual peculiarity, the monstrous seems to have led more significantly to a fictional discovery of the true depths of human nature than to a mere exploitation of the sensational and the perverse. By its insistence on singularity and exotic setting, the gothic novel seems to have freed the minds of readers from direct involvement of their superegos and allowed them to pursue daydreams and wish fulfilment in regions where inhibitions and guilt could be suspended. Those regions became thereby available to great writers who eventually demonstrated that sadism, indefinite guiltiness, mingled pleasure and pain (Maturin's "delicious agony"), and love-hate, were also deeply rooted in the minds of the supposedly normal.

Still, if we look to the earlier gothicists for psychological profundity we are bound to be disappointed. Horace Walpole's *Castle of Otranto* (1765) is most impressive for its early date. The plot is mechanical and the characterization primitive. That the mysterious helmet is larger than life and made of stone seems the main reason for calling it the prime ancestor of the gothic novel. In other respects the exoticism of the setting and the "naked" passions in it are surely outdone by such a work as *The Duchess of Malfi*. Ann Radcliffe's various novels, notably the *Romance of the Forest* (1791) and *The Mysteries of Udolpho* (1794), now seem more like childish fantasies than evocations of primal horror. Their dungeons, swart Italians, and rattling chains were properly and neatly satirized by Jane Austen in *Northanger Abbey*. That Catherine finds the mysterious documents to be only a roll of laundry lists seems a fitting rebuke to the pretensions of Mrs. Radcliffe and her school. Jane Austen thus enrolls herself among those who since Cervantes were to make their Juliens and Emmas victims of "bad literature."

. . .

With Matthew Gregory Lewis's *The Monk* (1796) and Mary Shelley's *Frankenstein* (1818) we are in a different fictional world. The urbane smile may well freeze on our faces and the titillating fantasies probe more deeply than we wish. . . . *Frankenstein* is not a mere tale of horror, but rather a significant fictional model of the mind. For the first time in gothic fiction characters take on the full symbolic resonance of inner psychological reality. To say flatly that the monster is Frankenstein's id on the rampage and that he subconsciously desires his family's extermination would be pretentious and anachronistic. Or to say that the monster uses murder as an attention-getting device would be foolishly reductive. It is quite different to argue that Frankenstein and his monster have much in common, that they are objectified parts of a single sensibility, and that they represent the intimate good and bad struggle in the human personality. Evil is within; in one's own works and creations. Good impulses are thwarted and evil ones encouraged by some inner perversity. The source of that perversity is perhaps a desire to be loved alone or an urge toward narcissism. Yet there is also the strong fascination with the gratuitous pursuit of one's evil nature. Frankenstein pursuing his monster is searching for his whole self. Human nature being what it is, total benevolence seems to create the spectre of monsters haunting the outskirts of Elysium: some sort of compromise must be made between the good and evil instincts of human nature in order to survive, since human nature deeply drives toward both good and evil; or at least some sort of modus vivendi must be found, most hopefully through full self-knowledge and self-discipline. While Ambrosio's unconscious incest was a form of unselfcritical narcissism, Frankenstein's rejection of his created monster was a denial of his nether forces for which he should have accepted a fully aware responsibility.

Such mythifying interpretations of gothic novels may seem obvious and unnecessary, a case of misplaced solemnity. Still, it may not be excessive to hazard a generalization. In its earlier and cruder forms the gothic novel made irresponsible use of such claptrap as chains and dungeons and prodigies of weather. With *The Monk* and especially with *Frankenstein* we find that the claptrap has begun to take on symbolic resonance. Ambrosio's descent into the tombs is a descent into evil. His rape of Antonia in those surroundings prompts him to say, "This sepulchre seems to me Love's bower," thus reviving the old mythic and Shakespearean theme of the sepulchral marriage bed. But in Mrs. Shelley's novel much wider echoes resound. The cottage where the monster received his "upbringing" is an Eden in which he is the unwilling serpent or the reluctant Cain: his uncomprehended desire to be loved has destroyed the tranquillity of the uncompre-

hending others. The icy reaches in which Walton first descries the
monster and his creator, and the brooding, glistening presence of Mont
Blanc are ambiguous symbols of nature's innocence and also her indifference or cruelty: we are well on the way to the whiteness of the
whale. Then, too, the moods of Frankenstein and his creature are often
at variance with those of nature; instead of a one-to-one correspondence,
often the sinister and the unnatural in men are heightened by nature's
own innocent or indifferent serenity. Nature in Mrs. Shelley's novel is
not the benevolently sympathetic or chastening nature of Byron and
Wordsworth. In social terms we witness in *Frankenstein* a failure of
"benevolence"; in personal terms, a mind incomplete without its
"other" mind. There is even the implication that in the idyllic family
life the "monster" must be or at least should be faced and laid and
caged, not avoided and left to roam the wilderness of marsh or mind.

The gothic hero easily shades into what is commonly called the
romantic hero; or, perhaps to put it better, both are members of the
same genus. Both share an essential loneliness and feeling of incom-
municability; both are generally scapegoats or guilt-haunted wanderers. Without attempting a perhaps futile contrast between the two,
we may provisionally confine ourselves to describing the gothic cousin.
Characteristically he harbors a nameless guilt. He is haunted by an
acute feeling of the discrepancy between good and evil. Indeed, both
qualities are present in him in heightened form. He possesses some
extraordinary virtue (scientific genius, strength, sanctity) which is
transformed somehow into an extraordinary vice. Finally, he is in touch
with nether forces, originally demonic but later inside the mind. Mrs.
Radcliffe and her like presented a rather crude mixture of sensibility
and sensationalism in which virtue laboriously triumphed over evil.
Lewis, though he makes his survivors happy at the end of his novel,
rejected the simplist notion that virture is always rewarded or, indeed,
that anyone has a monopoly of virtue. Ambrosio is close to becoming
a true villain-hero. Mrs. Shelley had the unusual courage to create a
chaotic world in which virtue is rewarded perhaps in heaven but not
necessarily on earth and in which evil is rampant still and in this life
may be inexorable.

In the course of development of the gothic hero and his setting one
also notices an evolution away from dependence for effect upon the
rigged supernatural and toward a recognition of what we might call,
for the sake of contrast, the "subnatural," that is, the irrational, the
impulse to evil, the uncontrollable unconscious. It is tempting to say

that that improbable mixture of sensibility and sensationalism, freed of the supernatural and concentrated in the mind, led eventually to the American and French versions of symbolism and to a recognition or rediscovery of myth as an expression of the psychic drama of the whole mind. To cast more widely, but perhaps more securely, it could be claimed that the development of the gothic novel foreshadows the future interest, both in art and science, in hidden workings, contradictory impulses, irrational and gratuitous evil, the intimacy of love and hate, whose effects are so diversely seen (whether expressed or suppressed) in Balzac, Dickens, Browning, Baudelaire, Dostoevsky and their heirs.

Is this a triumph of irrationalism in an age of rationalism? We may well have a sense that everything was happening in the nineteenth century, and all at once: symbolism and realism, rationalism and irrationalism, civilizing progress and utopian primitivism. If there is any convenient common denominator it might be a renewed sense of the profound, perhaps unfathomable, discrepancy between appearance and reality. The rejection of the supernatural and the descent into the mind may seem to reveal at the same time the "realities" of life and the irrational symbolism, quite impractical or unrealistic, of the unconscious. The plunge into the depths of the mind, so fateful for the age, seems to have revealed both a yearning for the utopian, simplist solution and an indulging of irrational impulses. The reductio ad absurdum occurred early in the stereotype of the villain with a heart of gold. It continues in mediocre literature today, where uncontrollable social forces have not taken over as prime movers. Such sentimental villain-heroes find some sort of salvation or justification in society. But the gothic hero and his immediate successors show an almost solipsistic struggle within themselves. In their struggle with society they do not become either victims or conformists; they are relatively free agents. Their trouble is both more cosmic and more personal.

It would be too simple to say that the "mystery tale" or the gothic novel arose in reaction to rationalism or empiricism or "science." In fact, it could be urged that it could arise only under their influence, since they create the right atmosphere for willing though temporary suspension of disbelief. *The Castle of Otranto* and *Vathek* are mainly titillations of sensuality, whether simple shudder or sadomasochism. They seem, strangely enough, still within the imaginative and moral scope of Voltaire and Dr. Johnson. With *The Monk* and with *Frankenstein* we enter upon new possibilities. *The Monk* is transitional, in that some attempt is made, despite the mere sensationalism, to delineate the complex psychological reactions to abnormal situations. But it is in *Frankenstein* that the mythic possibilities of the genre begin to emerge. Instead of a parade of horrors and marvels, the gothic novel has begun to suggest a mythology of the mind. Fantasy and exoticism, employed before as mere claptrap, become elemental and symbolic; decorative oddity becomes new myth. If these seem claims too large to be sustained so narrowly, the examples given may be urged as symptomatic of larger changes. We must at least allow that "realism" in the nineteenth century was "realistic" in plumbing mythic or symbolic depths, that such writers as Dickens and Browning were caught betwixt and between (between, for instance, merry old England and the gloomy old jungles of the mind), and that the continuity from *The Scarlet Letter* to *The Rose Tattoo* is fairly obvious.

The gothic hero's most successful immediate heirs are Heathcliff and Ahab. If one were to rehearse briefly the similarities between *Wuthering Heights* and *Moby Dick* one might catalogue the following: they are both set in remote or isolated surroundings; both novels are narrated by quite ordinary people; good impulses in the heroes have been thwarted or affronted and both are bent on massive and calculating revenge; both heroes bear marks of difference (Heathcliff's darkness suggesting the cursed race of Ham, and Ahab's scar the mark of Cain); the origins of both heroes are relatively vague; both are guilt-haunted wanderers whose skills for good (their omnicompetence in practical matters) are diverted to the service of "evil." Besides, both novels are quite unchristian, perhaps for the time daringly so: the pagan Queequeg comes off much better than the Quakers and the "grand, ungodly, godlike" Ahab pursues his quest under a ceremonial covenant with the crew of his own diabolistic invention; in *Wuthering Heights* religion is almost savagely parodied in the figure of the bigoted Joseph and supernatural reality in the novel is quite unsanctioned by conventional Christianity.

. . .

Ahab too is a distant cousin of Werther, the Ancient Mariner, and the Byronic figures. His neo-Faustian or neo-Promethean traits are clear enough. He belongs also in the company of guilt-haunted wanderers or reluctant scapegoats, bent on revenge or escape or expiation or simply knowledge. But he is neither reconciled, like Faust, nor confined by God, like Prometheus. The universe of *Moby Dick*, like that of *Wuthering Heights* and *Frankenstein*, is almost frighteningly without either God or devil; the God of conventional fiction, even a tyrant God, has effectually disappeared, just as the devil of earlier gothic diabolism has disappeared as the archfiend. In a universe without the presence of divine justice or retribution, notions of good and evil lose their simple polarity and generate shadowy and unexpected complexities. William Blake, to put it starkly, had called conventional good evil and conventional (in his sense of energetic, inventive, liberating) evil good. Again starkly, *Moby Dick* seems to ask what is good and what is evil, and to assert that the struggle is not between any external forces but rather within the turbulence of the mind. The solipsism or even narcissism of Ahab is quite evident: his wife and children receive only passing or even careless mention; he masterfully preserves his solitude though he is, to begin with, relatively isolated on the open seas; his monomaniacal interest is to pursue his savage and mysterious alter ego which, in costing him his leg, has consumed a part of him. Ocean, isolation, pursuit, monster: no wonder *Moby Dick* seems open to infinite exegesis.

It is at least arguable that the basic traits that make the novel so symbolically suggestive are those deriving eventually from the gothic novel: its simple unsocial setting, its omnicompetent hero, its embodiment of nether forces of the mind, and its "confusion" of conventional good and evil. Even of the claptrap of gothic fiction we discern significant though somewhat reinterpreted remnants.

.   .   .

One could construct some grandiose theory of the gothic mode and at the same time trace the whole course of its trajectory. In the Renaissance good and evil are distinct opposites, and good, with some exceptions, wins out in the end; in the Baroque good and evil are allowed a more intimate dialogue in which one seems to generate the other and the outcome becomes confusedly profound; in Neoclassicism the result is a mature, worldly-wise accommodation and compromise in which evil is acknowledged and harnessed to good; but in Romanticism good and evil reappear in starkly theatrical and dialectical form, attitudinizing and polemicizing, though strongly suggestive of unexpected new departures, such as that "evil" is really "good." Wicked old archetypes, like Don Juan and Faust, are "reconstructed" as ultimately good. While with Blake conventional "good" is evil and generative "evil" is good, his successors, like Baudelaire, Swinburne, and Lautréamont, attempted at times a kind of protesting diabolism or espousal of the devil as Promethean figure. That Milton's Satan was hailed as a prime ancestor is less reprehensible as an interpretation of seventeenth-century attitudes than it is revealing as a manifestation of nineteenth-century sensibility. Nowadays such diabolism is out of fashion. In fashion are a kind of social determinism (they are that way because society made them so) and a kind of universal sentimentality (they may be rough but they are rough diamonds). Both notions are optimistic, since the implication of even "existential" literature is that once everybody takes the proper view all will be well or at least as well as it will ever be.

To remain so on the surface is both exhilarating and risky. It may seem to the philosopher and theologian either frivolous or irreverent to discourse schematically and summarily on limitlessly profound matters like good and evil. Nevertheless, when notions of good and evil are represented in literature they are at once translated to the esthetic realm and thus exposed to the vicissitudes of convention and taste. Since for gothic novels, and for the novels that followed, the representation of good and evil was momentously important, it is surely a proper topic for literary and historical discussion. Surprisingly perhaps, we may well be convinced that the gothicists for all their outlandish oddities were in effect among the most fruitful literary explorers of the psyche. As citizens of the romantic revolution they plotted their diversionary intrigues and, scarcely aware, found themselves in the vanguard of literary history. Even if we may be inclined to disparage the gothic novel we must still grant that it boldly and often garishly presented fictionally fertile dilemmas of characterization and situation which slipped into the mainstream of Western literature and, along with many other things, helped bring about what we have now.

F. O. MATTHIESSEN

The Crucial Definition of Romance

Terms that Hawthorne used in the account of his imaginative life demand attention. His desire to provide "a neutral ground where the Actual and Imaginary may meet" happens to contrast significantly with a note of Whitman's that "imagination and actuality must be united. . . ."

When Whitman wrote in an early notebook, "Let facts and histories be properly told, there is no more need of romances," he was probably not thinking especially about Hawthorne, whose use of the term was peculiar to his own practice. But the poet would have been highly suspicious of Hawthorne's "neutral territory." It would have struck him as too suggestive of a drawn battle, as a sign that its author had not completely absorbed and mastered his material. Melville, in his increasing desperation while trying to compose *Pierre*, felt that it was impossible to write "without apparently throwing oneself helplessly open" to experience. That suggests his more passionate relation to life than Hawthorne's. It also shows his lack of the artist's "hard coldness," which would have prevented his becoming so involved in his personal suffering that *Pierre* turned out to be a gigantic failure. But by the same token it attests why Melville's exposure of himself to what Lawrence was to call "the sheer naked slidings of the elements" carried all his work, from *Moby-Dick* on, into a realm of emotional forces quite out of Hawthorne's range.

As usual Hawthorne was the first to note his own limitations. At the end of his account of how all vividness of imagination had deserted him during his tenure in the customhouse, he made his statement that a

better book than he would ever write had doubtless lain hidden in what
had struck him as the "dull and commonplace" routine.

> It was a folly, with the materiality of this daily life pressing so
> intrusively upon me, to attempt to fling myself back into another
> age. . . . The wiser effort would have been to diffuse thought and
> imagination through the opaque substance of to-day, and thus
> to make it a bright transparency; to spiritualize the burden that
> began to weigh so heavily; to seek, resolutely, the true and
> indestructible value that lay hidden in the petty and wearisome
> incidents, and ordinary characters, with which I was now con-
> versant.

The resolve to do this was what caused him to choose, as the settings
for his next two books, the existence with which he was most familiar,
an old house in Salem and the dramatic interlude of his experience at
Brook Farm. The prefaces to these books outline his definition of a romance, which bears only tangential relation to any of the other usages
then current. This definition, which is the most important text for his
conception of reality, needs to be read in strictest relation to his circumstances at the time. Out of that context, as it has usually been taken, a
sentence like this from the preface to *The Blithedale Romance* would
seem such an evasion of the artist's responsibility as to forfeit his book
all serious consideration: "In short, his present concern with the socialist community is merely to establish a theatre, a little removed from
the highway of ordinary travel, where the creatures of his brain may
play their phantasmagorical antics, without exposing them to too close
a comparison with the actual events of real lives."

But behind that remark lay an incident: the humorous sketch of his
companions in the customhouse had called down upon Hawthorne's
head a storm of vilification. Consequently, when he proceeded to draw
far more extensively on things he had observed near at hand, he
wanted to take every precaution to make clear that he was not copying
actual people, not even Margaret Fuller in Zenobia. He begged for the
license in creating atmosphere which the European reader took for
granted, but which the too literal-minded American public denied.
In making this plea he had already had a bitter encounter with the
dilemma that Cooper, once he had set himself to be a social satirist in
Homeward Bound, had found to be that of the American author. In
contrast with Europe, where bitter personalities excited disgust and
society was deemed fair game, the individual here was constantly
assailed, but no word was tolerated against the existing order—as

Hawthorne had quickly discovered as a result of his mildly ironic remarks on having been turned out of the surveyorship by the Whigs' resumption of power. No wonder that he ended his preface to *The Seven Gables* with the covering disclaimer that he "would be glad . . . if, especially in the quarter to which he alludes," his book might be read as "having a great deal more to do with the clouds overhead than with any portion of the actual soil of the County of Essex." These protective remarks had been necessitated by the fact that his relative weakness in invention had obliged him to borrow many suggestions, even though no whole character, from people he had observed. The nearest he came to a dangerous likeness was through using as a basis for Judge Pyncheon some traits of the politician who had been most instrumental in ousting him from his job.

But, more importantly, his prefaces also formulated his positive distinctions between the novel and the romance. The former, as Trollope was to reaffirm, "is presumed to aim at a very minute fidelity, not merely to the possible, but to the probable and ordinary course of man's experience." In contrast, Hawthorne went on to say, the writer of a romance could assume "a certain latitude, both as to its fashion and material." If he thought fit, he might "so manage his atmospherical medium as to bring out or mellow the lights and deepen and enrich the shadows of the picture." He might even, though he had best handle these ingredients sparingly, make some use of the strange and marvellous. This suggests Hawthorne's way of finding beauty in a moonlit room, beauty that could not exist "without some strangeness in the proportion," as the romantic movement had followed Bacon in affirming. Hawthorne's share of this feeling had come to him especially from his sense of the resistances that the artist's imagination had to overcome in a land where, as he was to say in the preface to *The Marble Faun*, actualities were so "terribly insisted on."

In his dedication of *Our Old Home* to Pierce in 1863, he had to admit that by then "the Present, the Immediate, the Actual," in the sense of the horrible fact of the war, had proved too potent for him. It had taken away not only his "scanty faculty," but even his "desire for imaginative composition"—remarks that recall how James was to find it impossible to continue *The Ivory Tower* after August 1914. Hawthorne had previously hoped that the notebook sketches he had made of English life should serve merely as a background for "a work of fiction . . . into which I ambitiously proposed to convey more of various modes of truth than I could have grasped by a direct effort." The furthest he got with this "abortive project" was in his notes for *The Ancestral Footstep*, the germ of whose idea, the return of an American to rediscover the older European life, bears a curious resemblance to that of the other book James was to leave unfinished at his death, *The Sense of the Past*.

The significant words in this last description of Hawthorne's aim are "various modes of truth," for these stem straight back to the crucial points he made about the romance in the preface to *The Seven Gables*, that "as a work of art, it must rigidly subject itself to laws," and that "it sins unpardonably so far as it may swerve aside from the truth of the human heart." Again in the context of the time, it must be remembered that though the major drift of fiction had set towards realism, the term had not yet been applied to the novel in English.[1] Hawthorne was therefore taking advantage of the unsettled standards of taste to make a plea for the assumptions that came to him from his past, for what could not be expressed by the "direct effort," for the freeing of the inner life through the mode of symbolizing. . . . Emerson equated "indirection" with the symbol, and Whitman was to follow Emerson's use of that word very closely. In one of the chapters of *The Confidence Man*, Melville was to tuck away a defense of his own method of heightening everyday life, which stemmed at least partly from Hawthorne. Melville found it strange that, in a work of fiction, "severe fidelity to real life should be exacted by anyone." In contrast, the readers for whom he aims will sit down as "tolerantly as they sit at a play, and with much the same expectations and feelings. They look that fancy shall evoke scenes different from those of the same old crowd round the customhouse counter, and the same old dishes on the boarding-house table." Was he thinking in that sentence of *The Scarlet Letter*, and even, possibly, of the contrast in *Moby-Dick* between the earth-bound scenes at Peter Coffin's Spouter Inn and the wild drama of Ahab?

> And as, in real life, the proprieties will not allow people to act out themselves with that unreserve permitted to the stage; so, in books of fiction, they look not only for more entertainment, but, at bottom, even for more reality, than real life itself can show. Thus, though they want novelty, they want nature, too; but nature unfettered, exhilarated, in effect transformed. In this way of thinking, the people in a fiction, like the people in a play, must dress as nobody exactly dresses, talk as nobody exactly talks, act as nobody exactly acts. It is with fiction as with reli-

[1] The earliest Oxford English Dictionary quotation for "realism" in relation to art or literature is from Ruskin's *Modern Painters* (1856).

gion; it should present another world, and yet one to which we feel the tie.

By this extension of the tendency of Hawthorne's prefaces, Melville formulated more exactly the kind of heightened reality they both wanted in their fiction. He also indicated how different their conceptions finally were from those, say, of the classic sculptors whom Hawthorne admired. Hawthorne himself, after a round of galleries, suggested the divergence: "I am partly sensible that some unwritten rules of taste are making their way into my mind; that all this Greek beauty has done something towards refining me, though I am still, however, a very sturdy Goth." (Incidentally, this was one of the two passages marked by Melville in *The French and Italian Notebooks*, which he acquired shortly after their publication, in 1872.) What Hawthorne implied by his contrast between Greek and Goth is subject to further definition, which will bring us even closer than we have yet come to the way his imagination apprehended reality. It will bring us also to the central reason why the mode of symbolizing, whether it remained richly allusive or whether it froze into a conventional and arbitrary allegory, was basic to the kind of Christian thought that conditioned Emerson and Thoreau as well as Hawthorne and Melville, and was still latent in Whitman's Quaker strain. That generalization does not mean that any of the group, except probably Melville, would have agreed with what Hawthorne experienced in his first full impression of a Gothic cathedral. When Emerson and Thoreau considered architecture, we have seen them primarily concerned with the primitive origin of its forms, with how man might have found the first hint for a nave in an aisle of trees. But Hawthorne, by the very fact of not looking for these universal analogies, but by remaining a provincial, uncovered the deeply buried and almost sole link between an American and the medieval world—a world that had still persevered in many of the folkways of our first settlers, as it had in the overhanging second story, leaded windows, and quaint carvings, "conceived in the grotesqueness of a Gothic fancy," of Hawthorne's house of the seven gables.

In visiting Lichfield Cathedral, he had not been the passionate pilgrim, since he had been drawn to the town chiefly by his interest in Johnson's birthplace. Nevertheless, as he looked at its bewilderingly varied form, it seemed, to his "uninstructed vision" to be "the object best worth gazing at in the whole world. . . ."

> A Gothic cathedral is surely the most wonderful work which mortal man has yet achieved, so vast, so intricate, and so pro-

foundly simple, with such strange, delightful recesses in its grand figure, so difficult to comprehend within one idea, and yet all so consonant that it ultimately draws the beholder and his universe into its harmony. It is the only thing in the world that is vast enough and rich enough.

Not that I felt, or was worthy to feel, an unmingled enjoyment in gazing at this wonder. I could not elevate myself to its spiritual height. . . . Ascending but a little way, I continually fell back and lay in a kind of despair, conscious that a flood of uncomprehended beauty was pouring down upon me, of which I could appropriate only the minutest portion. After a hundred years. . . . I should still be a gazer from below and at an awful distance, as yet excluded from the interior mystery. But it was something gained, even to have that painful sense of my own limitations, and that half-smothered yearning to soar beyond them. The cathedral showed me how earthly I was, but yet whispered deeply of immortality.

Citing this passage, Herbert Read has remarked that "this sense of an almost giddy vertiginous gulf between human finiteness and the infinity of the Absolute, whether in art or in religion, is the peculiar Northern or Gothic sensibility." This cleavage, as it was felt by Hawthorne, and by Melville in pressing his analogy between the operations of art and religion, was not the vague desire of the moth for the star. In their shared conviction that art "should present another world, and yet one to which we feel the tie," their roots were in the deepest Christian experience. The essence of Hawthorne's greatness, as Melville saw it, was that he breathed "that unshackled, democratic spirit of Christianity in all things." The range of implications that Melville compressed into that phrase will emerge only as we examine the development of his own handling of tragedy; but the fact that he became a tragic writer was owing to his widening sense of the gulf between the ideal and actuality, between the professions and practice of both democracy and religion. This sense was what separated him, as much as Hawthorne, from the transcendentalists, who bridged the gap between the finite and the Absolute by their assurance of "the infinitude of the private man."

Perhaps the chief reason why both Hawthorne and Melville succeeded in creating so few living characters, in contrast with Fielding and Jane Austen, or even with their own contemporaries Thackeray and Dickens, was that the Americans were more concerned with human destiny than with every man in his humor. Certainly it is true that long before he had seen a Gothic cathedral, Hawthorne had wanted to establish in the "laws" of his romances a related manner of multiple symbolizing of spiritual meanings. He too had wanted "strange, delightful recesses," liberties from literal verisimilitude. For the main concern of the romance was not external details, exactly presented settings, turns of speech, or characterizing gestures. It was "the life within the life."

DANIEL G. HOFFMAN

Fable as Reality

"When a writer calls his work a romance," Hawthorne asserts in his preface to *The House of the Seven Gables,* "he wishes to claim a certain latitude, both as to its fashion and material, which he would not have felt himself entitled to assume had he professed to be writing a novel." Indeed, the more closely one scrutinizes the "fashion" and the "material" of Hawthorne's fiction, and of *Moby-Dick, The Confidence-Man, Huckleberry Finn,* or, in our own day, Faulkner's sagas, the more difficult it becomes to make them all conform to any set of preconceptions. It is safe only to say that whatever else they may be individually, they cannot be satisfactorily described as novels of manners. They are significantly distinguished from the work of our novelists—Cooper, Howells, and James—by their authors' structural and thematic concerns with folklore, myth, and ritual. Their uses of these cultural survivals and primitive or subconscious patterns of experience dramatize their preoccupations with the instinctual and passional forces of life, with pre-conscious and pre-Christian values, with sub-rational and often anti-rational formulations of meaning. These values of course are almost invariably found in tensest tandem with their opposites: full consciousness, directed will, reason, Christianity.

It should not be surprising that the fictional development of primitivism loomed large on a continent whose early settlement had seemed, to the *philosophes* of the Enlightenment and the poets of Romanticism, to prove the justice of Rousseau's vision of the Noble Savage and the benignity of Nature. At the same time, America was the land of emergent rationalistic democracy and of capitalistic exploitation of the land. The conflicts, therefore, between Nature and Civilization, between a

From *Form and Fable in American Fiction,* by Daniel G. Hoffman, pp. 3–9, 353–59. Copyright © 1961, by Daniel G. Hoffman. Reprinted by permission of Oxford University Press, Inc.

275

prelapsarian Eden and the spoliation of Paradise necessary to the imposition of human values on an indifferent wilderness, between free will as a function of natural liberty and determinism as a result of surrender to society—these have been among the most fertile sources of tension in our national experience and our literature. In their dramatizations of these conflicts, the authors of our romances have tended to avoid the materials and forms of the conventional novel and to draw to an extraordinary degree upon folklore and myth. The social and literary situation in the American nineteenth century made the successful novel of manners a rarity and invited instead the development of fiction in another genre.

.   .   .

In yet another preface, to *The Blithedale Romance,* Hawthorne is careful to relinquish all claims to having written a novel of society, although such a case could yet be strongly made for that book. He proposes instead that his work conforms to that other genre, the romance, which . . . , he goes on to describe: The romance, he writes,

> while, as a work of art, it must rigidly subject itself to laws, and while it sins unpardonably so far as it may swerve aside from the truth of the human heart—has fairly a right to present that truth under circumstances, to a great extent, of the writer's own choosing or creation . . . He will be wise . . . to mingle the marvellous rather as a slight, delicate, and evanescent flavor, than as any portion of the actual substance of the dish offered to the public. He can hardly be said, however, to commit a literary crime, even if he disregard this caution.[1]

Such a situation is patently the result of our short history and of our egalitarian commitment. In the very decade which James describes, de Tocqueville had predicted that our cultural profession of equality would deny in theory and conceal in practice those differences between the varied stations of life which in aristocratic states are delineated and enforced by codes of manners. Egalitarian democracy would prove subversive of that distinctness of individual character at which the novelist must aim; for when everyone is equal how is anyone different from his fellows? Yet at the same time that egalitarianism denied such differences in the name of individual freedom, it cast the individual in his loneliest role in history. For he had no heritage, no tradition, no status ascribed to him by his past. He had to achieve everything he did or became, as though no man had lived on earth before him. The

---

[1]*Hawthorne* (New York: 1879), pp. 42–43.

political and institutional emphases of this lonely individualism were reinforced by Puritan theology. Man's relation to his God was un-mediated. The American had neither a class nor a history to fix his place in society, neither priest nor church to ameliorate his relation to the immensities.

Not only was our history short, but it was colonial. This circum-stance produced the inevitable cultural lag between the province and the motherland; and, more important perhaps, our Puritan founders represented a minority culture in the homeland itself. With their pre-dilection for allegory and distate for mimesis which we have observed, the realistic fashion emerging in late eighteenth-century fiction made small impact in America. Instead our prose writers were attracted to a fictional mode which in England flourished briefly as a minor, obverse reaction to the dominant realism of Defoe and Fielding and the senti-mentalized depiction of manners in Richardson.

Gothicism itself had been one of the heralds during the Age of Reason of the oncoming shift of sensibility to Romanticism. It brought together two already nascent Romantic themes—fascination with the past, and with those supernatural forces which defied the attempts of reason to comprehend and regulate experience. What is usually taken as the Gothic machinery of mystery calls for reinterpretation as the literary adaptation of supernatural folklore. In a sense the folk imagina-tion has always been Gothic in its acceptance of the inexplicable, of the supernatural. Gothicism in its attention to the medieval past focussed on the very period when the superstitious lore of modern times was being formed. This lore is the detritus of Europe's pagan past, a past which has lingered in country customs, seasonal festivals, the lore of witchcraft, and folk belief in revenants, stregas, fairies, and other un-Christian inhabitants of the world of spirit. Much of this lore came with the settlers to the American colonies, where it survived to nourish the imaginations of our own writers of romance. Thus the elements which Hawthorne termed "the marvellous" in his romances are at the same time "Gothic" and folkloristic. Much of "the marvellous" in the American romance takes advantage of folk superstition, whether actual-ly current in oral tradition or recovered for fictional use from the writings of antiquaries and historians. Thanks to the industrious collec-tion and classification of folklore by American scholars, it is possible to demonstrate the debt of the American romance to the varied strands of folk tradition.

.   .   .

The American author who would use this lore may either deal with it for its own sake, accepting its creations and its values, or he may view the heroes of native folk experience as one end of a cultural tug-of-war in which the other end of the rope is grasped by the heroes of European tradition. The former option leads to regionalism, the latter to a much more powerful literature. For, if I may extend the image, the rope that is drawn taut between Ben Franklin, the Yankee, the Kentucky Screamer, and Johnny Appleseed on the one side and Adonis, Prometheus, and Christ on the other, in its very length and tension represents the continuity of culture and the struggles of history. It is the opposition of the New World to the Old. The ties that bind both together can be cut or burst asunder only by main force or reckless daring. Yet it is the American hero's destiny to try to break these ties. It is his fate to endure the consequences of their breaking.

.   .   .

The core of the American experience has been a radical search for identity by attempting to free ourselves from old forms, old orders, old hierarchies of rank and belief, to discover the emergent man. Our culture has traditionally proposed as the basis for its new, indigenous forms the innate sanctity of the individual—his natural goodness, his "divine equality." Therefore the romance, as Hawthorne, Melville, and Mark Twain envisaged it, proved a form of art peculiarly consonant with the bias of our culture. Their inward vision and their concern with archetypal individual experience (as with Robin, Coverdale, Ishmael, and Huck) objectify these "real" values of American life.

Our romance writers have all taken the role of the artist to be the discoverer and revealer of truth. Rarely seeking that truth in contemporary reality, they found it disguised in the past of their ancestors or in their own childhoods or in symbol-freighted voyages abstracted from the economic and political life of their time. When they do treat social problems it is usually at a distance in time which makes the problems seem remote and "unreal" to the contemporary reader. Such may be the effect of Hawthorne's concentration on Puritan days to demonstrate that sin of pride for which contemporary examples were not lacking, and of Mark Twain's resolution of the moral problem of slavery in 1885—a quarter-century too late to exert any political influence on the issue. . . .

In form and spirit, as well as in content, the romance proved peculiarly adaptable to the needs of these authors. The absence of classical precepts governing its structure offered freedom to the writer who would develop his forms empirically from his materials. The form itself remains indeterminate, picaresque, enveloping interpolated tales. The romance tends to absorb or become pastoral idyl, satire, or representational novel, yet it retains its distinctive character. The traditions immediately antecedent to the American romance were, . . . allegorical, Gothic, and transcendental. In these works allegory was transformed into symbolism; the Gothic mode (despite its melodrama) assumed a seriousness unusual elsewhere by virtue of the communal values represented in supernatural folklore; and the transcendental aesthetic gave the whole work metaphoric consistency. In narrative method the romance tends to employ metaphor as a structural device. While the novel can get along in its absence, the romance cannot do without this unifying use of metaphor. Ernst Cassirer has shown the psychological identity of the metaphoric nature of language with the myth-making capacities of mind; in the American romance these two means for revealing the inherent forms of experience are readily linked, reinforcing each other at each juncture.

The unity these romances achieve is thus largely determined by both their "poetic" and their "mythic" dimensions. The romance is "poetic" in its use of the radical powers of self-discovery of the metaphor-making mind. It is "mythic" in appropriating from myth and folkore the patterns in which the archetypal themes of journey, quest, and initiation can best be organized. Since the romance is committed, as a form, neither to a tragic, a Christian, nor a comic resolution of its dilemmas, it was favored as an instrument for the discovery of meaning. Our authors, inheriting a disused Protestant orthodoxy, could not reconcile the absolute claims of faith with the moral ambiguities of life; tragic *hubris* to them exemplified the Romantic ego in its anarchy. Neither the tragic nor the Christian resolution appeared true to the life they knew. Comedy served them better with its implicit humanism, its tolerance of opposites, and its intrinsic offering of a masquerade in which the pursuit of truth may be clandestinely conducted. Insofar as they were concerned with the realistic aspects of culture they found such reality dramatized in the conflicts between indigenous and inherited values in American life. These tensions between their New and Old World heritages they envisaged most powerfully in re-creations of American folk characters and the legendary heroes of the past.

In tracing the shared debts of our romancers to these traditions it becomes clear that they do have common commitments to themes implicit in our national experience. Whether they treat native character in accordance with the vulgar optimism of popular comedy, or use comic stereotypes to explore in irony or satire the discrepancies between native self-assertion and what Melville called "the blackness of darkness" within us, these authors responded to the same elements in American life and together contribute to a significant tradition. Our recognition of these concerns they share should alter somewhat our sense of where the continuities lie in American literature. It is quite true that if we divide our writers into "Palefaces" and "Redskins," as Philip Rahv has suggestively proposed, we will think of Hawthorne taking tea with Oliver Wendell Holmes and Henry James, while Melville and Twain seek their dark-skinned camerados near Whitman's campfire in the wilderness. In assessing the traditions in our literature— as in defining its themes—I find pluralism more accurate than any prescriptive insistence upon mutually exclusive alternatives. Hawthorne, then, still wearing his undoubted pallor, can join the creators of Ishmael and Huck on the grounds he actually shares with them. His involvement with the themes they later drew upon, his pioneering development of forms they later used, indicate the profundity of his own mythmaking mind and the degree to which his sensibility, like theirs, was stirred by images of the subconscious primitive energies of fecundity and creation. Hawthorne's pallor comes from seclusion in the library. In the witchcraft documents and the pages of antiquarians he found his images akin to those that came to Melville and Twain not only from eclectic readings but from their own experiences in folk life. Yet even while we think of Hawthorne as a redskin indoors we must recall his own exposure to the folk life of a New England village with its population of Yankee characters and its local traditions of comic folktales, omens, and prophecies.

The traditions and themes these romancers share go beyond their responses to folk character and to folk-cherished images of the creative sources of life which Christianity and rationalism had repressed into the subconscious. In their sensibilities we see the conflict between pagan energy and Christian ethics, between primitivism and civilization, between free will and determinism, between optimism and despair. All of these dialectical conflicts may be subsumed in their exploration of the opposing claims of democracy and traditional order. The romancers all responded deeply to the promise of egalitarian freedom, a promise as indeterminate as it was all-encompassing. The free man in the free society would have to create his own order anew from the chaos out of which he had emerged; and that chaos seemed all the more threatening because it was largely by his own will that the established order of the social and the supernatural world had been destroyed. Yet the inherited order was itself an intolerable threat to the existence and self-knowledge of the individual, representing stasis, rigidity, the defeat of every force save inertia. In working out the destinies of such representative heroes as Robin Molineux, Hester, Holgrave, Miles Coverdale, Ishmael, Israel Potter, Pitch, and Huck Finn, our romancers made synoptic metaphors drawn from the folk traditions and the world-historical myths. Their imaginations placed these heroes in the crucial American experience: rebellion. They recognized that in his uncompromised rebellion the individual declares his independence from family, from social class, from church and God, from history.

Therefore in these romances the individual is defined not, as in the novels of Dickens, Flaubert, or Tolstoy, by his complex interrelationships with others who represent various social classes and their values. Instead he is defined by his relations to characters representing the contending forces in his own psyche or the alternative commitments of belief, value, and action available to him. The most significant relationships in the American romance, are those between the representative hero and characters who embody unfallen innocence or innate corruption, primitive purity or civilized guilt, intellectual isolation or passionate community.

. . .

The sensibility informing the romance has not been out-moded, nor is it likely to disappear as an active force on the American imagination. As we pass mid-century the work of William Faulkner looms as the most sustained achievement in American fiction since Henry James. And although Faulkner has practised many genres of fiction and has based his work more firmly on the documentation of social reality than any other major novelist of our time, his continuing affinity with the romance-novels we have examined is strong and clear. Their themes are his themes; the folklore that leavens their characters lives anew in his; the mythic patterns as antique as time that braced their experiences are the bulwarks still of his vision of the tensions between individual responsibility and the heritage of his culture. The forms and themes of the American romance are present too, in the work of authors younger than Faulkner—Saul Bellow, Ralph Ellison, and others. Their achievements, taken together, suggest that the romance tradition, coupled in our time with a more immediate social documentation than Hawthorne, Melville, or Twain allowed themselves, will long continue as a shaping force in American fiction.

RICHARD CHASE

Novel vs. Romance

Nothing will be gained by trying to define "novel" and "romance" too closely. One of their chief advantages is that, as literary forms go, they are relatively loose and flexible. But especially in discussing American literature, these terms have to be defined closely enough to distinguish between them, even though the distinction itself may sometimes be meaningless as applied to a given book and even though, following usage, one ordinarily uses the word "novel" to describe a book like Cooper's *The Prairie* which might more accurately be called a "romance" or a "romance- novel."

Doubtless the main difference between the novel and the romance is in the way in which they view reality. The novel renders reality closely and in comprehensive detail. It takes a group of people and sets them going about the business of life. We come to see these people in their real complexity of temperament and motive. They are in explicable relation to nature, to each other, to their social class, to their own past. Character is more important than action and plot, and probably the tragic or comic actions of the narrative will have the primary purpose of enhancing our knowledge of and feeling for an important character, a group of characters, or a way of life. The events that occur will usually be plausible, given the circumstances, and if the novelist includes a violent or sensational occurrence in his plot, he will introduce it only into such scenes as have been (in the words of Percy Lubbock) "already prepared to vouch for it." Historically, as it has often been said, the novel has served the interests and aspirations of an insurgent middle class.

By contrast the romance, following distantly the medieval example,

From *The American Novel and Its Tradition*, by Richard Chase, pp. 12–13, 21–28. Copyright © 1957 by Richard Chase. Reprinted by permission of Doubleday & Company, Inc.

282

feels free to render reality in less volume and detail. It tends to prefer action to character, and action will be freer in a romance than in a novel, encountering, as it were, less resistance from reality. (This is not always true, as we see in what might be called the static romances of Hawthorne, in which the author uses the allegorical and moral, rather than the dramatic, possibilities of the form.) The romance can flourish without providing much intricacy of relation. The characters, probably rather two-dimensional types, will not be complexly related to each other or to society or to the past. Human beings will on the whole be shown in ideal relation—that is, they will share emotions only after these have become abstract or symbolic. To be sure, characters may become profoundly involved in some way, as in Hawthorne or Melville, but it will be a deep and narrow, an obsessive, involvement. In American romances it will not matter much what class people come from, and where the novelist would arouse our interest in a character by exploring his origin, the romancer will probably do so by enveloping it in mystery. Character itself becomes, then, somewhat abstract and ideal, so much so in some romances that it seems to be merely a function of plot. The plot we may expect to be highly colored. Astonishing events may occur, and these are likely to have a symbolic or ideological, rather than a realistic, plausibility. Being less committed to the immediate rendition of reality than the novel, the romance will more freely veer toward mythic, allegorical, and symbolistic forms.

.   .   .

In order to amplify the discussion, in both the abstract and the concrete, it will be of value at this point to return, with the aid of Henry James's prefaces, to the question of definition. In doing so, I shall risk repeating one or two observations which have already been made.

The first four prefaces James wrote for the New York edition of his works set forth, or at least allude to, the main items of his credo as a novelist, and although they are perhaps well known, there may be some advantage in looking them over again before noticing what James had to say directly about the relation of the romance to the novel. The four prefaces are those to *Roderick Hudson*, *The American*, *The Portrait of a Lady*, and *The Princess Casamassima*.

We might take as a motto this sentence, from the Preface to *The Princess*: "Experience, as I see it, is our apprehension and our measure of what happens to us as social creatures." Although James himself does not overtly contrast his procedure with that of romance until he comes to the Preface to *The American*, we shall be justified in ourselves making the contrast, since James is obviously seeking to show, among other things, how the imperfections of romance may be avoided. And thus we reflect that, in a romance, "experience" has less to do with human beings as "social creatures" than as individuals. Heroes, villains, victims, legendary types, confronting other individuals or confronting mysterious or otherwise dire forces—this is what we meet in romances.

When James tells us that the art of the novel is the "art of representation," the practice of which spreads "round us in a widening, not in a narrow circle," we reflect on the relative paucity of "representation" in the older American romances and their tendency towards a concentrated and narrow profundity. Again we hear that "development" is "of the very essence of the novelist's process," and we recall how in romances characters appear really to be given quantities rather than emerging and changing organisms responding to their circumstances as these themselves develop one out of another. For if characters change in a romance, let's say as Captain Ahab in *Moby-Dick* or the Reverend Dimmesdale in *The Scarlet Letter* change, we are not shown a "development"; we are left rather with an element of mystery, as with Ahab, or a simplified and conventionalized alteration of character, as with Dimmesdale. Similarly, the episodes of romance tend to follow each other without ostensible causation; here too there is likely to be an element either of mystery or convention. To "treat" a subject, James says, is to "exhibit . . . relations"; and the novelist "is in the perpetual predicament that the continuity of things is the whole matter, for him, of comedy and tragedy." But in a romance much may be made of unrelatedness, of alienation and discontinuity, for the romancer operates in a universe that is less coherent than that of the novelist.

As for the setting, James says that it is not enough merely to report what it seems to the author to be, in however minute detail. The great thing is to get into the novel not only the setting but somebody's *sense* of the setting. We recall that in *The Scarlet Letter* the setting, although sketchy, is pictorially very beautiful and symbolically *à propos*. But none of the characters has a *sense* of the setting; that is all in the author's mind and hence the setting is never dramatized but remains instead a handsomely tapestried backdrop. In *Moby-Dick* the setting is less inert; it becomes, in fact, a kind of "enveloping action." Still, only in some of the scenes do we have Ishmael's sense of the setting; during most of the book Ishmael himself is all but banished as a dramatic presence.

The whole question of the "point of command" or "point of view" or "center of intelligence" is too complicated to go into here. Suffice it to say that the allotment of intelligence, the question of what character shall be specially conscious of the meaning of what happens to and around him so that we see events and people more or less through his eyes, thus gaining a sense of dramatic coherence—these questions are less and less pertinent as fiction approaches pure romance. Natty Bumppo need be conscious only of what the Indians are going to do next. Hawthorne's Chillingworth and Melville's Ahab are clairvoyant-ly conscious, but with a profoundly obsessive distortion of the truth. They are not placed in context in order to give concrete dramatic form to a large part of what the author sees, as is the "point of com-mand" in a James novel; all we learn from them is how *they* see. And as I shall suggest in speaking of *The Blithedale Romance*, the dyed-in-the-wool romancer like Hawthorne merely proves that you mustn't have a central observer in your story, because if you do you simply point up the faults of romance and admit your incapacity to follow out a fully developed novelistic procedure. In the romance too much de-pends on mystery and bewilderment to risk a generally receptive intelligence in the midst of things. Too often the effect you are after depends on a universe that is felt to be irrational, contradictory, and melodramatic—whereas the effect of a central intelligence is to pro-duce a sense of verisimilitude and dramatic coherence.

One or two further items from the prefaces may point up the contrast. A character, especially "the fictive hero," as James says, "successfully appeals to us only as an eminent instance, as eminent as we like, of our own conscious kind." He must not be "a morbidly special case"— but in romance he may well be. Again, says James, when economy demands the suppression of parts of the possible story they must not be merely "eliminated"; they must be foreshortened, summarized, com-pressed but nevertheless brought to bear on the whole. But in the looser universe of the romance, we may think "elimination" will be less criminal and unexplained hiatuses and discontinuities may positively contribute to the effect. To take an obvious case, in *Moby-Dick* we are content to think the sudden elimination of Bulkington an interesting oddity rather than a novelistic blunder and we gladly draw on the poetic capital Melville makes of it.

As for the moral significance of the novel, James sees a "perfect dependence of the 'moral' sense of a work of art on the amount of felt life concerned in producing it." We must ask, he says, "is it valid, in a word, is it genuine, is it sincere, the result of some direct impression or perception of life." These questions bear less on the romance, one of the assumptions of which is that it need not contain a full amount of felt life, that life may be felt indirectly, through legend, symbol, or allegory. Nor does the romance need the sincerity of the novel; indeed, as Lawrence points out, American romances, especially, tend to make their effect by a deep "duplicity" or ironic indirection.

To come finally to James's specific comments on the question we are considering. In the prefaces he follows his own advice as that had been expressed twenty-odd years earlier in "The Art of Fiction"—he sees no reason, that is, why the practicing writer should distinguish between novel and romance. There are good novels and bad ones, novels that have life and those that haven't—and this, for the novelist, is the only relevant question. The implication is that the novelist will be also the romancer if the "life" he is rendering extends into the realm of the "romantic." But if we are not, except as critics and readers, to distinguish between novel and romance, we still have to distinguish, within the novel that may be also a romance, the "romantic" from the "real." And this James essays in his Preface to *The American*.

In rereading this early novel James found a large element of romance in the free and easy way in which he had made his semilegendary hero Christopher Newman behave on his European travels. Particularly, James thought, the picture of the Bellegard family was "romantic." James had made them reject Newman as a vulgar manufacturer when actually common sense tells us that "they would positively have jumped at him." And James comments that "the experience here represented is the disconnected and uncontrolled experience—uncontrolled by our general sense of 'the way things happen'—which romance alone more or less successfully palms off on us." At the same time James finds an unexpected pleasure in rereading *The American*, which somewhat compensates for the lapses of verisimilitude. And his description of this pleasure makes a fair definition of the pleasure of romance—"the free play of so much unchallenged instinct . . . the happiest season of surrender to the invoked muse and the projected fable."[1]

"The disconnected and uncontrolled experience," then, is of the essence of romance, and any adequate definition must proceed from this postulate. First, however, one may clear out of the way certain

[1]See Melville's plea to his reality-minded readers for latitude in the depiction of character and incident. The ideal reader, he says, will "want nature . . . ; but nature unfettered, exhilarated, in effect transformed. . . . It is with fiction as with religion: it should present another world, and yet one to which we feel the tie." (*The Confidence Man*, Chapter 33.)

conventional but inadequate descriptions of romance. It is not "a matter indispensably of boats, or of caravans, or of tigers, or of 'historical characters,' or of ghosts, or of forgers, or of detectives, or of beautiful wicked women, or of pistols and knives"—although one might perhaps be a little readier than James to think that these things might be of service. Yet one follows him assentingly when he decides that the common element in sensational tales is "the facing of danger" and then goes on to say that for most of us the danger represented by caravans and forgers is certainly benign or impotent compared with the "common and covert" dangers we face in our everyday existence, which may "involve the sharpest hazards to life and honor and the highest instant decisions and intrepidities of action."

The "romantic" cannot be defined, either, as "the far and the strange," since, as such, these things are merely unknown, whereas the "romantic" is something we know, although we know it indirectly. Nor is a novel romantic because its hero or heroine is. "It would be impossible to have a more romantic temper than Flaubert's Madame Bovary, yet nothing less resembles a romance than the record of her adventures." Nor can we say the presence or absence of "costume" is a crucial difference, for "where . . . does costume begin or end."

James then arrives at the following formulation:

> The only *general* attribute of projected romance that I can see, the only one that fits all its cases, is the fact of the kind of experience with which it deals—experience liberated, so to speak; experience disengaged, disembroiled, disencumbered, exempt from the conditions that we usually know to attach to it and, if we wish so to put the matter, drag upon it, and operating in a medium which relieves it, in a particular interest, of the inconvenience of a *related*, a measurable state, a state subject to all our vulgar communities.

And James goes on in words that are particularly illustrative of his own art:

> The greatest intensity may so be arrived at evidently—when the sacrifice of community, of the "related" sides of situations, has not been too rash. It must to this end not flagrantly betray itself; we must even be kept if possible, for our illusion, from suspecting any sacrifice at all.

In a fully developed art of the novel there is, as James says, a "latent extravagance." In novelists of "largest responding imagination before the human scene," we do not find only the romantic or only reality but a "current . . . extraordinarily rich and mixed." The great novelist responds to the "need of performing his whole possible revolution, by the law of some rich passion in him for extremes."

To have a rich passion for extremes is to grasp both the real and the romantic. By the "real," James explains, he means "the things we cannot possibly *not* know, sooner or later, in one way or another." By the "romantic" he means "the things that, with all the facilities in the world, all the wealth and all the courage and all the wit and all the adventure, we never *can* directly know; the things that can reach us only through the beautiful circuit and subterfuge of our thought and our desire."

We hear much in these prefaces of the novelist's rich and mixed "current," of the possible "revolution" of his mind among extremes, of the "circuit" of thought and desire. James speaks, too, of the "conversion" that goes on in the mind of the novelist's characters between what happens to them and their *sense* of what happens to them, and of "the link of connection" between a character's "doing" and his "feeling." In other words James thinks that the novel does not find its essential being until it discovers what we may call the circuit of life among extremes or opposites, the circuit of life that passes through the real and the ideal, through the directly known and the mysterious or the indirectly known, through doing and feeling. Much of the best American fiction does not meet James's specifications. It has not made the circuit James requires of the "largest responding imagination." And the closer it has stuck to the assumptions of romance the more capital it has made, when any capital has been made, exactly by leaving the Jamesian circuits broken. That very great capital can be made in this way James does not acknowledge or know, and hence his own hostility, and that of many of his followers, to the more extreme forms of American fiction—those we associate, for example, with Brockden Brown, Poe, Melville, and Faulkner.

Nevertheless James's theory of the novel, his idea of the circuit of life which allows him to incorporate in his novels so many of the attributes of romance, is the most complete and admirable theory, as at their best James's are the most complete and admirable novels yet produced by an American. And it is against James's theory and often, though certainly not always, his practice that we have to test the achievements of his compatriots. But the danger is that in doing so we should lapse into an easy disapproval of that "rich passion . . . for extremes" which James praised on his own grounds but which may be seen operating to advantage on other grounds too.

CHESTER E. EISINGER

The Gothic Spirit
in the Forties

The American novel has dealt with property, money, and manners in a realistic way. The forties is heir to this realistic tradition. And it is heir to another tradition as well. For American fiction has been a divided stream. Strangely, given the nature of American culture, . . . the gothic and symbolic have played a part in American fiction almost from the beginning. The seeds of these literary modes also lay in those origins. Out of the quest for property on the frontier, for example, came the loneliness and terror of the gothic. Out of the Puritanism came the idealism which made a symbolic interpretation of experience thoroughly understandable. Critical opinion in recent years, in pointing out the distinction between the novel and the romance, has demonstrated that the romance as fiction is gothic and symbolic, antirealistic and melodramatic. It has insisted that most American fiction is written as parable and its real life is internal. It has shown how the power of blackness pervades much of nineteenth-century fiction. The forties is heir to this tradition, too. Indeed, often one has the impression that critics feel this is the only tradition at work upon modern American fiction.

. . . . .

The symbolic and gothic stream began with Charles Brockden Brown. In the nineteenth century Poe, Hawthorne, and Melville contributed to it, artists whose deepest spiritual needs, whose intimacy with the terrors of darkness and death, demanded and found symbolic expression. The American tradition which they initiate and

From *Fiction of the Forties*, by C. E. Eisinger, pp. 15–16, 235–40, 243, 258–60, 262–63. Published, 1963, by the University of California Press. Reprinted by permission of the publisher.

289

carry forward survives in the forties in the work of writers like Paul Bowles and Truman Capote and Carson McCullers, where we see the world of flight, childhood terror, estrangement, and perverted love.

.   .   .

One kind of new fiction draws heavily upon the gothic imagination. It is a kind especially at home in the South during the forties, breathing and thriving on the foul air of decadence it knows is rising from the historical and spiritual ruins there. This place and this time—the forties and the succeeding decade—seem particularly hospitable to the gothic. But gothicism is not the exclusive property of the South in our time or in an earlier one; and it does not belong exclusively to the new fiction. It is a way of apprehending experience that served, during the forties, in other areas as well and has served almost from the beginning of the American career in the imagination.

Fascinated with such devices as talking pictures and mechanical monsters, the early gothic revealed something juvenile in the American imagination. But presently, what seemed to have started in the sheer delight and curiosity of investigating the outré finds iself staring into an abyss of real horror, discovered, stumbled upon, inadvertently or unconsciously as it were. The gothic writer is like the gifted child, left alone to model what he will from the mud of the Nile; he creates out of the pure innocence of his impulse the image of those hideous prehistoric creatures who, before man ever appeared on the earth, might first have crawled out of the Nilotic slime. Such images rise from deep in his childish soul, escaping without conscious volition into the fingers that shaped the dream or the memory of that filth from which man might have sprung. In the intimacy with which the child lives with terror, in his innocence, and in his lack of restraint or knowledge of convention lay the truth of the horror he thus glimpsed. Such a version of the juvenile applies to the American gothic writer, who begins with the obvious and the melodramatic. But the truth is there beneath the monstrous trappings: the secret necrophilia made public, the necessity for flight confessed, the sadism no longer contained, the horror of real life recognized. To perceive this truth of the gothic vision, one must strike through the mask to discover that all men are victims or cripples. The mask not so much hides as symbolizes the essential flaw. So that the picture on the wall, the mansion with the broken columns, the metal robot stands for something, is the physical object that expands into a meaningful abstraction.

The gothic has a symbolic content, then, that links it to the new fiction. Even if it begins in the unconscious, a symbolic representation of reality may rise to the level of art. Then it becomes a self-conscious way of distorting reality. And this suggests that the rage for the gothic in the forties was the product of a preference for art over life. The truths of life that men could see in their daily experience were too harsh to assimilate, to have to confront face to face and to live with. The artist did not then decide to escape into fantasy, fantasy being so unreliable it might prove worse than the world. But he might have decided it is better to filter these truths through an art form and so come at them, when it is necessary to do so at all, at one remove. In this way art becomes a wall between men and the horror of life, a horror which we cannot take straight, so to speak. It is a wall which shuts us off from the real horror, but encloses a synthetic horror, a kind which has the truth in it that we do not have to pay for. The synthetic truth or synthetic decadence or synthetic horror takes the sting out of reality. Thus the purposes of art as ceremony are served. Thus art is dehumanized. The gothic is linked to the new fiction in its dedication to this doctrine of the dehumanization of art.

.   .   .

No one reveals more clearly, or more obviously, the uses of the gothic than Truman Capote. His work has no bearing at all upon the smiling aspects of American life. It has no relation to the area of public or ordinary experience; Capote has said he has no convictions, in an orthodox sense, about religion or politics. The world of his fiction is a world of terror, defeat, and loneliness in which children who are not childlike grope through a nightmarish reality. Everyone in this world is a cripple, a physical or emotional or mental defective. Everywhere is the thick air of the supernatural or the occult, in which the characters drown. But Capote's people do not will their own destruction. They yearn for fulfillment in love. They wish to open the channels of the spirit and flow toward each other in heartfelt communion. They wish to banish loneliness and discover in love their own identities. The gothic interpretation of experience is not an expression of Capote's appetite for sensationalism (although there is a taint of this) or a reaction of blank revulsion against the world. The gothic vision is a symbol of his conviction that both society and man frustrate the quest for the self. In this sense the gothic becomes, in Capote's hands, a variation on the pervasive theme of fiction in the forties: the inward-turning search for the dimensions of the self.

This quest—or is it more accurate to say the failure of this quest?—

is the subject of Capote's first novel, *Other Voices, Other Rooms* (1948). The protagonist is Joel Harrison Knox, the child of divorced parents. He has been given his mother's family name, but his mother has died as the story opens, and he goes to find his father, a man named Sansom. The boy, then, does not know who he is—does not know what his name is or who his father is, although he does know that he is descended from a Civil War general. The story takes place at Skully's Landing, a decayed plantation near Noon City, a stagnant little town in the South. The prose is fanciful, often gossamer-light; the manner is self-conscious and arty; the book has a contrived air.

Note, for example, the treatment of that not altogether novel subject, southern decadence. Skully's Landing is the mysterious bourne where Joel will make his quest. Capote has no difficulty in endowing it with decay and mystery. Part of it has been destroyed by fire; the columns in the front are broken; the garden in the rear is a jungle. One is tempted to make a game out of reading this evidence of ruin as symbol, but I shall confine myself to two comments. All the evidence attests to the collapse of a civilization, that of the ante-bellum South, that has been replaced by nothing else. The past exists only as a memory of faded grandeur or as a reproach to the present; surely the past has no vital connection with the present. As a result, the decadence here described is isolated, existing for its own sake. . . .

In this setting, so inauspicious for his tasks, Joel must find his father, establish his own identity, grow from childhood to manhood, and uncover a love that will sustain him in his enterprises. The quest for the father ends in the discovery that Sansom is a helpless paralytic who is condemned to a perpetual semicoma from which he can escape neither to sleep nor to full consciousness. Joel can expect neither love nor protection from his father, since these cannot flow from a paralyzed source that is neither dead nor alive. His effort to claim his masculinity is frustrated by a tomboy, Idabel, and by his own nature. . . .

Blocked at every exit into a relationship that might fulfill him, he retreats to the dream world of the self, which is the other room where all quests are satisfied and he can find admiration, his father, love. The dream world is sterile, having only Joel's incapacities to feed upon. All alternatives exhausted, Joel turns to Cousin Randolph and homosexuality. His growth from childhood to manhood is a development to an accepted perversion which was, from the beginning, latent within him.

.   .   .

The themes of this novel may be the authentic concerns of a serious writer. The search for identity, the portraits of loneliness, the ambiguity of reality as reflected in the distorting mirror, the cost of human imperfection, the meaning of a decadent culture—these constitute an impressive array of thematic material. Capote has made an impressive integration of these various matters. But for me, at least, the book exists more as a detached art object than as a felt, imaginative experience. Its emotional life is not genuine, as its themes are. It is a real question whether Capote has given us a meaningful view of the universal disorder that madly throbs in the human id. His themes demand profound reflection and tragic resolution; we get close but eccentric observation and a hothouse horror that arouses no emotion stronger than pity.

. . .

The *Grass Harp* is a modest success. In its concern with love and the individual personality, it is typical of Capote's work. But the Gothic element in his other work has been transmuted here into mellowed fantasy.

Capote's authentic gothic mode is carried forward in *The House of Breath* (1950), by William Goyen, the first novel of a promising talent who belongs really to the fifties. Goyen's gothic treatment of homosexuality, of southern degeneration, of futile lives embarked on futile flight from scenes dead to love—all this promises continuity to the kind of fiction Capote has written. Goyen has the characteristic southern talent for the evocation of place, and he commands the typical techniques of the new fiction: the Joycean stream of consciousness, the poetic prose, the addiction to symbols. The pessimism in this novel is set against a romantic conception of the unity of all things. Out of this sense of a universal relationship, which is reminiscent of Whitman, comes an urge toward life, expressed in the breath metaphors that appear constantly in the novel. The tension created by this ambivalence results not in a sense of resolution but of sterility, which is induced by the pervasive homosexuality of the novel.

In an essay on "The Understanding of Fiction," John Crowe Ransom argues that fiction brings us into a primitive world of spontaneous and natural affections. He opposes the primitive to the intellectual and sentiment to idea. Since an art work must touch the heart, the substance of fiction should be drawn from feeling and not mind. Such a theory becomes at once a justification of the poetic vision as a means of apprehending experience. It gives sanction to a writer's commerce in a fabulous rather than in a literal truth. Out of these rich implications, such a theory makes a beginning in the description of Carson Mc-Cullers' work. She is governed by the aesthetics of the primitive. This means that her overview is essentially antirealistic. She has cut herself off from the world of ordinary experience and ordinary human beings who might entertain ordinary ideas. Her people are bizarre, freakish, lonely, hermaphroditic. This aesthetic dictates an intense concentration on man's most urgent emotional needs: a communion of dialogue and love. For her, further, the truth of the fable is the truth of the heart. It is not concerned with abstractions about the structure of society or with ideological conflicts in the contemporary world. . . .

Out of the still and twisted world in which her imagination dwells, Mrs. McCullers has drawn some truths that come home to all men. She has illuminated the possibilities for loneliness and the capacities for deviant behavior that mark the human lot. But there is a troubling sense of something wanting in what she does. The world of the adolescent child is, after all, only a promise of life to come in adulthood. The crazy, private world of her freakish and tortured adults is on the periphery of our experience, even if a significantly disturbing one. It is a narrow corner of human existence that she has chosen to exploit in her fiction. Her view of man's fate, therefore, adds little, in the largest sense, to the dimensions of our understanding. The gothic view of life has conjured up the terror of life but has not weighed the consequences of that terror. Mrs. McCullers knows something of the conditions under which life must be carried on, but she has not gone beyond this to examine how men might endure under these conditions. There is no room in her work for the *consequences* of human action; there is no sense of the continuity of life. She has succeeded perhaps too well in creating an art form that is cut off from life. It is a form cut off from society, from morality, from religion, from ideas, from concern with man's burden or with man's hope. It is a special art form, and its special quality makes it symptomatic of the phenomena we have always with us—a disturbed psyche and a disturbed time.

The similarities between Eudora Welty and Carson McCullers are many. Eudora Welty is also on familiar terms with gothic abnormality, although not as deeply possessed by it. She uses her characters—*her* deaf mutes or mad, decadent aristocrats—out of the same preoccupation with the themes of isolation, love and separateness, communication. Like Mrs. McCullers, she constantly probes the problem of identity or of separateness which leads to isolation, while at the same time she forces upon her characters a recognition of the demands of love which can be fulfilled only through communication. The tensions established by this movement from pole to pole, from separateness to love, are the staples of her work. Like Mrs. McCullers, she shares in the southern tradition of the neo-conservatives, but her attitude toward the shape of southern society is, at best, passive. A defined social scheme is there in her work; it is a given. But it is hardly at the center of her concern as an artist. That center is occupied by an absorption with the mystery of personality.

Clearly, Miss Welty is a southern writer of the new fiction. Indeed, independent of literary coterie and scornful of literary fashion as she may be, she stands at the head of the southern gothic stream of the new fiction in the forties. Her work is a summation of all that it represents and a major contribution to American literature of the twentieth century. . . .

Her achievement was possible because Miss Welty is so intensely dedicated to the power and mystery of the imagination in the creation of prose fiction. This commitment as writer to the ineluctable, the vagrant, but perhaps the more profound aspects of the human personality has made her stories apparently formless: she confesses herself, indeed, unsympathetic to the systematic analysis of stories and will not promise symmetrical development in her own. It is this commitment that causes her to regard reason, as a writer's instrument, with deep suspicion, for a writer's choices are only incidentally reasonable; they are impelled by feeling, by art, and only last (if at all) by reason. Perhaps the best explanation of the writing process that Miss Welty herself makes is this: ". . . that subject, method, form, style, all wait upon— indeed hang upon—a sort of double thunderclap at the author's ears: the break of the living world upon what is stirring inside the mind, and the answering impulse that in a moment of high consciousness fuses impact and image and fires them off together." This passage, which occurs at the close of an essay entitled "How I Write," brings to mind Coleridge's ideas on the imagination. Miss Welty has already made a distinction between the imagination and analysis which is comparable to that of Coleridge between the imagination and the understanding. But a more specific similarity is to be found in her intense concentration upon the fusing function that welds external and internal experience. For Coleridge has claimed that the creative activity of man is to be seen in the work of the imagination, which fuses insights of reason with the sense impressions yielded up by the understanding. The imagination, says Coleridge, is "that reconciling and mediatory power, which incorporating the reason in images of the sense, and organizing (as it were) the flux of the senses by the permanence and self-circling energies of the reason, gives birth to a system of symbols, harmonious in themselves, and consubstantial with the truths of which they are the conductors."

. . .

Five of the first six stories in Eudora Welty's first volume deal with abnormal characters. Lily Daw is feeble-minded; the petrified man is an exhibit in a freak show; the Morgans are deaf and dumb; Keela, with a traveling circus, eats live chickens; the narrator in "Why I Live at the P. O." is at least eccentric if she is not suffering from dementia praecox, as Katherine Anne Porter seems to believe. At first blush it appears that we are to have a gallery of horrors, and certainly the impression is inescapable that Miss Welty, in this early stage of her career at least, was fascinated by the macabre and the freakish. She is, in this respect, like other southern writers of gothic fiction. But she is different in a significant way, because the abnormal characters do not exist as symbols of southern decadence in her stories, and neither personal nor social decay is her theme. In fact, a comic spirit informs three of these stories. It is a comedy quite different from the superiority that Erskine Caldwell, say, evinces toward his rural degenerates. It is a comedy that does not exploit the abnormal but, as it were, absorbs it. Feeble-minded Lily, in "Lily Daw and the Three Ladies" for example, comes off very well. Despite the efforts of the officious but conscientious ladies of the town to exercise their stewardship over Lily and protect her— she is a maturing girl—Lily has responded to her own needs and her own rhythm and given in to a traveling xylophone-player. The ladies, who were packing Lily off to an institution, prove surprisingly flexible and resourceful when they discover Lily's commitment, and pack her off, instead, into marriage. In the other two stories the comedy has a sharper bite, but again not at the expense of the abnormal character. Even when she does not invoke the comic spirit, Miss Welty manages to avoid lugubrious decay and still use the abnormal. Stories like "The Key" and "Keela, the Outcast Indian Maiden," two of these five, have the trappings of the outré but the quite legitimate themes of communication and guilt. The point is that the center of interest in Miss Welty's stories is not in any psychological or physical deviation. She uses her freaks and eccentrics much as she uses her regionalism: they are the specifics from which she launches herself toward those generalized conceptions that have universal meaning and appeal.